THE STOCK MARKET
Theories and Evidence

The Stock Market

THEORIES AND EVIDENCE

JAMES H. LORIE
*Professor of Business Administration and
Director of the Center for Research in Security Prices
Graduate School of Business, University of Chicago*

MARY T. HAMILTON
*Professor of Finance and
Chairman of the Department of Finance
School of Business Administration, Loyola University of Chicago*

 1973

RICHARD D. IRWIN, INC.   *Homewood, Illinois   60430*
IRWIN-DORSEY INTERNATIONAL   *London, England   WC2H 9NJ*
IRWIN-DORSEY LIMITED   *Georgetown, Ontario   L7G 4B3*

First Printing, March 1973
Second Printing, July 1973
Third Printing, December 1973
Fourth Printing, February 1974
Fifth Printing, June 1974
Sixth Printing, December 1974
Seventh Printing, April 1975

ISBN 0-256-01450-7
Library of Congress Catalog Card No. 72–95390

Printed in the United States of America

To
LOUIS H. ENGEL

who, while at Merrill Lynch, Pierce, Fenner & Smith, Inc., was more responsible than any other person for the establishment of the Center for Research in Security Prices (sponsored by Merrill Lynch, Pierce, Fenner & Smith, Inc.) at the Graduate School of Business of the University of Chicago. The Center has been of great importance to the authors and may have been useful to others.

Foreword

OVER THE YEARS, there has been a large stream of popular articles and books about the stock market. This is not surprising since many millions of Americans have owned and do own stocks and since changes in stock prices have had a great direct impact on the net worth of investors and on the vigor of the national economy.

These articles and books have, with some notable exceptions, made one of two points. The first is that it is relatively easy for the individual investor to make very substantial returns by investing according to some simple rules. The second point is that the individual investor is manipulated or exploited by the denizens of the Wall Street jungle or the financial institutions to such an extent that investing in common stocks is intolerably hazardous.

The scientific literature about the stock market compellingly refutes both points. For reasons which this book tries to make clear, simple rules for selecting investments cannot be expected to produce extraordinary returns. Nor is the small individual investor at a substantial disadvantage as compared with the professional investor or the financial institution.

This book is about recent scientific research on the stock market, though much of it also applies to other investments. In the last 20 years, there has been an enormous change in what we know about the stock market and in the way we think about it. The changes have occurred primarily because of three things: (1) the publication in

1952 of Harry Markowitz's article on portfolio theory;[1] (2) the development of the theory of efficient markets and of its implications for security analysis and portfolio management; and (3) the development of high-speed computers and large files of financial information in machine-readable form, permitting the testing and extension of theories and a large volume of empirical findings. These related developments have increased our understanding of the ways in which investors should and do behave. We have also learned much about the functioning of our capital markets whose efficiency is important in channeling funds into their most promising uses.

Although in some fields academic work seems to have few general, practical implications, academic work in investments has practical implications which are basic and important. When the academic work is understood, it can be used to manage assets. Unfortunately, much academic work is written in ways which are difficult to understand, and much work depends for a complete understanding upon familiarity with numerous related articles and books which have appeared over many years in many places. This book attempts to organize, summarize, translate into simple language, and interpret the voluminous theoretical and scientific literature.

The book is divided into three sections. The first deals with the behavior of the stock market and in particular with the behavior of stock prices and rates of return on stocks. It includes a discussion of the theory of efficient markets, the evidence regarding its validity, and its implications for investors.

The second section deals with the valuation of securities. Since balance sheets and income statements for large numbers of companies for many years have been transformed into machine-readable form, there have been vigorous and persistent efforts to measure the forces which determine stocks prices in order to predict them more accurately. The use of formal models and empirical inquiry has provided new knowledge and has cast light on the validity of some old and new theories of security valuation. Among the topics covered in this section are the effect of capital structure and dividend policy on the value of the firm and the effects of the rate of growth in, and the stability of, corporate earnings.

The final section deals with portfolio theory. It includes an ex-

---

[1] Harry Markowitz, "Portfolio Selection," *Journal of Finance,* vol. 7, no. 1 (March 1952), pp. 77–91.

planation of the principles of rational portfolio selection for investors who like high rates of return and dislike risk. Risk plays an important part in the theory of stock evaluation and in portfolio theory, and the book discusses current controversies about the definition and measurement of risk and current theories and findings about the relationship of risk to rates of return. The final section also includes a discussion of the way in which efficient markets would operate to determine the prices of risky assets, assuming that investors behave in accordance with the principles of modern portfolio theory. There is a concluding chapter on investment counselling. Modern developments in the field of investments have made counselling the dominant financial service, though it is probably the most neglected.

Acknowledgments

Hundreds of students and several colleagues in the academic and financial communities read the manuscript of this book and gave us helpful criticism. We wish to thank students in classes in investments at the Graduate School of Business of the University of Chicago during the fall, winter and spring of 1971–72, and wish to thank especially our colleagues Fischer Black, Lawrence Fisher, Roger Ibbotson, David Kleinman, and Ralph Wanger.

Merrill Lynch, Pierce, Fenner & Smith, Inc. and the Graduate School of Business of the University of Chicago through its Center for Research in Security Prices provided generous financial support, and we thank them.

Domenica Moroney and Czatdana Baxter transformed our scattered thoughts and semilegible writing into clean copy. We are grateful.

February 1973   J. H. Lorie
                                                   M. T. Hamilton

Contents

Section One
The Behavior of the Market

1. The Stock Market and the National Economy   3

   Introduction. Some Descriptive Statistics on the Market and Investors. The Determinants of the Level of Stock Prices. Some Empirical Relationships between the Stock Market and the National Economy. *Some Secular Relationships. Cyclical Relationships. Inflation.* The Timing Problem.

2. Rates of Return on Investment in Common Stocks   26

   Introduction. A Little Financial Arithmetic. Average Rates of Return on Common Stocks: *New York Stock Exchange. Rates of Return on Stocks Not on the New York Stock Exchange.* Variability in Rates of Return on Common Stocks. Rates of Return on Bonds.

3. Stock Market Indexes   51

   Introduction. Some Problems: *Sampling. Weighting. Methods of Averaging.* The Major Indexes: *The Dow Jones Industrial Average. The Standard & Poor's "500." The New York Stock Exchange Composite. The American Stock Exchange Price Level Index. The Value Line "1400" Composite Average. Investment Performance Indexes.* Relationship among the Indexes. Concluding Remarks.

4. The Efficient Market Hypothesis   70

Introduction. Some History: *Early Beginnings. Early Tests of the Weak Form.* Quest for a Theory: *Tests of the Semistrong Hypothesis. Tests of the Strong Form of the Hypothesis.* Conclusions.

5. Implications of the Efficient Market Hypothesis   98

Introduction. Security Analysis: *The State of the Art. Implications.* Portfolio Management: *The State of the Art. Appropriate Changes. Investment Counselling.* Conclusions.

Section Two
The Valuation of Securities

6. The Theory of Stock Valuation   113

Introduction: *Basic Principles.* Cash Flows: *Dividends. Earnings. The Dividend and Earnings Hypotheses Reconciled.* The Appropriate Rate of Discount. Conclusions.

7. Stock Valuation Models   125

Introduction. The Missing Discount Rate. Some Models: *The Value Line Ratings. The Whitbeck-Kisor Model. The Ahlers Model. Limited-Horizon Models.* Critical Issues: *Growth in Earnings. The Specification of the Price-Earnings Ratio. Forecasting Problems.* Conclusions.

8. Measuring Earnings   142

Introduction. Ambiguity in Reported Income because of Numerous Accounting Options. Other Elements of Ambiguity in Reported Income or Earnings per Share. Mergers. Conclusions.

9. Predicting Earnings   157

Introduction. Historical Earnings as a Predictor of Future Earnings. Predictions of Security Analysts. Interim Earnings as Predictors of Annual Earnings. Conclusions.

Section Three
Portfolio Management

10. The Theory of Portfolio Management   171

Introduction. The Markowitz Contribution: *Efficient Portfolios. Portfolios and Securities. The Efficient Frontier. Lending and Borrowing.* Utility, Risk Aversion, and Optimality. Conclusions.

11.   Further Developments in Markowitz's Work:
      The Capital Asset Pricing Model and Other Things   198

Introduction. A Simplification of the Markowitz Model. The Determination of Prices of Financial Assets: *The Assumptions*. The Realism of the Model: *Efficient Portfolios. Other Assumptions. Empirical Evidence on the Explanatory Power of the Model*. Conclusions.

12.   Risk: Measurement, Stability, and Relationship to Return   211

Some Early Empirical Studies of Risk and Return: *Bonds. Bonds Compared with Stocks. Common Stocks. Portfolios*. The Beta (and Alpha) Coefficients: *Alpha*. Conclusions.

13.   The Evaluation of the Performance of Portfolios   228

The Study of the Bank Administration Institute: *Rate of Return. Risk. Combining Measurements of Rate of Return and Risk*. Bench Marks. Measurements of Different Parts of the Portfolio. Reaching a Conclusion.

14.   Diagnosing the Causes of Performance   248

Introduction. Skill in Selecting Particular Assets. Skill in Switching between Classes of Assets. Efficiency of Diversification. Degree of Adherence to Prescribed Policies. Transaction Costs. Taxes. Management Fees.

15.   A Note on Investment Counselling   260

Introduction. The Needs and Resources of Investors. The Specification of Investment Policy. Conclusion.

Glossary   267

Notes   277

Complementary Readings   291

Index   295

THE BEHAVIOR
OF THE MARKET

1

The Stock Market and the
National Economy

INTRODUCTION

MANY INVESTORS, including professionals, look upon investing as a kind of game in which the sole purpose is to pick the winners. Such an outlook can lead to myopic concentration on short-run changes in the prices of stocks and to neglect of the extremely important role which the capital markets play in the real economy. We shall exemplify that myopia for most of this book, but not in this first chapter.

Some commentators, looking for an explanation of the apparently superior vitality and efficiency of much American enterprise when compared with that in most other countries, have said that the efficiency of capital markets in this country is the major explanation. The large scale of public markets for stocks and bonds in this country, the high standards of disclosure imposed upon corporations by the exchanges and the government, and the very broad participation of individuals and institutions as investors have combined to reduce the cost of capital to American enterprise and to cause funds to be channeled into investments in reasonable accordance with their promise of productivity and profit.

In the United States, publicly held corporations constitute a much larger proportion of the total value of business enterprise than in most other countries. Although some commentators are concerned about a separation of ownership and control in the publicly held corporation, others think that it is beneficial for management to be subjected to pressures from numerous outside owners and that the American economy, as a consequence, is less subject to the dangers of nepotism than economies in which the privately held corporation is of greater relative importance.

This first chapter is about the relationship between the stock market and the national economy. Changes in the market affect the economy and, more obviously, changes in the economy affect the market. An understanding of that interrelationship might help with one of the two main problems of investing—the problem of timing movements into and out of common stocks in anticipation of general movements in the level of stock prices. The preceding sentence is phrased cautiously because solution of the "timing problem" seems to be difficult as judged by the record of investors.

The chapter has four sections after this brief introduction. The following section contains some simple descriptive statistics about securities markets and investors. The next section discusses the theory which bears upon the determination of the level of stock prices. After that is a discussion of empirical relationships between changes in the real economy and changes in stock prices. Finally, there is discussion of the timing problem.

SOME DESCRIPTIVE STATISTICS ON THE MARKET AND INVESTORS

At the end of 1969 the market value of corporate equities in the United States was approximately $925 billion.[1] The value of shares listed on the New York Stock Exchange was over $600 billion, about two thirds of the total. At the end of 1971, there were on the New York Stock Exchange 17.5 billion shares listed in 1,927 issues of common and preferred stocks in 1,426 companies.[2] Most of the empirical work on the stock market in this country has been on stocks listed on this exchange. This is explained in part by the fact that most of the data in machine-readable form is on these stocks. The fact that the New York Stock Exchange is by far the most important market for common stocks in the world makes this necessary restriction of empirical work easier to bear.

The next most important stock exchange in this country is the American Stock Exchange whose 1,249 issues had a market value at the end of 1970 of $38 billion.[3] The over-the-counter market has more than 20,000 issues whose aggregate market value at the end of 1970 was somewhat greater than that of issues on the American

Stock Exchange but only a minor fraction of the value of issues on the New York Stock Exchange.

The number of issues on the New York Stock Exchange is substantially less than 10 percent of the number of publicly traded issues of stock in this country, but the value of stocks on the NYSE is about two thirds of the total. There is great concentration of value within the list of stocks on the New York Stock Exchange. For example, at the end of 1971 the market value of the common stock of International Business Machines was over $38 billion. The second most valuable stock issue on the New York Stock Exchange was American Telephone and Telegraph whose value was almost $25 billion. As a way of seeing the degree of concentration, the 5 most valuable issues had a value equal to about 17 percent of the total value of all issues listed on the exchange, and the 50 most valuable had a value equal to about 45 percent.

This great concentration of value has some implications for the construction of indexes of price movements and the achievement of effective diversification as is described in chapter 3.

In order to contribute further to a general feeling about the nature of the market, it is worth noting who the investors are. One kind of summary is given in table 1–1.

Although individuals own directly about 72 percent of all outstanding equities, their importance in determining the prices of common stocks is far less. In the first place, many of the holdings of individuals are managed for them by financial institutions. In 1971, individuals accounted for only 24.4 percent of the total value of shares traded on the New York Stock Exchange. Financial institutions and intermediaries accounted for 52.4 percent; members of the exchange, 23.2 percent.[4] The relative importance of trading by institutions and intermediaries has been rising rapidly. As recently as 1960, individuals accounted for more than half of the New York Stock Exchange volume as measured by shares traded and more than 40 percent as measured by value.

THE DETERMINANTS OF THE LEVEL OF STOCK PRICES

Although there has been, during the past 25 years, a very pronounced moderation in the amplitude of fluctuations in the level of output, income, employment, and other measures of activity in the national economy, there continue to be very substantial fluctuations

TABLE 1–1
Estimated Holdings of NYSE-Listed Stocks by Financial Institutions (in billions)

	Year End				
Type of Institution	*1949*	*1959*	*1969*	*1970*	*1971*ᴾ
Insurance companies:					
Life.	$ 1.1	$ 2.9	$ 10.2	$ 11.7	$ 15.2
Nonlife.	1.7	5.7	11.7	12.2	15.5
Investment companies:					
Open-end	1.4	11.6	39.1	39.0	46.4
Closed-end.	1.6	5.2	4.1	4.1	5.0
Noninsured pension funds:					
Corporate	0.5	11.8	52.4	57.2	72.2
Other private	*	0.7	3.1	3.5	4.8
State & local government . . .	*	0.4	6.2	8.2	12.3
Nonprofit institutions:					
College & university					
endowments.	1.1	3.0	6.7	6.9	7.8
Foundations.	1.1	5.4	12.1	12.2	14.9
Other.	1.0	4.4	8.9	9.0	10.1
Common trust funds	*	1.4	4.1	4.1	4.6
Mutual savings banks	0.2	0.3	1.0	1.2	1.4
Total	$ 9.7	$ 52.8	$159.6	$169.3	$210.2
Market value of all NYSE					
listed stock	$76.3	$307.7	$629.5	$636.4	$741.8
Estimated percent held by					
above institutions.	12.7%	17.2%	25.4%	26.6%	28.3%

* Less than $50 million.
ᴾ Preliminary estimates.
Source: *1972 Fact Book*, New York Stock Exchange, p. 50.

in the level of stock prices (table 1–2). Since the end of World War II, there have been six occasions in which comprehensive indexes of stock prices have declined more than 19 percent in a period of 12 months or less and 9 periods of 12 months in which the market has risen by more than 20 percent. When these large and rapid movements in the level of comprehensive indexes occur, almost all stocks are affected, though in different degrees. Since the ability to anticipate such large, rapid, and general movements in the level of stock prices is a potential source of great enrichment, an understanding of the determinants of the level of prices may be worth seeking.

The value of a corporation's stock is determined by expectations regarding future earnings of the corporation and by the rate at which those earnings are discounted. In a world of certainty, all securities would offer a certain return equal to the real rate of return on capital. In a world of uncertainty, returns are not so easily explained. In our uncertain world, feelings about securities can be summarized in one

TABLE 1–2
Major Bear and Bull Markets, 1929–1970 (Standard & Poor's Composite [1941–43 = 10])

Dates	Duration (Months)	Peak Value	Trough Value	Change (Points)	Change (Percent)
Sept. 1929–June 1932 33		31.30	4.77	−26.35	− 84.8
June 1932–Feb. 1934 20		4.77	11.32	6.55	137.3
Feb. 1934–Mar. 1935 13		11.32	8.41	− 2.91	− 25.7
Mar. 1935–Feb. 1937 23		8.41	18.11	9.70	115.3
Feb. 1937–Apr. 1938 14		18.11	9.89	− 8.22	− 45.3
Apr. 1938–Oct. 1939 18		9.89	12.90	3.01	30.4
Oct. 1939–Apr. 1942 30		12.90	7.84	− 5.06	− 39.2
Apr. 1942–May 1946 49		7.84	18.70	10.86	138.5
May 1946–June 1949 37		18.70	13.97	− 4.73	− 25.3
June 1949–Jan. 1953 43		13.97	26.18	12.21	87.4
Jan. 1953–Sept. 1953 8		26.18	23.27	− 2.91	− 11.1
Sept. 1953–July 1956 34		23.27	48.78	25.51	109.6
July 1956–Dec. 1957 17		48.78	40.33	− 8.45	− 17.3
Dec. 1957–July 1959 19		40.33	59.74	19.41	48.1
July 1959–Oct. 1960 15		59.74	53.73	− 6.01	− 10.1
Oct. 1960–Dec. 1961 14		53.73	71.74	18.01	33.5
Dec. 1961–Oct. 1962 10		71.74	56.17	−15.57	− 21.7
Oct. 1962–Jan. 1966 39		56.17	93.32	37.15	66.1
Jan. 1966–Oct. 1966 9		93.32	77.13	−16.19	− 17.3
Oct. 1966–Dec. 1968 26		77.13	106.48	29.35	38.1
Dec. 1968–May 1970 17		106.48	76.06	−30.42	− 28.6

way by a personal estimate of the likelihood of various changes in future earnings. The weighted average or mean of these possible changes is called the *expected* change. (The weights are equal to the probabilities of occurrence.) There are several measures of the variation in the possible changes, but the standard deviation is most frequently used.

The greater the mean or expected value of the possible changes, the higher the prices of stocks, other things being equal. There is also strong evidence that most persons do not like increased uncertainty. As a consequence, an increase in the standard deviation of possible changes represents an undesired decrease in the confidence of investors in predicting the future and will be accompanied by a reduction in the level of prices, other things being equal.

What we have said so far is that two determinants of the level of stock prices are the expected level of earnings and the degree of uncertainty of investors in estimating what future earnings will be. The third determinant of the level of stock prices is the rate at which a prospective stream of *certain* earnings is discounted to determine its present value. The present value of any stream of earnings is obviously affected by the rate at which it is discounted—the higher the rate, the lower the value. The rate at which earnings should be discounted is related to or determined by the rate of return that can be earned on alternative investments. Since, in the discussion above, risk or uncertainty is explicitly taken into account—usually in estimating a risk premium—by consideration of the standard deviation of possible changes in earnings, the relevant rate of return on alternative investments is the rate of return on assets which do not entail risk.

The academic literature in finance often glibly discusses the "risk-free rate," and there are rates which seem to be virtually risk free, at least in nominal terms. For example, 180-day Treasury bills can be bought at a known price and will be presumably redeemed 180 days later at a known price. Indubitably, the federal government will have the power to redeem the bill, assuming the absence of nuclear holocaust, revolution, or fits of insanity, and thus—according to one's pessimism about catastrophe—the bills are risk free or virtually risk free. When the relevant time period is longer—say, five years—there is no security which is equally risk free. Even if the market price were known and the probability of default were virtually nil, the total rate of return on a five-year government bond depends in part on the rates at which periodic interest payments can be reinvested, and these rates cannot be known with precision. Nevertheless, the range of uncertainty in the total nominal rate of return on the bond is small.[5] Uncertainty concerning changes in the level of all prices, i.e., inflation, continues to exist and be a problem.

In discounting future streams of corporate earnings to determine their present value, these so-called risk-free rates for relevant time periods are the rates which are conventionally used.

Since all interest rates are interrelated, though in different ways at different phases of the business cycle, it is convenient to say that the rate at which corporate earnings should be discounted is determined by the level of interest rates. These have fluctuated widely in recent years. For example, at the end of 1960, the yield to maturity or rate of return on 90-day Treasury bills was about 2.25 percent, while the corresponding rate at the end of the second quarter of 1970 was 6.67 percent. This almost certainly helps explain why the price-earnings ratio of stocks in the Dow Jones Industrial Average was 19.1 at the earlier and 12.8 at the later date.

To give some additional concreteness to the discussion of determinants of the level of stock prices, let us examine the most dramatic change in stock prices during a brief period since the end of World War II—the decline of about 37 percent in the level of the New York Stock Exchange Composite Index between May 14, 1969 and May 26, 1970. What caused this rapid and large decline? First, a minor recession began "officially" according to the National Bureau of Economic Research during the third quarter of 1969 and brought with it virtual certainty of a decline in corporate earnings. In fact, between the second quarter in 1969 and the second quarter in 1970, corporate earnings declined by almost 14 percent, at seasonally adjusted annual rates. Second, the yield to maturity on 90-day Treasury bills and three-to-four-year government bonds rose from about 6.2 percent and 6.6 percent to 6.7 percent and 7.8 percent, respectively.* Those two factors alone could plausibly account for a substantial decline in stock prices.

For an explanation of the balance of the decline, one must rely on conjecture. Although American society was noticeably distinguishable from either Utopia or the Garden of Eden in early 1969, dissatisfaction did not seem to be as acute and violent prior to 1969 as it did in 1969 and 1970. In the later period, the extension of the war into Cambodia and Laos and the accompanying domestic reactions and other factors could have increased social malaise and caused decreased confidence in the future of the American society, the American economy, and the value of American corporations.

Added to all of the above was the disarray—some felt the near dissolution—of Wall Street. What happened to Wall Street in 1969 and 1970 is well described and analyzed in Donald Regan's *A View From the Street*.[6] For a variety of ancient fundamental causes and current precipitating causes, many brokerage firms disappeared through bankruptcy or absorption into stronger firms. Confidence in the soundness of basic financial institutions was shaken.

Thus, a decline in profits, a rise in interest rates, foreign wars, domestic violence, and apprehension and disarray in Wall Street plausibly accounted for the sharp decline in stock prices, but it would have been more difficult to predict it. Prediction would have required a gift of prophecy not often possessed by economists, investors, politicians, or even investment counselors. It would have been necessary to foresee the recession, the continued rise in interest rates, the course of foreign affairs, and the progressive alienation of American youth.

---

* The figures are quarterly averages.

Of course, those rare individuals with either the gift of prophecy or good luck, who got out of the stock market (and the bond market) or who even sold stocks short, did very well by comparison with investors less gifted or lucky. The gifted or lucky ones may have acquired not only money but also the reputation for wisdom, which is valuable even when ill founded.

SOME EMPIRICAL RELATIONSHIPS BETWEEN THE STOCK MARKET AND THE NATIONAL ECONOMY

The subject of empirical relationships between the stock market and the national economy is vast, and the National Bureau of Economic Research has filled more than a five-foot shelf with work on the subject. Nevertheless, in this introductory chapter, which is to serve as a background for the more serious, subsequent discussions, we shall deal with this subject only briefly.

Industrious students of the national economy and seekers of profit in the stock market have studied the interrelationships among hundreds of economic time series. Numerous persistent relationships have been identified and analyzed. Three time series are of especial interest: stock prices, corporate profits, and price-earnings ratios. By far the most important determinant of the level of stock prices is corporate profits. (See figure 1–1.) During the Great Depression, both profits and stock prices fell by over 75 percent. In all subsequent periods, there was a remarkable correspondence between major movements in the two series, with the exception of the period immediately after World War II. At that time, profits rose rapidly and stock prices lagged badly for several years. The relationship is reflected in the dramatic decline in price-earnings ratios after the War. (See figure 1–2.) If one can forecast profits and the ratio of prices to profits, one can obviously forecast stock prices and become very wealthy. The task is formidable, however. The balance of this chapter will discuss this subject.

Some Secular Relationships

From time to time economists and investors wonder whether the stock market is "unreasonably" high or low relative to the level of economic activity. Interesting examples of such speculation are numerous. We have chosen two for discussion because they are well done

FIGURE 1-1

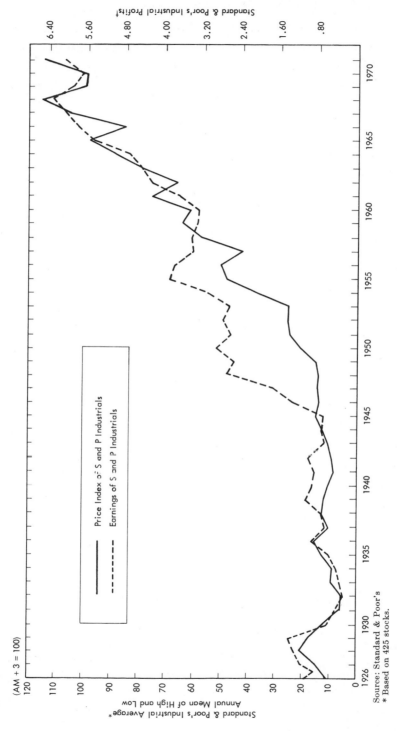

(AM + 3 = 100)

Standard & Poor's Industrial Average*
Annual Mean of High and Low

Standard & Poor's Industrial Profits†

Price Index of S and P Industrials
Earnings of S and P Industrials

Source: Standard & Poor's
* Based on 425 stocks.

FIGURE 1–2

Price-to-Earnings Ratios

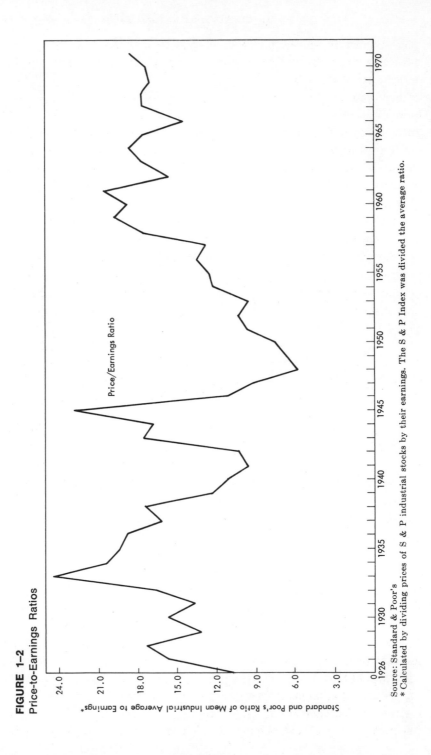

Price/Earnings Ratio

Standard and Poor's Ratio of Mean Industrial Average to Earnings*

Source: Standard & Poor's
*Calculated by dividing prices of S & P industrial stocks by their earnings. The S & P Index was divided the average ratio.

and sufficiently ancient to permit assessment of the accuracy of the projections and thus to illustrate the pitfalls of even the most intelligent treatments of the subject.

Solomon, in 1955, analyzed the relationship between common stock prices and economic growth.[7] He recognized the dangers in mechanical extrapolation of historical relationships and at the same time recognized that such relationships in developed societies do not often change dramatically in short periods of time. Thus, history is a useful though imprecise guide to the future. His method was to measure the relationship between changes in gross national product and changes in the level of the Standard & Poor's Index of 425 industrial stock prices. In order to eliminate the effects of changes in the price level, both series were deflated by the same price index. On the basis of these measurements, Solomon divided the period between 1874 and 1955 into two overlapping periods, estimating an average annual rate of real growth in gross national product (compounded annually) of 4 percent for the period 1874–1913 and of 3 percent for the period 1909–1955. The corresponding growth rates for stock prices for the two periods were 2.667 percent and 2 percent. Solomon concluded that, "Over the period as a whole, the real growth in stock values has proceeded at about two-thirds of the rate of the real growth in gross national product."[8] In the short run, there are, of course, marked changes in the relative growth rates, but Solomon felt that there is some stability to the longer-term relationship. As a consequence of more detailed analysis than we present here, Solomon concluded that the level of stock prices in 1955 was extremely close to what would have been predicted if one had based the prediction on the growth in gross national product and the historical relationship between that growth and stock prices.

Solomon did not make forecasts about the future course of the economy or of stock prices, but it is mildly interesting to note what stock prices would have been at the end of 1969, given the level of gross national product and a continuation of the long-term historical relationship between it and stock prices. If both series were deflated by the implicit price deflator for gross national product, the estimated increase in the Standard & Poor's 425 Price Index between 1955 and 1969 would have been about 35 percent; the actual increase was about 98 percent. The explanation of the marked discrepancy is that price-earnings ratios have been consistently higher in recent years than during most of the period between 1874 and 1955. These higher ratios were only partially offset by the fact that corporate profits failed to rise as rapidly in response to growth in the real economy as in earlier periods. For example, price-earnings ratios generally ranged between 5.9 and 17.6 during the 15 years before 1955, and between 12.9 and 20.6 during the 15 years after 1955. (There was an anomaly in 1945 when the ratio was 23.0.) Contrariwise, percentage changes in real corporate profits on the average were 1.42 times as great as percentage changes in real gross national product during the earlier period and less than half as great during the later period.

In 1956, Weston dealt with the same subject in "The Stock Market in Perspective."[9] Weston pointed out that there is a close relationship between gross national product and sales by businesses, a close relationship between sales and profits, a close relationship between profits and dividends, and finally, a close relationship between dividends and stock prices. This led predictably to the conclusion that there is a close relationship between gross national product and the level of stock prices. Rather than rely on average annual rates of growth in these series, Weston estimated the average relationship between changes in the two series for the period 1868 through 1955.* Weston, like Solomon, felt that stock prices in 1955 were just about right. Unlike Solomon, Weston was rash enough to predict what stock prices would be in 1960, 1965, and 1975. His predictions are given in table 1–3.

Weston's errors were substantial. This was due, in part, to the inaccuracy of the projections of gross national product. However, even if he had possessed perfect foresight with respect to levels of gross national product, his estimating relationships would have given bad results. For example, his estimate for the Standard & Poor's Industrial Index, using actual gross national product figures, would have been low by 24 percent in 1960 and by 45 percent in 1965. Estimates of the Dow Jones Industrial Index would also have been low, though by smaller amounts. The percentage errors are given in table 1–4.

Perhaps fortuitously, the forecast for the Standard & Poor's Index would have been very close to its actual level in 1970.

Cyclical Relationships

Studying long-term relationships is interesting and hazardous and undoubtedly will continue to be a popular activity. A related activity

---

* Weston used annual data to estimate the relationship for the period 1909–40 (omitting the years 1928–32) and decade data to estimate the relationship from 1868 through 1928.

TABLE 1–3

Projections of Gross National Product and Stock Prices, 1960, 1965, 1975, Related to Bench-Mark Years

Year		Gross National Product— 1953 Dollars* (in Billions)	Standard & Poor's Industrial Index— 420 Stocks†	Dow Jones Industrial Average— 30 Stocks‡
1929	Actual	$177.7	171.1	311.2
1955	Actual	385.0	340.7	442.7
1960	Projected	436.0	342.0	450.0
1965	Projected	535.0	416.2	545.8
1975	Projected	634.0	490.5	641.6

* Projected figures from Joint Committee on the Economic Report, *Potential Economic Growth of the United States*, 1954, p. 35.

† Projected figures derived by formula $SP = 15 + .75GNP$ (described in text).

‡ Projected figures derived by formula $DJ = 28.20 + .9675GNP$ (method similar to that described in text).

Note: The correlation coefficients for the above relationships are all statistically significant. The standard errors of estimate are small.

Source: Weston, "The Stock Market in Perspective," *Harvard Business Review*, vol. 34, no. 2 (March–April, 1956), pp. 71–80.

TABLE 1–4

Errors in Forecasts Based on Weston's Equations[a]
(forecasted level relative to actual level)

	Standard & Poor's Industrial Index	Dow Jones Industrial Average
1960	−24.4%	−19.9%
1965	−45.4%	−31.9%
1970	− 0.7%	+28.9%

[a] Estimates computed using actual figures for gross national product.

is the analysis of shorter-term movements in stock prices and other economic phenomena. Two findings are especially pertinent. Fluctuations in output, income, and employment have become progressively milder and are now quite mild by standards as recent as 30 or 40 years ago. For example, the most recent "recession," in 1969–70, produced a decline in real Gross National Product of only about 1.5 percent from peak to trough, an increase from 3.3 to 6.1 percent in unemployment, and an *increase* in real disposable personal income in every quarter except the last in 1970. That decline was a modest 0.65 percent. Depressions and recessions in the 1930s and 1940s were several times as severe, as measured by these criteria. Even in the 1950s and early 1960s, recessions were much more severe.

Burns explained the increasing stability of the economy in his presidential address to the American Economic Association in 1959.[10] His main points were:

1.   Increased reliance by the federal government (and even by state governments) on income taxes for revenue and the withholding of income taxes and quarterly payments means that government revenues are quickly responsive to changes in levels of employment and output and affect income in an appropriate counter-cyclical way.

2.   The vast increase in unemployment compensation and in welfare programs has sharply reduced the sensitivity of personal income to changes in the level of economic activity. A relatively minor contributor to this same phenomenon is the great increase in common stock ownership by the American public and the relative stability of corporate dividends as compared with corporate earnings. This increased stability in personal incomes has apparently caused much greater stability in consumption expenditures.

3.   There has been a great change in the structure of employment. First, services have come to be of much greater importance relative to manufacturing, and services are relatively stable. Second, even within manufacturing, "white-collar" employment has come to constitute a larger proportion of employment in manufacturing. White-collar employment in manufacturing is more stable than blue-collar employment.

4.   Monetary policy has become more stable and predictable and has contributed to the increased stability of the economy.

Stock prices, however, are not determined or primarily influenced by the level of output, employment, and income; as has been said, stock prices respond more to corporate profits. At the same time that the economy has been becoming more stable, corporate profits have been becoming increasingly sensitive to those relatively small fluctuations in the real economy which persist. Andersen presents the relevant data in his "Trends in Profit Sensitivity."[11] The point is well made by the data in table 1–5.

In the most recent recession, 1969–70, the relationship between changes in nominal GNP and nominal corporate profits is astonishing. Nominal GNP rose in every quarter while corporate profits declined 21 percent between the third quarter of 1969 and the fourth quarter of 1970. Under these circumstances, the calculation of a sensitivity ratio is obviously absurd.

The reason for the increased sensitivity of profits is a change in

TABLE 1–5
Measuring Profit Sensitivity during Four Postwar
Recessions*

Period of Decline	Change in GNP	Change in Corporate Profits	Profit Sensitivity Ratio
4Q48–4Q49	–4.3%	–15.4%	3.6
2Q53–1Q54	–2.8%	–18.8%	6.7
3Q57–1Q58	–3.8%	–27.3%	7.2
2Q60–1Q61	–0.8%	–14.2%	17.8

* Theodore A. Andersen, "Trends in Profit Sensitivity," *Journal of Finance*, vol. 18, no. 4 (December 1963), p. 638. All data are seasonally adjusted and in current dollars. All profits are calculated pretax.

the structure of business costs. Fixed costs have become an increasingly large proportion of total costs so that fluctuations in the level of output and sales can, and generally will, have a magnified impact on profits. Since profits are the difference between revenues and costs, profits respond more violently to changes in revenues if it is increasingly difficult to reduce costs in response to reduced output and sales. The increased importance of fixed costs is caused primarily by increases in the capital intensiveness in manufacturing and in wholesale and retail distribution, the increased relative importance of the white-collar labor force, the increased cost of labor turnover as the work force becomes more technically trained and specialized, with a consequent increase in the willingness of firms to retain employees who are not fully occupied, and by the increased importance of research and development expenditures.

Inflation

Stock prices are clearly of great interest to investors, and, in an era of virtually continuous inflation, there has been an understandable interest in the relationship between changes in prices in general and changes in the prices of common stocks. The major work in this field is by Kessel and Alchian.[12] The common belief, derived in part from the writings of Keynes[13] and Fisher,[14] is that inflation is advantageous to owners of common stock because it reduces the burden to corporations of servicing and repaying their debt. A second line of argument, derived from Hamilton[15] and Mitchell,[16] states that stockholders receive additional benefits from inflation because, typically, prices for the products which corporations sell rise before and faster than wage rates.

The assertions with respect to the relationships between price inflation and the burden of debt and labor costs rest upon some questionable assumptions which deserve scrutiny. As Kessel points out, even a casual look at dramatic inflations in industrialized countries in modern times should cause skepticism about the universal validity of the assertions of Keynes, Fisher, Hamilton, and Mitchell.

The Keynes-Fisher hypothesis regarding the benefits to owners of common stock during inflation would be true if business firms were debtors and if the interest rates which they pay on their debt failed to reflect the future changes in the price level. There is some reason to doubt that either of those assumptions is generally true. Although many firms have debt in their capital structure, it is a mistake to believe that that fact alone causes them to be debtors. Kessel and Alchian point out that it is necessary to look at both the assets and liabilities of business firms in order to determine whether they are debtors or creditors. The necessity of this view is most dramatically illustrated by banks. Superficially, banks appear to be creditors, since their business is primarily lending money. But it is also true that a large proportion of their liabilities—primarily deposits—offsets their fixed-dollars assets—primarily loans. That is, their assets from which they receive a "fixed" number of dollars are more than offset by their liabilities which cost a "fixed" number of dollars. By taking both sides of the balance sheet into account, banks turn out to be not creditors but debtors. Thus, if it is true that debtors benefit from inflation, banks should benefit.

Kessel found that when the debtor or creditor position of business firms is viewed in this way, a surprisingly high proportion of business firms are not debtors but are creditors. The basis for this conclusion was analysis of the relative magnitude of the following monetary assets and liabilities:

Monetary Assets	*Monetary Liabilities*
Cash	Accounts payable
Marketable securities	Notes payable
Accounts receivable	Tax liability reserve
Tax funds receivable	Bonds
Notes receivable	Preferred stock
Prepaid insurance	
Gold	

There is also reason to doubt that interest rates fail to reflect the future course of the price level. Figure 1–3 illustrates the course of

FIGURE 1–3
Yields on Highest Grade Corporate Bonds

* Estimates of "real" interest rates were obtained from statistical regressions of nominal interest rates on current and lagged price changes and on variables thought to influence "real" interest rates (i.e., the level of and changes in output and changes in the deflated money stock). See William P. Yohe and Denis S. Karnosky, "Interest Rates and Price Level Changes, 1952–69." *Review.* Federal Reserve Bank of St. Louis, December 1909.
   Latest data plotted: November estimated.
   Prepared by Federal Reserve Bank of St. Louis.

interest rates on long-term corporate bonds of high quality between 1962 and 1970. The nominal rate of return on these bonds rose from approximately 4.5 percent to 8.5 percent. During most of the period, the real rate of return on the bonds, i.e., the nominal rate adjusted for changes in prices, was remarkably stable. It was about 3.5 percent in 1962 and about 4 percent in 1969. Only during the last part of 1969 and the first half of 1970 did real rates rise substantially to a level of 4.35 percent.

The belief that wages lag behind prices during inflation, with a consequent reduction in real labor costs and an increase in corporate profits, is also of questionable validity. Kessel and Alchian examined various bodies of data from Spain, France, England, Germany, and the United States and concluded that "a reading of this evidence suggests that the wage-lag hypothesis ought to be regarded as essentially untested."[17] The foreign data indicate a general tendency for labor costs to decline during inflation, but there are various plausible explanations of this aside from a lag in wages. American data relating changes in stock prices to the ratio of wages to equity for corporations indicate the opposite of what the wage-lag hypothesis implies. During the inflationary period of 1939–52, stock prices of firms for which wages were relatively unimportant increased more rapidly than stock prices for firms for which wages were of greater relative importance. Thus, the evidence is fragmentary and conflicting, and the validity of the hypothesis remains to be determined.

The problem of interpreting economic time series is always complicated by the fact that almost all such series in growing economies have strong, upward, secular trends. This frequently causes persons to assume causal relationships between series which climb together, when the causes of the parallel upward movements lie in the general growth of the economy. This problem is present to some extent in interpreting the effect of price inflation on stock prices. The problem is diminished in importance by considering the relationship between general prices and rates of return on common stocks rather than prices themselves.

It is particularly instructive to note the generally persistent high rates of return between 1954 and 1965 when the American economy had relatively stable prices. In contrast, between 1965 and 1972 there was substantial inflation and a lower level of rates of return—frequently negative—on common stocks.

Although rising prices cannot be counted upon to produce rising profits and increased stock prices, stocks have for almost all periods produced rates of return in real terms which are superior to those on fixed-dollar assets. The data presented in table 1–6 bring this out. Since 1965, although refined measurements are not available, rates of return on bonds have exceeded rates for stocks for many periods.

THE TIMING PROBLEM

The increased stability of the economy has undoubtedly contributed to an upward adjustment in price-earnings ratios, but the increased sensitivity of corporate profits to fluctuations in the economy continues to cause large fluctuations in stock prices. Thus the timing problem continues to be exciting and potentially profitable.

TABLE 1–6

Rates of Return on Stocks[a] and Bonds[b] for Specified Periods, 1926–65 (average annual rates of return compounded annually)

Period[c]	Stocks (percent)	Bonds (percent)
1925–65	9.3	3.7
1930–65	12.0	3.5
1935–65	12.6	2.8
1940–65	16.0	2.4
1945–65	12.6	2.1
1950–65	14.5	1.9
1955–65	12.5	2.1
1960–65	15.9	3.5
1930–40	4.7	6.3
1940–50	19.0	2.5
1950–60	14.9	1.1

[a] Data taken from Lawrence Fisher and James H. Lorie "Rates of Return on Investments in Common Stocks: The Year-by-Year Record, 1926–65," *Journal of Business*, vol. 41, no. 3 (July 1968). Data are based on assumption of equal initial investment in all stocks on NYSE at beginning of period and reinvestment of dividends.

[b] Data taken from Lawrence Fisher and Roman L. Weil, "Coping with the Risk of Interest-Rate Fluctuations: Returns to Bondholders from Naïve and Optimal Strategies," *Journal of Business*, vol. 44, no. 4 (October 1971), pp. 408–31. Data are based on assumption of investment in Standard & Poor's High Grade (AAA) Bond Indexes. These are based on 20-year bonds.

[c] Period is from year-end to year-end.

The starting point for many investors is the work of the National Bureau of Economic Research. In their more than 50-year quest for an understanding of the interrelationships among economic time series, some relevant findings have emerged. Stock prices are one of the 12 economic time series considered a *leading indicator*. Major movements in a leading indicator generally or typically precede movements in the general economy as reflected by such comprehensive measures as gross national product. In the 20 most recent business cycles, common stock prices have led changes in gross national product on the average by four months. The average lead is the same for peaks and troughs. Many of the other leading indicators have substantially longer average lead times with reference to peaks. The average leads for the 12 indicators which have exhibited the most consistent relation in past business cycles are shown in the table 1–7.

There has been an understandable tendency to look to those leading

TABLE 1–7
Leading Indicators of Business Activity (record of timing of selected statistical indicators at business cycle turns)

	Peaks		Troughs	
	Number of Cycles	*Avg. Lead Months*	*Number of Cycles*	*Avg. Lead Months*
Leading indicators				
(1) Average hours worked	9	– 6	10	–4
(2) Nonagricultural placements	5	–11	5	–1
(3) Net business formation.	5	–20	5	–3
(4) Durable goods new orders	10	– 8	10	–2
(5) Plant & equip. contracts, orders.	4	– 8	4	–3
(6) Housing permits.	11	–13	11	–5
(7) Mfg. & trade inventory change	5	–14	5	–6
(8) Industrial materials prices	10	– 6	11	0
(9) Common stock prices	22	– 4	22	–4
(10) Corporate profits (net).	10	– 6	10	–2
(11) Price/unit labor cost	10	–11	11	–3
(12) Consumer debt change	7	–12	7	–4

Source: Sprinkel, *Money and Markets* (Homewood, Ill.: Richard D. Irwin, Inc. 1971), p. 138.

indicators which have led stock prices in order to solve the timing problem. The disconcerting thing is that the average leads conceal a great deal of variability from cycle to cycle. Indeed, in some cycles, the leading indicators do not lead at all. These irregularities in the temporal interrelationships of the time series make it absurd to rely upon any simple mechanical scheme for reacting to the more leading "leading" indicators. In fact, the problem is so difficult that even sophisticated and subtle interpretations of the data often lead investors astray.

Since the publication of Friedman and Schwartz's *Monetary History of the United States*[18] and especially since Friedman's monetary theories have been so widely discussed, substantially confirmed by experience, and increasingly accepted, much attention has focused on changes in the money supply as a precursor of changes in general economic conditions and even of stock prices themselves. Sprinkel, a true believer in the Friedman church, has written two interesting books on the relationship between changes in the rate of change in the money supply and changes in stock prices. In his second book,[19] his major conclusions were the following:

1. Changes in the growth rate of the money supply have a "usually decisive" effect on business conditions and stock prices.

2.   Competent monetary analysis can detect relevant changes in monetary policy by reviewing policy statements of the Federal Reserve Board and analyzing current changes in the money supply and other monetary statistics.

3.   Understanding the relationships between the stock of money and the real economy can contribute to the solution of the timing problem, but the solution itself will continue to be difficult and its

FIGURE 1–4

Monetary Growth and S&P's Index of 425 Industrials* (annual rate of

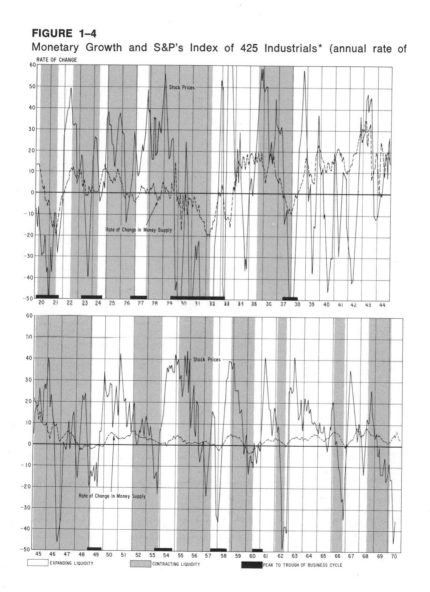

value may diminish through time if cyclical fluctuations in stock prices diminish.

For a substantial period of time, changes in the rate of expansion in the money supply seem to provide reasonably reliable clues to future changes in the level of stock prices. The relationship is illustrated in figure 1–4. Since 1918, there have been only three sharp market declines which were not preceded by a period of monetary contraction. These occurred in 1939–40, 1962, and 1966. The lead of changes in the money supply over bear markets is variable, but on the average is about nine months. The lead for bull markets is typically shorter and averages two to three months. Data relating to major market movements are given in table 1–8.

Unfortunately, such regularity almost inevitably is diminished through time as it is noted and as investors react to it. In very recent periods, there is some evidence that changes in the rate of growth in the money supply lead changes in stock prices by shorter periods or are coincidental.

Common sense would reject the idea of a single time series which reliably led the market, thus simply providing the secret of great wealth. Investors with common sense who play the timing game successfully must anticipate better than other investors the course of the

TABLE 1–8
Turning Points in Money and Stock Prices—1918–70

	Lead before Downturns		
*Monetary Growth Rate Peaks**	*Stock Price Peaks*	*Months Series Lead*	
December 1918.	October 1919	10	
September 1922.	March 1923	5	
November 1924.	February 1926	15	
December 1928 (April 1928). . . .	September 1929	9	(17)
July 1936 (June 1935)	March 1937	8	(21)
January 1945.	May 1946	16	
December 1951.	January 1953	13	
February 1955.	July 1956	17	
November 1958.	July 1959	8	
January 1962.	December 1961	–1	
January 1966 (October 1964) . .	January 1966	0	(15)
July 1968 (July 1967)	December 1968	5	(17)
	Range	17 to –1	(21 to –1)
	Average	8.8	(12.8)

* Computed on a 6-month moving average.
Money = Demand deposits and currency.
Source: Federal Reserve; Dow Jones; Harris Trust and Savings Bank.

TABLE 1–8 (continued)
Turning Points in Money and Stock Prices—1918–70

	Lead before Upturns	
Monetary Growth Rate Troughs	*Stock Price Troughs*	*Months Series Lead*
June 1921.	August 1921	2
August 1923.	October 1923	2
December 1926.	December 1926	0
March 1932.	June 1932	3
December 1937.	May 1938	5
February 1949 (July 1948)	June 1949	4 (11)
November 1953 (March 1954)	September 1953	−2 (−6)
January 1958.	December 1957	−1
May 1960.	October 1960	5
September 1962.	October 1962	1
November 1966.	October 1966	−1
December 1969 (February 1970) . . .	June 1970	6 (4)
	Range	6 to −2 (11 to −6)
	Average	2.0 (2.1)

general economy, corporate profits, and interest rates; and, this task seems to require a comprehensive and perceptive analysis of national and international economic, political, and social developments. The visible record of professionally managed portfolios indicates that many play the timing game and that few, if any, win it.

2

Rates of Return on Investment in Common Stocks

INTRODUCTION

SCIENTIFIC PROGRESS in any field depends crucially on accurate measurement. Many measurements are interesting in themselves, but their most important scientific role is to test the validity of theory. Since most financial theory is focused on an explanation of the level, structure, and behavior of rates of return, their accurate measurement is essential if the theory is to be tested and improved.

The very great growth in the value of assets managed by financial institutions since 1945 has provided an additional stimulus to the need for measurement. The trust departments of commercial banks in this country now manage almost $300 billion. The assets of mutual funds are approximately $60 billion. Other financial institutions, including investment counselors, manage or control assets far in excess of $100 billion. With this increase in the value of assets managed by institutions and with the general availability of powerful digital computers, there has come an increased effort to manage assets scientifically.

This effort includes discrimination among different investment strategies and assessment of the effects on rates of return of various relevant variables such as dividends, interest rates, risk, and rates of growth in earnings. In order for these efforts at scientific management to be successful, it is essential that there be refined measurements of rates of return on the various assets being managed.

Although there have been satisfactory studies of the rates of return on investments in bonds,[1] until fairly recently there were only crude and rudimentary measures of rates of return on investments in common stocks. As recently as 1964, Herzog could write that ". . . it is very disturbing to find that the financial literature contains little information on realized or *ex post* yields."[2] In an effort to remedy this, Herzog presents some crude measurements of yields on three classes of corporate securities for the period 1929–62. His randomly selected sample is restricted to industrial securities rated "A" by Moody's Investors Service in 1929 and includes ten commons, ten preferreds, and ten bonds. As Herzog recognizes, the sample has limitations. In addition, however, he fails to take into account such things as commissions and taxes which significantly affect rates of return.

Only in 1964 did the financial community have, for the first time, refined measurements of the rates of return on common stocks listed on the New York Stock Exchange.[3] The data presented in 1964 covered all stocks listed on the exchange for 1926–60. The measurements were detailed, taking into account all relevant capital changes, taxes, and commissions. This original work in 1964 was updated in 1968[4] and supplemented in 1970 by comparable data on the variability of rates of return.[5] These studies will be discussed in this chapter.

Before presenting the most recent data on rates of return on common stocks, there will be a discussion of some common problems and errors in computing rates of return and of some of the earlier efforts to estimate rates of return on common stocks.

Almost all of the data presented in this chapter relate to common stocks listed on the New York Stock Exchange. There will be incidental data and commentary on rates of return on bonds, United States common stocks not listed on the New York Stock Exchange, and common stocks and bonds in the United Kingdom. The emphasis on the common stocks listed on the New York Stock Exchange is necessary, because data on other common stocks and other types of financial assets are not nearly so adequate. Although the loss of comprehensiveness is to be regretted, the stocks listed on the New York Stock Exchange have a market value substantially exceeding that of all other common stocks publicly traded in the United States. Also, the common stocks listed on the New York Stock Exchange have a value vastly exceeding—perhaps by a factor of five to one—common stocks listed on any other stock exchange in the world. The Stock Exchange of London lists many more stocks than are listed on the New York Stock Exchange, but their aggregate value in recent years has been only about one fifth of that of the New York Stock Exchange.

The value of stocks listed on exchanges in the many other countries of the world with organized exchanges is, in each instance, very much less than the value of those listed on the Stock Exchange of London.

A LITTLE FINANCIAL ARITHMETIC

All data on rates of return presented in this chapter are based upon changes in the market value of assets and on the value of things received during the relevant period by the owners of those assets. The things received are interest, dividends, rights, and occasionally other things.

Computers deal most easily with rates of return compounded continuously while most people seem to prefer rates compounded annually. This difference can cause difficulties and errors and should therefore be understood.

The annual rate of return compounded continuously on any investment is the natural logarithm (log_e) of the ratio of the value of the investment at the end of the year to the value at the beginning. For example, if the investment were initially worth $100 and one year later was worth $110, the wealth ratio would be 1.1 and its natural logarithm would be 0.09531. The annual rate of return compounded continuously would be 9.531 percent. If the growth to $110 had taken place in six months, the annual rate compounded continuously would have been twice as great or 19.062 percent; if the growth had taken two years, the annual rate would have been half as much or 4.765 percent.

The annual rate of return compounded annually is one less than the value of the exponential function e^x where x is the annual rate compounded continuously. For example, if the annual rate of return compounded continuously were 10 percent, the rate compounded annually would be given by the following expression:

$$e^{.10} - 1 = 1.1052 - 1 = .1052$$

Thus, the rate compounded annually would be 10.52 percent.*

For all wealth ratios greater than 1.0, rates compounded continuously are less than the corresponding rates compounded annually. For wealth ratios less than 1.0, the reverse is true.[6]

One common error in using rates of return is to assume that the

---

* If y is the rate compounded annually, $y = e^x - 1$, where x is the rate compounded continuously. Values of e^x can be found in most books of mathematical tables.

average annual rate of return, compounded annually, for a period of several years is equal to the arithmetic mean of the annual rates of return for the individual years. That is, if the annual rates of return compounded annually for a three-year period were 8, 10, and 12 percent respectively, one might assume that the average rate of return for the three-year period were 10 percent. This is an error. The correct answer is to be found in either of two ways. The first is to calculate the geometric mean of the annual rates of return compounded annually.* In the example presented above, the correct average annual rate of return for the three-year period would be the cube root of the annual rates as follows:

$$\text{Average annual rate} = \sqrt[3]{1.08 \times 1.10 \times 1.12} - 1 = 0.09988$$
$$= 9.99 \text{ percent}$$

The second correct way to calculate the average annual rate of return compounded annually is to compute the arithmetic mean of the annual rates compounded continuously and then find the corresponding rate compounding annually. In the example given above, the successive annual rates compounding continuously are 7.696, 9.531 and 11.333. Their mean is 9.52 and the corresponding rate compounding annually is 9.99 percent.

The point is made dramatically by considering an initial investment of $100 which is worth $200 in one year and $100 in two years. The successive annual rates, compounded annually, are 100 percent and −50 percent. The arithmetic mean of the two rates is 25 percent. The true rate is clearly 0 percent. This is the result if we take the geometric mean as follows:

$$\sqrt{2.0 \times 0.5} - 1 = 0.$$

Another source of error in some efforts to calculate rates of return is the assumption that dividends, interest, or rights are received in the middle of the relevant time period, uniformly through the time period, or at the beginning or end of the time period rather than at the time they were actually received. Since there is strong seasonality in the distribution of interest and dividends, the simplifying assumptions which are sometimes used introduce small, but occasionally significant, errors into the calculation of actual rates of return.

---

* In order to deal with negative rates of return, wealth ratios are used in computing the geometric mean. The average annual rate is then the geometric mean minus one.

There are some special problems in calculating the variability of rates of return. These are discussed in the section of this chapter dealing with that subject.

AVERAGE RATES OF RETURN ON COMMON STOCKS

New York Stock Exchange

The best of the early efforts to measure returns was by Alfred Cowles[7] who measured rates of return on all common stocks on the New York Stock Exchange for the period 1871–1937. Cowles assumed that an investor bought at the beginning of 1871 all stocks listed on the New York Stock Exchange in proportion to their market value and redistributed the holdings each month in order to preserve the proportionality. Without going into much detail, it can be said that Cowles found an average annual rate of return from such an investment policy of approximately 6.6 percent per year, compounded annually. This rate included price changes and dividends. Cowles failed to take account of brokerage charges and taxes. Since Cowles's period ended during a depression, the returns during the period which he studied are not sharply at variance with the more refined measures which were later made for subsequent periods.

A recent and comprehensive study by Fisher and Lorie[8] covers all common stocks listed on the New York Stock Exchange for the period 1926–60. The rates are average annual rates compounded annually, and assume initial equal investments in each listed common stock. Such an investment policy is possible for individual investors, but could not of course be carried out by all investors without dramatically changing the relative prices of common stocks. Only a policy of investing in common stocks in proportion to their market value is possible for all investors considered together. The policy of making equal initial investments was chosen because of its simplicity and because it implied absolute neutrality of judgement with respect to the relative attractiveness of different investments. The rates presented in this study are refined in the sense that they take account of the following: (1) commissions that would actually have been paid on round lot transactions; (2) all relevant capital changes; (3) the exact time when dividends and rights were received; (4) the tax status of these dividends; and (5) all other things that would have affected the actual rates of return from the prescribed investment policy.

The original study, covering the period 1926–60, was extended through 1965 in an article published in July 1968.[9] Since the findings of the earlier study are included in the latter, some of the major tables of the latter study are presented as tables 2–1 and 2–2.*

The findings are extremely numerous and will not be retold in the text, but a few of the highlights deserve emphasis. Over the entire period 1926–65, the average annual rate of return compounded annually (assuming reinvestment of dividends and that the investor was tax exempt) was 9.3 percent. This differs somewhat, but not greatly, from findings for earlier periods by Cowles and from the findings by Merrett and Sykes[10] for the United Kingdom. For most of the periods after World War II, rates were abnormally high. The average annual rate between the end of 1945 and the end of 1965 was 12.6 percent.†

The effect of taxes is quite noticeable. The terminal wealth of the tax-exempt investor in 1965 would have been 2.26 times as great as that of the investor in the tax category corresponding to a taxable income of $50,000 in 1960.

It is possibly interesting, though certainly not exciting, to note that rates of return with reinvestment of dividends differ slightly from rates without reinvestment. The curious thing is that rates with reinvestment need not be higher. Of course, the terminal wealth is greater if dividends are invested rather than consumed, but the rate of return may be either higher or lower. Rates of return are based upon the relationship between ending wealth and beginning wealth. Reinvestment of dividends causes terminal wealth to be greater, but it also causes the amount invested to be greater. Whether the reinvestment causes rates of return to be greater or less depends upon whether rates are greater or less after the larger amount has been invested.

The 1964 study by Fisher and Lorie attracted a great deal of attention in the press and generated some misunderstandings and passionate controversy. The rates of return reported in that study indicate by implication the rates of return that could have been achieved by the random selection of common stocks listed on the New York Stock Exchange. This fact and the fact that the reported rates were surprisingly high—higher, in fact, than rates actually achieved on many professionally managed portfolios—caused some to question the

---

* The complete tables are Appendix A.

† Although refined measures are not available for the period 1966–72, rates have been substantially below the long-term average.

TABLE 2-1

Rates of Return on Investment in Common Stocks Listed on the New York Stock Exchange with Reinvestment of Dividends (percent per annum compounded annually)

To	FROM 1/26	12/26	12/27	12/28	12/29	12/30	12/31	12/32	12/33	12/34	12/35	12/36	12/37	12/38	12/39	12/40	12/41	12/42	12/43	12/44
12/26	-1.6																			
12/27	15.3	30.0																		
12/28	23.9	37.7	45.5																	
12/29	7.8	9.6	0.1	-30.0																
12/30	-2.3	-3.5	-13.0	-31.7	-37.2															
12/31	-11.1	-13.5	-21.7	-36.3	-40.8	-47.8														
12/32	-11.0	-12.7	-19.0	-30.3	-32.1	-31.0	-11.1													
12/33	-2.7	-3.2	-7.7	-15.6	-11.8	-1.3	36.9	108.4												
12/34	-1.2	-1.6	-5.2	-11.3	-7.0	2.4	28.2	55.0	13.8											
12/35	2.2	2.1	-0.8	-5.7	-0.5	9.3	32.9	53.5	31.2	50.4										
12/36	6.6	5.5	3.1	-0.4	5.3	15.3	37.5	54.5	40.9	56.8	63.9									
12/37	0.5	0.1	-2.3	-6.2	-2.8	3.3	16.1	23.1	8.2	6.6	-10.9	-46.0								
12/38	2.8	2.5	0.4	-2.9	0.9	7.0	18.7	25.1	12.9	12.4	1.1	-16.2	30.7							
12/39	2.6	2.3	0.3	-2.6	0.9	6.0	15.7	20.5	10.1	9.0	1.1	-11.2	12.9	-3.3						
12/40	1.9	1.6	-0.2	-3.0	0.2	4.7	13.0	16.9	7.9	6.4	-1.1	-9.8	6.3	-5.0	-9.0					
12/41	1.2	0.9	-0.8	-3.3	-0.5	3.5	10.8	13.8	5.8	4.2	-1.9	-0.2	2.6	-5.5	-9.0	-10.2				
12/42	2.0	1.9	0.4	-0.4	0.9	4.8	11.6	14.3	7.2	6.0	0.9	-0.9	6.1	0.6	1.1	7.6	31.1			
12/43	3.5	3.4	2.2	1.7	3.1	7.2	13.8	16.5	10.2	9.7	5.5	0.9	12.3	9.4	12.1	22.2	47.1	56.7		
12/44	4.6	4.7	3.5	3.5	4.7	8.7	15.2	17.9	11.3	12.0	8.4	4.6	15.7	13.7	17.1	26.8	45.6	49.3	38.1	
12/45	6.3	6.5	5.5	5.5	7.0	11.3	17.6	20.4	15.4	15.5	12.4	9.3	20.3	19.4	23.7	33.6	51.4	55.4	50.1	59.8
12/46	5.5	5.7	4.7	3.2	6.0	9.9	15.6	18.0	13.3	13.1	10.2	7.2	16.3	15.0	17.8	24.2	34.8	34.5	26.0	20.2
12/47	5.3	5.6	4.6	3.1	5.8	9.3	14.6	16.8	12.4	12.1	9.4	6.7	14.7	13.5	15.5	20.3	27.5	26.3	18.9	13.2
12/48	5.1	5.2	4.2	2.8	5.8	8.5	13.5	15.5	11.3	11.1	8.4	5.8	12.7	11.7	13.3	17.0	22.5	20.8	14.2	9.1
12/49	5.7	5.8	4.9	3.6	6.0	9.1	13.8	15.7	11.7	11.5	9.1	6.8	13.3	12.3	13.9	17.3	22.2	20.8	15.2	11.4
12/50	6.5	6.7	5.9	4.6	7.0	10.2	14.9	16.7	12.9	12.8	10.6	8.5	14.8	14.1	15.6	19.0	23.5	22.4	17.9	15.0
12/51	6.9	7.1	6.4	5.1	7.5	10.6	15.1	16.7	13.1	13.1	11.0	9.0	14.8	14.1	15.6	18.6	22.6	21.6	17.7	15.2
12/52	7.0	7.2	6.5	5.3	7.6	10.5	14.8	16.4	13.0	13.0	11.0	9.0	14.5	13.8	15.1	17.9	21.5	20.4	16.8	14.5
12/53	6.6	6.8	6.1	5.0	7.1	9.8	13.9	15.3	12.2	12.1	10.2	8.3	13.3	12.5	13.7	16.1	19.3	18.1	14.8	12.5
12/54	8.1	8.2	7.6	6.5	8.7	11.6	15.3	16.8	14.3	14.4	12.7	10.5	15.5	14.8	16.2	18.7	21.9	21.0	18.2	16.4
12/55	8.4	8.6	8.0	6.9	9.2	11.9	15.9	17.4	14.6	14.6	12.7	11.1	15.9	15.2	16.6	18.8	21.8	21.1	18.6	16.9
12/56	8.5	8.7	8.1	7.0	9.2	11.8	15.7	17.1	14.4	14.4	12.6	11.1	15.6	15.1	16.2	18.2	20.8	20.2	17.9	16.4
12/57	7.8	7.9	7.3	6.3	8.3	10.7	14.3	15.5	13.2	12.4	11.2	9.7	14.0	13.5	15.1	17.5	18.3	17.5	15.1	13.6
12/58	8.8	9.0	8.4	7.6	9.5	12.1	16.0	16.9	14.4	13.9	12.7	11.3	15.1	15.0	16.0	17.6	20.2	19.4	17.3	16.0
12/59	8.9	9.1	8.5	7.6	9.7	12.1	15.6	16.8	14.4	14.5	12.8	11.5	15.6	15.0	16.0	17.6	19.9	19.1	17.1	15.8
12/60	8.8	9.0	8.3	7.5	9.4	11.6	16.1	16.1	13.9	14.0	12.3	11.1	14.8	14.2	15.1	16.6	18.7	17.9	15.9	14.6
12/61	9.3	9.5	8.9	8.1	9.9	12.2	15.4	16.6	14.4	14.5	13.0	11.8	15.4	15.0	15.8	17.3	19.3	18.5	16.5	15.4
12/62	8.6	8.8	8.2	7.3	9.1	11.1	14.3	15.3	13.3	13.3	11.8	10.7	14.0	13.5	14.3	15.6	17.3	16.5	14.6	13.5
12/63	8.9	9.1	8.5	7.7	9.5	11.6	14.5	15.6	13.5	13.6	12.2	11.0	14.3	13.8	14.6	15.8	17.4	16.7	14.9	13.9
12/64	9.1	9.3	8.8	7.9	9.6	11.6	14.9	15.6	13.6	13.7	12.4	11.3	14.4	14.0	14.7	15.8	17.4	16.7	15.0	14.0
12/65	9.3	9.5	9.0	8.2	10.0	12.0	14.9	15.9	13.9	14.0	12.6	11.6	14.6	14.2	14.9	16.0	17.5	16.9	15.4	14.4

TABLE 2-1 (continued)

FROM

To	12/45	12/46	12/47	12/48	12/49	12/50	12/51	12/52	12/53	12/54	12/55	12/56	12/57	12/58	12/59	12/60	12/61	12/62	12/63	12/64
12/46	-9.9																			
12/47	-4.4	-0.5																		
12/48	-3.5	-1.0	-2.9																	
12/49	1.9	5.4	8.2	19.3																
12/50	7.8	12.4	16.6	27.0	35.8															
12/51	9.4	13.3	16.4	23.1	25.2	14.9	8.9													
12/52	9.4	12.9	15.2	19.7	19.8	12.4	3.5	-3.1												
12/53	7.9	10.5	12.1	15.0	13.7	7.5	18.5	22.8	54.8											
12/54	12.5	15.5	17.7	21.3	21.6	17.9	19.1	22.2	37.2	19.0										
12/55	13.4	16.2	18.2	21.4	21.7	18.5					6.5									
12/56	13.3	15.6	17.2	19.8	20.0	17.0	16.9	18.6	26.7	13.3	6.5	-12.9								
12/57	10.5	12.3	13.5	15.3	14.8	12.0	11.1	11.1	14.5	3.4	-3.7	17.4	57.9							
12/58	13.3	15.3	16.7	18.7	18.6	16.5	16.5	17.5	21.9	14.5	13.0	17.6	36.0	14.4						
12/59	13.2	15.3	16.6	18.6	18.6	16.6	16.6	17.6	21.2	15.0	14.0	13.1	21.9	6.4	-1.9					
12/60	12.2	14.0	15.2	16.8	16.5	14.9	14.8	15.3	17.8	12.4	11.2									
12/61	13.2	14.9	16.0	17.5	17.3	16.0	16.0	16.6	19.0	14.6	13.9	16.1	23.7	13.6	12.9	27.6	-13.3			
12/62	11.3	12.8	13.7	14.9	14.5	13.1	12.8	13.0	14.7	10.5	9.4	10.4	15.1	6.3	3.8	5.9	2.0	17.7		
12/63	11.8	13.2	14.0	15.2	14.9	13.5	13.3	13.5	15.0	11.3	10.4	11.5	15.7	8.7	7.4	10.4	7.6	18.5	16.3	
12/64	12.1	12.1	13.4	14.5	14.3	13.3	13.3	13.8	15.3	11.9	11.2	12.3	16.2	10.4	9.7	12.8	12.9	22.6	23.4	28.3
12/65	12.6	14.1	14.9	15.9	15.8	14.5	14.3	14.7	16.2	13.1	12.5	13.6	17.7	12.7	12.4	15.9	12.9	22.6	23.4	28.3

Note: Part A—Cash-to-portfolio, tax exempt.
Source: Fisher and Lorie "Rates of Return: Year-by-year Record," p. 296.

TABLE 2–2

Rates of Return on Investment in Common Stocks Listed on the New York Stock Exchange without Reinvestment of Dividends (percent per annum compounded annually)

FROM

To	1/26	12/26	12/27	12/28	12/29	12/30	12/31	12/32	12/33	12/34	12/35	12/36	12/37	12/38	12/39	12/40	12/41	12/42	12/43	12/44
12/26	-1.8																			
12/27	14.9	29.9																		
12/28	23.3	37.5	45.6																	
12/29	8.0	10.1	0.6	-30.0																
12/30	-1.2	-2.3	-12.1	-31.5	-36.9															
12/31	-8.9	-11.3	-20.1	-35.8	-40.5	-47.6														
12/32	-9.1	-11.0	-18.1	-30.5	-32.4	-31.4	-11.5													
12/33	-2.5	-3.0	-8.0	-16.9	-13.1	-2.4	36.3	108.8												
12/34	-1.4	-1.8	-5.9	-12.9	-8.4	1.3	27.9	55.5	13.7											
12/35	1.5	1.5	-1.8	-7.5	-2.1	8.3	32.7	54.0	31.1	50.4										
12/36	6.3	4.9	2.2	-1.9	4.0	14.5	37.5	55.3	41.1	57.2	64.2									
12/37	0.4	0.0	-2.9	-7.5	-3.7	3.2	17.4	25.5	17.4	8.0	-9.9	-45.9								
12/38	2.1	1.9	-0.6	-4.7	-0.5	6.4	19.5	27.0	13.6	13.2	1.2	-16.9	30.5							
12/39	1.9	1.7	-0.7	-4.4	-0.5	6.5	16.6	22.5	10.8	9.7	-0.3	-12.2	12.8	-3.6						
12/40	1.5	1.2	-1.1	-4.6	-1.0	4.2	14.2	19.3	8.6	7.0	-1.2	-10.7	6.3	-5.3	-10.1					
12/41	1.0	0.7	-1.4	-4.7	-1.5	3.4	12.4	16.6	6.8	5.1	-2.0	-10.1	2.8	-5.7	-9.1	-10.1				
12/42	1.5	1.4	-0.6	-3.7	-0.5	4.3	12.8	16.7	7.8	6.4	0.4	-6.2	5.9	-0.0	0.4	7.1	31.1			
12/43	2.6	2.6	0.9	-1.9	1.4	6.2	14.5	18.3	10.3	9.6	4.6	2.7	11.7	8.4	11.2	21.8	47.7	57.8		
12/44	3.4	3.5	1.9	-0.6	2.8	7.6	15.5	19.3	12.0	11.6	7.2	6.7	14.8	12.5	16.0	26.3	46.3	50.2	38.2	
12/45	4.7	5.0	3.6	1.3	4.8	9.7	17.4	21.2	14.6	14.6	10.9	7.1	19.1	17.8	22.3	32.9	52.0	56.1	50.1	59.8
12/46	4.2	4.4	3.0	0.9	4.1	8.6	15.8	19.4	12.9	12.7	9.1	5.4	15.7	14.1	17.1	24.2	36.1	35.9	26.7	20.9
12/47	4.2	4.4	3.0	0.9	4.0	8.2	15.2	18.5	12.2	11.9	8.5	4.9	14.4	13.0	14.4	20.7	29.2	28.1	19.8	13.8
12/48	4.1	4.2	2.8	0.8	3.7	7.8	14.6	17.6	11.5	11.1	7.7	4.4	12.9	11.5	13.4	18.0	24.8	23.1	15.5	10.0
12/49	4.5	4.6	3.3	1.4	4.2	8.1	14.5	17.6	11.8	11.4	8.2	5.2	13.3	12.0	13.8	18.1	24.4	22.8	16.1	11.8
12/50	5.1	5.2	4.0	2.2	5.0	8.9	15.3	18.2	12.5	12.3	9.4	6.6	14.3	13.3	15.1	19.4	25.2	23.9	18.3	14.8
12/51	5.4	5.5	4.4	2.7	5.4	9.2	15.4	18.1	12.7	12.6	9.8	7.0	14.4	13.3	15.1	19.0	24.4	23.1	18.1	15.1
12/52	5.3	5.5	4.4	2.9	5.5	9.2	15.2	17.9	12.7	12.5	9.3	7.2	14.2	13.1	14.9	18.5	23.5	22.2	17.4	14.5
12/53	5.3	5.4	4.4	2.7	5.3	8.8	14.7	17.4	12.2	12.0	9.3	6.8	14.8	13.8	15.5	17.3	21.9	20.4	15.8	13.0
12/54	6.1	6.3	5.3	3.8	6.3	9.8	15.5	18.1	13.2	13.2	10.6	8.3	14.8	13.8	15.5	18.9	23.4	22.3	18.2	15.9
12/55	6.4	6.6	5.7	4.2	6.7	10.1	15.8	18.3	13.5	13.5	11.0	8.8	15.1	14.1	15.8	19.0	23.3	22.2	18.5	16.3
12/56	6.5	6.7	5.8	4.3	6.8	10.1	15.6	18.1	13.5	13.4	11.0	8.8	14.9	14.1	15.5	18.5	22.5	21.5	18.0	15.9
12/57	6.1	6.3	5.4	3.9	6.3	9.5	15.0	17.4	12.7	12.6	11.1	8.0	13.9	12.9	14.3	17.1	20.9	19.8	16.1	13.9
12/58	6.9	7.0	6.1	4.7	7.1	10.3	15.6	17.9	13.5	13.5	11.1	9.3	14.9	14.1	15.4	18.2	22.0	20.9	17.5	15.6
12/59	6.9	7.1	6.2	4.9	7.2	10.4	15.6	17.9	13.5	13.5	11.0	9.3	14.9	14.1	15.4	18.1	21.7	20.7	17.3	15.5
12/60	6.8	7.0	6.1	4.8	7.1	10.1	15.3	17.6	13.3	13.2	11.0	9.1	14.4	13.6	14.9	17.4	21.0	19.9	16.5	14.7
12/61	7.2	7.4	6.5	5.2	7.5	10.5	15.5	17.8	13.5	13.6	11.4	9.6	14.8	14.0	15.3	17.8	21.2	20.1	16.9	15.2
12/62	6.8	7.0	6.1	4.8	7.0	10.2	15.1	17.3	12.9	12.9	10.7	8.9	14.0	13.2	14.4	16.8	20.2	19.0	15.7	13.9
12/63	7.0	7.2	6.3	5.1	7.3	10.2	15.1	17.3	13.1	13.1	10.9	9.1	14.2	13.4	14.6	16.9	20.1	19.0	15.8	14.1
12/64	7.1	7.3	6.5	5.3	7.4	10.2	15.1	17.3	13.1	13.1	11.0	9.3	14.2	13.4	14.6	16.9	20.1	19.0	15.9	14.3
12/65	7.3	7.5	6.7	5.5	7.7	10.5	15.3	17.4	13.3	13.3	11.2	9.6	14.4	13.6	14.8	17.0	20.1	19.0	16.1	14.5

TABLE 2–2 (continued)

FROM

To	12/45	12/46	12/47	12/48	12/49	12/50	12/51	12/52	12/53	12/54	12/55	12/56	12/57	12/58	12/59	12/60	12/61	12/62	12/63	12/64
12/46	-9.8																			
12/47	-4.6	-0.7																		
12/48	-3.6	-1.0	-2.8																	
12/49	1.2	4.9	7.7	18.9																
12/50	6.6	11.4	15.7	26.5	35.7															
12/51	8.1	12.4	15.8	23.1	25.6	15.0														
12/52	8.3	12.1	14.8	20.0	20.3	12.5	8.8													
12/53	7.2	10.2	12.2	15.8	14.6	7.9	3.6	-3.2												
12/54	10.9	14.4	16.9	21.1	21.5	17.3	17.8	22.1	54.8											
12/55	11.8	15.0	17.4	21.2	21.6	18.0	18.5	21.8	37.7	19.0										
12/56	11.7	14.6	16.5	19.8	20.1	16.6	16.6	18.5	27.4	13.5	6.6									
12/57	9.8	12.2	13.7	16.3	15.7	12.4	11.6	11.8	15.9	4.0	-3.3	-12.7								
12/58	11.9	14.4	16.2	18.9	18.8	16.2	16.2	17.4	22.5	14.3	12.6	16.9	58.1							
12/59	12.0	14.4	16.2	18.8	18.8	16.3	16.4	17.5	21.8	14.9	13.7	17.3	36.5	14.6						
12/60	11.3	13.6	15.2	17.4	17.2	15.0	14.9	15.6	18.7	12.5	11.1	13.1	22.6	6.6	-2.1					
12/61	12.0	14.2	15.8	17.9	17.7	15.8	15.8	16.6	19.7	14.4	13.6	15.9	24.2	13.5	12.7	27.9				
12/62	10.7	12.7	14.0	15.8	15.5	13.4	13.1	13.5	15.8	10.7	9.4	10.6	15.9	6.5	3.8	6.1	-13.5			
12/63	11.0	13.0	14.3	16.0	15.7	13.7	13.5	13.8	16.0	11.4	10.4	11.6	16.5	8.8	7.2	10.6	1.8	18.0		
12/64	11.3	13.2	14.4	16.1	15.8	13.9	13.7	14.1	16.2	11.9	11.0	12.3	16.7	10.3	9.4	12.8	7.3	18.6	16.4	
12/65	11.7	13.7	14.9	16.5	16.3	14.5	14.3	14.8	16.9	13.0	12.2	13.5	18.1	12.4	12.1	15.8	12.5	22.7	23.4	28.3

Note: Part A—Cash-to-portfolio, tax exempt.
Source: Fisher and Lorie "Rates of Return: Year-by-year Record."

legitimacy of the findings and others to assert that the authors had recommended random selection as a sensible investment policy. The authors made no comment on what would be a sensible investment policy; they merely presented the results. The question of whether random selection is a sensible policy is discussed at considerable length in later chapters of this book, especially, those dealing with efficient markets and with portfolio theory.

Rates of Return on Stocks Not on the New York Stock Exchange

At about the same time that the work on rates of return on the New York Stock Exchange was being carried out, Merrett and Sykes were doing similar work for common stocks in the United Kingdom.[11] Although their studies did not take into account commissions and differed in other ways from the studies by Fisher and Lorie, the results are roughly comparable in conception and generality. The average rates of return are quite similar, though on the average somewhat lower. For example, for the period 1919–1966, an initial lump-sum investment in the shares represented by the De Zoete and Gorton Index* would have yielded an average annual return net of taxes of 8.5 percent. Merrett and Sykes also present the returns resulting from lump-sum investments for one-year periods in both real and money terms. These are summarized in table 2–3.

TABLE 2–3
Annual Rates of Return, Compounded Annually for One-Year Period Investments

	Real Terms	Money Terms
Prewar 1919–39.	12.4	10.3
War 1939–49	0.3	5.9
Postwar 1949–66	7.4	11.2
Whole Period 1919–66	8.0	9.7

Source: Merrett and Sykes, "Return on Equities."

In both series, the rates of return appear to divide into three broad groups, and, as in the United States, the nominal rates appear abnormally high in the postwar period.

There is fragmentary evidence regarding average rates of return on stocks not on the New York Stock Exchange. The National Quota-

---

* This is an index based on stocks of major companies.

tion Bureau publishes an over-the-counter industrial stock average consisting of 35 leading stocks. Between January 1960 and June 1968, the annual rate of price appreciation on these stocks was 15.5 percent as compared to 6.7 percent for the New York Stock Exchange Composite Index. The American Stock Exchange also publishes a price level index.* For the period April 1964 through June 1968, the annual rate of appreciation was 25.4 percent and the corresponding figure for the New York Stock Exchange composite index was 6.5 percent.

While interesting, the usefulness of these data in comparing rates of return is limited. The National Quotation Bureau and American Stock Exchange indexes refer to price levels, not rates of return. It seems likely that dividend yields are higher for stocks on the New York Stock Exchange than for those on the other exchanges so that differences in rates of price appreciation overstate differences in the rates of return. A further drawback lies in the methods used to construct the indexes. Both are similar to the Dow Jones Averages in that the effect of a change in the price of a component stock is not related to its price. The effect of a change of $1 in a stock selling for $10 per share is the same as that of an identical change for a stock selling for $100 per share.

VARIABILITY IN RATES OF RETURN ON COMMON STOCKS

The studies by Fisher and Lorie already discussed refer to average rates of return, assuming equal initial investments in common stocks listed on the New York Stock Exchange. These studies contain no information about the variability of rates of return among individual issues. A subsequent study by Fisher and Lorie[12] contains such information. This subject will be discussed in the chapters of this book dealing with risk and return from investments in common stocks. Nevertheless, the subject also is appropriate here as a complement to the discussion of average rates of return. The major findings on variability are presented as tables 2–4 and 2–5.

The tables are reasonably clear without detailed comment. In general, the mean wealth ratios increase with the length of the holding period. Distributions for longer holding periods tend to have greater dispersion than distributions for shorter periods, both absolutely and relatively. For all periods studied, skewness of the distribution was positive. Such a finding is almost inevitable in view of the fact that

---

* The American Stock Exchange Index is not available prior to April 1964.

TABLE 2–4

Frequency Distributions of Wealth Ratios for Investments in Individual Stocks Listed on the NYSE, 1926–65

					Centiles of the Frequency Distributions						
Period of Investment	5th	10th	20th	30th	40th	(Median) 50th	60th	70th	80th	90th	95th
(1)	(2)	(3)	(4)	(5)	(6)	(7)	(8)	(9)	(10)	(11)	(12)

ONE-YEAR PERIODS

1/30/26-12/31/26	.429	.560	.722	.845	.917	.991	1.060	1.115	1.183	1.316	1.485
12/31/26-12/31/27	.640	.752	.888	1.053	1.132	1.225	1.330	1.457	1.601	1.834	2.274
12/31/27-12/31/28	.725	.834	.976	1.064	1.153	1.251	1.376	1.512	1.711	2.136	2.795
12/31/28-12/31/29	.197	.279	.405	.518	.604	.700	.774	.873	.977	1.123	1.218
12/31/29-12/31/30	.205	.265	.367	.442	.521	.593	.674	.757	.868	.986	1.106
12/31/30-12/31/31	.158	.215	.292	.347	.401	.467	.536	.615	.738	.909	1.044
12/31/31-12/31/32	.353	.449	.561	.654	.729	.828	.931	1.035	1.173	1.377	1.662
12/31/32-12/30/33	.657	.856	1.189	1.402	1.628	1.849	2.075	2.394	2.742	3.331	4.338
12/30/33-12/31/34	.566	.645	.759	.849	.938	1.029	1.134	1.262	1.428	1.728	2.017
12/31/34-12/31/35	.761	.864	1.029	1.134	1.232	1.353	1.492	1.656	1.927	2.342	2.747
12/31/35-12/31/36	.854	.943	1.052	1.154	1.235	1.334	1.446	1.583	1.773	2.130	2.461
12/31/36-12/31/37	.276	.315	.373	.420	.472	.517	.562	.624	.687	.798	.888
12/31/37-12/31/38	.693	.838	.986	1.090	1.186	1.260	1.350	1.458	1.594	1.798	2.020
12/31/38-12/30/39	.554	.626	.704	.790	.869	.947	1.021	1.089	1.183	1.319	1.478
12/30/39-12/31/40	.477	.584	.713	.795	.852	.904	.952	1.005	1.069	1.194	1.331
12/31/40-12/31/41	.445	.545	.666	.751	.820	.879	.947	1.016	1.096	1.234	1.412
12/31/41-12/31/42	.844	.907	.986	1.054	1.120	1.190	1.273	1.380	1.527	1.766	2.106
12/31/42-12/31/43	1.032	1.088	1.195	1.249	1.331	1.403	1.499	1.624	1.812	2.130	2.560
12/31/43-12/30/44	1.029	1.088	1.151	1.202	1.245	1.304	1.372	1.441	1.556	1.750	2.025
12/30/44-12/31/45	1.179	1.238	1.316	1.372	1.427	1.500	1.578	1.672	1.805	2.074	2.329
12/31/45-12/31/46	.529	.592	.698	.785	.847	.898	.944	1.002	1.083	1.187	1.308
12/31/46-12/31/47	.617	.701	.795	.857	.910	.962	1.025	1.091	1.175	1.312	1.456
12/31/47-12/31/48	.600	.703	.798	.858	.916	.967	1.007	1.050	1.107	1.212	1.321
12/31/48-12/31/49	.840	.906	.997	1.061	1.122	1.178	1.233	1.302	1.374	1.481	1.617
12/31/49-12/30/50	.904	.965	1.047	1.123	1.207	1.298	1.384	1.487	1.614	1.817	2.015
12/30/50-12/31/51	.832	.905	.981	1.039	1.081	1.122	1.172	1.228	1.294	1.419	1.554
12/31/51-12/31/52	.771	.841	.920	.980	1.037	1.088	1.137	1.184	1.245	1.333	1.424
12/31/52-12/31/53	.602	.704	.805	.864	.918	.969	1.021	1.064	1.112	1.221	1.320
12/31/53-12/31/54	1.095	1.164	1.251	1.327	1.407	1.480	1.565	1.660	1.786	1.995	2.256
12/31/54-12/30/55	.829	.924	1.003	1.049	1.093	1.144	1.193	1.261	1.354	1.516	1.687
12/30/55-12/31/56	.711	.789	.880	.941	.989	1.026	1.082	1.141	1.236	1.378	1.518
12/31/56-12/31/57	.496	.567	.658	.721	.791	.856	.923	.996	1.060	1.149	1.228
12/31/57-12/31/58	1.112	1.199	1.294	1.363	1.434	1.491	1.552	1.647	1.780	2.001	2.326
12/31/58-12/31/59	.759	.845	.934	.988	1.028	1.080	1.149	1.214	1.323	1.527	1.715
12/31/59-12/30/60	.591	.652	.749	.825	.887	.948	1.022	1.100	1.196	1.325	1.447
12/30/60-12/29/61	.852	.935	1.037	1.114	1.176	1.235	1.301	1.373	1.460	1.621	1.818
12/29/61-12/31/62	.544	.616	.696	.761	.813	.856	.909	.965	1.019	1.114	1.207
12/31/62-12/31/63	.808	.894	.985	1.041	1.089	1.137	1.186	1.247	1.344	1.488	1.657
12/31/63-12/31/64	.765	.875	.978	1.049	1.099	1.142	1.194	1.248	1.323	1.466	1.622
12/31/64-12/31/65	.856	.923	.995	1.056	1.116	1.196	1.275	1.387	1.510	1.732	1.963

FIVE-YEAR PERIODS

1/30/26-12/31/30	.041	.095	.192	.340	.518	.682	.876	1.116	1.443	1.884	2.476
12/31/30-12/31/35	.098	.227	.417	.660	.897	1.147	1.412	1.766	2.293	3.296	4.601
12/31/35-12/31/40	.119	.218	.364	.539	.673	.832	.959	1.134	1.336	1.736	2.061
12/31/40-12/31/45	1.459	1.721	2.084	2.408	2.708	3.155	3.688	4.335	5.556	7.601	10.036
12/31/45-12/30/50	.477	.627	.865	1.007	1.148	1.302	1.481	1.702	1.960	2.409	2.838
12/30/50-12/30/55	.853	1.142	1.440	1.691	1.907	2.107	2.337	2.621	3.002	3.775	4.568
12/30/55-12/30/60	.532	.707	.939	1.130	1.292	1.477	1.656	1.883	2.181	2.708	3.396
12/30/60-12/31/65	.761	.977	1.256	1.440	1.605	1.778	1.979	2.241	2.595	3.402	4.445

TEN-YEAR PERIODS

1/30/26-12/31/35	.016	.048	.152	.256	.461	.688	1.007	1.368	1.850	2.730	4.297
12/31/35-12/31/45	.614	1.056	1.592	1.912	2.210	2.557	2.999	3.493	4.216	5.500	7.664
12/31/45-12/30/55	.621	.982	1.505	1.895	2.302	2.750	3.270	4.059	5.100	7.169	9.001
12/30/55-12/31/65	.836	1.157	1.654	2.035	2.427	2.814	3.208	3.681	4.289	5.473	7.075

20-YEAR PERIODS

1/30/26-12/31/45	.000	.052	.324	.772	1.273	1.864	2.772	3.914	5.133	7.395	11.389
12/31/45-12/31/65	.912	1.886	3.357	4.549	6.269	8.242	10.111	12.529	16.068	21.992	30.115

40-YEAR PERIOD

1/30/26-12/31/65	.000	.258	1.283	3.724	8.257	14.323	21.581	33.613	50.787	82.532	127.554

Source: Fisher and Lorie, "Studies of Variability of Returns," pp. 106–7.

* Gini's mean difference tells the expected value of the difference in returns between two portfolios of any given size, including portfolios of one stock.

† For a discussion of the interpretation of the coefficient of concentration, see Fisher and Lorie, "Studies of Variability of Returns," p. 104.

Period of Investment	Minimum	Maximum	Arithmetic Mean	Standard Deviation	Mean Deviation	Gini's Mean Difference	Coefficient of Variation	Relative Mean Deviation	Coefficient of Concentration	Skewness	Kurtosis	Number of Companies
(13)	(14)	(15)	(16)	(17)	(18)	(19)	(20)	(21)	(22)	(23)	(24)	(25)
				ONE-YEAR PERIODS								
1/30/26-12/31/26	.073	2.970	.985	.343	.242	.355	.348	.245	.180	1.304	8.891	510
12/31/26-12/31/27	.000	7.889	1.300	.577	.374	.546	.444	.288	.210	3.660	36.275	543
12/31/27-12/31/28	.398	13.226	1.453	.904	.498	.712	.622	.343	.245	5.844	60.390	589
12/31/28-12/31/29	.0C0	1.851	.700	.318	.259	.361	.454	.370	.258	.261	2.718	627
12/31/29-12/31/30	.046	2.105	.620	.286	.229	.318	.461	.369	.257	.685	4.047	717
12/31/30-12/31/31	.000	2.204	/ .522	.291	.221	.311	.558	.425	.298	1.323	6.365	737
12/31/31-12/31/32	.000	3.308	.891	.435	.319	.455	.488	.358	.255	1.481	7.462	732
12/31/32-12/30/33	.000	20.841	2.083	1.366	.873	1.253	.656	.419	.301	4.686	54.283	709
12/30/33-12/31/34	.090	9.481	1.139	.574	.364	.517	.504	.319	.227	5.358	67.343	707
12/31/34-12/31/35	.C00	6.077	1.507	.675	.485	.687	.448	.322	.228	1.830	9.327	7C6
12/31/35-12/31/36	.178	17.234	1.483	.814	.424	.605	.549	.286	.204	10.719	197.482	719
12/31/36-12/31/37	.109	1.372	.541	.195	.153	.215	.360	.283	.199	.815	4.073	744
12/31/37-12/31/38	.000	7.187	1.307	.497	.320	.469	.380	.245	.179	3.998	44.628	780
12/31/38-12/30/39	.000	2.830	.967	.313	.234	.334	.324	.242	.173	1.140	6.735	775
12/30/39-12/31/40	.000	2.748	.901	.276	.195	.288	.306	.216	.160	.823	8.584	778
12/31/40-12/31/41	.C00	2.941	.898	.312	.227	.330	.348	.253	.184	1.101	7.515	788
12/31/41-12/31/42	.560	5.907	1.311	.501	.320	.452	.382	.244	.172	3.358	21.015	797
12/31/42-12/31/43	.293	7.469	1.564	.644	.389	.550	.412	.249	.176	4.134	30.193	8C0
12/31/43-12/30/44	.417	4.389	1.383	.353	.237	.339	.256	.171	.123	2.451	14.494	810
12/30/44-12/31/45	.649	4.700	1.598	.422	.283	.400	.264	.177	.125	2.807	16.262	826
12/31/45-12/31/46	.254	2.230	.901	.242	.184	.266	.268	.204	.147	.609	4.739	853
12/31/46-12/31/47	.348	2.577	.994	.260	.195	.280	.262	.196	.141	1.031	5.812	9C4
12/31/47-12/31/48	.337	4.544	.969	.259	.169	.250	.268	.175	.129	3.571	44.575	939
12/31/48-12/31/49	.095	2.885	1.194	.254	.189	.271	.213	.158	.114	.967	7.704	963
12/31/49-12/30/50	.645	3.917	1.358	.378	.283	.397	.279	.208	.146	1.622	8.628	990
2/30/50-12/31/51	.135	4.047	1.149	.242	.168	.245	.211	.146	.107	2.249	24.699	1,010
2/31/51-12/31/52	.113	1.866	1.089	.201	.157	.223	.185	.144	.103	.207	3.915	1,029
2/31/52-12/31/53	.C00	2.135	.968	.215	.162	.234	.222	.168	.121	.389	4.939	1,044
2/31/53-12/31/54	.608	5.441	1.548	.392	.279	.397	.253	.180	.128	2.205	15.744	1,045
2/31/54-12/30/55	.163	2.886	1.190	.270	.194	.280	.227	.163	.118	1.391	7.370	1,052
2/30/55-12/31/56	.142	4.282	1.065	.268	.188	.273	.251	.176	.128	2.342	24.249	1,055
2/31/56-12/31/57	.268	2.266	.864	.242	.191	.268	.280	.221	.155	.638	5.395	1,056
2/31/57-12/31/58	.803	5.077	1.579	.440	.285	.412	.279	.181	.131	2.873	16.763	1,077
2/31/58-12/31/59	.428	3.372	1.144	.310	.219	.314	.271	.191	.137	1.824	9.521	1,067
2/31/59-12/30/60	.253	2.380	.981	.276	.215	.303	.282	.219	.154	.886	5.001	1,088
2/30/60-12/29/61	.0C0	3.810	1.276	.330	.229	.335	.259	.180	.131	1.885	12.084	1,119
2/29/61-12/31/62	.146	1.741	.865	.206	.159	.228	.239	.184	.132	.364	4.102	1,142
2/31/62-12/31/63	.C00	3.214	1.176	.287	.198	.291	.244	.168	.124	1.680	1C.576	1,162
2/31/63-12/31/64	.326	3.130	1.163	.265	.188	.278	.228	.162	.120	1.043	7.656	1,191
2/31/64-12/31/65	.289	5.426	1.282	.410	.283	.401	.320	.221	.156	2.554	16.991	1,227
				FIVE-YEAR PERIODS								
1/30/26-12/31/30	.000	4.487	.877	.778	.6C0	.822	.887	.684	.468	1.412	5.405	510
2/31/30-12/31/35	.CC0	11.841	1.568	1.585	1.079	1.506	1.011	.688	.480	2.463	11.345	737
2/31/35-12/31/40	.000	10.457	.949	.822	.519	.741	.867	.547	.391	4.460	41.754	719
2/31/40-12/31/45	.C00	48.855	4.264	3.990	2.289	3.150	.936	.537	.369	5.010	41.665	788
2/31/45-12/30/50	.063	6.514	1.455	.771	.576	.811	.530	.396	.279	1.525	7.489	853
2/30/50-12/30/55	.113	10.794	2.335	1.217	.861	1.240	.521	.369	.266	1.836	9.107	1,010
2/30/55-12/30/60	.102	35.876	1.701	1.508	.737	1.067	.886	.433	.314	12.294	257.373	1,055
2/30/60-12/31/65	.159	18.598	2.086	1.382	.851	1.221	.663	.408	.293	4.087	34.270	1,119
				TEN-YEAR PERIODS								
1/30/26-12/31/35	.000	24.674	1.238	1.852	1.086	1.480	1.496	.877	.598	5.481	56.199	510
2/31/35-12/31/45	.CC0	74.724	3.226	3.675	1.708	2.459	1.139	.529	.381	11.440	205.680	719
2/31/45-12/30/55	.047	21.753	3.526	2.766	2.012	2.779	.785	.571	.394	1.958	8.668	853
2/55-12/31/65	.084	22.340	3.241	2.350	1.506	2.166	.725	.465	.334	3.278	20.969	1,055
				20-YEAR PERIODS								
1/30/26-12/31/45	.CC0	40.763	3.361	4.759	2.943	4.018	1.416	.876	.598	3.718	22.395	510
2/45-12/31/65	.116	110.916	10.766	10.593	7.083	9.866	.984	.658	.458	3.111	19.804	853
				40-YEAR PERIOD								
1/30/26-12/31/65	.000	1715.239	35.124	89.807	36.247	48.377	2.557	1.032	.689	13.439	242.255	510

TABLE 2–5
Aggregated Frequency Distributions of Wealth Ratios from Investments in Individual Stocks Listed on the NYSE, 1926–65

		Periods				
Statistic	*40 One-Year*	*20 One-Year (1926-45)*	*20 One-Year (1946-65)*	*8 Five-Year*	*4 Ten-Year*	*2 Twenty-Year*
5th centile	.466	.356	.663	.201	.130	.052
10th centile	.613	.480	.763	.391	.340	.288
20th centile	.796	.675	.879	.726	.894	1.006
30th centile	.911	.828	.961	.990	1.416	1.871
40th centile	1.003	.958	1.026	1.240	1.833	3.028
50th centile (median) . . .	1.085	1.075	1.091	1.491	2.245	4.222
60th centile	1.173	1.192	1.161	1.762	2.709	5.626
70th centile	1.277	1.326	1.245	2.096	3.282	7.940
80th centile	1.423	1.500	1.359	2.564	4.099	11.194
90th centile	1.675	1.830	1.551	3.581	5.479	17.263
95th centile	1.975	2.230	1.743	4.875	7.451	22.878
Minimum	0.000	0.000	0.000	0.000	0.000	0.000
Maximum	20.841	20.841	5.441	48.855	74.724	110.916
Mean	1.148	1.158	1.138	1.904	2.808	7.064
Standard deviation	.554	.699	.355	2.064	2.892	9.008
Mean deviation	.351	.447	.255	1.145	1.761	5.956
Gini's mean difference . . .	.518	.653	.367	1.640	2.505	8.052
Coefficient of variation. . .	.483	.604	.312	1.084	1.030	1.275
Relative mean deviation	.306	.386	.224	.601	.627	.843
Gini's coefficient of concentration	.226	.282	.161	.431	.446	.570
Skewness.	5.339	5.062	1.791	7.197	7.315	3.485
Kurtosis	111.090	86.788	12.734	107.852	144.189	24.393
Number of cases.	35,407	14,394	21,013	6,791	3,137	1,363

Source: Fisher and Lorie, "Studies of Variability of Returns," p. 108.

it is impossible to lose more than 100 percent of one's investment (assuming that one does not buy on margin or sell short) while it is possible to make much more than 100 percent when one is lucky or wise. As a consequence of the positive skewness, the mean is almost invariably greater than the median.

The distributions depart from normality in another way. There are more observations near the mean than would be expected if the distributions were normal, and there are more observations in the extreme tails. These empirical results confirm other conjectures and studies suggesting that rates of return and wealth ratios depart from normality in these ways. These departures from normality affect the relative attractiveness of different measures of dispersion in returns as proxies for risk, as will be discussed later.

Another subject which is discussed at some length in subsequent chapters, is the effect of diversification on variability of wealth ratios or returns. (See table 2–6.) Distributions are presented for portfolios of different sizes, ranging from one stock to all stocks listed on the New York Stock Exchange. The portfolios designated with the letter *E* or *S* were formed by a simple random selection of individual stocks. Portfolios designated with the letter *R* were selected by random selection, subject to the constraint that not more than one stock could be in a single industry. As can be seen from observation of the measures of relative dispersion, diversification can lead to substantial reductions in the variability of wealth ratios, even if the selection is according to a random process.

Another interesting fact is the rapidity with which the possibility or reducing dispersion by diversifying is exhausted. (See table 2–7.) That is, usually about 90 percent of all possible reduction in relative dispersion is achieved by the time the portfolio contains only 16 stocks. For reasons discussed later, it can be worthwhile to achieve much more than 90 percent of possible reduction in dispersion. So, portfolios of many more than 16 stocks may be justified. The main advantages are a much enhanced ability to predict sensitivity of the portfolio to market movements and an improved opportunity to minimize taxes.

The tables on frequency distributions can be used in various ways. One is to measure the relative frequency of losses or gains of various magnitudes for various periods. Another is to evaluate returns on actual portfolios by seeing their place in the frequency distribution of returns on randomly selected portfolios. Although something is learned by comparisons with mean rates on such portfolios, something more is learned by reference to the frequency distributions.

RATES OF RETURN ON BONDS

Reference has already been made to some early studies of rates of return on bonds. We will comment here only on Hickman's[13] since it is one of the first to present estimates of actual, as opposed to promised, rates of return. He investigated straight corporate bonds* offered during 1900–1943 and those outstanding on January 1, 1900. The sample included almost all large straight issues (offerings of $5 million

---

* Straight corporate bonds are defined as fixed-income single-maturity bonds offered by domestic corporations and held by the domestic investing public. Such bonds are not convertible.

TABLE 2–6

Aggregated Frequency Distributions of Wealth Ratios from Investments in Randomly Selected Portfolios Containing Specified Numbers of Stocks Listed on the NYSE, 1926–65

Number and Length of Periods	Size of Portfolio/ Sampling Method	Centiles of the Aggregated Frequency Distributions										
		5th	10th	20th	30th	40th	50th (Median)	60th	70th	80th	90th	95th
(1)	(2)	(3)	(4)	(5)	(6)	(7)	(8)	(9)	(10)	(11)	(12)	(13)
PERIODS						40 YEARS 1926–1965						
40 ONE-YEAR	1E	.466	.613	.796	.911	1.003	1.085	1.173	1.277	1.423	1.675	1.975
	2E	.539	.681	.838	.939	1.021	1.099	1.182	1.280	1.409	1.622	1.855
	8S	.582	.745	.883	.964	1.044	1.121	1.196	1.286	1.406	1.569	1.719
	8R	.584	.747	.883	.964	1.045	1.122	1.198	1.288	1.407	1.570	1.718
	16S	.583	.763	.893	.965	1.046	1.129	1.202	1.290	1.408	1.561	1.680
	16R	.587	.763	.894	.965	1.046	1.130	1.205	1.293	1.409	1.566	1.684
	32S	.581	.775	.899	.964	1.043	1.136	1.205	1.295	1.408	1.555	1.648
	32R	.588	.768	.902	.968	1.041	1.140	1.214	1.299	1.406	1.565	1.657
	128S	.576	.781	.900	.966	1.035	1.147	1.200	1.301	1.403	1.555	1.606
	All	.580	.782	.900	.968	1.030	1.147	1.192	1.303	1.418	1.556	1.588
8 FIVE-YEAR	1E	.201	.391	.726	.990	1.240	1.491	1.762	2.096	2.564	3.581	4.875
	2E	.418	.605	.879	1.109	1.328	1.553	1.803	2.110	2.555	3.444	4.533
	8S	.678	.804	1.021	1.239	1.435	1.627	1.842	2.101	2.473	3.355	4.278
	8R	.680	.805	1.023	1.242	1.437	1.631	1.848	2.107	2.480	3.423	4.366
	16S	.748	.847	1.036	1.287	1.470	1.661	1.847	2.093	2.405	3.508	4.308
	16R	.746	.845	1.036	1.292	1.473	1.650	1.866	2.113	2.415	3.695	4.490
	32S	.794	.868	1.023	1.336	1.491	1.639	1.845	2.097	2.360	3.674	4.327
	32R	.769	.849	1.018	1.347	1.503	1.665	1.916	2.171	2.404	4.051	4.672
	128S	.851	.891	.976	1.416	1.517	1.633	1.818	2.109	2.316	3.987	4.335
	All						1.635					
4 TEN-YEAR	1E	.130	.340	.894	1.416	1.833	2.245	2.709	3.282	4.099	5.479	7.451
	2E	.360	.683	1.250	1.727	2.129	2.496	2.885	3.340	3.959	5.086	6.235
	8S	.736	.979	1.607	2.233	2.571	2.838	3.097	3.383	3.746	4.324	4.881
	8R	.754	.992	1.618	2.255	2.596	2.861	3.118	3.404	3.763	4.335	4.786
	16S	.870	1.065	1.545	2.452	2.749	2.968	3.173	3.387	3.661	4.062	4.436
	16R	.888	1.080	1.551	2.504	2.804	3.016	3.221	3.433	3.690	4.090	4.447
	32S	.972	1.123	1.471	2.636	2.889	3.061	3.226	3.389	3.603·	3.904	4.172
	32R	.898	1.026	1.334	2.797	3.036	3.207	3.357	3.524	3.696	3.992	4.314
	128S	1.109	1.185	1.351	2.895	3.070	3.185	3.284·	3.384	3.525	3.671	3.829
	All						3.233					
2 TWENTY-YR	1E	.052	.288	1.006	1.871	3.028	4.222	5.626	7.940	11.194	17.263	22.878
	2E	.517	.959	1.893	2.763	3.722	4.981	6.601	8.647	11.282	15.653	20.082
	8S	1.608	2.010	2.661	3.390	4.465	6.201	7.895	9.424	11.129	13.516	15.839
	8R	1.660	2.060	2.717	3.464	4.531	6.242	7.888	9.408	11.100	13.468	15.770
	16S	2.012	2.360	2.911	3.502	4.335	6.359	8.501	9.845	11.135	12.984	14.497
	16R	2.100	2.437	2.992	3.587	4.418	6.423	8.523	9.856	11.105	12.924	14.378
	32S	2.350	2.665	3.070	3.514	4.078	6.467	9.058	10.174	11.110	12.523	13.417
	32R	2.293	2.569	2.980	3.393	3.848	6.376	9.147	10.206	11.092	12.449	13.352
	128S	2.791	2.962	3.272	3.506	3.739	6.377	9.924	10.447	10.971	11.494	12.574
	All						7.064					

or more) of railroads, public utilities, and industrial corporations and a representative 10-percent sample of small straight issues, adjusted by weighting to cover all small issues. In the years 1900–1943, $71.5 billion par amount of straight bonds were offered to and acquired by the public. For the entire period, the estimated weighted average annual rate of return was 5.6 percent, compounded annually. Astonishingly, this was equal to the promised yield as a result of offsets between capital losses on defaulted issues and capital gains on irregular offerings or others called at a premium or selling at a premium in 1944. Yields on bonds offered and extinguished in different periods

Number and Length of Periods	Size of Portfolio and Sampling Method	Sample Minimum	Sample Maximum	Arithmetic Mean	Standard Deviation	Mean Deviation	Gini's Mean Difference	Coefficient of Variation	Relative Mean Deviation	Coefficient of Concentration	Skewness	Kurtosis	Number of Portfolios Examined
(14)	(15)	(16)	(17)	(18)	(19)	(20)	(21)	(22)	(23)	(24)	(25)	(26)	(27)
PERIODS						40 YEARS 1926–1965							
ONE-YEAR	1E	.000	20.841	1.148	.554	.351	.518	.483	.306	.226	5.339	111.090	35,407
	2E	.000	14.428	1.148	.451	.307	.449	.393	.268	.196	3.097	41.128	16,357,749
	8S	.164	6.272	1.148	.354	.265	.381	.308	.231	.166	1.028	7.606	5,242,880
	8R	.185	6.171	1.148	.353	.264	.381	.307	.230	.166	1.037	7.837	2,621,440
	16S	.273	4.434	1.148	.335	.257	.367	.292	.224	.160	.680	5.069	2,621,440
	16R	.284	4.406	1.149	.334	.257	.367	.290	.223	.160	.661	5.075	1,310,720
	32S	.344	3.533	1.148	.325	.253	.359	.283	.220	.157	.502	4.136	1,310,720
	32R	.373	3.261	1.150	.324	.253	.359	.281	.220	.156	.474	4.074	655,360
	128S	.434	2.525	1.148	.318	.249	.353	.277	.217	.154	.380	3.618	655,360
	All	.522	2.083	1.148	.315	.247	.350	.275	.216	.152	.345	3.493	40
FIVE-YEAR	1E	.000	48.855	1.904	2.064	1.145	1.640	1.084	.601	.431	7.197	107.852	6,791
	2E	.000	45.698	1.904	1.623	.995	1.417	.852	.523	.372	4.713	47.629	3,023,639
	8S	.103	16.196	1.904	1.190	.827	1.171	.625	.434	.307	2.239	11.032	1,048,576
	8R	.122	15.239	1.918	1.209	.837	1.189	.631	.436	.310	2.212	10.601	524,288
	16S	.268	11.391	1.905	1.103	.787	1.113	.579	.413	.292	1.794	7.059	524,288
	16R	.278	10.258	1.934	1.145	.809	1.154	.592	.418	.298	1.754	6.528	262,144
	32S	.427	8.355	1.903	1.051	.762	1.075	.552	.401	.282	1.557	5.316	262,144
	32R	.428	7.618	1.966	1.145	.814	1.165	.582	.414	.296	1.537	4.981	131,072
	128S	.668	5.713	1.906	1.019	.745	1.043	.535	.391	.274	1.409	4.293	131,072
	All	.877	4.264	1.904	1.007	.743	1.021	.529	.390	.268	1.362	4.017	8
TEN-YEAR	1E	.000	74.724	2.808	2.892	1.761	2.505	1.030	.627	.446	7.315	144.189	3,137
	2E	.000	51.189	2.808	2.144	1.418	2.039	.763	.505	.363	4.564	62.253	1,307,279
	8S	.049	16.967	2.804	1.325	.991	1.431	.472	.354	.255	1.037	8.955	524,288
	8R	.079	16.527	2.824	1.342	.994	1.436	.475	.352	.254	1.205	10.180	262,144
	16S	.192	10.241	2.807	1.137	.881	1.254	.405	.314	.223	.104	3.940	262,144
	16R	.228	9.974	2.849	1.164	.898	1.270	.409	.315	.223	.236	4.525	131,072
	32S	.475	6.930	2.806	1.030	.822	1.131	.367	.293	.201	-0.459	2.580	131,072
	32R	.476	7.813	2.896	1.150	.940	1.239	.397	.325	.214	-0.371	2.801	65,536
	128S	.797	4.637	2.804	.942	.786	.974	.336	.280	.174	-0.945	2.255	65,536
	All	1.238	3.526	2.808	.914	.785	.860	.326	.280	.153	-1.094	2.293	4
TWENTY-YR	1E	.000	110.916	7.064	9.008	5.956	8.052	1.275	.843	.570	3.485	24.393	1,363
	2E	.000	94.155	7.064	6.883	4.983	6.778	.974	.705	.480	2.327	12.326	493,173
	8S	.172	41.127	7.070	4.702	3.903	5.189	.665	.552	.367	.893	3.586	262,144
	8R	.154	36.448	7.086	4.656	3.857	5.139	.657	.544	.363	.893	3.591	131,072
	16S	.545	28.019	7.063	4.221	3.735	4.748	.598	.529	.336	.510	2.265	131,072
	16R	.646	24.726	7.095	4.156	3.678	4.679	.586	.518	.330	.498	2.237	65,536
	32S	1.208	21.171	7.058	3.961	3.701	4.438	.561	.524	.314	.272	1.603	65,536
	32R	1.190	19.714	7.002	3.999	3.769	4.465	.571	.538	.319	.243	1.522	32,768
	128S	2.213	14.266	7.061	3.758	3.699	4.033	.532	.524	.207	.065	1.127	32,760
	All	3.361	10.766	7.064	3.702	3.702	3.702	.524	.524	.262	.000	1.000	2

varied considerably. In general, actual yields on bonds offered and extinguished either prior to 1932 or subsequent to 1931 exceeded those on bonds issued before the depression and extinguished later. Table 2–8 is illustrative.

In assessing Hickman's findings, two things should be remembered. First, his estimates are derived from bonds held to maturity or until called or defaulted. In addition, the averaging of returns over time periods implicitly assumes reinvestment of interest and proceeds from redemption at a rate of return equivalent to that of the bond up until the time of its redemption.

TABLE 2-6 (continued)

Number and Length of Periods	Size of Portfolio/ Sampling Method	Centiles of the Aggregated Frequency Distributions										
		5th	10th	20th	30th	40th	(Median) 50th	60th	70th	80th	90th	95th
(1)	(2)	(3)	(4)	(5)	(6)	(7)	(8)	(9)	(10)	(11)	(12)	(13)
PERIODS							20 YEARS 1926-1945					
20 ONE-YEAR	1E	.356	.480	.675	.828	.958	1.075	1.192	1.326	1.500	1.830	2.230
	2E	.438	.545	.718	.859	.979	1.098	1.218	1.344	1.497	1.761	2.070
	8S	.510	.582	.760	.892	1.001	1.145	1.272	1.378	1.497	1.675	1.891
	8R	.512	.584	.760	.893	1.002	1.149	1.275	1.380	1.499	1.677	1.887
	16S	.524	.583	.771	.902	.995	1.167	1.295	1.389	1.498	1.649	1.837
	16R	.527	.587	.769	.903	.998	1.173	1.298	1.392	1.504	1.656	1.828
	32S	.530	.581	.779	.908	.986	1.189	1.311	1.396	1.496	1.622	1.816
	32R	.532	.588	.769	.913	.994	1.196	1.318	1.400	1.505	1.640	1.796
	128S	.533	.576	.781	.909	.976	1.221	1.322	1.400	1.501	1.593	1.766
	All	.531	.580	.795	.900	.976	1.219	1.309	1.418	1.495	1.581	1.841
4 FIVE-YEAR	1E	.100	.207	.435	.673	.920	1.200	1.561	2.022	2.722	4.123	6.168
	2E	.286	.421	.622	.798	.983	1.206	1.535	2.091	2.878	4.217	5.517
	8S	.586	.678	.804	.914	1.036	1.195	1.454	2.028	3.222	4.243	5.082
	8R	.591	.680	.806	.917	1.039	1.199	1.460	2.035	3.303	4.327	5.177
	16S	.677	.748	.847	.935	1.038	1.194	1.461	1.895	3.472	4.307	4.950
	16R	.677	.746	.845	.934	1.039	1.201	1.480	1.909	3.658	4.489	5.113
	32S	.740	.794	.868	.937	1.023	1.194	1.482	1.795	3.674	4.327	4.783
	32R	.712	.769	.849	.924	1.018	1.222	1.527	1.844	4.051	4.672	5.080
	128S	.821	.851	.891	.929	.976	1.191	1.536	1.680	3.987	4.335	4.549
	All						1.258					
2 TEN-YEAR	1E	.036	.133	.386	.772	1.255	1.702	2.084	2.596	3.367	4.578	6.213
	2E	.195	.362	.700	1.043	1.427	1.859	2.277	2.725	3.302	4.273	5.435
	8S	.590	.736	.979	1.246	1.621	2.108	2.498	2.842	3.236	3.812	4.350
	8R	.607	.754	.992	1.258	1.631	2.141	2.537	2.891	3.293	3.870	4.400
	16S	.749	.870	1.065	1.268	1.545	2.217	2.640	2.925	3.221	3.639	4.055
	16R	.763	.888	1.080	1.276	1.551	2.307	2.740	3.037	3.344	3.788	4.268
	32S	.871	.972	1.123	1.271	1.471	2.242	2.756	2.994	3.233	3.568	3.911
	32R	.813	.898	1.026	1.157	1.334	2.305	3.073	3.326	3.590	3.991	4.961
	128S	1.043	1.109	1.185	1.264	1.351	1.967	2.952	3.109	3.270	3.481	3.672
	All						2.232					

TABLE 2-6 (concluded)

Number and Length of Periods	Size of Portfolio/ Sampling Method	Centiles of the Aggregated Frequency Distributions										
		5th	10th	20th	30th	40th	(Median) 50th	60th	70th	80th	90th	95th
(1)	(2)	(3)	(4)	(5)	(6)	(7)	(8)	(9)	(10)	(11)	(12)	(13)
PERIODS							20 YEARS 1945-1965					
20 ONE-YEAR	1E	.663	.763	.879	.961	1.026	1.091	1.161	1.245	1.359	1.551	1.743
	2E	.746	.820	.913	.982	1.042	1.100	1.162	1.236	1.335	1.497	1.650
	8S	.829	.876	.944	1.005	1.063	1.114	1.163	1.218	1.299	1.454	1.567
	8R	.831	.876	.944	1.005	1.062	1.113	1.163	1.219	1.300	1.454	1.566
	16S	.847	.887	.948	1.007	1.069	1.120	1.165	1.214	1.285	1.450	1.557
	16R	.849	.888	.948	1.005	1.067	1.120	1.166	1.216	1.287	1.448	1.559
	32S	.857	.891	.951	1.004	1.074	1.127	1.167	1.210	1.277	1.453	1.558
	32R	.860	.894	.954	1.003	1.065	1.128	1.174	1.219	1.282	1.443	1.560
	128S	.864	.887	.962	.994	1.078	1.140	1.169	1.199	1.277	1.456	1.561
	All	.865	.883	.968	.987	1.077	1.147	1.169	1.192	1.279	1.453	1.563
4 FIVE-YEAR	1E	.579	.797	1.057	1.264	1.460	1.656	1.875	2.131	2.474	3.149	3.916
	2E	.861	1.015	1.227	1.399	1.560	1.724	1.903	2.116	2.407	2.924	3.481
	8S	1.175	1.280	1.427	1.554	1.678	1.810	1.953	2.115	2.312	2.600	2.865
	8R	1.177	1.281	1.428	1.556	1.682	1.816	1.960	2.121	2.316	2.602	2.868
	16S	1.267	1.351	1.473	1.583	1.702	1.837	1.982	2.130	2.291	2.506	2.688
	16R	1.267	1.350	1.471	1.586	1.712	1.855	2.004	2.148	2.305	2.516	2.702
	32S	1.331	1.397	1.495	1.590	1.710	1.863	2.016	2.151	2.284	2.448	2.573
	32R	1.329	1.393	1.494	1.600	1.743	1.942	2.099	2.219	2.336	2.483	2.610
	128S	1.400	1.435	1.507	1.603	1.712	1.923	2.054	2.165	2.267	2.364	2.431
	All						1.894					
2 TEN-YEAR	1E	.749	1.073	1.576	1.960	2.358	2.787	3.233	3.843	4.661	6.361	8.260
	2E	1.290	1.590	2.003	2.340	2.661	2.992	3.361	3.824	4.483	5.610	6.839
	8S	2.144	2.350	2.620	2.836	3.034	3.241	3.463	3.719	4.068	4.643	5.146
	8R	2.160	2.364	2.630	2.845	3.040	3.244	3.465	3.718	4.059	4.628	5.118
	16S	2.439	2.614	2.831	2.993	3.151	3.308	3.479	3.669	3.922	4.290	4.620
	16R	2.451	2.626	2.845	3.005	3.161	3.313	3.479	3.663	3.906	4.256	4.559
	32S	2.661	2.800	2.962	3.105	3.224	3.342	3.472	3.613	3.785	4.020	4.268
	32R	2.721	2.867	3.020	3.153	3.262	3.371	3.493	3.619	3.773	3.992	4.201
	128S	2.924	3.021	3.147	3.219	3.291	3.363	3.445	3.535	3.625	3.738	3.904
	All						3.383					

Source: Fisher & Lorie, "Studies of Variability of Returns", pp. 110-13.

Number and Length of Periods	Size of Portfolio and Sampling Method	Sample Minimum	Sample Maximum	Arithmetic Mean	Standard Deviation	Mean Deviation	Gini's Mean Difference	Coefficient of Variation	Relative Mean Deviation	Coefficient of Concentration	Skewness	Kurtosis	Number of Portfolios Examined
(14)	(15)	(16)	(17)	(18)	(19)	(20)	(21)	(22)	(23)	(24)	(25)	(26)	(27)

PERIODS

20 YEARS 1926-1945

Number and Length of Periods	Size of Portfolio and Sampling Method	Sample Minimum	Sample Maximum	Arithmetic Mean	Standard Deviation	Mean Deviation	Gini's Mean Difference	Coefficient of Variation	Relative Mean Deviation	Coefficient of Concentration	Skewness	Kurtosis	Number of Portfolios Examined
ONE-YEAR	1E	.000	20.841	1.158	.699	.447	.653	.604	.386	.282	5.062	86.788	14,394
	2E	.000	14.428	1.158	.569	.399	.574	.492	.344	.248	2.880	31.712	5,246,994
	8S	.164	6.272	1.158	.448	.355	.493	.387	.306	.213	.869	5.628	2,621,440
	8R	.185	6.171	1.159	.447	.354	.492	.386	.306	.212	.874	5.805	1,310,720
	16S	.273	4.434	1.158	.425	.348	.476	.367	.301	.205	.529	3.691	1,310,720
	16R	.284	4.406	1.159	.422	.347	.474	.364	.300	.204	.507	3.709	655,360
	32S	.344	3.533	1.157	.412	.345	.465	.356	.298	.201	.358	2.993	655,360
	32R	.373	3.261	1.162	.410	.345	.464	.353	.297	.200	.322	2.946	327,680
	128S	.434	2.525	1.158	.403	.343	.455	.348	.296	.196	.237	2.606	327,680
	All	.522	2.083	1.158	.400	.341	.450	.346	.295	.194	.204	2.514	20
FIVE-YEAR	1E	.000	48.855	1.914	2.615	1.485	2.050	1.366	.776	.535	6.257	75.783	2,754
	2E	.000	45.698	1.914	2.091	1.355	1.825	1.092	.708	.477	3.996	32.107	969,210
	8S	.103	16.196	1.914	1.588	1.226	1.561	.830	.640	.408	1.805	6.781	524,288
	8R	.122	15.239	1.937	1.615	1.244	1.591	.834	.642	.411	1.762	6.447	262,144
	16S	.268	11.391	1.917	1.490	1.196	1.494	.778	.624	.390	1.413	4.158	262,144
	16R	.278	10.258	1.962	1.549	1.235	1.557	.789	.629	.397	1.346	3.765	131,072
	32S	.427	8.355	1.912	1.431	1.177	1.442	.748	.615	.377	1.212	3.056	131,072
	32R	.428	7.618	1.999	1.562	1.258	1.577	.781	.629	.395	1.147	2.761	65,536
	128S	.668	5.713	1.917	1.397	1.170	1.394	.729	.611	.363	1.070	2.391	65,536
	All	.877	4.264	1.914	1.383	1.175	1.347	.722	.614	.352	1.032	2.223	4
TEN-YEAR	1E	.000	74.724	2.232	3.075	1.845	2.302	1.378	.826	.516	10.879	225.901	1,229
	2E	.000	51.189	2.232	2.284	1.550	1.935	1.023	.695	.433	6.927	98.839	387,916
	8S	.049	16.967	2.227	1.415	1.189	1.459	.636	.534	.328	2.162	14.642	262,144
	8R	.079	16.527	2.269	1.473	1.202	1.497	.649	.530	.330	2.326	15.430	131,072
	16S	.192	10.241	2.229	1.222	1.091	1.327	.548	.489	.298	1.079	5.646	131,072
	16R	.228	9.974	2.316	1.322	1.134	1.420	.571	.490	.307	1.191	5.836	65,536
	32S	.475	6.930	2.230	1.113	1.039	1.239	.499	.466	.278	.511	2.630	65,536
	32R	.476	7.813	2.390	1.398	1.268	1.540	.585	.530	.322	.562	2.448	32,768
	128S	.797	4.637	2.228	1.023	1.000	1.118	.459	.449	.251	.103	1.233	32,768
	All	1.238	3.226	2.232	.994	.994	.994	.445	.445	.223	.000	1.000	2

Number and Length of Periods	Size of Portfolio and Sampling Method	Sample Minimum	Sample Maximum	Arithmetic Mean	Standard Deviation	Mean Deviation	Gini's Mean Difference	Coefficient of Variation	Relative Mean Deviation	Coefficient of Concentration	Skewness	Kurtosis	Number of Portfolios Examined
(14)	(15)	(16)	(17)	(18)	(19)	(20)	(21)	(22)	(23)	(24)	(25)	(26)	(27)

PERIODS

20 YEARS 1945-1965

Number and Length of Periods	Size of Portfolio and Sampling Method	Sample Minimum	Sample Maximum	Arithmetic Mean	Standard Deviation	Mean Deviation	Gini's Mean Difference	Coefficient of Variation	Relative Mean Deviation	Coefficient of Concentration	Skewness	Kurtosis	Number of Portfolios Examined
ONE-YEAR	1E	.000	5.441	1.138	.355	.255	.367	.312	.224	.161	1.791	12.734	21,013
	2E	.174	4.951	1.138	.287	.216	.307	.252	.189	.135	1.233	7.080	11,110,755
	8S	.534	2.644	1.138	.223	.174	.246	.196	.153	.108	.769	3.673	2,621,440
	8R	.535	2.580	1.138	.222	.174	.246	.195	.153	.108	.772	3.654	1,310,720
	16S	.637	2.214	1.138	.210	.165	.233	.185	.145	.103	.708	3.259	1,310,720
	16R	.658	2.141	1.138	.210	.166	.233	.184	.146	.103	.710	3.228	655,360
	32S	.697	1.989	1.138	.203	.160	.227	.179	.141	.100	.681	3.059	655,360
	32R	.711	1.930	1.139	.202	.161	.226	.178	.142	.099	.670	3.007	327,680
	128S	.777	1.765	1.138	.198	.156	.221	.174	.137	.097	.664	2.917	327,680
	All	.864	1.579	1.138	.197	.154	.218	.173	.136	.096	.659	2.875	20
FIVE-YEAR	1E	.063	35.876	1.894	1.296	.806	1.152	.684	.425	.304	6.646	129.423	4,037
	2E	.107	24.524	1.894	.947	.635	.903	.500	.335	.238	4.318	57.353	2,054,429
	8S	.553	7.417	1.894	.557	.428	.597	.294	.226	.158	1.458	8.981	524,288
	8R	.639	7.554	1.899	.562	.430	.600	.296	.226	.158	1.528	9.500	262,144
	16S	.846	5.052	1.894	.460	.377	.514	.243	.199	.136	.699	3.666	262,144
	16R	.886	4.934	1.906	.470	.383	.524	.247	.201	.138	.732	3.866	131,072
	32S	.910	3.507	1.895	.404	.348	.462	.213	.184	.122	.309	2.168	131,072
	32R	1.022	3.471	1.932	.422	.370	.484	.218	.191	.125	.167	1.972	65,536
	128S	1.197	2.746	1.894	.355	.320	.408	.187	.169	.108	.052	1.596	65,536
	All	1.455	2.335	1.894	.340	.316	.378	.179	.167	.100	.004	1.461	4
TEN-YEAR	1E	.047	22.340	3.383	2.571	1.677	2.485	.760	.496	.367	2.499	13.148	1,908
	2E	.064	21.851	3.383	1.820	1.286	1.865	.538	.380	.276	1.775	8.049	919,363
	8S	.837	9.564	3.381	.917	.793	1.004	.271	.235	.148	.915	4.242	262,144
	8R	1.035	9.523	3.380	.902	.787	.990	.267	.233	.146	.886	4.139	131,072
	16S	1.451	7.562	3.385	.653	.671	.726	.193	.198	.107	.668	3.613	131,072
	16R	1.523	6.935	3.381	.630	.662	.703	.186	.196	.104	.611	3.488	65,536
	32S	1.999	5.787	3.382	.469	.605	.527	.139	.179	.078	.494	3.230	65,536
	32R	1.912	5.420	3.401	.425	.613	.479	.125	.180	.070	.358	3.029	32,768
	128S	2.600	4.409	3.379	.256	.572	.290	.076	.169	.043	.289	2.821	32,768
	All	3.241	3.526	3.383	.143	.143	.143	.042	.042	.021	.000	1.000	2

TABLE 2–7

Percent of Possible Reduction in Relative Dispersion Achieved through Increasing the Number of Stocks in the Portfolio (based on portfolios of stocks from NYSE for 1926–65 or as specified)

Measure of Relative Dispersion for Holding Period(s)	*Number of Stocks in Portfolio*						
	1	*2*	*8*	*16*	*32*	*128*	*All (Market)*
Coefficient of Variation							
40 one-year	0	43	84	92	96	99	100
20 one-year (1926–45).	0	43	84	92	96	99	100
20 one-year (1946–65).	0	43	84	92	96	99	100
8 five-year	0	42	83	91	96	99	100
4 ten-year	0	38	79	89	94	99	100
2 twenty-year	0	40	81	90	95	99	100
Relative Mean Deviation							
40 one-year	0	42	84	91	95	98	100
20 one-year (1926–45).	0	45	87	94	96	99	100
20 one-year (1946–65).	0	39	80	89	94	99	100
8 five-year	0	37	79	89	95	99	100
4 ten-year	0	35	79	90	96	100	100
2 twenty-year	0	43	91	99	100	100	100
Gini's Coefficient of Concentration							
40 one-year	0	41	81	90	94	98	100
20 one-year (1926–45).	0	39	79	87	93	98	100
20 one-year (1946–65).	0	40	81	89	94	98	100
8 five-year	0	36	76	85	91	97	100
4 ten-year	0	28	65	76	84	93	100
2 twenty-year	0	29	66	76	83	92	100

Source: Fisher and Lorie, "Studies of Variability of Returns," p. 116.

TABLE 2–8

Weighted Average Realized Yields, Large Issues Only

Years		*Realized Yield (Percent)*
Offered	*Extinguished*	
1900–31	1900–31	6.4
1900–31	1932–43	4.6
1932–43	1932–43	6.0

Source: Hickman, *Corporate Bond Quality.*

More recently, Weil[14] and Fisher and Weil[15] have made estimates for 1926–68 of the nominal return* on holdings for one or more years of a portfolio of 4 percent, 20-year bonds. In contrast to Hickman's analysis, the study does not assume that bonds are held to maturity. The estimated returns are those in the first year of ownership of a high-grade, 20-year maturity, corporate bond portfolio. To measure this, the portfolio is assumed to consist of a "pseudo-bond" whose investment performance can be calculated from an index. The one used is Standard & Poor's Corporate AAA Bond Yields. The initial investment is the purchase of a 20-year, 4 percent bond. It is sold one year later when it has become a 19-year bond, and the proceeds together with the interest just received ($4.04) are used to purchase a new 20-year bond. This avoids not only the problem of having bonds of differing maturities in the portfolio, but also the question of the reinvestment rate.

For the entire period, the mean nominal one-year holding period return was 3.9 percent. If the investment were made in December 1925 and held (with alteration each year to maintain a term to maturity of approximately 20 years) until December 1968, the return would have been 3.3 percent. The estimated returns are probably biased upward because of the use of the Standard & Poor's Index whose bonds are never in default, and because commissions and taxes are ignored. Table 2–9 presents returns for various holding periods and is directly comparable to the Fisher-Lorie rates of return on common stocks in table 2–1.

One of the major decisions which investment managers must make is the allocation of funds between equities, primarily common stock, and fixed-income assets, primarily bonds. The relative attractiveness of returns on these two classes of investments has been of interest over the past century. One of the pioneer studies was that of Edgar Lawrence Smith.[16] Writing in 1924, Smith surmised that bonds would outperform stocks in periods when the price level falls. His data relate to four separate holdings of stocks and bonds covering various overlapping periods of about 20 years from 1866 to 1922. The stock samples were selected by three arbitrary methods. For each of 11 test periods, Smith assumed an initial investment of approximately $10,000 in the common stocks of ten different companies, and an investment

---

* In their terminology, the nominal return is the realized yield uncorrected for changes in the price level. All returns discussed so far in this book have been nominal returns.

TABLE 2–9

Annual Returns on a Constant Portfolio of 20-Year AAA Bonds (percent per annum compounded annually)

ANNUAL RETURNS TO HOLDING A CONSTANT PORTFOLIO OF TWENTY-YEAR AAA BONDS

FROM	12/25	12/26	12/27	12/28	12/29	12/30	12/31	12/32	12/33	12/34	12/35	12/36	12/37	12/38	12/39	12/40	12/41	12/42	12/43	12/44
To
12/26	7.2
12/27	7.0	6.7
12/28	5.4	4.5	2.3
12/29	4.4	3.5	1.9	1.6
12/30	5.6	5.2	4.7	5.9	10.4
12/31	4.7	4.2	3.5	3.9	5.1	0.1
12/32	4.7	4.3	3.8	4.1	5.0	2.4	4.8
12/33	5.1	4.9	4.6	5.0	5.9	4.4	6.7	8.6
12/34	6.2	6.1	6.0	6.7	7.7	7.0	9.5	11.9	15.3
12/35	6.6	6.5	6.5	7.1	8.1	7.6	9.6	11.3	12.6	9.9
12/36	6.7	6.7	6.6	7.2	8.0	7.6	9.2	10.4	11.0	8.8	7.7
12/37	6.3	6.3	6.2	6.7	7.3	6.9	8.1	8.7	8.8	6.6	5.0	2.4
12/38	6.3	6.2	6.2	6.6	7.1	6.7	7.7	8.2	8.2	6.4	5.3	4.1	5.8
12/39	6.2	6.1	6.1	6.4	6.9	6.5	7.4	7.7	7.6	6.1	5.2	4.3	5.3	4.8
12/40	6.1	6.0	6.0	6.3	6.7	6.3	7.1	7.4	7.2	5.9	5.1	4.4	5.1	4.8	4.8
12/41	5.9	5.8	5.7	6.0	6.4	6.0	6.6	6.8	6.6	5.4	4.7	4.1	4.5	4.1	3.7	2.6
12/42	5.7	5.6	5.5	5.8	6.1	5.7	6.3	6.4	6.2	5.1	4.4	3.9	4.2	3.8	3.4	2.7	2.9
12/43	5.6	5.5	5.4	5.6	5.9	5.5	6.0	6.1	5.9	4.9	4.3	3.8	4.0	3.7	3.4	2.9	3.1	3.3
12/44	5.5	5.4	5.3	5.5	5.8	5.4	5.9	6.0	5.7	4.8	4.3	3.8	4.0	3.8	3.6	3.2	3.5	3.7	4.2
12/45	5.5	5.4	5.3	5.5	5.7	5.4	5.8	5.9	5.7	4.8	4.3	3.9	4.1	3.9	3.8	3.6	3.8	4.1	4.5	4.8
12/46	5.3	5.2	5.1	5.3	5.5	5.2	5.6	5.6	5.4	4.6	4.2	3.8	4.0	3.7	3.6	3.4	3.6	3.7	3.9	3.7
12/47	5.0	4.9	4.8	5.0	5.2	4.9	5.2	5.2	5.0	4.2	3.7	3.4	3.5	3.2	3.0	2.8	2.8	2.8	2.7	2.1
12/48	5.0	4.9	4.8	4.9	5.1	4.8	5.1	5.1	4.9	4.2	3.7	3.4	3.5	3.3	3.1	2.9	3.0	3.0	2.9	2.6
12/49	5.0	4.9	4.8	5.0	5.1	4.9	5.1	5.2	4.9	4.3	3.9	3.6	3.7	3.5	3.4	3.2	3.3	3.4	3.4	3.2
12/50	4.9	4.8	4.7	4.8	5.0	4.7	4.9	4.9	4.7	4.1	3.7	3.5	3.5	3.3	3.2	3.1	3.1	3.1	3.1	2.9
12/51	4.6	4.4	4.4	4.4	4.6	4.3	4.5	4.5	4.3	3.7	3.3	3.0	3.0	2.8	2.7	2.5	2.5	2.4	2.3	2.1
12/52	4.5	4.4	4.3	4.4	4.5	4.3	4.5	4.5	4.3	3.7	3.3	3.1	3.1	2.9	2.8	2.6	2.6	2.5	2.4	2.2
12/53	4.4	4.3	4.2	4.3	4.4	4.2	4.4	4.4	4.1	3.6	3.2	3.0	3.0	2.8	2.7	2.5	2.5	2.5	2.4	2.2
12/54	4.5	4.4	4.3	4.4	4.5	4.2	4.4	4.4	4.2	3.7	3.4	3.1	3.2	3.0	2.9	2.8	2.8	2.8	2.7	2.6
12/55	4.3	4.2	4.1	4.2	4.3	4.0	4.2	4.2	4.0	3.5	3.2	2.9	3.0	2.8	2.7	2.5	2.5	2.5	2.4	2.3
12/56	4.0	3.9	3.8	3.8	3.9	3.6	3.8	3.8	3.6	3.0	2.7	2.5	2.5	2.3	2.2	2.0	2.0	1.9	1.8	1.6
12/57	4.0	3.9	3.8	3.9	4.0	3.7	3.9	3.9	3.7	3.2	2.9	2.7	2.7	2.5	2.4	2.3	2.2	2.2	2.1	1.9
12/58	3.8	3.7	3.6	3.7	3.8	3.5	3.7	3.6	3.4	3.0	2.7	2.4	2.4	2.3	2.1	2.0	2.0	1.9	1.8	1.4
12/59	3.7	3.6	3.5	3.5	3.6	3.3	3.4	3.4	3.2	2.7	2.5	2.2	2.2	2.1	1.9	1.8	1.7	1.7	1.6	1.4
12/60	3.8	3.7	3.6	3.6	3.7	3.5	3.6	3.6	3.4	2.9	2.7	2.5	2.5	2.3	2.2	2.1	2.0	2.0	1.9	1.8
12/61	3.8	3.7	3.6	3.6	3.7	3.5	3.6	3.6	3.4	3.0	2.7	2.5	2.5	2.4	2.3	2.1	2.1	2.1	2.0	1.9
12/62	3.9	3.8	3.7	3.7	3.8	3.6	3.7	3.7	3.6	3.1	2.9	2.7	2.7	2.6	2.5	2.4	2.4	2.4	2.3	2.2
12/63	3.8	3.7	3.7	3.7	3.8	3.6	3.7	3.7	3.5	3.1	2.9	2.7	2.7	2.6	2.5	2.4	2.4	2.3	2.3	2.2
12/64	3.8	3.8	3.7	3.7	3.8	3.6	3.7	3.7	3.5	3.1	2.9	2.7	2.8	2.6	2.6	2.5	2.5	2.4	2.4	2.3
12/65	3.7	3.7	3.6	3.6	3.7	3.5	3.6	3.5	3.4	3.0	2.8	2.6	2.6	2.5	2.4	2.4	2.3	2.3	2.3	2.2
12/66	3.6	3.5	3.4	3.4	3.5	3.3	3.4	3.3	3.2	2.8	2.6	2.4	2.4	2.3	2.2	2.1	2.1	2.1	2.0	1.9
12/67	3.4	3.3	3.2	3.2	3.3	3.1	3.2	3.1	3.0	2.6	2.4	2.2	2.2	2.1	2.0	1.9	1.9	1.8	1.8	1.7
12/68	3.3	3.3	3.2	3.2	3.2	3.1	3.1	3.1	2.9	2.6	2.4	2.2	2.2	2.1	2.0	1.9	1.9	1.8	1.8	1.7
12/69	3.3	3.2	3.1	3.7	3.2	3.0	3.1	3.1	2.9	2.6	2.4	2.2	2.2	2.1	2.0	1.9	1.9	1.9	1.8	1.7

ANNUAL RETURNS TO HOLDING A CONSTANT PORTFOLIO OF TWENTY-YEAR AAA BONDS
PAGE 2 (CONTINUED)

FROM	12/45	12/56	12/47	12/48	12/49	12/50	12/51	12/52	12/53	12/54	12/55	12/56	12/57	12/58	12/59	12/60	12/61	12/62	12/63	12/64	12/65	12/66	12/67
To
12/46	2.6
12/47	0.8	-0.9
12/48	1.8	1.4	3.9
12/49	2.8	2.9	4.9	5.9
12/50	2.6	2.5	3.7	3.7	1.5
12/51	1.6	1.4	2.0	1.4	-0.8	-3.1
12/52	1.9	1.8	2.4	2.0	0.7	0.3	3.9
12/53	1.9	1.8	2.3	2.0	1.0	0.8	2.9	1.8
12/54	2.3	2.3	2.8	2.6	1.9	2.0	3.8	3.8	5.7
12/55	2.0	2.0	2.3	2.1	1.5	1.5	2.7	2.3	2.5	-0.7
12/56	1.3	1.2	1.4	1.1	0.4	0.3	0.9	0.2	-0.3	-3.2	-5.7
12/57	1.7	1.6	1.9	1.7	1.2	1.1	1.8	1.4	1.3	-0.1	0.2	6.4
12/58	1.4	1.3	1.5	1.3	0.8	0.7	1.2	0.8	0.6	-0.6	-0.6	2.0	-2.2
12/59	1.1	1.0	1.2	1.0	0.5	0.4	0.8	0.4	0.1	-1.0	-1.0	0.6	-2.2	-2.2
12/60	1.6	1.5	1.7	1.5	1.1	1.1	1.6	1.3	1.2	0.5	0.7	2.4	1.1	2.7	7.9
12/61	1.7	1.6	1.8	1.7	1.3	1.3	1.8	1.5	1.5	0.9	1.2	2.6	1.7	3.0	5.7	3.6
12/62	2.1	2.0	2.2	2.1	1.8	1.8	2.3	2.1	2.2	1.7	2.1	3.4	2.9	4.2	6.4	5.6	7.7
12/63	2.1	2.0	2.2	2.1	1.8	1.9	2.3	2.1	2.2	1.8	2.1	3.2	2.7	3.7	5.3	4.4	4.9	2.1
12/64	2.2	2.2	2.3	2.2	2.0	2.0	2.4	2.3	2.4	2.0	2.3	3.4	3.0	3.9	5.1	4.4	4.7	3.3	4.5
12/65	2.1	2.0	2.2	2.1	1.9	1.9	2.2	2.1	2.1	1.8	2.1	3.0	2.6	3.3	4.2	3.5	3.4	2.1	2.1	-0.3
12/66	1.8	1.7	1.9	1.8	1.5	1.5	1.9	1.7	1.7	1.4	1.6	2.3	1.9	2.4	3.1	2.3	2.0	0.7	0.2	-1.9	-3.5
12/67	1.5	1.5	1.6	1.5	1.3	1.2	1.5	1.4	1.4	1.0	1.1	1.8	1.3	1.7	2.2	1.5	1.1	-0.2	-0.7	-2.4	-3.4	-3.4
12/68	1.5	1.5	1.6	1.5	1.3	1.3	1.5	1.4	1.3	1.0	1.2	1.8	1.4	1.7	2.2	1.5	1.2	0.1	-0.3	-1.4	-1.8	-0.9	1.5
12/69	1.6	1.5	1.6	1.5	1.3	1.3	1.5	1.4	1.4	1.1	1.2	1.8	1.4	1.7	2.1	1.5	1.2	0.3	0.1	-0.8	-0.9	-0.1	1.6

Source: Fisher and Weil, "Coping with Interest-Rate Fluctuations," p. 425.

of the same amount in high-grade bonds. He then compared: (1) the terminal market value (without reinvestment of interest or dividends) of the stock portfolios with those of the bond portfolios, and (2) the income accounts. Although the tests were biased in favor of bonds since he assumed no depreciation or default for the latter, in ten of the eleven periods, stocks outperformed bonds. In three of the periods, the price level fell. In no test period was there a loss in stocks. Although the methodology is crude, the results are interesting in the light of more recent investigations.* Donald Kemerer[17] also compared the performance of stocks and bonds for the period 1900–1950. Looking at the real (deflated by a price index) gains in indexes of stock and bond prices for 41 ten-year periods, he found that stocks were the better investment in 35 and bonds in only 6. Moreover, if dividend yields had been considered, stock investment would have been even more favorable.

The Fisher-Weil[18] study permits refined comparisons between rates of return on stocks and bonds. In addition to their rates of return discussed earlier, they developed an index of the investment perfor-

TABLE 2–10

Statistics on Ratios of Terminal Wealth to Initial Investment for High-Grade Bonds and Common Stocks

Statistic (1)	Bonds (2)	Stocks per Index (3)	Stocks per Fisher-Lorie Study (4)
40 One-Year Periods Beginning in December of 1925, 1926, . . . , 1964			
Minimum.	0.943	0.542	0.527
Maximum	1.153	2.376	2.104
Mean	1.038	1.178	1.153
Standard Deviation	.040	.343	.318
Mean Deviation	.030	.257	.249
Gini's Mean Difference · · · · · · · · ·	.044	.368	.354
8 Five-Year Periods Beginning in December of 1925, 1930, . . . , 1960			
Minimum.	1.036	.775	0.886
Maximum	1.444	4.626	4.307
Mean	1.208	2.095	1.923
Standard Deviation	.125	1.136	1.017
Mean Deviation	.104	.867	.750
Gini's Mean Difference	.140	1.205	1.031

Source: Fisher and Weil, "Coping with Interest-Rate Fluctuations," p. 412.

---

* Smith's work was updated in 1954 by Winthrop B. Walker. His results which appeared in *A Re-examination of Common Stocks as Long Term Investments* (Portland, Maine: The Anthoensen Press, 1954) cover the period 1923–51 and support the earlier findings.

mance of long-term, high-grade bonds when a naïve strategy is followed. This is directly comparable to an index of the investment performance of common stocks.[19] From these it is possible to estimate the ratio of final wealth to initial investment for an investor who bought stocks or bonds at various dates, assuming no commissions, taxes, or other expenses. They found for the period 1926–68 that "long-term bonds have given both lower average return and more than proportionately lower dispersion than would have been obtained from holding a well-diversified portfolio of common stocks listed on the New York Stock Exchange."[20] Some of their results are summarized in table 2–10.

Merrett and Sykes[21] also looked at returns on fixed-interest securities relative to those on equities for the United Kingdom. The average return from year-to-year investments in consols* for the period 1919–66 was 2.3 percent, as compared to an average return of 8.5 percent on equities. Of particular interest is the fact that almost without exception, the returns for lump-sum investments for ten-year periods are substantially larger for equities than for bonds.

---

* Consols are bonds with no maturity; they are "perpetuities."

3

Stock Market Indexes

INTRODUCTION

FOR SEVERAL REASONS, it is necessary to include a discussion of stock market indexes. In talking about investments, it is necessary to talk about movements in "the market" and it is interesting to compare such movements with other things such as industrial production, changes in the money supply, and corporate profits. Rates of return on the market itself can be a valuable bench mark for judging the performance of actual portfolios. Further, modern portfolio theory requires knowledge of the relationship of prices of individual stocks to movements in the market in order to allocate funds rationally among stocks. For these and other purposes it is essential that there be a summary measure of the behavior of the market. Indexes serve this purpose. Since there are several in general use, it seems sensible to discuss the principles underlying them, the uses for which each is best suited, and the relationships among changes in them.

SOME PROBLEMS

We do not present a detailed, technical discussion on indexes in general since such discussions are available in numerous books on statistics.[1] Nevertheless, we shall discuss the following three important issues which arise in constructing indexes:

1. Selecting stocks for inclusion.
2. Determining the relative importance or weight of each included stock.
3. Combining or averaging included stocks.

In briefer terms, there are the problems of sampling, weighting, and averaging.

Sampling

An index can be based on a sample of stocks or upon all of them. Movements in the New York Stock Exchange could be represented by movements of, say, 100 stocks or by movements in the entire list. When indexes were first constructed, the burden of data processing made it impractical to include more than a few stocks. For example, when the Dow Jones Industrial Average was first published in 1884, only 11 stocks were included. Modern computers make it relatively easy to include large numbers of stocks. As a result, the two newest important indexes—those of the New York Stock Exchange and the American Stock Exchange—are based on all stocks listed on the respective exchanges.

Since there are indexes of the two major exchanges which include all stocks, it may seem unnecessary to discuss the sampling problem. But, such discussion is helpful since two important measures of the market, the Standard & Poor's Indexes and the Dow Jones Averages, are based on samples and because there is no comprehensive index of stocks which are not listed on any exchange, i.e., over-the-counter stocks. The usefulness of indexes based on samples is importantly influenced by the degree to which one can confidently infer movements in excluded stocks on the basis of movements in included stocks. For stocks on the New York and American stock exchanges, at least, such inferences can be made with great confidence from both the Standard & Poor's Index and the Dow Jones Average.

The adequacy of indexes based on samples is caused by two things: (1) the fact that stocks of relatively few companies constitute a large proportion of the value of the stocks of all companies, and (2) the tendency of all stocks to move together.

For some purposes, the very substantial concentration of value in relatively few companies contributes to the power of small samples. If each company is considered to be equally important, this concentration is of no help. If, however, large companies are considered more important than small, as it true when one is interested in changes in the market value of all stocks, the concentration of value is very helpful. (The extent of this concentration has been discussed in chapter 1.)*

Almost half of the variation in the prices of individual stocks between 1926 and 1965 was accounted for by movements in the market.[2] Although the proportion has been declining, it is still substantial. Obviously, if all stocks moved together in perfect lock step, a single stock would represent the market with perfect fidelity. Although the degree of co-movement is not that high, it is still sufficient to help make relatively small samples valuable as indicators of general market movements.

The extent to which these factors cause small samples to represent accurately movements in the general market is indicated by a recent study of the variability in prices of stocks listed on the New York Stock Exchange.[3] For random samples of as few as eight stocks, the degree of conformity is striking. For example, for the 40 individual years ending in 1965, the cumulative frequency distributions of wealth ratios of all stocks in each year and the cumulative frequency distributions of ratios for portfolios of eight stocks selected at random were virtually identical except for the extreme tails, as is indicated in figure 3–1. Although almost indistinguishable, there are two curves.

The degree of conformity of portfolios of size 16 and 32 stocks is even greater. This means that rates of return based on samples of 16 or 32 can be expected to provide good estimates of rates of return on all stocks. In 1965, for example, the mean wealth ratio of all stocks at year-end relative to the beginning of the year was 1.28; randomly selected portfolios of size 16 could be expected to be between 1.38 and 1.18 about two thirds of the time.

If one deliberately tries to pick portfolios which are not representative, the degree of conformity will obviously be much less. This is true of some mutual funds which are specialized by industry. Thus the Chemical Fund or the Oceanographic Fund should not be expected to be representative of stocks in general. Unless there is a deliberate attempt at specialization, almost any sample of stocks of reasonable size will tend to represent well movements in all stocks. The best example is the Dow Jones Industrial Average of only 30 stocks

---

* See p. 5.

FIGURE 3–1
Aggregated Frequency Distributions of Wealth Ratios from In-
vestments in Randomly Selected Portfolios of All Stocks and
Eight Stocks

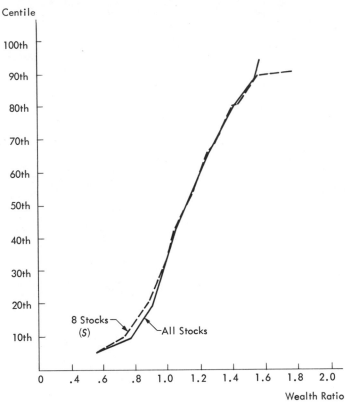

Note: The portfolios of eight stocks were selected by simple random sampling
without replacement, designated by the letter *S* in the study.

whose properties and degree of conformity with general market movements are discussed below.

When the purpose of the index is to represent changes in the value
of all stocks, small samples can be used with very great confidence.
For example, the stocks included in the Standard & Poor's "500"
stock index constituted in 1970 about 80 percent of the value of all
stocks listed on the New York Stock Exchange. Even the Dow Jones
Industrial Average based on only 30 stocks, included stocks having
a value equal to about 30 percent of all stocks listed in December
1970.

Weighting

The prices of each stock included in an index must be combined in order to determine the value of the index. For that purpose, it is necessary each time the index is computed to determine the relative importance of each included stock.

Even if the persons computing the index do not recognize the weighting problem, they deal with it. For example, the Dow Jones Industrial Averages are constructed so as to give each included stock a weight proportional to its price. No one has ever been able to devise a rational justification for this except simplicity. Yet, the Dow Jones Averages are widely used and are valuable indicators of general market movements.

The reason for weighting is to insure that the index reflects the relative importance of each stock in a way suited to the purpose of the index. The two most common ways of weighting stocks are in accordance with market value or by assigning equal weights to equal relative price changes. The former method is appropriate for indicating changes in the aggregate market value of stocks represented by the index, while the latter is more appropriate for indicating movements in the prices of typical or average stocks. Changes in general market value are more important for studies of relationships between stock prices and other things in the national economy. Value-weighted indexes also have the desirable property of "macro-consistency." That is, it is possible for all investors to hold portfolios in which the individual stocks have a relative importance equal to the relative values of all outstanding shares.

On the other hand, indexes based upon equal weighting* are better indicators of the expected change in prices of stocks selected at random. For some purposes, such as index is a more appropriate bench mark than a value-weighted index.

An intuitive feeling for the major implications of the two most common ways of weighting can be achieved by realizing the simple fact that value-weighted indexes attach relatively great importance to large companies and that the stocks of those companies may behave differently from the stocks of small companies. The main expected

---

* By equal weighting, we mean an index based on the assumption that equal dollar amounts are invested in each stock. We do not mean the process used in constructing the Dow Jones Averages by which the prices of included stocks are added up and divided by the number of stocks (adjusted for stock splits).

difference is the greater volatility in the fortunes and stock prices of small companies and the greater tendency for the price of stocks of large companies to be moved by the general economic tides in the economy as a whole.

Although the stocks in the Dow Jones Averages are not value weighted, the selection produces almost the same results. That is, the stocks included are the stocks of very large companies. As a consequence, movements in the Dow Jones Averages are similar, with respect to volatility and trend, to indexes based on value weighting.

Another property of value weighting is the automatic adjustment for stock splits. If there is no change in aggregate market value of outstanding shares of the stock that is split, its relative importance remains the same and the index is not affected. Indexes which are not weighted by market value have no such automatic adjustment. If the method of adjustment changes the relative importance of the split stock, it may impart a bias to the index. When one of the stocks in the Dow Jones Average is split, adjustment is made by changing the divisor used in the calculation of the value of the average. The adjustment process is illustrated by the following simple hypothetical example:

TABLE 3–1
Hypothetical Average Adjusted for Stock Split

Stock	*Before Split*		*After Split*	
	No. Shares	*Price per Share*	*No. Shares*	*Price per Share*
A	10	$20	20	$10
B	10	$10	10	$10
C	10	$ 6	10	$ 6
Total	30	$36	40	$26
Divisor		3		2.1667
Average		12		12

* The divisor for the average after stock A splits is reduced from 3 to 2.1667 in order to preserve the value of the index.

Although an adjustment is necessary to avoid the absurdity of causing a change in the value of the average in response to stock splits, the adjustment process and the method of weighting can produce a bias. Since stocks in the Dow Jones Averages are weighted according to their market price, the adjustment for a stock split reduces the relative importance of that stock. If stocks that split behave differently from others, the Dow Jones Averages will be biased. There is some evidence that stocks which split are those of companies which have been doing particularly well.[4] If such stocks should continue to do particularly well, the weighting and adjustment process for the Dow Jones Averages would produce a downward bias.

Methods of Averaging

Given a group of prices of common stocks, either weighted or unweighted, one has to combine them into a single number in order to create a descriptive measure. Although statistics books list and discuss several kinds of averages or measures of central tendency, and although in the history of stock market indexes many different kinds of averages have been used, at the present time in the United States only two kinds of averages are used in constructing the major stock market indexes. These are the arithmetic mean and the geometric mean.* All of the most widely used indexes such as the New York Stock Exchange Indexes, the Standard & Poor's Indexes, the Dow Jones Averages, and the American Stock Exchange Index are based on arithmetic means of prices or price changes. The only index based on a geometric mean is Value Line's.

Before going into the question of methods of averaging, it is worth noting that indexes, though typically based on averages, are not quite the same as averages. The difference consists of the fact that the index is constructed by assigning some arbitrary, but usually rounded, number to the value of the average at some point in time in order to facilitate comparisons of the value of the index at subsequent (or previous) points in time. For example, many federal economic statistics are indexes which were arbitrarily assigned a value of 100 for the base period 1967. The Consumer Price Index in August 1972 had a value of 125.7, meaning that the index was 25.7 percent greater than the base period, 1967. The value of the Standard & Poor's Index of prices of 425 industrial stocks in January 1969 was 110.97, and in the base period of 1941–43 the value of the index was 10.0. An average, on the other hand, does not involve the selection of an arbitrary value for some base period; it is simply an average. The Dow Jones Averages are not indexes, technically; they are simply the arith-

---

* Strictly speaking, an approximation of the geometric mean must be used since it is computed by multiplication rather than addition. If the price of a stock falls to zero, the index would be zero.

metic means of the prices of the stocks included at each point in time, adjusted for stock splits. Table 3–2 illustrates the difference:

TABLE 3–2

Stock	Base Period Price	Current Period Price
X	$100	$125
Y	$ 50	$ 75
Z	$ 30	$ 15
Average.	$ 60	$ 71.67
Index	100	119.45

Note: The average of the stock prices was $60 in the base period. In the current period, the average is $71.67 or about 19 percent above the base average. The index is therefore 119.45. One additional point is worth noting. The index in the example refers to an unweighted arithmetic average of prices so the $25 or 25 percent increase in the price of stock X has the same effect on the index as the $25 or 50 percent increase in the price of Y.

For some purposes, it is important to understand the differences which result from the different methods of averaging. The example above used an arithmetic average. If there is any variation through time in the prices making up the index, there will be a difference between the value of an arithmetic mean and a geometric mean of the prices. An index based on the geometric mean will increase more slowly and decrease more rapidly than an index based on the arithmetic mean. The degree of divergence increases with the degree of variability in the component prices. This is illustrated by an example of indexes based on three stocks which go up for two successive periods and then decline for two successive periods. (See table 3–3.)

TABLE 3–3
Indexes Based on Arithmetic and Geometric Averages of Stock Prices

Stock	Base	1	2	3	4
X	$10	$12	$15	$10	$ 6
Y	$10	$15	$20	$15	$ 2
Z	$10	$21	$31	$ 8	$ 4
Average					
Arithmetic	$10	$16	$22	$11	$ 4
Geometric	$10	$15.6	$21	$10.6	$ 3.6
Index					
Arithmetic	100	160	220	110	40
Geometric	100	156	210	106	36

Table 3–3 illustrates not only the differences between movements in arithmetic and geometric indexes when stock prices rise and fall but also the methods of computing an arithmetic mean and a geometric mean. The arithmetic mean is the sum of the individual prices divided by the number of prices while the geometric mean is the nth root of the product of the prices.

Some people claim that the arithmetic mean has an upward bias and some that the geometric mean has a downward bias. In one sense, the arithmetic mean is biased upwards. For example, if a $10 stock moves to $20, and a $20 stock falls to $10, the arithmetic average of the relative changes is 25 percent. If each stock returns to its original price, the arithmetic average of the relative change is still 25 percent. However, the total value of the stocks is unchanged. The geometric mean adjusts for this. A corollary of this property of arithmetic averages is that over long periods of time, an arithmetic index will outperform most of the components. This is due in part, however, to the economic characteristics of stock prices; since there is a lower, but no upper, limit to price changes, their distribution will not be symmetric.*

It is interesting to consider the magnitude of the differences in indexes that can be caused by the choice of the method of averaging. It has been estimated that a geometric average of the Dow Jones stocks would have 2.4 percentage points less gain per year than the arithmetic average, whereas an arithmetic index of the Value Line stocks would have increased on average 3.0 percentage points more per year than the geometric index. Similarly, Standard & Poor's Industrial Index was about 17 in June 1950 and about 90 in July 1966. If a geometric average had been used, the index would have been only about 60 in July 1966.[5]

An interesting solution to the problem is that used by Fisher.[6] For the period 1926–60, he computed both an arithmetic and a geometric index of equally weighted relative price changes. When compared to the Fisher-Lorie rates of return presented in chapter 2, he found the arithmetic index had an upward bias and the geometric a downward bias, greater in magnitude. He therefore computed a combined index with weights of 0.56 and 0.44 for the arithmetic and geometric indexes respectively. Movements of this index relative to some of those currently available are considered in a subsequent section.

---

* More specifically, the distribution of price changes is positively skewed so the median value falls below the mean value.

THE MAJOR INDEXES

There is a variety of indexes of stock prices currently available. They differ in construction and in purposes for which they are best suited. We will limit our discussion to five of the most widely known. We will also comment briefly on investment performance indexes, which are a better measure of total returns.

The Dow Jones Industrial Average

The Dow Jones Industrial Average is probably the most familiar of stock price measures and the most widely quoted by professional investors and taxicab drivers. At the same time, it is often the most misunderstood. Essentially, the measure is an unweighted arithmetic average of the prices of 30 industrial stocks. The term "unweighted" is somewhat of a misnomer in that the influence of a particular stock on the change in the average is proportional to its price. For example, an increase of 10 percent in the price of a $100 stock has twice the effect of a 10 percent increase in a $50 stock.

The average has undergone changes both in composition and in computation since its appearance in 1884 in a daily letter issued by Dow Jones & Co. At that time, it included 11 stocks. A twelfth was soon added. In 1916, the sample was enlarged to 20, and in 1928, to 30. Upon occasion there have been substitutions in the stocks included in order to improve the representativeness of the average. There have been approximately 30 changes since 1928.[*]

Originally, the average was computed by summing the prices of the component stocks and dividing by the number of included stocks. Adjustments for stock splits or dividends of 10 percent or more[†] were made by multiplying the new price of the affected stock by an appropriate factor. For example, if a stock split two for one, the new price was multiplied by two in order to compute the average. In 1928, this procedure was changed. Since then, instead of summing the prices (some with multipliers) and dividing by the number of stocks, the price totals (with no multipliers) have been divided by a number adjusted so that the average is unaffected on the transition date. Each new stock split or dividend reduces the divisor so that by December 1972, the divisor was approximately 1.7. One result is that there is no

---

[*] The most noted is the substitution in 1939 of AT&T for IBM.

[†] Stock dividends of less than 10 percent were ignored.

exact equivalence between points in the average and dollars and cents. A change of $1 in each stock in the index would cause the average to change by about 18 points.

A more important feature of the adjustment, however, is that the change in the divisor reduces the importance of the split stock relative to that of the other stocks. The possibility of bias resulting from this computation was mentioned in the preceding section. The actual DJI stood at 192.91 at the end of 1945 and 969.26 at the end of 1965. If a constant divisor had been used throughout this period, with adjustments made in the original way, the average would have been 1086.59 at the end of 1965.[7]

Despite the popularity of the Dow Jones Industrial Average, criticisms are abundant. A frequent, but superficial, objection is that it is widely misconstrued as being the actual stock price average. More fundamental criticisms are aimed at the representativeness of the sample and the method of computation. The 30 stocks are of large, well-established companies; in 1970, they constituted about 30 percent of the market value of all stocks on the New York Stock Exchange. It has been argued that these "blue chips" are not representative of an average portfolio and are therefore poor measures of market performance.

The major criticisms of the methodology focus on the whimsical system of implicit price weights, the possibility of bias resulting from the adjustments, and the failure to adjust for small stock dividends. The latter are usually added to the reported cash dividend total. For example, in 1964 the value of small stock dividends for which no adjustment was made constituted 19 percent of total dividends reported.[8]

Some proponents of the DJI who accept the sample have suggested changing the computational procedure by introducing explicitly market value or equal weights. Some also argue for replacing the arithmetic mean with a geometric mean. One proponent has actually recomputed the DJI using market value weights and arithmetic and geometric means with equal weights. If the value of each of these variants was 192.91 at the end of 1945 (the actual value of the DJI), by the end of 1965 they would have the following values in comparison to the actual DJI of 969.26:[9]

Market value weights 1026.84
Equal weights–arithmetic average. 1096.92
Equal weights–geometric average 813.40

The relationship between the 1965 value of the various averages is what one would expect, given the properties of different methods of computation. Over the 20-year period, the performance is quite similar, but for short periods, there can be considerable diversity in the changes of the averages.

The Standard & Poor's "500"

The Standard & Poor's Composite Index of 500 stocks includes 425 industrials, 25 railroads, and 50 utilities. In contrast to the Dow Jones Averages, the relative importance of the prices of the component stocks is determined by the value of shares outstanding. The index is officially described as a "base-weighted aggregative," but in fact, the weights are adjusted for stock dividends, new issues, etc. The aggregate market value of the stocks in the index is expressed as a percentage of the average market value in the period 1941–1943. This percentage is divided by ten which was selected as the value of the index in the base period. This was done in order to make the index in line with the actual average of stock prices.*

The present index of daily prices was first published in 1957, although other less comprehensive indexes were published before that. It has been extended back to 1928 on a daily basis. In coverage, it is considerably broader than the DJI. In 1965, the aggregate market value of the 500 stocks was about 80 percent of all stocks on the New York Stock Exchange. Interestingly, the market value of Dow Jones Industrial stocks on that date—all of which are included in the 500—was about 40 percent of the "500" market value. The importance of individual stocks in the indexes can be very different. For example, the implicit weight of AT&T in the Dow Jones Industrial was 2.8 percent in 1965. In the Standard & Poor's "500" its market value weight was 7.5 percent. If the Dow Jones Industrial used market value weights, that of AT&T would have been 18.6 percent.

A composite index such as Standard & Poor's has several advantages. The coverage is broad, and the weighting is explicit. Moreover, no adjustments for splits is necessary. Critics have argued that the index is dominated by large companies and that value weights can create an upward bias. These criticisms are much less universal than those aimed at the Dow Jones Industrials.

---

* When the present index was first published in 1957, its value was 47; the average price of all shares on the New York Stock Exchange was $45.23.

The New York Stock Exchange Composite

In 1965, the New York Stock Exchange inaugurated its own composite index covering all common stocks listed on the exchange. It is similar in concept to the Standard & Poor's Indexes in that it is an index of market value or, alternatively, a value-weighted price index. It is intended to measure changes in the average stock price which result from market action alone. The aggregate market value is related to the value in the base period, December 31, 1965. The index on that date was set at 50; the actual stock price average was $53.33.

No adjustment for splits is needed, but the base is adjusted to account for any changes in capitalization and new listings or delistings. The adjustment is such that the relationship between the adjusted base value and the current market value after the change is the same as that between the current market value before the change and the prior base value. In this way, the index is unaffected by factors other than price changes in the market. The index of daily closing prices have been extended back to May 28, 1964.

The American Stock Exchange Price Level Index

The American Stock Exchange also developed its own index in 1966. This is an unweighted index of price *movements* of all its traded stocks and warrants, derived by adding or subtracting the average net price change each day to the previous index value. It is therefore quite different from the usual stock market measures. Since only net changes are considered, no account is taken of the relationship of the net change to the price of a stock. In this sense, it is comparable to the Dow Jones Averages.

The use of net price changes has several interesting features. It avoids the problem of splits in that the only time the index is affected is on the day after the split. In practice, the previous day's closing index is adjusted when stock splits, dividends, or cash dividends occur. When new listings appear, the divisor used to obtain the average net change is increased correspondingly.

The base price is $16.88, the average price on April 29, 1966. Since values for the other periods are calculated by adding or subtracting net price changes, the index would more appropriately be called an average. It is available back to October 1, 1962.

The official ASE index differs markedly in its behavior from an index based on an unweighted average of actual prices. The official index has risen more in strong markets and fallen less in weak markets as indicated by figure 3–2.

FIGURE 3–2
The Official American Stock Exchange Index and an Index Based on an Average of Actual Prices, 1966–72

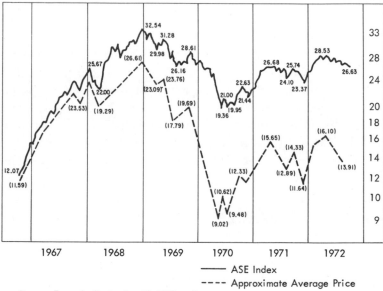

Source: *Barron's*, September 18, 1972, p. 9.

The Value Line "1400" Composite Average

The Value Line Composite Average first appeared in 1963. It consists of 1,217 industrials, 154 utilities, and 29 rails. It is the only widely used index which is based on a geometric average of relative price changes of the component stocks. Although labeled an average, it is in fact, an index with a value of 100 on June 30, 1961. The adjustment for stock splits or dividends is made by adjusting the closing price of the stock on the previous day to compute the relative change.

Investment Performance Indexes

An investment performance index is essentially an index of rates of return. It differs from a price index in that it takes into account cash dividends. Alfred Cowles[10] was the first to publish a time series of this type. Although no performance indexes are available on a current basis, Fisher has developed an index based on all of the 1,715 common stocks listed on the New York Stock Exchange for all or part of the period from the end of January 1926 through the end of December 1960. We will not go into the details of the construction, but it is interesting to look at some of the effects of taking dividends into account. Table 3–4 presents changes for selected periods in the

TABLE 3–4
Rates of Change in Two Indexes of Common Stock Performance

	Period					
	1/26–12/60		12/40–12/60		12/50–12/60	
Security Group	IPI[a]	PI[b]	IPI[a]	PI[b]	IPI[a]	PI[b]
Railroads.	4.0	0.5	17.1	12.0	6.8	2.0
Local and highway transportation	5.6	–0.4	16.7	8.6	11.6	5.5
Water transportation	4.4	–1.7	14.2	5.3	9.4	1.4
Airlines	3.6	2.4	6.1	4.0	5.0	2.1
All common stocks	8.9	4.0	16.0	9.9	13.3	7.9

a Investment performance index.
b Price index.
Source: Fisher, "Stock Market Indexes."

investment performance index and a comparable price index by industry.

The different indexes can lead the uncautious to different conclusions. For example, for the period 1926–60, the price indexes in table 3–4 indicate that rails outperformed stocks in local and highway transportation companies while the more comprehensive investment performance indexes indicate the reverse.

RELATIONSHIP AMONG THE INDEXES

The preceding discussion raises an obvious question: Of what practical importance is the choice of an index? Some insight can be derived from looking at comparative movements over time of the various indexes. In figure 3–3, the Dow Jones Industrial Average and the Standard & Poor's "500" are plotted at quarterly intervals from 1926 to 1960. (These have been shifted to a base of 1960 = 100.) Fisher's Combination Index also appears for the same period.

FIGURE 3–3

Comparative Movements of Three Prices Indexes and Two Investment Performance Indexes

Source: Fisher, "New Stock Market Indexes," p. 204a.

At first glance one might conclude that differences in coverage and construction are of little importance since the major indexes do move together over long periods of time. The Dow Jones Industrial Average and Standard & Poor's "500" exhibit great similarity over the 45-year period, and no doubt the New York Stock Exchange Composite, if available, would have behaved in much the same way. This similarity is inevitable, given the coverage of the indexes. On December 31, 1970 the market value of the Dow Jones Industrials was about $200 billion. This represents about 30 percent of the market value of all common stocks listed on the New York Stock Exchange and about 38 percent of the market value of the Standard & Poor's "500." The

---

* The Combination Index is the weighted average of the arithmetic and geometric averages referred to on p. 59 of this chapter.

overlap makes it unlikely that there will be marked divergence in the long run. Between 1926 and 1970, the Dow Jones Industrial Average increased 399 percent while the Standard & Poor's "500" increased 622 percent. Within the period, the two indexes crossed 17 times. The Combination Index crossed each of the other two 15 times.

The close relationships between various indexes is illustrated further in table 3–5. The simple correlation between each pair of indexes

TABLE 3–5

Correlations between Indexes of Prices of Stocks on the New York Stock Exchange[a]

Index	Period	Correlation Coefficient
Dow Jones Composite and:		
Dow Jones Industrial.	Jan. 1926–Dec. 1966	0.969
Standard & Poor's "500"	Jan. 1926–Dec. 1966	0.977
Standard & Poor's "425"	Jan. 1926–Dec. 1966	0.959
New York Stock Exchange Composite[b]	Jan. 1939–Dec. 1966	0.906
Dow Jones Industrial and		
Standard & Poor's "500"	Jan. 1926–Dec. 1966	0.976
Standard & Poor's "425"	Jan. 1926–Dec. 1966	0.969
New York Stock Exchange Composite[b]	Jan. 1939–Dec. 1966	0.908
Fisher's Combination Price Index	Jan. 1926–Dec. 1960	0.985
Standard & Poor's "500" and		
Standard & Poor's "425"	Jan. 1926–Dec. 1966	0.981
New York Stock Exchange Composite[b]	Jan. 1939–Dec. 1966	0.913
Fisher's Combination Price Index	Jan. 1926–Dec. 1960	0.919
Standard & Poor's "425" and		
New York Composite	Jan. 1926–Dec. 1966	0.909

[a] Correlations are between closing values on the last Friday of the month.
[b] Although the New York Stock Exchange Index was started in 1966, it was extended back to 1939 on the basis of linkage with Securities Exchange Commission Stock Price Index.

measures the degree to which they tend to move up and down together.* All of the correlations are above 0.9, indicating that movements in the indexes correspond closely. A coefficient of 0.9 means

---

* The range of the correlation coefficient is -1 to $+1$. A value of $+1.0$ or -1.0 would indicate perfect correlation, while a value of 0.0 would indicate no correlation.

that over 80 percent of the variance in one index is "explained" by the variation in the other.

Although long-run movements are similar, indexes may differ markedly over short periods of time. This is reflected both in turning points and volatility. On one occasion, there was a significant difference in the turning points of the market as a whole as measured by a comprehensive equal-weighted index and the Dow Jones Averages or Standard & Poor's Indexes. In 1929, the equal-weighted index reached its peak six months before the month-end peak in the other two. This suggests that the prices of stocks in relatively small companies turned down before the prices of stocks in large companies. In this instance at least, the use of the index giving greater weight to small companies could have had enormous value. The equal-weighted index also reached its trough in 1932, one month before either of the other two indexes. All other turning points occurred in the same month.

Some indication of the relative volatility of various indexes is illustrated in table 3–6. The mean relative monthly price changes and

TABLE 3–6
Relative Monthly Changes in Stock Market Indexes (July 1964–June 1969)

Index	*Mean*	*Standard Deviation*	*Mean Deviation*
Dow Jones Composite	0.06%	3.36	2.66
Dow Jones Industrial	0.14%	3.38	2.67
Standard & Poor's "500"	0.35%	3.08	2.48
Standard & Poor's "425"	0.40%	3.19	2.59
New York Stock Exchange Composite[a]	0.41%	3.33	2.59
New York Stock Exchange Industrial[a]	0.39%	3.95	3.11
Value Line Composite	0.61%	4.02	3.08
Value Line Industrial	0.76%	4.29	3.28
American Stock Exchange	1.95%	5.60	4.33

[a] Period covered is January 1966–June 1969.

two measures of disperions are presented for nine indexes. The period covered is July 1964 to June 1969 except for the New York Stock Exchange Indexes which are for the period since January 1966.

The mean relative price change in the Dow Jones Composite was 0.06 percent. For the Standard & Poor's Composite, the mean change was 0.35 percent, almost six times larger. In other words, the volatility of two measures designed to represent the New York Stock Exchange was dramatically different.

CONCLUDING REMARKS

Irwin Friend et al. found that the average annual rate of return (compounded annually) on investment in 136 mutual funds was 10.7 percent for the period January 1960 through June 1968; the rate from equal investment in all listed stocks would have been 12.4 percent and the rate from investment in all stocks in amounts proportional to their initial market value would have provided a return of 9.9 percent.[11] Their findings illustrate two points: (1) for some purposes, understanding the construction of indexes can make a crucial difference in interpreting the results of research, and (2) differences among available indexes are not likely to be great.

4

The Efficient Market
Hypothesis

INTRODUCTION

DURING THE DECADE of the 1960s, there was a curious and extremely important controversy about the process which determines the prices of common stocks. Initially, the controversy focused on the extent to which successive changes in the prices of common stocks were independent of each other. In more technical terms, the issue was whether or not common stock prices follow a random walk. If they do, knowledge of the past sequence of prices cannot be used to secure abnormally high rates of return.

As evidence accumulated that the walk is random, the focus of academic attention shifted to an investigation of the kind of market-making process which would produce such a result. This led to the theory of efficient markets in which prices adjust rapidly to new information. Both Samuelson[1] and Mandelbrot[2] have proven rigorously that independence of successive price changes is consistent with an efficient market.

It is difficult to know the most effective technique of exposition of a complicated economic and statistical argument. After experimenting with various approaches, we came to feel that greater insight into the controversy and its significance can be achieved by tracing, somewhat chronologically, the course of the argument and of the work related to it rather than by a simple exposition of the logic of the argument.

As the controversy and related work have progressed through the

70

years, students have come to distinguish three forms of the efficient-market (formerly, the random-walk) hypothesis: (1) the weak form; (2) the semistrong form; and (3) the strong form. The weak form asserts that current prices fully reflect the information implied by the historical sequence of prices. In other words, an investor cannot enhance his ability to select stocks by knowing the history of successive prices and the results of analyzing them in all possible ways. The semistrong form of the hypothesis asserts that current prices fully reflect public knowledge about the underlying companies, and that efforts to acquire and analyze this knowledge cannot be expected to produce superior investment results. For example, one cannot expect to earn superior rates of return by reacting to annual reports, announcements of changes in dividends, or stock splits. The strong form asserts that not even those with privileged information can often make use of it to secure superior investment results.

If these startling hypotheses are true, their practical importance is enormous. They would affect profoundly security analysis, portfolio management, and the selection of an investment strategy. One cannot assert for certain whether these hypotheses are true or not, but one can confidently assert that the evidence regarding their validity is sufficiently persuasive so that all informed investors should be fully aware of the hypotheses themselves, the evidence concerning their validity, and their implications for investors.

This chapter indicates how the controversy arose, the evidence relating to it, and the general significance of the findings. The next chapter discusses the implications of these findings for investors.

SOME HISTORY

Early Beginnings

The term "random walk" has been of interest to statisticians for almost seventy years. It is believed that the term was first used in an exchange of correspondence appearing in *Nature* in 1905.[3] The exchange provided the proper answer to a common, vexing problem: If one leaves a drunk in a vacant field and wishes to find him after a lapse of time, what is the most efficient search pattern? It has been demonstrated that the best place to start is the point where the drunk was left. That position is an unbiased estimate of his future position, since the drunk will presumably wander without purpose or design in a random fashion.

Even before the correspondence in *Nature,* Louis Bachelier had studied commodity prices and concluded that they followed a random walk, though he did not use the term.[4] Bachelier asserted and presented convincing evidence that commodity speculation in France was a "fair game." This meant that neither buyers nor sellers could expect to make profits. In other terms, the current price of a commodity was an unbiased estimate of its future price. Or, still again, if the *expected* price on each day were subtracted from the *actual* price, the sum of those differences, on the average, would be zero.

Bachelier's earlier work was pregnant with meaning for investors, but the gestation period was one of the longest on record. There was some corroborating work in other contexts and with other data by Working,[5] Cowles,[6] and Kendall,[7] but the burgeoning of modern work on this subject did not begin until 1959. In that year, two original and provocative papers were published.

In one, Roberts indicated that a series of numbers created by cumulating random numbers had the same visual appearance as a time series of stock prices.[8] An observer with a predisposition to see familiar patterns in these wavy lines could detect the well-known head-and-shoulders formations and other patterns both in the series representing stock prices and in the random series. Roberts also pointed out the first differences of the numbers generated by the random process looked very much like the first differences of stock prices. Robert's interesting pictures are given in figures 4–1 and 4–2. Roberts suggested research on the subject to see whether his tentative finding that stock prices appeared to be the result of a random process were confirmed by more detailed and exhaustive investigation.

The second work appearing in 1959 which provoked controversy and stimulated research was by Osborne.[9] He was a distinguished physicist with the Naval Research Laboratory in Washington, D.C. when the article was published. Although Osborne has learned a great deal about the stock market since 1959, he professed (probably incorrectly) to be ignorant about the market at that time. He chose to look at the numbers representing stock prices to see whether they conformed to certain laws governing the motion of physical objects. In particular, he was interested in seeing whether the movements of prices were of the sort that characterizes the movements of very small particles suspended in solution—so-called "Brownian motion." He found a very high degree of conformity between the movements of stock prices and the law governing Brownian motion. Specifically, the variance of price

FIGURE 4–1

Actual and Simulated Levels of Stock Market Prices for 52 Weeks

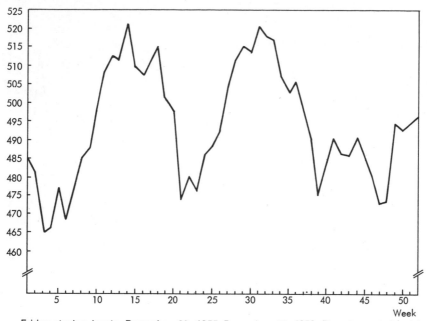

Friday closing levels, December 30, 1955–December 28, 1956, Dow Jones Industrial Average

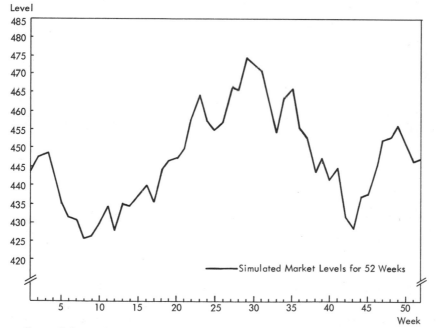

Source: Roberts, "Stock Market Patterns," pp. 5–6.

FIGURE 4–2

Actual and Simulated Changes in Weekly Stock Prices for 52 Weeks

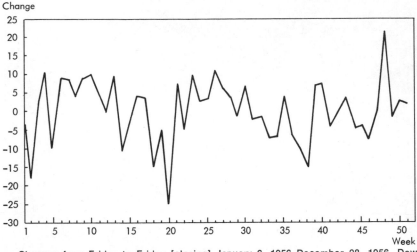

Changes from Friday to Friday [closing] January 6, 1956–December 28, 1956, Dow Jones Industrial Average

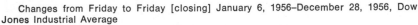

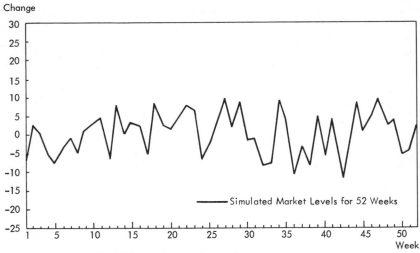

Source: Roberts, "Stock Market Patterns," pp. 5–6.

Friday closing levels, December 30, 1955–December 28, 1956, Dow Jones Industrial Average

changes over successively longer intervals of time increases as the square of the length of time. This implies that the logarithms of price changes are independent of each other. Although Osborne's point of view is different, his findings are consistent with Roberts'.

Early Tests of the Weak Form

The work by Osborne and Roberts at first was taken seriously only by a small group of academicians. Both pieces of work suggested, on the basis of preliminary and tentative investigation, that changes in stock prices were random. The first reactions in the academic community were to devise various ingenious tests of this randomness using bodies of data considerably more extensive than those used by either Osborne or Roberts. These tests by Moore (1962),[10] Fama (1965),[11] Granger and Morgenstern (1963),[12] and others, provided substantial support for the tentative conclusions of Osborne and Roberts. On the basis of measurements of serial correlations between prices changes, through investigation of the number of successive changes of given sign, and in other ways, these workers tested the statistical independence or the randomness of successive changes in stock prices. They uniformly found only insignificant departures from randomness.

Since there is general agreement, we will present only a few highlights. Moore was one of the first to look at the serial correlation between successive price changes of individual stocks. The interpretation of this sort of test is that a low coefficient suggests that previous price changes cannot be used to predict future changes. Moore examined weekly changes of 29 randomly selected stocks for 1951–58 and found an average serial correlation coefficient of -0.06. This value is extremely low, indicating that data on weekly changes are valueless in predicting future changes. Fama studied the daily proportionate price changes of the 30 industrial stocks in the Dow Jones Average for approximately five years, ending in 1962. The serial correlation coefficients for the daily changes are all very small, the average being 0.03. The investigation was extended to test the possibility that lagged price changes show some dependence. Again, the coefficients do not differ substantially from zero. Fama's results are shown in table 4–1. The correlation coefficients are very low. While the evidence is impressive, correlation coefficients have an unfortunate attribute. They may be dominated by a few extreme and unusual observations.

To test this, Fama looked at the signs rather than size of successive

TABLE 4–1
Daily Serial Correlation Coefficients for Lags of 1, 2, . . . , 10 Days

Stock	1	2	3	4	5	6	7	8	9	10
Allied Chemical	.017	-.042	.007	-.001	.027	.004	-.017	-.026	-.017	-.007
Alcoa	.118*	.038	-.014	.022	-.022	.009	.017	.007	-.001	-.033
American Can	-.087*	-.024	-.034	-.065*	-.017	-.006	.015	.025	-.047	-.040
A.T.&T.	-.039	-.097*	.000	.026	.005	-.005	.002	.027	-.014	.007
American Tobacco	.111*	-.109*	-.060*	-.065*	.007	-.010	.011	.046	.039	.041
Anaconda	.067*	-.061*	-.047	-.002	.000	-.038	.009	.016	-.014	-.056
Bethlehem Steel	.013	-.065*	.009	.021	-.053	-.098*	-.010	.004	-.002	-.021
Chrysler	.012	-.066*	-.016	-.007	-.015	.009	.037	.056*	-.044	-.021
Du Pont	.013	-.033	.060*	-.027	-.002	-.047	.020	.011	-.034	.001
Eastman Kodak	.025	.014	-.031	.005	-.022	.012	.007	.006	.008	.002
General Electric	.011	-.038	-.021	.031	-.001	.000	-.008	.014	-.002	.010
General Foods	.061*	-.003	.045	.002	-.015	-.052	-.006	-.014	-.024	-.017
General Motors	-.004	-.056*	-.037	-.008	-.038	-.006	.019	.006	-.016	.009
Goodyear	-.123*	.017	-.044	.043	-.002	-.003	.035	.014	-.015	.007
International Harvester	-.017	-.029	-.031	.037	-.052	-.021	-.001	.003	-.046	-.016
International Nickel	.096*	-.033	-.019	.020	.027	.059*	-.038	-.008	-.016	.034
International Paper	.046	-.011	-.058*	.053*	.049	-.003	-.025	-.019	-.003	-.021
Johns Manville	.006	-.038	-.027	-.023	-.029	-.080*	.040	.018	-.037	.029
Owens Illinois	-.021	-.084*	-.047	.068*	.086*	-.040	.011	-.040	.067*	-.043
Procter & Gamble	.099*	-.009	-.008	.009	-.015	.022	.012	-.012	-.022	-.021
Sears	.097*	.026	.028	.025	.005	-.054	-.006	-.010	-.008	-.009
Standard Oil (Calif.)	.025	-.030	-.051*	-.025	-.047	-.034	-.010	.072*	-.049*	-.035
Standard Oil (N.J.)	.008	-.116*	.016	.014	-.047	-.018	-.022	-.026	-.073*	.081*
Swift & Co.	-.004	-.015	-.010	.012	.057*	.012	-.043	.014	.012	.001
Texaco	.094*	-.049	-.024	-.018	-.017	-.009	.031	.032	-.013	.008
Union Carbide	.107*	-.012	.040	.046	-.036	-.034	.003	-.008	-.054	-.037
United Aircraft	.014	-.033	-.022	-.047	-.067*	-.053	.046	.037	.015	-.019
U.S. Steel	.040	-.074*	.014	.011	-.012	-.021	.041	.037	-.021	-.044
Westinghouse	-.027	-.022	-.036	-.003	.000	-.054*	-.020	.013	-.014	.008
Woolworth	.028	-.016	.015	.014	.007	-.039	-.013	.003	-.088*	-.008

Column headers labeled under: *Lag*

* Coefficient is twice its computed standard error.
Source: Fama, "The Behavior of Stock Market Prices," p. 72.

changes to see if runs tended to persist. The daily changes in the prices of each of the 30 Dow Jones stocks were classified as zero, positive, or negative. A sequence of $++--+++--0$, for example, would be made up of five runs. If runs do tend to persist (i.e., if there are trends), the total number of runs will be less and the average length of a run longer than if the series were random. Fama's findings are in table 4–2. In general, the actual number of runs conforms very closely to the numbers expected, although there is a slight tendency for runs in daily changes to persist. This is also suggested by the predominately positive correlation coefficients for daily changes. The departure from randomness is negligible, however, and the evidence is strong support for the random-walk hypothesis. The financial community seemed to be unaware of or indifferent to this work.

Some advocates of technical analysis argued that these tests were unfair because they were too rigid and that possible complicated dependencies in successive price changes must be investigated. This led to an interesting effort to refute the implications of the work of Roberts, Osborne, Fama, and the others. Alexander[13] tried to devise trading rules based solely on price changes which could produce abnormally high rates of return. If he could find such rules, they would imply that price changes followed patterns and were not random. Alexander's trading rule was of the following form: Wait until stock prices have advanced by x percent from some trough and then buy stocks; next, hold those stocks until they have declined y percent from some subsequent peak and then sell them or sell them short. Continue this process until bankrupt or satisfied.

Alexander's first efforts to refute the assertions of randomness appeared to be successful, since his results implied the existence of trends or persistence of movements in stock prices. His so-called filter technique produced enormous rates of return. On the basis of corrections in his work suggested and carried out by Fama[14] and Fama and Blume,[15] the profits disappeared. The major shortcomings of Alexander's early work were the failure to realize that dividends were a cost rather than a benefit when stocks were sold short, the failure to take transaction costs into account, and the assumption that stocks could be bought or sold at the precise price at which the signal to buy or sell was given. Fama and Blume demonstrated that filter schemes cannot, in general, provide returns larger than a naïve policy of buying and holding stocks. Very small filters can generate larger profits before commissions, suggesting some persistence in short-term price movements. This is corro-

TABLE 4-2
Total Actual and Expected Numbers of Runs for One-, Four-, Nine-, and Sixteen-Day Periods

Stock	Daily		Four-Day		Nine-Day		Sixteen-Day	
	Actual	Expected	Actual	Expected	Actual	Expected	Actual	Expected
Allied Chemical	683	713.4	160	162.1	71	71.3	39	38.6
Alcoa	601	670.7	151	153.7	61	66.9	41	39.0
American Can	730	755.5	169	172.4	71	73.2	48	43.9
A.T.&T.	657	688.4	165	155.9	66	70.3	34	37.1
American Tobacco	700	747.4	178	172.5	69	72.9	41	40.6
Anaconda	635	680.1	166	160.4	68	66.0	36	37.8
Bethlehem Steel	709	719.7	163	159.3	80	71.8	41	42.2
Chrysler	927	932.1	223	221.6	100	96.9	54	53.5
Du Pont	672	694.7	160	161.9	78	71.8	43	39.4
Eastman Kodak	678	679.0	154	160.1	70	70.1	43	40.3
General Electric	918	956.3	225	224.7	101	96.9	51	51.8
General Foods	799	825.1	185	191.4	81	75.8	43	40.5
General Motors	832	868.3	202	205.2	83	85.8	44	46.8
Goodyear	681	672.0	151	157.6	60	65.2	36	36.3
International Harvester	720	713.2	159	164.2	84	72.6	40	37.8
International Nickel	704	712.6	163	164.0	68	70.5	34	37.6
International Paper	762	826.0	190	193.9	80	82.8	51	46.9
Johns Manville	685	699.1	173	160.0	64	69.4	39	40.4
Owens Illinois	713	743.3	171	168.6	69	73.3	36	39.2
Procter & Gamble	826	858.9	180	190.6	66	81.2	40	42.9
Sears	700	748.1	167	172.8	66	70.6	40	34.8
Standard Oil (Calif.)	972	979.0	237	228.4	97	98.6	59	54.3
Standard Oil (N.J.)	688	704.0	159	159.2	69	68.7	29	37.0
Swift & Co.	878	877.6	209	197.2	85	83.8	50	47.8
Texaco	600	654.2	143	155.2	57	63.4	29	35.6
Union Carbide	595	620.9	142	150.5	67	66.7	36	35.1
United Aircraft	661	699.3	172	161.4	77	68.2	45	39.5
U.S. Steel	651	662.0	162	158.3	65	70.3	37	41.2
Westinghouse	829	825.5	198	193.3	87	84.4	41	45.8
Woolworth	847	868.4	193	198.9	78	80.9	48	47.7
Averages	735.1	759.8	175.7	175.8	74.6	75.3	41.6	41.7

Source: Fama, "The Behavior of Stock Market Prices," p. 75.

borated by some of the evidence presented earlier. However, the trends are so short that the profits are wiped out by commissions. The only ones to be enriched by using filter techniques to buy and sell stocks would be the brokers; the investors themselves would be bankrupt.

Although attempts by others to demonstrate the value of trading rules for New York Stock Exchange stocks were equally unsuccessful,[16] Dryden[17] found some evidence of persistence in trends in United Kingdom share prices. He applied the filter technique to three stock price indexes. If transaction costs are ignored, the filter technique generally produces rates of return substantially higher than a buy-and-hold policy for small and medium size filters. From this he concludes, "The high rates of return . . . obtainable from the application of filters together with the absence of the pattern of relationships which would be expected in the presence of series following random walks, suggest that considerably more dependence might exist in U.K. shares than in those of U.S."[18] He properly cautions against accepting the conclusions until the analysis has been more extensive.

All of these early investigations were tests of the so-called "weak form" of the random-walk hypothesis. That is, they tested the statistical properties of price changes themselves without reference to the relationship of these changes to other kinds of financial information. The evidence strongly supports the view that successive price changes are substantially independent. It also indicates that knowledge of the negligible dependencies cannot be used to enhance profits because of transaction costs.

QUEST FOR A THEORY

In the early 60s, academic workers continued to investigate the randomness of stock prices, and the financial community continued to be indifferent, indignant, or only amused. The indifference, indignation, or amusement stemmed from disbelief in the validity of the findings or from the misconception that randomness implied a kind of senselessness in the determination of stock prices. After a substantial body of evidence had accumulated that stock prices did indeed seem to follow a random walk, the more inquisitive members of the academic community began to wonder about the economic process which could produce such results.

The explanation of the apparent randomness of stock prices lies in understanding the market-making mechanisms. In an efficient market where information is freely available, the price of a security can be expected to approximate its "intrinsic" value because of competition among investors. Intrinsic values can change as a result of new information. If, however, there is only a gradual awareness of new information and all that it implies, successive price changes will exhibit dependence. If the adjustment to information is virtually instantaneous, successive price changes will be random. Although implicit in the work of many, including Boness,[19] Sprenkle,[20] Moore,[21] and probably even Adam Smith, the first specification of efficient markets and their relationship to the randomness of prices of things traded in that market is attributable to Samuelson (1965)[22] and Mandelbrot (1966).[23] If a market has zero transaction costs, if all available information is costless to all interested parties, and if all participants and potential participants in the market have the same time horizons and homogeneous expectations with regard to prices, the market will assuredly be efficient and, as Samuelson has proved, prices in such a market will fluctuate randomly.

These utopian conditions, of course, do not exist, but they are not necessary in order for a market to be efficient and for prices to fluctuate randomly. Following Fama,[24] the necessary conditions for efficiency are far less stringent and are merely that information be readily available to a "sufficient" number of investors, that transaction costs be "reasonable,"* and that, in the absence of agreement about the implications of current information and expectations regarding price movements, there be no evidence of consistent superiority or inferiority by significant participants in the market. The existence of these less stringent conditions cannot be definitively determined directly, but much of the work to which reference is made later in this chapter indicates that the market for stocks listed on the New York Stock Exchange seems quite efficient and this efficiency implies that the sufficient conditions are reasonably descriptive of actual markets.

The assertion that a market is efficient is vastly stronger than the assertion that successive changes in stock prices are independent of each other. The latter assertion—the weak form of the efficient market hypothesis—merely says that current prices of stocks fully reflect all that is implied by the historical sequence of prices so that a knowledge of that sequence is of no value in forming expectations about future prices. The assertion that a market is efficient implies that current prices reflect and impound not only all of the implications of the his-

---

* Even this is not strictly necessary. Exhorbitant transaction costs might restrict the frequency of transactions but not distort the prices at which they take place.

torical sequence of prices but also all that is knowable about the companies whose stocks are being traded. This stronger assertion has proved to be especially unacceptable or unpalatable to the financial community, since it suggests the fruitlessness of efforts to earn superior rates of return by the analysis of all public information. Although some members of the financial community were willing to accept the implications of the weaker assertion about the randomness of price changes and thereby to give up technical analysis, almost no members of the community were willing to accept implications of the stronger form and thereby to give up fundamental analysis.

One of the objections to the assertion that markets are efficient and that current prices impound or reflect all that is knowable about companies is the misconception that these assertions contradict the observable fact that the market has risen over almost all reasonably long periods of time. How can it be that current prices are unbiased estimates of future prices or that current prices impound all that is knowable about the future if investors as a whole usually earn positive rates of return on common stocks as a consequence of their upward secular trend? The problem is not so vexing as it first seems. For example, it is possible to construct a coin which on the average comes up heads six times in ten. The sequence in outcomes from tossing the coin will follow a random walk, even though heads come up more frequently. The probability of a head on any toss is totally unaffected by the outcomes of previous tosses. Thus, it is quite possible that the probability that the market will go up is greater than 0.5 and at the same time that the probability of its going up in any day, week, or month is not affected by the sequence of price changes in preceding days, weeks, or months. In other words, the distribution of price changes has a nonzero mean. Further, knowledge of the true probabilities of this biased coin, if generally understood, would not permit anyone to earn "abnormal" returns.

Perhaps a better explanation is provided by the reflection that investors would be willing to incur the risk of holding common stocks only if there were an expectation of positive rates of return—and, the expected rates would have to exceed the rates on less risky assets such as insured savings accounts. Efficiency in a market for such stocks would result in prices at each point in time which led, on the average, to the expected rates of return. This is a modification of the earlier formulation that current prices are unbiased estimates of future prices. The more reasonable assertion is that current prices produce rates of return that, on average, will be positive after taking into account taxes, transaction costs, and other costs. It is not necessary that the expected rates of return for different stocks be the same. In fact, it would be astounding if they were. The rates of return which people anticipate would have to be different for different stocks in order for investors to be willing to hold them. In general, as will be demonstrated later, rates of return on the average are expected to be higher for stocks believed to subject the investor to greater risk.

Once it was realized that the theory of efficient markets provided an explanation of the observed substantial randomness of successive changes in stock prices, the controversy became one about the efficiency of the market. As indicated, efficiency implies a good deal more than substantial randomness in successive price changes; it implies the probable fruitlessness of analyzing public information as a means of securing superior rates of return. This has come to be known as the semistrong form of the random-walk hypothesis.

Testing the profit to be gained from the analysis of public information was made considerably easier by the creation of Compustat tapes and the tapes of the Center for Research in Security Prices.* The Compustat tapes provided a particularly rich resource for scientific inquiry into the usefulness of conventional financial information of the sort to be found on balance sheets and income statements in identifying undervalued and overvalued stocks. Since about 100 major financial institutions lease Compustat tapes at substantial cost, it can be presumed that a large number of ingenious efforts have been made to interpret balance sheets and income statements for the purpose of predicting changes in the prices of the related common stocks. It is quite possible that there exists some secret method of looking at these data which does produce superior investment results, but a large number of public efforts have uniformly resulted in failure. Although it has proved possible and even rather easy to analyze the data on the Compustat tapes to explain what has happened to stock prices, it apparently has proved an insoluble problem to use these data to predict what will happen. These efforts are described in more detail in chapter 7, which is on common stock valuation.

The results of tests of the weak form of the efficient market hypothe-

* Compustat tapes supplied by Standard & Poor's subsidiary, Investment Management Services, have been available since 1964. The tapes of the Center for Research in Security Prices (CRSP) were created by the Center at the Graduate School of Business of the University of Chicago with a grant from Merrill Lynch, Pierce, Fenner & Smith Inc. and are now distributed by Investment Management Services. These tapes also first became available in 1964.

Tests of the Semistrong Hypothesis

sis were consistent with market efficiency but did not test it directly.* Investigations of the semistrong form of the hypothesis are concerned with market efficiency and the extent to which prices fully reflect public knowledge. The focus of the empirical tests is the speed of adjustment to new information. Fama, Fisher, Jensen, and Roll[25] looked at the effect of stock splits on stock prices. The folklore with respect to stock splits was that the total value of an issue of common stocks was increased by increasing the number of shares. Efforts to explain this apparent irrationality were numerous and untested. The various explanations seemed to have in common the belief that investors, for various reasons, preferred stocks with low prices per share and that this preference led to an increased demand for stocks at low prices, even though the level of earnings, volatility of earnings, and other underlying economic variables remained unchanged.

Believers in the efficiency of markets and the rationality of investors were skeptical about the folklore. There would seem to be no reason why splitting a stock should change its aggregate value unless the split implied something about the company. Fama, Fisher, Jensen, and Roll subjected the folklore to its first comprehensive and rigorous scientific test. Their hypothesis was that splits, which are usually accompanied by dividend increases, were interpreted by the market as a predictor of a dividend change. A dividend change can convey information about management's confidence about future earnings. In an efficient market, the only price effects of a split would be those associated with the information implied by a possible dividend change.

Both the methods and the findings of the investigators are of considerable interest. They examined all stock splits of 25 percent or more on the New York Stock Exchange from January 1927 through December 1959. The investigators did not try to find out whether prices went up or down after stock splits; they tried to find out whether stock prices went up or down more than could have been expected. This required that they abstract from the influence of general market conditions during months surrounding the time of the split.

Their first step was to determine the relationship between rates

---

* Roll's study of the Treasury bill market is an exception. It is a test of the weak form of the hypothesis in terms of the "fair-game" rather than the random-walk model. He concluded that the market is efficient. See Richard Roll, "The Efficient Market Model Applied to U.S. Treasury Bill Rates" (Ph.D. diss., University of Chicago, 1968).

of return on individual stocks in the study and rates of return on the market as a whole except for the period around the split. For each of the 622 securities* in the study, they estimated statistically the relationship of the monthly rates of return of individual stocks to the rates of return on all listed stocks on the New York Stock Exchange.† The estimated relationships are based on the 420 months during the 1926–60 period with the exception of the 15 months before and the 15 months after the month of the split. These months were excluded because unusual price behavior in months surrounding the split would obscure the long-term relationship.

The market would be judged to have been efficient if the split did not alter this relationship, except to the extent that the split contained information which altered expectations about rates of return on the stocks which split. New information would be reflected in deviations of rates of return from normal relations to the market rates. The next step in the analysis was to compute the average deviation or residual, using all of the splits studied, for each of the 29 months prior to the split and 30 months after the split. In figures 4–3 through 4–5, month zero is defined as the month in which the split is effective. It is not the same chronological date for all stocks. Month 1 is the month immediately following the split, and month −1 is the month preceding, and so forth. The vertical axis in the figures measures the average *cumulative* deviation of returns from the normal relationships with the market.

Figure 4–3 shows that the deviations before the split are positive and therefore that rates of returns for stocks that split tend to be high, relative to the market as a whole, by comparison with their longer term historical relationship. After the split, however, the rates of return on these stocks, on the average, have the normal relationship to rates of return on the market as a whole.‡ Figure 4–4 summarizes data for stocks which had dividend increases within a year of the time when the stocks were split. A dividend increase (or decrease) occurred, by definition, if the ratio of dividends paid in the year following the

---

* Some of the stocks in the sample split more than once, so the number of splits studied was 940.

† The rationale for this approach—the "market model"—is discussed more fully in chapter 11.

‡ The deviations shown in the figures are cumulative, so a rising curve means the deviations are positive. A leveling off in the curve indicates a return to the normal relationship.

FIGURE 4–3
Cumulative Average Residuals—All Splits

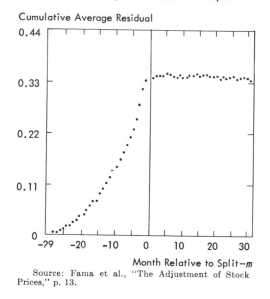

Source: Fama et al., "The Adjustment of Stock Prices," p. 13.

FIGURE 4–4
Cumulative Average Residuals for Dividend "Increases"

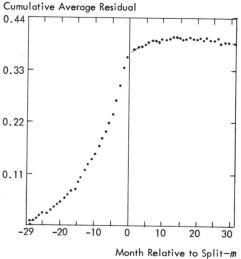

Source: Fama et al., "The Adjustment of Stock Prices," p. 15.

FIGURE 4–5
Cumulative Average Residuals for Dividend "Decreases"

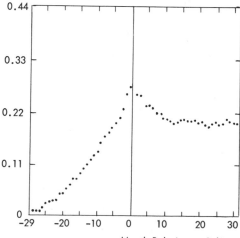

Source: Fama et al., "The Adjustment of Stock Prices," p. 15.

split to those paid in the year preceding the split was larger (or smaller) than the ratio for the exchange as a whole. Following the split, there is a very slight upward drift in the rates of return on stocks with dividend increases relative to the market by comparison with the normal relationship. By the end of 30 months, however, the normal relationship has been resumed. Of particular interest is the fact that the rise in average rates of return begins well before the split. Since information about a split is received on the average only two to four months in advance, the rise cannot be accounted for by the split. A more likely explanation is that splits occur after periods of unusual prosperity for the company which is reflected in the prices of the stocks.

Figure 4–5 shows that after a split, stocks that did not have a subsequent dividend increase had declining rates of return relative to the market by comparison with the normal relationship. The authors interpret these findings as indicating that the announcement of a stock split implies the strong likelihood of a subsequent increase in dividends. The likelihood is substantial but not certain. When these expectations are fulfilled by a subsequent dividend increase, there is a slight feeling of relief on the part of investors and a slight enhancement in the rates of return on the affected stocks relative to what could be expected in the absence of the stock split and accompanying dividend increase. When expectations are disappointed, there is a decline in rates of return relative to the market, reflecting the disappointment of investors.

In summary, the authors regard their work as providing strong support for the hypothesis that the market is efficient. Stock splits have no effect on rates of return, independent of the effect created by the presumption that the stock split contains information regarding future dividend changes and therefore earnings potential. In Fama's words, ". . . apparently the market makes unbiased forecasts of the implications of a split for future dividends, and these forecasts are fully reflected in the price of the security by the end of the split month."[26]

A second ingenious research effort bears on the extent to which the market for stocks is efficient. Scholes[27] studied the price effects of large secondary offerings in order to separate the effects of the distribution *per se* from the informational content of the distribution. Following the methodology of Fama, Fisher, Jensen, and Roll, he found that on the average, the price of a common stock declines between 1 and 2 percent when a secondary offering is made. Scholes does not attribute this to selling pressure, since he found no relationship between the size of the block, either absolutely or as a percentage of the outstanding stock, and the size of the decline. He concludes that the decline is caused by the information implicit in the offering. When offerings are classified by type of vendor, those made by corporations or corporate officers are associated with the largest relative price declines. Moreover, the full price effects of the secondary offering are reflected within six days. Since the Securities and Exchange Commission (SEC) does not require identification of the vendor until six days after the offering, this implies that the market anticipates the informational content of the offering. Scholes extended his analysis to new issues, and these results also support the notion of market efficiency.

A third kind of public announcement was studied by Ball and Brown.[28] For the period 1946–66, the deviations from "normal" rates of return for 261 firms were examined to detect the effect of annual earnings announcements. The authors classified the firms into two groups: those whose earnings for a given year increased relative to the market and those whose earnings decreased relative to the market.* They found that the average rates of return for stocks with "increased earnings" rose throughout the year preceding the announcement. For stocks with "decreased earnings," the opposite was true. In other words, most of the information in the earnings announcement had been anticipated by the market.

Further support for the efficient market hypothesis comes from a study of the effects of announcements of discount rate changes by the Federal Reserve Banks.[29] Waud analyzed the deviations of daily returns on the Standard & Poor's "500" Index from the average daily return and found a statistically significant announcement effect on the next trading day. However, the effect is small—0.5 percent or less—and he concludes that the announcement is anticipated by the market. Possibly, of course, discount rate changes do not have substantial impact on stock prices.

Tests of the Strong Form of the Hypothesis

So far, in this chapter, there has been discussion of the weak and the semistrong forms of the efficient market hypothesis. Substantial evidence has been produced to show that the weak form is valid.

---

* Increases and decreases were defined in a manner similar to that used for dividends by Fama, Fisher, Jensen, and Roll.

The studies on this subject have indicated no exploitable dependencies in successive changes in stock prices. There is also substantial support for the semistrong form of the hypothesis. Four studies were cited to indicate that market prices adjust very promptly to the release of public information such as stock splits, secondary offerings, reports of earnings, and changes in the Federal Reserve Board's rediscount rate.

Now it is time to examine the strong form of the hypothesis— namely that prices of stocks reflect not only what is generally known through public announcements but also what may not be generally known. Certain groups have monopolistic access to information. Also, the ardent quest of legions of security analysts for original insights and small revealing clues could confer superior ability to predict the future course of stock prices. Tests of the strong form consist of analyses of the performance of portfolios managed by groups which might have special information.

These tests consist of an examination of the performance of professionally managed portfolios. The argument is that performance by professionally managed portfolios that was consistently superior to the performance of the market as a whole or to relevant subsets of stocks in that market would indicate an element of inefficiency in the price-making process. Consistent superiority would suggest that some people have superior access to relevant information not reflected in the prices of stocks.

The most visible of the professionally managed portfolios are the mutual funds. They are required by law to present all of the information necessary to compute rates of return on their portfolios. Fortunately for the brevity of this discussion, the results of investigations of mutual fund performance are rather uniform. The first reasonably comprehensive and serious study of mutual fund performance was by Irwin Friend and his associates at the Wharton School.[30] This study was undertaken at the request of the Securities and Exchange Commission and was published under their auspices. The study covered 189 funds from the period December 1952 to September 1958. The major conclusion in the context of this chapter was that, on the average, the performance of the mutual funds studied was insignificantly different from the performance of an unmanaged portfolio with similar asset composition. Rates of return on the latter were measured by the Standard & Poor's Indexes. About one half of the funds performed worse and one half better than the unmanaged portfolios.

There was no evidence of consistently superior performance by any of the funds. Comparisons with rates of return on an unmanaged portfolio fully invested in common stocks as represented by the Standard & Poor's Composite Index indicated that few of the funds did as well. Those which did were shares in specialized funds.

The next major study differs in design and coverage from the first, but the conclusions are consistent with it. William F. Sharpe studied the performance of 34 mutual funds for the period 1954–63.[31] Unlike the earlier study, the Sharpe study takes account not only of rates of return but also of risk, as measured by variability in rates of return of the individual funds. (The analytic framework of the study is the "capital asset pricing model" developed by Sharpe[32] and Lintner.[33] This is discussed in detail in chapter 11.)

Briefly, the model indicates that under certain conditions the relationship between the expected return on a portfolio and its expected variability is linear if the portfolio is efficient. "Efficiency" in this context means that the portfolio provides maximum return for a given level of risk; or equivalently, minimum risk for a given level of return. An investor can vary the risk level associated with a particular portfolio either by investing part of his funds in a risk-free asset or by borrowing additional funds for equity investment (at the same risk-free rate). This is illustrated in figure 4–6. M is the market portfolio, $E(R_M)$ is the expected return on the market portfolio, R_f is the riskless rate of return, and σ_M is the variability of returns on the market portfolio. If M is the market portfolio or one highly correlated with it and equally volatile, any point on the line R_fMY can be obtained by lending or borrowing. Portfolios lying above the line are "superior" to randomly selected portfolios of equal riskiness while portfolios below the line are "inferior."

Sharpe found that, if the expenses of the funds are ignored, 19 of the 34 outperformed the Dow Jones Industrial Average, after taking risk into account. If expenses are considered, only 11 funds did better than the Dow Jones "portfolio" while 23 did worse. Sharpe estimates that the odds are more than 100 to 1 against the possibility that these results were affected by the particular choice of a sample.[34] There were some persistent measurable differences in the performance of individual funds, but these were accounted for, to a major extent, by differences in expenses incurred. This finding lends "support to the view that the capital market is highly efficient and that good managers concentrate on evaluating risk and providing diversification,

FIGURE 4–6

The Theoretical Relationship between Risk and Return for Efficient Portfolios

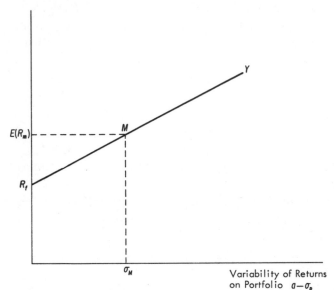

Expected Return
on Portfolio $E(R_p)$

$E(R_m)$

R_f

M

Y

σ_M

Variability of Returns
on Portfolio $a - \sigma_p$

spending little effort (and money) on the search for incorrectly priced securities."[35] Sharpe's major conclusion, therefore, is that mutual fund performance provides evidence that the market for common stocks and other financial assets is highly efficient. Even the professional managers of mutual funds failed consistently to outperform a comprehensive market index.

A more comprehensive study of mutual fund performance by Michael Jensen[36] covered the performance of 115 mutual funds for the period 1955–64. He followed Sharpe in that he did not take account of rates of return alone. Recognizing that variations in fund performance could be expected on the basis of differences in the degree of risk assumed, Jensen compared the performance of individual mutual funds with the performance that could have been expected from randomly selected portfolios of equal riskiness.[37] There is a serious problem in defining the bench mark against which performance of the mutual funds is evaluated, and this problem is discussed at length in chapter 13. In the meantime, we must remain content with a rather brief explanation of the bench mark. Within the context of the "capital asset pricing model," it is possible by artificially constructing portfolios consisting of varying proportions of riskless assets—generally government debt securities—and a portfolio of all stocks listed on the New York Stock Exchange, to create portfolios of different riskiness that would have been selected on the average by random selection. These have a range of riskiness covering that experienced by the mutual funds. Since the riskiness of these randomly selected portfolios depends only upon the proportion invested in the riskless asset and the proportion invested in the market portfolio, the portfolios representing different degrees of riskiness lie on a straight line. The market portfolio in Jensen's work is defined as the Standard & Poor's Composite Index. The measure of risk which he uses is a measure of the sensitivity of a fund's return to changes in the return on the market as measured by the index.* Jensen's major results are illustrated in the figure 4–7.

In figure 4–7, the straight line represents the risk and return on randomly selected portfolios, and the individual dots represent the performance of individual mutual funds. The figure presented above indicates the results on the assumption that mutual funds had no expenses other than brokerage commissions. It can be observed that about half of the dots lie above the line and about half below. This is the result that would be expected if the market were highly efficient with market prices fully reflecting all that was knowable through public announcement or ascertainable through the efforts of individual security analysts.

Figure 4–8 indicates comparisons between mutual fund performances and randomly selected portfolios of equal riskiness after mutual funds are charged with the expenses which they incurred. Naturally, a much smaller proportion of the mutual funds did as well as the randomly selected portfolios. In fact, only 43 out of 115 mutual funds had superior performance. On the average, for the ten-year period, the terminal value of the mutual funds, assuming reinvestment of dividends, would have been about 9 percent less than the terminal value of the randomly selected portfolios, assuming reinvestment of dividends and interest. When loading charges are taken into account, the comparisons are even more adverse from the point of view of mutual

* Sharpe uses the standard deviation of a fund's return to measure variability. The measure of sensitivity used by Jensen is the "beta coefficient." The differences between these two approaches are discussed in chapter 11.

FIGURE 4–7

Scatter Diagram of Risk and (Gross) Return for 115 Open-End Mutual Funds in the Period 1955–64

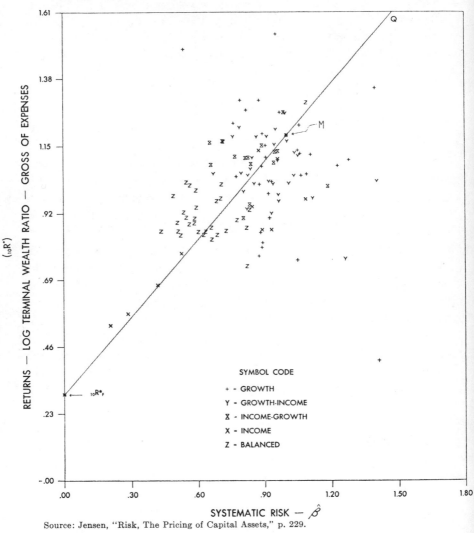

Source: Jensen, "Risk, The Pricing of Capital Assets," p. 229.

funds. At the end of the ten-year period, the average terminal value of the funds was 15 percent less than that of the randomly selected portfolios.

Although Jensen's results indicate that mutual funds on the average did not outperform randomly selected portfolios of equal riskiness,

FIGURE 4–8

Scatter Diagram of Risk and (Net) Return for 115 Open-End Mutual Funds in the Ten-Year Period, 1955–64

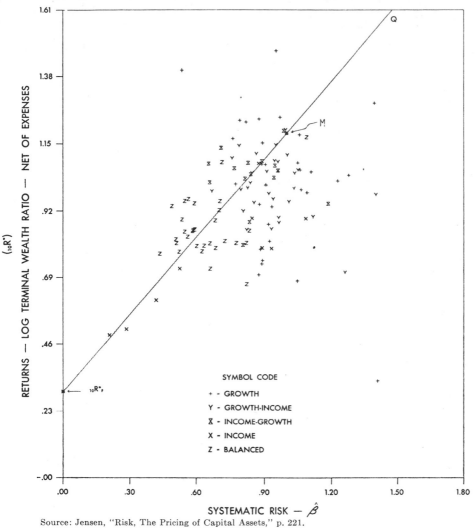

Source: Jensen, "Risk, The Pricing of Capital Assets," p. 221.

there remains the possibility that some mutual funds consistently outperform randomly selected portfolios. Such a finding would represent a partial invalidation of the strong form of the random walk hypothesis. Jensen, in his study, looked into this matter to some degree, though he admitted that further investigation is warranted. On the basis of his preliminary inquiry, Jensen found that a mutual fund which was superior to a randomly selected portfolio in one period was superior to a randomly selected portfolio in a subsequent period about half the time. Obviously, about half the time the performance of the mutual fund in the subsequent period was inferior to the randomly selected portfolio. Jensen also sought to determine whether any fund was more frequently superior to randomly selected portfolios during the ten-year period than would be expected on the basis of chance alone. He found no evidence of such superiority. In sum, Jensen's investigation of mutual fund performance provided additional support for the strong form of the random-walk hypothesis. Mutual fund managers did not appear to have monopolistic access to information. Moreover, large expenses were not associated with high rates of return.

Friend, Blume, and Crockett studied mutual fund performance for the period January 1960 to mid–1969.[38] The period is particularly interesting because of the growth of mutual funds. The market value of equities in fund portfolios increased from $26.7 billion in 1964 to $50.9 billion in 1968. For the whole period, the study indicated that a portfolio with equal dollar amounts in all New York Stock Exchange common stocks would, on the average, have slightly outperformed the 136 funds examined. In contrast, the average performance of the funds was slightly superior to that of a portfolio of all New York Stock Exchange stocks with investments proportional to market values. In the 1968–1969 period, the weighted portfolio surpassed the funds. The rates of return reflect dividends and capital gains, are net of expenses, and include loading fees. The rates are summarized in table 4–3.

A comparison of funds with random portfolios of equal riskiness indicated that high- and medium-risk funds outperformed weighted

TABLE 4–3
Average Rates of Return on Managed and Unmanaged Portfolios[a]

| | Portfolio of All NYSE Common Stocks | | |
Period	136 Funds	Equally Weighted	Value Weighted
Jan. 1960–June 1968	10.7%	12.4%	9.9%
Jan. 1960–Mar. 1964	9.0%	7.0%	9.9%
Apr. 1964–June 1968	12.8%	17.8%	9.8%
July 1968–July 1969	–3.8%	b	–3.3%

Source: Friend et al., pp. 50–68
[a] Annual rate, compounded monthly
[b] Not available

random portfolios during 1960–68 and that low-risk funds provided inferior rates of return. None of the groups outperformed unweighted random portfolios.

The most recent evaluation of mutual funds appears in the *Financial Analysts Journal* for November–December 1972. Williamson studied 180 mutual funds for 1961–70. The results are familiar. In general, the funds did average. One fund out-performed the market in eight years, but chance alone could reasonably account for that. The funds did not show superior judgment either in picking stocks or anticipating general market movements.[39]

One can readily imagine that findings such as those of Friend, Sharpe, Jensen, and Williamson did not create strong euphoria in the mutual fund industry. The least happy interpretation of the findings cited above was that mutual fund managers were incompetent. Even if one avoided that *misinterpretation,* it was possible to conclude—although erroneously—that mutual funds provided no useful function. In fact, neither charges of incompetence nor of uselessness are justified.

The fact that mutual funds did not outperform randomly selected portfolios could mean, and probably does mean, merely that mutual fund managers compete in an efficient market with other portfolio managers of approximately equal competence. Mutual fund managers must compete with the managers of trust departments of commercial banks, with professional individual investors, and with other professionals in investment counseling firms, insurance companies, and elsewhere. Since mutual fund managers must maintain a portfolio of at least 20 securities, and since these are usually widely diversified, it is not at all surprising or indicative of incompetence that on the average these portfolios do not do significantly better or worse than portfolios of equal riskiness selected from the market as a whole.

Even if this is true, mutual funds have important functions to perform. Perhaps the most important has been persuading large numbers of individual investors that common stocks are an appropriate investment for ordinary people of modest wealth. The long history of rates of return on common stocks as compared with other financial investment media suggests that this persuasion by managers of mutual funds has, on the average, over long periods of time proved beneficial to the investing public. In addition, mutual funds may provide a very efficient way for a relatively small investor to achieve effective diversification, something which is usually highly desirable. Mutual funds also provide useful bookkeeping and custodial services and are increasingly able to buy brokerage services on relatively favorable terms. Thus, we can conclude that evidence on mutual fund performance supports the strong form of the random-walk hypothesis but does not indicate either lack of competence by mutual fund managers or the foolishness of individual investors who use mutual funds as an outlet for their savings.

Investigations of the investment behavior of investors other than managers of mutual funds who might have access to monopolistic information are less numerous. There is some evidence, however, that inside information is a potential source of inefficiency in the market. Niederhoffer and Osborne[40] examined the trading of specialists on major exchanges. They concluded that information on unexecuted orders can be used profitably. The finding that the price declines following a secondary offering are larger if the vendor is a corporation or corporate officer indicates that insiders may benefit from privileged information.[41] Lorie and Niederhoffer[42] also found evidence of profitability in insider trading. They analyzed insider trades from January 1950 to December 1960 of 105 New York Stock Exchange companies. They conclude that:

proper and prompt analysis of data on insider trading can be profitable. . . . When insiders accumulate a stock intensively, the stock can be expected to outperform the market during the next six months. Insiders tend to buy more often than usual before large price increases and to sell more often than usual before price decreases.[43]

They also found that a change in direction of trading activity can be an important clue to insider expectations concerning their stock.

These findings, while meager in comparison to the evidence in support of the efficient market hypothesis, do suggest there are minor departures from complete efficiency. There is no evidence however, that groups other than specialists or corporate insiders can use special information to earn above normal profits.

CONCLUSIONS

This chapter has attempted to trace the development of the random-walk hypothesis. At first, investigators studied the properties of changes in stock prices and found them to be substantially independent. This independence caused stock prices to follow a random walk. This result was surprising and interesting. The quest for an explanation led to the theory of efficient markets which has implications far beyond the mere statistical independence of successive changes in stock prices. An efficient market is one in which a large number of buyers and sellers react through a sensitive and efficient mechanism to cause market prices to reflect fully and virtually instantaneously what is knowable about the prospects for the companies whose securities are being traded. This way of looking at things caused a transformation from the so-called random-walk hypothesis, with which investigators started, to the so-called efficient market hypothesis which now dominates most discussion of this subject.

There are three forms of this hypothesis: the weak form, the semistrong form, and the strong form. The weak form asserts that successive changes in stock prices are substantially independent. A number of investigators have found strong evidence to support this hypothesis. The semistrong form asserts that public information is fully reflected in stock prices. Several competent inquiries into this subject have indicated the very prompt and unbiased adjustment of market prices to new public information. The strong form of the hypothesis asserts that not only public information but also the kind of information available to security analysts through their private and individual inquiries is fully reflected in stock market prices. Several studies of the performance of mutual funds, whose performance is visible, support the contention that professionally managed portfolios do not outperform randomly selected portfolios of equal riskiness. These findings are consistent with the strong form of the hypothesis. The only evidence that suggests deviations from the strong form concerns specialist and insider trading. These deviations, however, appear to be only minor inefficiencies in the market-making process.

5

Implications of the Efficient Market Hypothesis

INTRODUCTION

IN THE LAST CHAPTER, we presented substantial evidence regarding the validity of the various forms of the efficient market hypothesis. The hypothesis is not that superior performance is impossible; merely that consistently superior performance for a given risk level is extremely rare. If the hypothesis is substantially or generally true, security analysis and portfolio management would be quite different than if the hypothesis were not generally true.

There is a curious paradox. In order for the hypothesis to be true, it is necessary for many investors to disbelieve it. That is, market prices will promptly and fully reflect what is knowable about the companies whose shares are traded only if investors seek to earn superior returns, make conscientious and competent efforts to learn about the companies whose securities are traded, and analyze relevant information promptly and perceptively. If that effort were abandoned, the efficiency of the market would diminish rapidly.

The paradox is striking, but it is not very different from the paradox of all effectively competitive markets. Entrepreneurs continue trying to compete though the competitive process itself can reduce the rate of profits to zero. Investors continue to compete in an effort to arrive at superior judgments. The likelihood of being consistently superior is apparently quite small, but the rewards for success can be enormous. Clearly, it is a game worth winning, although it may not be a game worth playing.

This chapter discusses appropriate strategy for investors who accept the major conclusions of the preceding chapter. The next section of this chapter deals with the implications of the efficient market hypothesis for security analysis; the subsequent section, for portfolio management.

SECURITY ANALYSIS

The State of the Art

Security analysis is carried out by almost all investors and financial institutions. The individual investor typically makes casual inquiry based upon conversation with brokers, scrutiny of the financial pages of the press, reading annual reports, and the like. Financial institutions are obviously more systematic and professional in their approach. They employ about 11,000 security analysts whose credentials are sufficient to entitle them to membership in the various financial analysts' societies in the United States. Although the methods of the amateur and professional security analysts differ substantially, they have in common the effort to identify undervalued and overvalued securities. Implicit in this identification process is the notion of "intrinsic value." The security analysts try to assess the magnitude of negative and positive differences between current market prices and what the prices *should* be—that is, intrinsic value.

Various theories of security valuation will be discussed in chapter 6. All of them attach great importance to the level of earnings per share, expected growth in earnings per share, riskiness, and dividend payments. The estimates of the impact of these different variables upon intrinsic value vary according to the statistical techniques used or according to the types of intuition brought to bear upon the problem. The activity is carried out with the belief that portfolios resulting from the process will provide rates of return superior to those produced by any other process, especially random selection. As indicated in the previous chapter, there is very substantial evidence that the classical process of security evaluation for the purpose of identifying undervalued and overvalued securities does not produce the superior rates of return which are sought. This seems to be true even though some financial institutions perform the task of security evaluation extremely well. With the use of large files of financial information in machine-readable form and highly trained staffs of economists and statisticians, sophisticated models of security valuation are created and large numbers of securities are evaluated. Unfortunately, all of this, competent though it be, does not, on the average, seem to produce the desired results.

Implications

The most general implication of the efficient market hypothesis is that most security analysis is logically incomplete and valueless. A typical analytical report is based on public information, perhaps supplemented by a company visit, and indicates the prospects for either improvement or deterioration in the company's profitability. After what is often a detailed, lucid, accurate, and perceptive analysis, the analyst concludes with a recommendation that the stock be bought, held, sold, or sold short. The logical incompleteness consists in failing to determine or even consider whether the price of the stock already reflects the substance of the analysis. For true believers in efficient markets, a recommendation to buy or sell cannot rest solely on one's own opinion about a company, but rather must be based on a significant difference between that opinion and the opinion of other investors who determine the current price of the stock. A very optimistic forecast of a company's future earnings is no justification for buying the stock; it is necessary that the analyst's forecast be significantly more optimistic than other forecasts. Such marked differences in opinion are the basis of abnormal gains and losses. A proper analytical report will include evidence of the existence of such a difference and support for the analyst's own view.

Another implication of an efficient market is the possibility of economies of scale in security analysis and portfolio management. The quest for undervalued and overvalued securities costs about the same whether the amount available for investment is $1,000 or $1 billion. If the occasional success of the quest—and nothing has been said which should suggest its inevitable failure—could produce superior returns of, say, 0.5 percent, this would produce additional returns of $5 on the investment of $1,000 and of $5 million on the investment of $1 billion. Clearly, the quest might make sense for large financial institutions having billions of dollars to manage, while it would not make sense for investors with smaller sums.

A third implication is the extreme unlikelihood that one can consistently earn superior rates of return by analyzing public information in conventional ways. Although originality may be coupled with un-soundness and thereby be unproductive, the only hope for superiority in results lies in seeking unique ways of forming expectations about the prospects for individual companies.

An example of originality in the analysis of financial information is provided by the work of Charles Callard.[1] Almost every seemingly new idea has recognizable antecedents, and Callard's ideas certainly bear recognizable relationship to work which went before.[2] Neverthe-less, Callard has made sufficient changes in the earlier work so that his system of security analysis can be fairly termed original.

The presentation of Callard's work is not intended as certification that it contains the secret of great wealth. The work is presented as an example of an ingenious and plausible effort to understand the workings of corporations on the basis of public information so as to achieve a greater ability to forecast future profitability.

Callard's system is based upon the belief that intelligent scrutiny of several time series of financial data for individual corporations can reveal to the perceptive analyst the likely near-term course of corporate profits. The basic time series in the Callard system are gross operating assets, sales and earnings as a percentage of this asset base, assets per dollar of book value, the debt-equity ratio of the corporation, the dividend yield, and the cost of capital.

The potential insight to be derived from a consideration of these data can be illustrated by reference to two hypothetical corporations, A and B. Corporation A has had an average annual growth in earnings per share of 7 percent for the last 20 years. The corporation operates in an industry which is expanding, and a conventional scrutiny of the industry and of the historical profitability of the firm might lead to quite optimistic estimates of the future. A look at the time series listed above might reveal the following facts: (1) the asset base has been expanding; (2) profits, as a percentage of the asset base, have been declining; (3) the financing of the expansion of assets has been largely through the issuance of debt securities, so that now the debt-equity ratio of the corporation is high by comparison with other firms in similarly cyclical industries; (4) the average rate of return on the asset base is now less than the firm's cost of capital; and (5) the cost of capital has risen rapidly with the rise in interest rates during the last 15 years. In summary, the increase in earnings per share over the last 10 to 15 years has been made possible by a rapid expansion in assets financed by issuing debt securities. The ability of the firm to continue to expand assets in this way is nearly exhausted, so that continued growth in earnings per share at the historical rate is unlikely. If the price-earnings ratio of the stock is at the same levels which have prevailed in recent years, one might conclude that the market is overestimating future prospects for the company and that the company's stock is overvalued.

In contrast to Company A is Company B. Company B has had the same average annual rate of growth in earnings per share as A. Its asset base has been expanding slowly, it owes no money, and the rate of return on its asset base is in excess of 25 percent. At the same time, the firm's cost of capital is only 11 percent. All of this information suggests that the firm has the potential to increase its earnings per share. What is needed is for the firm to use some of its available credit in order to expand its asset base. Such an expansion, assuming a rate of return on the acquired assets comparable to or even moderately lower than that on existing assets, would result in increased earnings per share. Careful attention to statements by the chief executive officer at annual meetings and before financial analysts' societies, and other information, can provide advance clues to the intentions of the company with regard to the expansion of its assets. If these clues are numerous and strong, indicating a more rapid expansion of the asset base, and if the price earnings ratio of the stock is at the same levels that have existed in recent years, one might conclude that the market is undervaluing the security and that it should be bought.

A somewhat similar approach has been developed by Babcock.[3] His general argument is that the observed trend in earnings per share can be quite misleading. Part of the growth in earnings is sustainable, but part is merely transitory. To separate these parts, he looks at the components of growth, such as the profit margin on sales, the turnover ratio of sales to total capital, the leverage effect of debt on common equity, and a pull-through rate (one minus the tax rate). By definition, the product of these is the after-tax rate of return on common equity. Earnings per share are the product of the rate of return and book value, or common equity per share. Analysis of the trends and deviations from trend in each of the component variables is then used to isolate sustainable from transitory movements. If actual growth in earnings per share has been substantially in excess of sustainable growth, a downturn in the rate of growth is expected. If actual earnings have grown less rapidly than sustainable growth, the expectation would be for accelerated growth.

The difficulty in deciding whether to make investment decisions on the basis of analyses such as the foregoing is that of deciding whether the current market price of the stocks being analyzed already reflects the knowledge gained by the analysis.

These ways of looking at the financial data of a corporation may or may not be useful. If they should prove to be useful, that fact would almost certainly become known. As a consequence, the widespread use of these approaches to security analysis would quickly end their profitability. Current prices of common stocks would soon reflect what was learnable about their prospects from these methods of security analysis.

The intent of this discussion of the ways of looking at financial data by Callard and Babcock is to provide examples of the possibility of ingenious modifications of conventional methods of security analysis. There are many other modifications. Some of them will prove useful and others will not. The only thing which seems virtually certain is that the useful methods will soon be used on a scale sufficient to cause market prices to reflect the lessons which such new forms of analysis can provide.

A different type of originality is illustrated by the practices of Meyer A. Berman, as reported in the *Wall Street Journal* on January 23, 1970.[4] Berman's originality—and it is not unique—consists in scrutinizing, very promptly, public sources of information which are available only to those who take more trouble than is necessary to read the financial pages of the daily press. Berman makes a practice of reading all of the reports filed at the Securities and Exchange Commission for clues to future prospects of reporting companies. A dramatic example cited in a *Wall Street Journal* article concerned Acme Missiles Corporation. Acme Missiles had been highly regarded because of its lucrative contracts to build launching pads for missiles. Berman noted in his reading that Acme Missiles had lost its construction bond. Since the federal government does not sign contracts with firms not having a construction bond, the implications for Acme were important. Berman sold Acme short at 38 and happily watched the stock decline rapidly to 5.

Lorie and Niederhoffer, in their study of insider trading, indicate the possibility of occasionally superior profits from the very prompt scrutiny of information on insider trading.[5] Certain patterns of trading by insiders, if noticed very promptly, can produce a small margin of superiority in trading in those stocks. The opportunities are not glittering since the patterns with predictive power occur only rarely, but profits on those occasions can make the effort worthwhile.

It may also be possible for a security analyst to develop a profound understanding of the impact of new developments such as changes in technology or in economic policies. This type of ability can be valuable and is undoubtedly rare. If one has it, however, there is nothing in the Securities and Exchange Commission disclosure rules to prevent the quest for relevant information.

So far, it has been pointed out that even if the efficient market hypothesis is true, there is a role for security analysis if the magnitude of investable funds is sufficient, or if there is sound originality in the process of analysis. There is still another role for the security analyst. The objectives, tastes, and needs of different investors differ substantially. Most of these differences can be summarized in terms of the risks and associated expected level of returns which are suitable for the investor. Even though it may be extremely difficult for security analysts to demonstrate consistently superior ability in specifying expected earnings for individual corporations, it is not so difficult to estimate the riskiness of investments in different securities. There tends to be considerable stability through time in the variability of both earnings per share and of prices of common stocks.[6] This means that the careful analysis of variability can be used to help in choosing portfolios appropriate to the needs of the individual investor.

A belief in an efficient market is not exactly equivalent to a disbelief in the possibility of superior security analysis. There can be individuals in the world who have a quicker or more profound understanding of the economic consequences for individual firms of changes in the economic environment or changes within the firm itself. The truly talented professional portfolio manager tries to make sure that he can identify such rare and valuable talent if he should encounter it. This requires a systematic effort to assess the value of advice or the quality of predictions made by the security analysts available to him. Sometimes all of these analysts work for the same firm as the portfolio managers; sometimes, they work for brokers and investment counselors with whom the professional manager has contact.

One method of assessing the value of predictions has been developed by a firm with a large staff of analysts. Each analyst is responsible for expressing an opinion about a group of stocks in his industry. These opinions are classified in one of six categories. The number "1" indicates that the stock should be bought because of its very bright prospects; "2" indicates that it is acceptable to buy the stock; "3", that the stock may be held but should not be acquired; "4", that it is acceptable to sell the stock if it is held; and "5", that the stock must be sold. "6" indicates no opinion. This categorization of analysts' opinions enables the portfolio manager to ascertain whether the individual analyst has the capacity to discriminate among the stocks for which he is responsible. Perhaps, some analysts have great discriminatory powers and others little. Either judgment should be reached only after the passage of a considerable period of time, perhaps as much as two years or more.

The ultimate purpose of assessing the value of the information and predictions of security analysts is to improve the quality of the analysis upon which decisions are based. This is achieved in two ways. The most obvious is to pay more and more attention to those analysts whose record is superior, and less and less attention—perhaps none at all—to analysts whose record has proved to be inferior. Successful discrimination would reduce the enormous flow of information which comes to portfolio managers and increase the usefulness and profitability of the advice which is received.

A second way in which the evaluation of security analysis can lead to its improvement is by changing the methods of analysis used. The simplest changes would consist of diminishing the ambiguity or increasing the precision of the predictions or advice which is conveyed. More basic and more difficult is changing the ways in which security analysts look at the world in order to derive their data and other basic information, and the way in which they interpret it for the purpose of selecting promising investments. This is not the place for a prolonged treatise on security analysis, but it is appropriate to point out that discrimination among security analysts in order to identify the best and the worst provides rich material for the identification of the methods which seem to work well and those which seem to work badly. (A more detailed discussion of techniques of security valuation is to be found in chapter 8.)

PORTFOLIO MANAGEMENT

The State of the Art

At the present time, portfolio management as practiced by professionals in financial institutions is fairly easily described. Security analysts do their work and classify securities in categories according to their attractiveness as investments. Investment committees consider the recommendations of security analysts and create a list of securities which are approved for purchase by portfolio managers. These lists vary in length from time to time and from institution to institution, but it would not be unusual to find an approved list of 200 securities in a large financial institution.

Portfolio managers then select securities from the approved list as a result of their own appraisals of relative attractiveness and in response to the individual needs and tastes of the clients whose funds are being invested. In creating the individual portfolios, the portfolio manager is often constrained by general policies specifying the minimum number of securities which must be held, the maximum proportion of the portfolio which can be in any single security or in any single industry, the minimum number of industries in which investments must be held, and so forth. The entire process is sufficiently straightforward so that Geoffrey Clarkson and Alan Meltzer could write a computer program to reproduce almost exactly the portfolio which a professional portfolio manager selected.[7]

Adjusting portfolios to the needs and tastes of the individual investor is amusingly described by Brealey.

It is a commonly held view that the mix of common stocks maintained by an investor should depend on his willingness to bear risk. According to this view, a broker or investment counselor is a kind of financial interior decorator, skillfully designing portfolios to reflect his client's personality.[8]

Appropriate Changes

Those who believe, as Brealey does, in the efficient market hypothesis would change the process of professional portfolio management. Except on rare occasions, no money or energy would be expended in trying to predict the rates of return on individual securities. The rare occasions would arise when a portfolio manager had really strong reason to believe that the security analyst or some other member of his financial institution had either confidential information or an especially original and valuable insight into the prospects for an individual corporation. On other occasions, the professional portfolio manager would consider the following things:

1. *The degree of diversification.* At its simplest, this means that the portfolio manager should insure that virtually all of the variations in rates of return on the portfolio are determined by fluctuations in the general market for common stocks. As is discussed later (chapter 11), the market, on the average, provides superior rates of return for that risk which cannot be avoided (i.e., risk of owning securities in general), but does not provide superior returns for risks which can be avoided (i.e., risks caused by the independent fluctuations in the value of a group of common stocks apart from fluctuations of the market as a whole). The task of achieving sufficient diversification is easy. As was indicated in chapter 2, even simple random selection leads to portfolios which approximate the market very closely when only 16 or 20 stocks are held.

2. *The riskiness of the portfolio.* The level of risk which the client or beneficiary should assume must be determined either by consultation with the client or independently by the professional advisor when the clients views are of no value as would be the case when the client is an infant, a senile person, or possibly a woman.* The appropriate level of risk is determined by the client's resources, needs, and tastes, whether the client is an individual, a corporate trustor, or an endowed institution.

3. *The maintenance of the desired risk level.* The portfolio should be selected and maintained in accordance with the level of risk which is deemed appropriate. Brealey has asserted that the conventional view is that this task requires a good deal of custom tailoring to the client's needs. Modern portfolio theory, on the other hand, asserts that all clients can hold the same group of common stocks and that the appropriate level of risk is to be achieved by dampening volatility through the injection of short-term government securities or by increasing volatility through buying on margin. There will be much more discussion of this view later, but even at this point it can be seen that the suggestion lacks practicality in some instances. The lack of practicality stems from a variety of sources, including the limited size of the market for many securities, the impossibility of executing orders instantaneously so that the relative attractiveness of assets can change dur-

---

* An article in the *Wall Street Journal* provides evidence of the belief—though not of its validity—that women are not wise investors. *Wall Street Journal,* April 5, 1970, p. 1.

ing the process of establishing or liquidating a position, and differences in the tax status and time horizons of investors.

4. *The tax status of the investor.* Returns on investments almost always consist, in part, of interest or dividends and, in part, of capital gains. For investors subject to taxation, the proportions of the total return coming from these sources matter since they are taxed at different rates.

5. *Transaction costs.* Possibilities for reducing transaction costs have increased substantially in recent years with the growth of the "third" and "fourth" markets, creation of automated quotation systems for over-the-counter trading in listed stocks, and negotiated rates for trades of large value on the New York Stock Exchange.

In accordance with all the foregoing, Black[9] has advocated that almost all portfolio managers should be passive. That is, they should select a diversified portfolio, lever it through borrowing to a higher degree of risk or dampen it through the purchase of government securities to a lower degree of risk, maintain the appropriate degree of risk, realize tax losses when appropriate, meet the needs of the investor for funds, maintain efficient diversification through periodic shifts in securities, and use professional skill in minimizing transaction costs. These tasks are difficult and important, but they are not the tasks conventionally believed to be the necessary ones for the professional portfolio manager. The professional portfolio manager needs periodically to review the circumstances of the investor to make sure that the portfolio's riskiness is at all times appropriate for the client.

Investment Counselling

If markets are efficient, choosing an investment policy will generally have a much greater influence on rates of return than security analysis or conventional portfolio management. Investment counselling deserves more research and resources than it traditionally receives. It is discussed in chapter 15.

CONCLUSIONS

The accumulating evidence regarding the validity of the random-walk or efficient market hypothesis has changed some conceptions as to the appropriate form of security analysis and the appropriate role of the portfolio manager. The ardent quest for undervalued or over-valued securities by 11,000 trained security analysts has made it extremely unlikely that more than very small and transient margins of superiority can be achieved by any of these analysts. The small and transient margins can be profitably exploited only by portfolio managers of financial institutions with very large amounts of assets to manage. The obviousness of great economies of scale in the performance of security analysis has already been stressed.

Originality, when sound, still has potential for providing rewards. Large financial institutions can seek this originality in techniques of analysis of conventional information, hoping to improve the speed and accuracy with which public information is organized, analyzed, and interpreted. Other security analysts must seek to develop their originality in other ways. Perhaps it will prove fruitful to seek new kinds of objective data on corporate performance; perhaps, to view old data in fresh perspectives in order to get a clearer vision of future profitability of individual corporations.

Even though stocks are bought and sold in efficient markets, there still remains an important need for estimates of the contributions which individual securities make to the riskiness of diversified portfolios. This riskiness tends to change only slowly through time so that careful analysis of historical data can still have value. Knowledge of the relationship between risk and reward is one of the very few kinds of knowledge whose value is not diminished seriously by its general dissemination.

The role of the portfolio manager, too, has been changed by increasing conviction that the market for securities is efficient. Unless one has a strong feeling, buttressed by hard evidence, that the portfolio manager has superior skill, much is to be said for a strategy of passivity. Under this strategy, the portfolio manager has the following tasks to perform: (1) a determination of the appropriate level of risk for the portfolio under management; (2) achievement of the desired level of risk by constructing a portfolio of well diversified common stocks which is either dampened through inclusion of riskless assets or levered by purchasing on margin; (3) the periodic review of the appropriateness of the level of risk; (4) the maintenance of the desired level of risk; (5) management of additions to and deletions from the portfolio in order to minimize taxes and provide either for necessary additional investment or for the reduction of investment in order to make disbursements; and (6) minimization of transaction costs.

In addition to these functions, the portfolio manager should constantly be in search of analysts with superior insight. The task is difficult because the superior analyst is rare and because the identification of that superiority is difficult and subject to error. There is also a responsibility to measure performance in order to provide the basis for identifying the causes of inferiority or superiority.

Investment counselling is the selection of an appropriate investment policy. It is an important, neglected subject.

THE VALUATION
OF SECURITIES

6

The Theory of Stock Valuation

INTRODUCTION

Basic Principles

FEW READERS will be astounded by the assertion that investments are valuable because of the desirable things which they provide to the investor. This is true whether the investment is in art objects, stamps, wine, or in financial assets such as stocks and bonds. Investments having aesthetic qualities are difficult to value because some of the consequences are not financial. Fortunately, this chapter and this book deal only with investments in financial assets, so the problem of valuation is somewhat simplified. That is, all of the relevant consequences of investment are financial, and therefore the value of an investment is purely monetary.

Difficulties begin to arise only when one attempts to identify and estimate the prospective financial consequences of an investment and to determine their impact on value. A list of such prospective consequences includes the following: (1) changes in the market value of the asset; (2) distributions of valuable things such as dividends, interest, and rights to the owner; and (3) changes in the riskiness of the asset.

In a certain world, all assets would provide the same return which would be equal to the marginal productivity of capital. In our uncertain world, prices of assets are determined by what investors expect to be the financial consequences of owning them. Differences of opinion create the opportunities to make abnormal gains and to lose money. The purpose of security analysis is to detect differences between the value of a security as determined by the market and a security's "intrinsic value"—that is, the value that the security *ought* to have and will have when other investors have the same insight and knowledge as the analyst.

The value of an asset in our uncertain world is the present value of the future cash flows which the asset provides to its owners. The cash flows have two components: (1) periodic payments of such things as dividends and interest; and (2) the price of the asset when it is sold. The present value is determined by discounting these cash flows at a rate which includes the rate of interest on risk-free assets and an additional rate which is the risk premium on the particular asset.

There are controversies both about the cash flows to be discounted and about the rate of discounting. This chapter is organized around these controversies.

We first discuss the controversy as to whether it is the future stream of dividends to the stockholder or the stream of earnings of the corporation which should be considered and discounted in determining the present value of the stock.

The second disagreement is about the appropriate rate for discounting future cash flows. Everyone, even economists of the Soviet Union, understands that a dollar today is more important than a dollar in the future, and that therefore some discounting of future cash flows is essential for rational economic behavior. Although a certain claim to $100 five years hence is less valuable than a certain claim to $100 today, not all would agree on the difference in value.

A third controversy stems from differing conceptions of and techniques for assessing the investor's confidence in the prediction of cash flows. This is another way of saying that there is disagreement about measuring uncertainty or risk. Although there is general agreement that almost all investors desire to avoid risk and that it is associated with the degree of unpredictability of future returns, there is considerable disagreement regarding the best ways to assess or estimate that degree of unpredictability and the ways in which the unpredictability of returns on individual securities contribute to the riskiness of entire portfolios.

The next section discusses the cash flows to be discounted; the following section discusses the rate of discount and its relation to risk.

CASH FLOWS

Miller and Modigliani in a famous article[1] state that one can find at least the following four approaches to the valuation of shares: (1) the discounted cash-flow approach; (2) the current-earnings-plus-future-investment-opportunities approach; (3) the stream-of-dividends approach; and (4) the stream-of-earnings approach. Miller and Modigliani demonstrate that the approaches, properly understood, are logically equivalent. In the discussion in this chapter, the four equivalent approaches will be reduced to two for simplicity. The first is a combination of the stream-of-dividends approach and the discounted cash-flow approach. The most obvious difference between them is that the discounted cash-flow approach explicitly takes account of the terminal market value of the asset while the stream-of-dividends approach avoids that consideration either by assuming that the asset is held in perpetuity[2] or by implicitly assuming that the terminal market value is simply the value of unpaid future dividends.

The two other approaches discussed by Miller and Modigliani focus on earnings. One values the stream of earnings whereas the other considers current earnings and future investment opportunities. The latter is converted into the former by transforming investment opportunities into rates of return on investments.

Dividends

One of the earliest and ablest proponents of the view that dividends determine the investment value of stock was John Burr Williams. He says, "Let us define the investment value of a stock as the present worth of all dividends to be paid upon it."[3] In specific terms the value of a share of stock is as follows:

$$V_o = \frac{D_1}{(1 + i)} + \frac{D_2}{(1 + i)^2} + \cdots \frac{D_N}{(1 + i)^N}$$

where V_o is the present value of the share, D_1 is the first dividend, D_2 the second dividend, and so forth, and i is the rate at which the dividends are discounted.

He goes on to say,

Most people will object at once to the foregoing formula for stocks by saying that it should use the present worth of future *earnings* not future *dividends*. But should not earnings and dividends both give the same answer under the implicit assumptions of our critics? If earnings not paid out in dividends are successfully reinvested at compound interest for the benefit of the stockholder, as the critics imply, then these earnings should produce dividends later; if not, then they are money lost. Furthermore, if these reinvested earnings will produce dividends, then our formula will take account of them when it takes account of all future dividends; but if they will not, then our formula will rightly refrain from including them in any discounted annuity of benefits.

Earnings are only a means to an end, and the means should not be mistaken for the end. Therefore, we must say that a stock derives its value from its dividends, not its earnings. In short, a stock is worth only *what you can get out of it*. Even so spoke the old farmer to his son:

> A cow for her milk
> A hen for her eggs
> And a stock, by heck
> for her dividends.

> An orchard for fruit,
> Bees for their honey,
> And stock, besides,
> For their dividends.[4]

Williams avoids the awkward question of the effect of changes in the market value of stocks by emphasizing that he is talking only about the "investment value" of stocks. This allows him to assume that the investment is held for a very long period and that therefore the discounted value of a change in market value has a negligible impact on present value. In the discussion which follows, the assumption about the irrelevance of very distant changes in the market value of assets will be dropped since it is not essential to the argument. If one wishes to assume shorter periods, one can easily convert the Williams approach to a more comprehensive one which includes changes in market value simply by discounting the stream of dividends plus money received at the time the asset is sold. The controversy about the relative importance of earnings and dividends remains and deserves discussion.

Williams's subsequent discussion deals with some possible complications. He considers the appropriate rate of discounting, the effects of stock rights and assessments, risk premiums, the effect of the capital structure of the firm, and the marketability of the security. His treatment of these various subjects leads to the grand conclusion that the investment value of a stock is determined by discounting the "expected" [authors' term] stream of dividends at the discount rate appropriate for the individual investor as determined by his "minimum wages for abstinence" from current consumption.

Williams was a great pioneer, stating many important ideas which subsequently have been incorporated formally into a comprehensive theory of corporation finance and investments. His work on the crucial importance of dividends in determining stock values has been elaborated and quantified by subsequent workers.

One of the more recent tillers of this vineyard is M. J. Gordon who discusses the controversy as to the relative importance of dividends and earnings in his article, "Dividends, Earnings, and Stock Prices."[5] Gordon's statement of the dividend hypothesis is derived from John Burr Williams. The contrasting earnings hypothesis is, according to Gordon:

> . . . that the investor buys the income per share when he acquires a share of stock. The rationale is that regardless of whether they are distributed to him, the stockholder has an ownership right in the earnings per share. He receives the dividend in cash and the retained earnings in a rise in the share's value, and if he wants additional cash, he can always sell a fraction of his equity. In short, the corporate entity is a legal fiction that is not material with respect to his rights in the corporation or to the value he places on them.[6]

Gordon asserts that this view is widely held and is set forth most systematically in Lutz and Lutz.[7]

Gordon attempts to resolve the controversy by a study in which he estimates the relationship among the following variables: dividends, retained earnings, changes in dividends, and changes in retained earnings, all deflated by book value. Gordon feels that the issue as to the relative correctness of the dividend hypothesis and the earnings hypothesis can be resolved by seeing whether the price-earnings ratio of the stock is independent of the dividend-payout ratio. Lutz and Lutz and others who believe that earnings are all that matter, would have to believe that the dividend-payout ratio does not significantly affect the price-earnings ratio. Gordon, Williams, and others would have to believe that the payout ratio does make a difference. Gordon found that the payout ratio and changes in the payout ratio had a very significant impact upon price-earnings ratios in common stocks and therefore concluded that dividends were the primary determinant of share value.

Other workers have reached the same conclusion by other routes. By purely theoretical means, James Walter reached the conclusion that over longer periods of time stock prices reflect the present value of expected dividends.[8] He distinguishes between growth stocks and others by identifying the former as those corporations whose expected rates of return on additional internal investments exceed market capitalization rates of the common stocks. This finding does not lead to a modification of the dividend hypothesis; rather it is an explanation of variations in payout ratios, each of which has its own implications with respect to future dividends.

Earnings

When one reads the arguments in support of the dividend hypothesis, it is easy to be persuaded that no other approach could be sensible. It is easy to believe that all that is to be valued in an asset is represented by what it pays to the owner—dividends, in the case of common stocks—and the change in its market value during the time it is held. Nevertheless much of the academic literature, the popular press, and the professional financial community discuss the importance of earnings *per se* as the primary determinant of share value. Although some of the discussion treats earnings as being important only as an instrument for the payment of dividends, other discussion concentrates on the earnings themselves.

One's skepticism regarding the dominant importance of dividends might be stimulated by observing that there are some stocks which have never paid a dividend and a larger number which have not paid a dividend for many years, and that these stocks are in successful companies whose owners have in some instances enjoyed high rates of return. Litton Industries, Inc., for example, has never paid a dividend on its common stock, except stock dividends which do not count, yet the common stock has at all times sold for a positive price per share and for several years Litton was one of the most spectacular performers on the New York Stock Exchange.

Further support for a belief in the primacy of earnings could come from attending almost any meeting of financial analysts or of investment committees responsible for managing portfolios. Frequently, perhaps usually or almost always, discussions about prospects for prices of different stocks hinge upon discussions of prospects for earnings of these same stocks. Discussions of dividends are rare, although it is often tacitly recognized that dividends can be expected to change when there are large changes in earnings from other than transient causes.

Further, there is an intuitive appeal to the analogy between the value of the ownership of the assets of the corporation as represented by its common stock and the value of the direct ownership of any piece of income-producing property. Both the corporation and the income-producing property can easily be thought of as being valued because of the profit or income which they produce rather than because of that fraction of the profit or income which the owner chooses to transfer to his personal account for either consumption or investment in other things.

The Dividend and Earnings Hypotheses Reconciled

As has been stated, there is an intuitive plausibility to the belief that dividends (and changes in market value) should determine the value of a common stock and also to the belief that it is really earnings that matter. A choice between these plausible and superficially inconsistent beliefs is unnecessary, because, as Miller and Modigliani[9] have shown, once the underlying assumptions are made explicit and understood, the two hypotheses are equivalent. At least, the two approaches would be equivalent in a world of certainty without taxes and without transaction costs. The introduction of these unpleasant realities causes a modification, but only a minor one, in the demonstration of basic equivalence between the two hypotheses.

The reconciliation lies in making explicit the capital expenditure program of the corporation whose stock is being valued. Once one accepts a given program, Miller and Modigliani show the irrelevance of the dividend-payout ratio in valuing shares. In their words, "Values there (i.e., in a rational and perfect economic environment) are determined solely by 'real' considerations—in this case the earning power of the firm's assets and its investment policy—and not by how the fruits of the earning power are 'packaged' for distribution."[10] They mean that the value of a firm is determined solely by its earnings. Dividend policy has no effect.

To see why they say this, let us start simply with a firm which finances its internal investments with retained earnings and whose dividends are what remains after this investment. If the dividend were increased, the shareholder would be affected in two ways. He would benefit from the increased cash receipt, but he would also suffer since retained earnings would no longer suffice to finance internal investment and the deficiency would make it necessary to issue new shares. This would reduce the proportion of the firm owned by existing shareholders. Miller and Modigliani show that the value of the increase in the dividend is equal to the reduction in the value of a share caused by issuing new shares. If the total increase in dividends were $100,000, the firm would have to sell additional shares having a value of $100,000, thus reducing the value of previously outstanding shares by that amount. The result of these two effects would be to leave existing shareholders neither better nor worse than before the increase in dividends.

The reasoning is symmetrical if dividends were reduced. The reduction in the value of the cash receipt is precisely offset by the increase in value per share caused by the reduction in the number of outstanding shares that would be possible if the firm used its excess retained earnings to buy shares in the open market. It is always assumed, of course, that there are no transaction costs or taxes. In their article, Miller and Modigliani demonstrate rigorously that correct valuation formulae can be derived mathematically from either the stream of earnings or the stream of dividends. The two streams are identical.

The equivalence arises because once one knows the investment policy of the firm one knows its earnings. Changes in dividends would have the precisely offsetting effects just described. One might think that if dividends were increased and became large enough to require external financing for investment, the present value of the two streams would be different; earnings would remain the same and dividends would be larger than in the simple case. This way of looking at things is wrong. The stream of future dividends could not be larger for *existing* shareholders, since the necessary increase in the number of shares which would be required to finance internal investment would prevent dividends per share from being larger. In sum, earnings are all that matter.

There are various ways to become confused in thinking about the preceding propositions, and the literature contains examples of most of them. One mistake is to assume that dividend policy determines the amount available for internal investment which in turn affects earnings and the value of the firm. Dividend policy might affect internal investment, but it need not and generally should not.

Another mistake is in the calculation of earnings. The correct calculation takes into account the cost of capital used internally, whether financed by retained earnings or otherwise. Apparent earnings are greater than real economic earnings because apparent earnings do not take account of the cost of equity capital that is employed. Earnings, defined correctly, have the same present value as dividends.

The assertions so far about valuation all apply to a world of certainty without transaction costs or taxes. In a world of uncertainty, the theory of valuation becomes more complicated. Miller and Modigliani assert and demonstrate, however, that even in a world of uncertainty, dividend policy does not affect the value of shares. Their conclusion has been challenged by Gordon,[11] who states that a dollar paid out in dividends is valued more highly in the market than a dollar retained, because the financial consequences of retention by the company are more uncertain than the financial consequences of dividends received. Since risk aversion characterizes almost all investors, the higher uncertainty attached to the retained earnings, according to his argument, causes retained earnings to have less value than an equal number of dollars paid out in dividends.

Gordon's argument seems wrong. The investor can consume the dollar he receives in dividends, but he could also achieve a dollar of consumption if the dividend had not been paid by selling a dollar's worth of stock. Or, the investor can abstain from consumption of the dividend and invest it. In order for the dollar paid in dividends to be less risky and valued more highly than the dollar retained by the corporation, it would be necessary to assume that investment by the dividend recipient would be less risky than internal investment by the firm which might have paid the dividend. There is no *a priori* reason to believe in the existence of that superiority or in the irrationality of the firm, and therefore there is no reason to believe that earnings paid out will be valued more highly than earnings retained.

Miller and Modigliani also deal with other departures from their original, unrealistic assumptions. They consider the existence of debt in the capital structure of the firm and demonstrate its irrelevance to the proof of the equivalence between the present values of the stream of dividends and the stream of earnings.

Miller and Modigliani also considered the possibility that transaction costs or taxes could result in an investor preference for dividends or capital appreciation. Transaction costs of course can have a small effect, but it is unclear what it will be. Taxes conceivably can have a large effect, but their importance has diminished in recent years because of the growing importance of investors such as endowed institutions, pension funds, and retired individuals with low incomes for whom there are no taxes and for whom, therefore, a dollar of dividends is exactly as valuable as a dollar of capital gains. The conclusion is that uncertainty and market imperfections do not create large differences between the present value of the two streams.

One final question remains to be asked in this discussion of the importance of dividend policy. Do changes in dividends convey information which alters investors' expectations with regard to corporate profits? If increases in dividends cause investors to expect future earnings to be greater than they would be expected to be on the basis of other information, then increased dividends can be expected to cause higher share prices. Reduced dividends would of course have the contrary effect. It is the change in expectations, not the dividend policy itself, which would be the influence on price. Although these assertions are plausible, the existence of these effects has never clearly been demonstrated. In order for changes in dividends to convey important information, it would be necessary to assume that corporate management, corporate boards, and corporate accountants have been unwilling or unable to reveal the future prospects for corporate earnings except in the extraordinarily difficult and indirect way of changing the level of dividends. Recent work by Ross Watts suggests the information conveyed by dividend changes is not great.[12]

THE APPROPRIATE RATE OF DISCOUNT

The preceding discussion was designed to show that the value of a firm's shares is the present value of either its stream of dividends or its stream of earnings, adjusted to take account of the cost of capital employed. The two streams must be equivalent, given the investment policy of the firm. A vexing problem still remains: At what rate should these streams be discounted in order to ascertain their present value?

In theory, the answer is simple. The appropriate rate for each investor in discounting the expected stream of earnings or dividends is the opportunity cost of making the investment, i.e., the expected rate of return on alternative assets of similar riskiness. In a world of certainty, such a rate is completely market determined since, in equilibrium, the prices of shares of all corporations would be such that the rate of return on all investments would be the same. This market determined rate is *the* appropriate rate of discount for all investors for all securities. In the real world, the discount rate is more complex since varying degrees of uncertainty regarding the outcomes of alternative investments create different opportunity costs and rates of discount. It is unlikely that the discount rate for two securities chosen at random would be the same. For a particular security, the appropriate rate is market determined in one sense and subjective in another. It is market determined in that the investor should seek to ascertain the expected return in the market on assets of equal risk. The rate is subjective in that the estimation of risk can never be completely objective, nor can the determination of the expected return on other assets of similar risk.

Risk is the main subject of chapter 12. In this chapter, risk is given cursory treatment.

Future returns on any investment are uncertain. A measure of the degree of uncertainty is generally accepted as an estimate of risk. A major tenet of modern investment theory is that it is incorrect to estimate the risk of individual stocks considered in isolation. Since most investors are averse to risk, they choose to hold diversified portfolios. Hence, the riskiness of an individual security should be judged by its effect on the riskiness of such a portfolio.

That the distinction between the two ways of measuring risk can be important is easily illustrated. Consider a security which, on the basis of past performance, is believed to have a very uncertain future, i.e., be very risky, when judged in isolation. Perhaps, however, the security has had and is expected to have a pattern of price changes opposite to that of the market as a whole. The security goes down when the market goes up and vice versa. The security, though risky in isolation, would contribute to the stability and thereby reduce the riskiness of a diversified portfolio.

The logic and algebra necessary for understanding the process by which the investor can achieve a numerical estimate of the riskiness of an individual security is worked out well and clearly in William Sharpe's fine book, *Portfolio Theory and Capital Markets.*[13] At this point, we indicate only his conclusion: The proper measure of the riskiness of an individual security is its sensitivity to movements in the market. The appropriate rate of discount for future earnings or dividends in determining the present value of a stock is the expected rate of return on assets whose riskiness—sensitivity to movements in the market—is similar to that of the security in question.

Obviously, judgment is required. If a security tends on the average to rise and fall at the same speed as the market, the appropriate rate of discount would be about 9 percent. This has been approximately the long-term annual rate of return for the market as a whole. If the sensitivity of the security were less, the rate of discount would be lower; if the sensitivity were greater, the rate of discount would be higher than 9 percent to reflect the greater riskiness of the security.

CONCLUSIONS

This chapter has attempted to demonstrate the following:

1.   The value of a stock is equal to the present value of the firm's future earnings.

2.   Dividend policy does not affect the value, if one assumes no taxes, no transaction costs, and a fixed internal investment program.

3.   Given the foregoing assumptions, the present value of future dividends and future earnings are equal. This may seem impossible since earnings, ordinarily defined, exceed dividends for almost all firms for almost all years. It is possible if earnings are *correctly* defined. Correctness requires that ordinary earnings be reduced by the cost of capital that is retained or acquired for internal investment.

4.   The present value of earnings (or dividends) depends not only on their amount but also on the rate of discount. This rate is the opportunity cost of capital, defined as the expected foregone return on assets of equal riskiness.

5.   Risk for an individual security should be estimated by determining its effect on the riskiness of a diversified portfolio. This is equal to the sensitivity of the return on the security to changes in the return on the market as a whole. A reasonable rule of thumb is to assume a 9 percent annual rate of return for average stocks (i.e., those whose changes in rates of return are about the same as for the market). A lower number is appropriate for so-called *defensive* stocks; a higher number, for *aggressive* stocks.

7

Stock Valuation Models

INTRODUCTION

STOCK VALUATION MODELS are designed to identify undervalued and overvalued securities. An undervalued security is one whose price is judged to be less than it would be if other investors had the same perception of the company as that produced by the use of the valuation model. Contrariwise, an overvalued security is one whose market price is greater than it would be if all investors had the same perception of the company as that provided by the model.

Stock valuation models are not designed to answer the question as to whether it is desirable to own stocks as opposed to other assets such as cash or bonds, but rather to indicate which stocks seem relatively attractive and should therefore be bought and which seem relatively unattractive and should therefore be sold or sold short.

True believers in efficient markets have little faith in valuation models and are neither important producers nor consumers of them. The financial institutions which design and use such models are not run by true believers. The nonbelievers obviously think that the use of models will provide superior rates of return. So far, there is little public evidence that their belief is justified.

The preceding chapter discussed the theory of stock valuation, and stock valuation models make use of that theory. The theory states that in a world of certainty the current value of the corporation is the stream of future dividends or future earnings, properly defined, discounted to perpetuity. Under the simple assumption of a constant rate of growth in earnings or dividends per share,* it can be shown mathematically that the present value of the firm (if its value is finite†) is a function of dividends in the current period, the discount rate, and the rate of growth in dividends per share. Alternatively, one can express the value of the firm as a function of current earnings, the rate of growth of earnings, the internal rate of return, and the discount rate.[1]

The rate of return, given this unrealistic, but useful, assumption and also a constant payout ratio and price-earnings ratio, is $R = \dfrac{D}{P} + g$, where R is the rate of return, D is the current dividend, P is the price per share, and g is the constant rate of growth in dividends. Thus, if American Telephone is selling for 45, has a current dividend of 2.50, and an expected rate of growth of 5 percent annually, the rate of return is approximately $\dfrac{2.50}{45} + .05 =$ .106 or 10.6 percent. The formula, $R = \dfrac{D}{P} + g$, is a helpful rule of thumb for mature companies, but is not refined and is inappropriate for companies which are changing rapidly.

In our uncertain world with an investment community averse to risk, it is also necessary to take into account the confidence with which future earnings or dividends can be predicted. As one would expect, therefore, the valuation models uniformly include as variables expectations regarding future cash flows and the riskiness attached to those expectations. Typically, models also include as variables the dividend payout ratio and the "marketability" of the stock.

The following section of this chapter discusses the odd fact that discount rates do not appear in valuation models. The next sections discuss some models and critical issues in designing them.

---

* The rate of growth of total dividends will be the same as the rate of growth of earnings. The rate of growth of dividends *per share* will be the same only if all investment is financed internally; otherwise it will be less.

† This requires that the discount rate exceed the growth rate—a plausible assumption over long periods of time. See pages 135–36 of this chapter. Also see David Durand, "Growth Stocks and the Petersburg Paradox," *Journal of Finance,* vol. 12, no. 3 (September 1957), pp. 348–63; and M. J. Gordon, "Dividends, Earnings, and Stock Prices," *Review of Economics and Statistics,* vol. 41, no. 1 (May 1959), pp. 99–105.

THE MISSING DISCOUNT RATE

Valuation theory asserts that the price of an asset in a certain world is the present value of the future stream of cash payments to the owner. The present value of any future stream clearly depends on the rate at which the individual payments are discounted. Yet, valuation models do not contain a term representing this discount rate explicitly.

The explanation is complex. In the last chapter we pointed out that in our uncertain world, the appropriate rate of discount is not the same for all securities because expectations about earnings are held with varying degrees of confidence. In other words, the appropriate rate of discount is the risk-free rate plus some risk premium. Ideally, stock valuation models should include a discount variable explicitly, but this is not done in practice, at least not in any recognizable form. Most models rely on some measure of risk rather than on a discount rate.

This practice is logically incorrect, though the logical blemish is probably not important. The error exists because the present value of the cash flows resulting from owning an asset depends not only on the riskiness of the asset but also on the riskless rate of interest. The use of a measure of risk rather than a discount rate takes account of only one component of the discount rate. A change in the risk-free rate of return will affect the discount rate and most valuation models ignore this.

SOME MODELS

The Value Line Ratings

One of the early efforts to apply valuation theory systematically was by Value Line. It rated stocks on the basis of the relationship between current price and average forecasted price. The first ratings appeared in a book of charts, *The Value Line Ratings,* published in 1937. This was later expanded to a monthly service. The rating for a stock was based on a visual estimate of the normal relationship between its price, its earnings, and its book value. The "right" price was estimated to be some constant multiple of earnings plus a percentage of book value. In 1949, the approach was refined. Two more variables, dividends per share and price in the preceding period, were added to the estimating equation. Using multiple correlation techniques, the relationship between the price of a stock and the four independent variables was estimated from 20 years of historical data. To predict the price over the next 12 months, the analyst first forecast earnings, book value, and dividends per share for that period. Using these values and current price, he estimated price for the next 12 months from the equation.

The Value Line rating methods described above were conspicuously unsuccessful in predicting the performance of individual stocks. Their primary value in this discussion is in illustrating some pitfalls in using "scientific" methods. One defect was the use of time-series analysis that did not discriminate among stocks. The price of a stock was related only to its own earnings, book value, etc. In the words of Mr. Bernhard:

Of what use was it to say that a stock was 40 percent undervalued in a particular year, if in that particular year it did not perform better than other stocks that were less undervalued? The answer might be, "well, eventually it will." That is true, provided the earnings and dividends stick. But who can say where the earnings and dividends will be five years hence?*

Mr. Bernhard might have gone on to ask who can say where earnings and dividends will be *one* year hence. The estimates of future prices would be correct only if the *forecasts* of independent variables were correct, the relationship between them and prices did not change, and if the correlation between the independent and dependent variables were perfect.

The most serious problem is that historical relationships need not persist. This is demonstrated dramatically by the changes in price-earnings ratios in the post–World War II period. As we discussed in chapter 1, there are sound reasons for the near doubling of these ratios. Any forecasting model that included a constant earnings multiple derived from an earlier period was unlikely to predict correctly the postwar performance of stock prices. The Value Line Ratings, while indicating that many stocks were "undervalued" in the late 40s, also suggested substantial "overvaluation" in the 50s.

---

* Arnold Bernhard, *The Evaluation of Common Stocks* (New York: Simon and Schuster, 1959), p. 90. The Value Line Ratings are no longer based on the time-series analysis described above.

Finally, there are technical issues which can result in forecasting pitfalls. For example, economic time series tend to move together so that levels of these series are highly correlated. This means that the observed correlation between the independent and dependent variables is misleading. Also, the correlation between the independent variables often results in one variable being swamped by another so that it is impossible to distinguish between their separate effects.

These kinds of problems are common to all forecasting models and are handled more satisfactorily in more recent efforts. Value Line now uses a valuation model which seems to work well.[2]

The Whitbeck-Kisor Model

One of the best known articles in the field of investments in recent years is "A New Tool in Investment Decision-Making."[3] This article was the first published account of attempts to use regression analysis based on modern theory of stock valuation. The authors at that time worked in the trust department of the Bank of New York and their article stimulated a great deal of discussion and influenced subsequent efforts to solve the valuation problem from the point of view of the investor seeking superior returns.

In the Whitbeck-Kisor model, theoretical price-earnings ratios of stocks depend upon the projected average annual long-term growth rate in earnings per share, a measure of risk, and the expected dividend-payout ratio. The price-earnings ratio in the model is the ratio of the current price of the stock to "normalized" earnings, defined as earnings is a "normal" year and usually considered to be the average of earnings during the past three to five years. Normalized earnings are used since the price-earnings ratios of cyclical stocks are inversely related to earnings. That is, during recessions, price-earnings ratios are abnormally high and during booms, abnormally low.

Before going on to discuss the model in detail, it is probably desirable to consider the inclusion of the dividend-payout ratio, since Miller and Modigliani persuasively demonstrated, as discussed in the last chapter, that dividend-payout ratios should have no significant effect upon the valuation of common stocks. Although the inclusion of the variable in the Whitbeck-Kisor model is at variance with the Miller-Modigliani analysis, the contradiction is not what it seems.

Miller and Modigliani showed that in a world without transaction costs and taxes *and in equilibrium,* the dividend-payout ratio for a given firm should not affect the price of its stock, if one assumes that the investment policy of the firm is given. The inclusion of a variable to represent the dividend-payout ratio of a stock in a valuation formula is not at variance with the findings of Miller and Modigliani. Recall that the valuation formula or model is designed to indicate the relative attractiveness of different stocks. If two different stocks have the same expected level of future earnings and the same riskiness and have different payout ratios, there are legitimate grounds for preferring the stock with the higher dividend-payout ratio. Such a stock will provide the same growth in earnings with the same risk and at the same time provide higher dividends. Clearly it is better to have more rather than less. The ability of a stock to have the same growth in earnings as another stock with a lower payout ratio depends upon the former stock's having a higher rate of return on its internal investments. This higher rate of return on the assets of the company is, of course, what justifies the higher value placed upon its shares.

In equilibrium, rates of return at the margin for all investments of equal risk would, of course, be equal. Miller and Modigliani were talking about such an equilibrium position. Investors who use valuation models are trying to detect departures from equilibrium. If they are successful in identifying stocks that are "too high" or "too low," they can profit by selling or buying. Their actions will restore equilibrium by lowering the price of the stock that is too high and raising that of the stock that is too low.

The Whitbeck-Kisor decision model attempts to measure the relative attractiveness of common stocks at a particular date. This requires estimating the relationships between "normalized" price-earnings ratios and the independent variables. Their results are as follows:*

Theoretical $P/E = 8.2 + 1.5$ (growth rate) $+ 6.7$ (payout ratio)
$- 0.2$ (standard deviation of earnings about trend)

The values of the independent variables in the model are supplied by security analysts who base their judgments on historical data and an appriasal of current conditions. Risk is measured by the anticipated standard deviation of a firm's earnings about trend. Similarly, the dividend-payout ratio is that expected by the analysts.

The underlying proposition of the analysis is that at a given date, the relationship between the theoretical price-earnings ratio and the

---

* The equation was estimated using data for June 8, 1962.

other variables is the same for all common stocks, although the relationship may vary over time. To apply the model to investment decisions, the estimated theoretical price of each stock is compared with the actual market price to identify undervalued or overvalued stocks. In their words, "Given the theoretical or normalized price of any stock, we assume that the market price of the stock will seek this level faster than the theoretical price itself will change. . ."[4]

The model was tested on a sample of 135 stocks "of general market interest."[5] The rule adopted by Whitbeck and Kisor was that a stock was under- or overvalued if the actual price differed from the theoretical price by 15 percent or more. Their criterion for success was based on a comparison of the performance of "undervalued" stocks and "overvalued" stocks with the Standard & Poor's "500." The changes in the prices of the stocks in the three months after four different valuation dates seemed to indicate that the model was useful. The stocks identified as undervalued outperformed the index and the index outperformed those identified as undervalued.

Elating as this may have been, the results are far from conclusive. The published tests of the model refer only to four dates in 1960 and 1961 and to performance in each of the subsequent three-month periods. Different results might be obtained for other valuation dates and longer holding periods.[6] Also, the estimating equation is given for only one of the four valuation dates, so we do not know the magnitude of differences in the coefficients at different points in time. If market sentiment changes rapidly, causing marked changes in the estimating equation, market price may not move toward intrinsic value or the theoretical price as fast as the theoretical price itself changes.

The Ahlers Model

The model developed by David Ahlers[7] is essentially an extension and refinement of the Whitbeck-Kisor model, and retains its basic philosophy. Unlike the Whitbeck-Kisor model, analysts' judgements are incorporated directly in the statistical estimates of "steady-state" earnings. For each security, the forecast of quarterly earnings per share is based on current earnings seasonally adjusted and the previous quarter's estimate of steady-state earnings adjusted for the most recent estimate of the quarterly trend. The analysts' judgements—forecasts of annual earnings—are used to determine the best weights to be assigned to past and current data. This is a procedure which provides current estimates of normalized earnings, the trend in normalized earnings, and seasonal adjustments. The estimates of growth in earnings, the forecast error, and observed dividend yield are then included as explanatory variables in a relative valuation equation.

Although the equation is similar to that used by Whitbeck and Kisor, there are some important differences. First, the form of the equation is multiplicative rather than additive. Ahlers found this to be superior.[8] Second, the independent variables are reformulated. The growth rate in earnings forecast by the model is the growth in normalized earnings. Although Whitbeck and Kisor imply their growth factor measures the rate of growth in normalized earnings, Ahlers asserts that it is actually an estimate of the growth trend based on 15 years of historical data, adjusted for analysts' subjective beliefs.[9] Also, Ahlers uses dividend yield rather than the payout ratio. This he justifies on the grounds that "the POR (payout ratio) is not a relative measure between securities when considering the return to investors."[10] Finally, the measure of risk is the coefficient of variation rather than the standard deviation associated with the earnings forecast. Ahlers argues that some of the variability from the trend of actual earnings, measured by the standard deviation, may be explained by cyclical or seasonal factors. If "investors are more concerned with the unexpected portion of earnings variability than with the total variability,"[11] the coefficient of variation, or unexpected forecast error is a better measure of risk.

The model was tested for 1964 using 24 stocks randomly selected from the portfolio of a large eastern bank.[12] The forecasting equation was derived from data beginning with the first quarter of 1958. The performance criterion was based on total return rather than price appreciation alone, using the Standard & Poor's "425" as a bench mark. The stocks identified as undervalued by the model outperformed the index in three quarters, while those identified as overvalued were outperformed in three quarters. Ahlers also compares the ability of the model to discriminate among stocks with the ability of analysts and found that the model's "primary advantage lies in its ability in this test to identify undervalued stock with a better than an even chance of success."[13]

The model seems promising in that it is explicit in incorporating analysts' beliefs with historical data. A particularly interesting feature involves feedback and control which enables analysts to improve their forecasting. The predictive value of the model needs more extensive testing, but it is probably helpful to security analysts even if not the key to vast fortune.

Limited-Horizon Models

The two models discussed above imply an infinite horizon. That is, the growth rate which is estimated is expected to continue indefinitely. An alternative approach is to assume the growth rate cannot be projected beyond a certain number of years. The present value of the stock is then the discounted stream of earnings or dividends for a limited period plus the terminal value of the stock. Malkiel[14] has developed a model which assumes that dividends and earnings will grow at a constant rate to the horizon. At that time, the price-earnings ratio of all stocks is expected to be the same. Given this assumption, the price-earnings ratio is a function of the payout ratio and the growth rate. Implicit however, is the additional assumption that the appropriate rate of discount is similar for all securities regardless of risk. The choice of the time horizon is arbitrary. For these reasons the usefulness of the model is slight.

A more promising approach to the limited-horizon case has been adopted by Goldman, Sachs & Company.[15] In their model, the time horizon is determined empirically. Since the estimate of the growth in earnings varies with the number of years of historical data used, the procedure calls first for estimating the growth trend using five years of historical data and the available projections of an analyst. The growth horizon is the future point at which the expected deviation of earnings from trend is 7 percent. This process is repeated, adding one more year of historical data, until the growth horizon begins to decrease. This method of estimating the growth horizon is selective in that historical data which cease to be relevant are not taken into account.[16]

This model, unlike Malkiel's, does not specify in advance the price-earnings ratio at the horizon, since this would imply something about the growth prospects beyond the horizon. To avoid this, the analysis is limited to a group of companies with similar *long-term* growth potential and levels of risk. The price-earnings multiples at the horizon and the rate of return on the investment would be expected to be the same for all of the securities in the group. Under these assumptions, the price-earnings ratio at the horizon and the return on investment can be estimated using regression techniques.[17] The usefulness of the model has been tested for electric utilities by comparing rates of return on unmanaged portfolios with those on managed portfolios. Two thousand portfolios including up to 12 stocks were selected randomly.* The rates of return for several holding periods were computed for each assuming: (1) a simple buy-and-hold strategy with reinvestment of dividends; and (2) use of the valuation model subject to certain trading restrictions. After three years, the performance of over 90 percent of the portfolios was improved by management, and after five years, the performance of all portfolios was improved. The average improvement in the annual rates of return was 1.1 percentage points after three years and 1.7 percentage points after five years. Although transaction costs have been taken into account there was no allowance for taxes. The results are therefore inconclusive, but do suggest the model may be useful at least in investing new cash flows.

CRITICAL ISSUES

Growth in Earnings

As has been seen, expected growth in earnings is the most important variable in valuation models currently in use. The major difficulty is that most security analysts—and perhaps even most managements—do not even pretend to be able to make accurate forecasts of earnings very far into the future. Once one goes beyond the period for which one has explicit quantitative forecasts, one is left with the necessity of adopting some rule of thumb about average rates of growth in succeeding years. At the cost of considerable oversimplification, one can divide methods for solving this problem into three groups: (1) those which extrapolate into the indefinite future recent average annual rates of growth; (2) those which extrapolate recent growth rates for a few years and then assume a gradual regression in growth rates toward the mean rate for the national economy; and (3) those which extrapolate current rates into the future and then postulate a sudden change to the rate of growth in the national economy. Sometimes the three general methods just described are modified by reference to growth rates for a particular industry rather than for the economy as a whole, and sometimes other variants are used.

Almost everyone acknowledges the necessity of allowing extraordi-

---

* The portfolios were started between December 31, 1962 and September 30, 1964.

narily high growth rates in earnings to regress toward mean growth rates for an industry or for the economy as a whole. The compulsion to allow for such regression is illustrated by the following hypothetical situation. In 1970, IBM earned about $1 billion after taxes. In many recent years, IBM has enjoyed an annual rate of growth in earnings of 18 percent or more. If a rate of 18 percent were to be assumed for the next 20 years, IBM's profits after taxes in the year 1995 would be almost $63 billion. If during the same period, total corporate profits after taxes grew at an annual rate of 3.6 percent, total corporate profits after taxes in the year 1995 would be approximately $100 billion. The simple extrapolation of these two growth rates would result in IBM's profits after taxes being about five eighths of total corporate profits for the United States. Although such a result is not impossible, it strains the credulity of most analysts and investors so much that some reduction in IBM's growth rate is introduced into the valuation models relating to the price of its stock.

The need for allowing for decay or regression in extraordinarily high growth rates is indicated not only by appeals to common sense in examples such as that just presented, but also by the logic of growth rates which exceed rates of discounting for the indefinite future. Theoretically, if growth in earnings per share is expected at all times in the future to exceed the rate at which those earnings are discounted, the price of the stock to which those rates apply should be infinite. David Durand discusses this problem in his well-known article, "Growth Stocks and the Petersburg Paradox."[18] For the moment, let us assume that the earnings of a particular stock are discounted at a rate, i, and that the earnings grow at a constant rate. If the price of the stock is the discounted value of the stream of earnings, the value of this stock could be represented as follows:

$$V = \frac{E}{1+i} + \frac{E(1+g)}{(1+i)^2} + \frac{E(1+g)^2}{(1+i)^3} + \cdots + \frac{E(1+g)^{t-1}}{(1+i)^t}$$

where V is the value of the stock, E is earnings, g is the rate of growth in earnings, and i is the rate at which the earnings are discounted.

If one factors out the term $\dfrac{E}{1+i}$, the result is the following:

$$V = \frac{E}{1+i}\left(1 + \frac{1+g}{1+i} + \frac{(1+g)^2}{(1+i)^2} \cdots + \frac{(1+g)^{t-1}}{(1+i)^{t-1}}\right)$$

If g is greater than i, one can see that the value of this infinite series is infinite. Conversely, if i is greater than g, the series has a finite sum and $V = \dfrac{E}{i - g}$.

The resolution of the "Petersburg Paradox"—namely, theory indicates that a stock whose growth rate in earnings exceeds the discount rate will have an infinite value while no one has even been known to pay so high a price—lies in a refusal to believe that g can consistently and indefinitely exceed i. Growth rates are assumed to regress toward some mean rate. Also, it is reasonable to believe that i increases through time to allow for the increased uncertainty of more distant earnings.[19] A complementary explanation is that there is diminishing marginal utility of wealth.

People deal with the lack of realism in the indefinite extrapolation of extraordinarily high growth rate in various ways. It is not clear that any one way has been shown to be markedly superior to others. This may be a realm in which the application of ingenuity and effort will yield a margin of superiority in security analysis which alone has the promise of making possible superior rates of return.

Another interesting way of looking at this problem is provided by Charles Holt in his article, "The Influence of Growth Duration on Shares Prices."[20] Holt's article is designed to indicate the length of time that current growth rates must continue if the existing price-earnings ratio for the stock is justified. If the mean ratio for all stocks on the New York Stock Exchange at some point in time is, say, 15, and the ratio for IBM is, say, 40, how long does one have to assume that IBM's current growth rate will last in order to justify a ratio for its stock that is two and two-thirds times as great as the average for all stocks on the New York Stock Exchange? Holt's article does not solve the analytical problem of forecasting what earnings are going to be, but he does provide a way to judge intuitively whether the assumptions underlying current stock prices seem reasonable.

The Specification of the Price-Earnings Ratio

In almost all valuation models, the dependent variable is the price-earnings ratio. There are some difficulties in its specification. They arise from the need to define earnings. Among the possibilities are earnings for the most recent 12 months, earnings for the most recent fiscal year, predicted earnings for the forthcoming year, or the strange and useful number, "normalized earnings." Another difficulty arises when it is necessary to express earnings per share. Should these earnings be in terms of shares of common stock currently outstanding, the average number outstanding during the most recent fiscal year, or in terms of the number of shares that would be outstanding if all convertible securities were converted and all options to buy common shares were exercised?

All of the difficulties just listed are in addition to the most important difficulty which is the subject of the next chapter, namely, the actual measurement of corporate earnings at any point in time. This last difficulty stems from the ambiguity of many accounting practices and the conceptual and empirical difficulties in measuring the financial impact of the firm's activities.

Perhaps the first choice is between the use of earnings for some very recent period and the use of predicted earnings for some future period. The evidence is overwhelming that financial analysts should begin with an attitude of open-minded skepticism about their ability to predict earnings. It seems to be extraordinarily difficult for anyone to predict earnings consistently better than "the Street." Perhaps the effort is worth making, but there is no point in using predicted earnings in valuation models until there has been some demonstration of superiority on the part of the person predicting earnings for use in the models.

A second and considerably easier problem is the choice between actual earnings as reported and some "normalized earnings." Almost all addicts of valuation models recognize the need to use normalized earnings, at least for those industries marked by substantial cyclicality in earnings. The failure to use normalized earnings leads to some gross anomalies or absurdities. These arise in an especially acute form whenever the earnings in a cyclical industry are at their cyclical lows. Consider the following example: At the end of 1962, Latrobe Steel's price was about seven times its earnings for the year; at the end of 1969, the ratio was about 38. The extremely high price-earnings ratio in 1969 was evidence neither of extreme optimism regarding its future nor of derangement on the part of investors regarding its current value. Rather, investors believed that there was a transient cyclical depression in Latrobe's earnings and rationally adjusted their valuation to take account of this fact. In the earlier period, earnings per share were extraordinarily high and the price-earnings ratio was low, indicating the belief that future earnings would be lower. A failure to use normalized earnings for companies such as Latrobe would cause the user of valuation formulas to regard them as extremely overvalued at the times of their cyclical lows and undervalued at cyclical highs, when in fact there is no reason to believe that such misconceptions exist.

Whitbeck and Kisor in their 1963 article[21] discuss the tendency of some earnings ratios to move contracyclically with the market, suggesting that investors have some concept of normalized earnings. In figure 7–1 they present evidence on the cyclical behavior of price-earnings ratios from 1950 to 1960 for a sample of stocks.

FIGURE 7–1
Cyclical Behavior of Price-Earnings Ratios

1956-'58 = 100

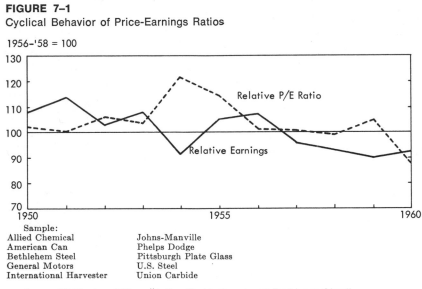

Sample:
Allied Chemical   Johns-Manville
American Can   Phelps Dodge
Bethlehem Steel   Pittsburgh Plate Glass
General Motors   U.S. Steel
International Harvester   Union Carbide

Source: Whitbeck and Kisor, "A New Tool in Investment Decision-making."

There is substantial agreement about the need to "normalize" earnings and some difference of opinion about the best way to do it. Whitbeck and Kisor recommended that earnings be normalized by adjusting them to what they would have been had the firm been having a "normal" or mid-cyclical year. Their published works are silent on the way to make the adjustment. One method, of course, is to resort to authority, which usually means asking someone whose pretentions to knowledge exceed one's own. Another method is to use a moving average for each of the past three, four, five, or more years. Still another way would be to regress earnings per share on GNP to see how much most recent earnings are inflated above or deflated below normal because of departures in GNP from its long-term trend. There is a need to "normalize" earnings, and there are a number of ways to do this. No one has demonstrated the importance of the differences among the ways or the superiority of any of them.

The final issue mentioned earlier in specifying the price-earnings ratio is the choice between expressing earnings per share in terms of current shares outstanding and the number that would be outstanding if all convertible issues were converted and all options were exercised. Once again, it is very easy to indicate how easily one could be misled if all one knew were earnings per share for currently outstanding common shares. Consider two companies, A and B. A earns $1 million and has one million shares of common stock outstanding. Company B earns $1 million and has only 500,000 shares of common stock outstanding. Company B also has 500,000 shares of convertible preferred outstanding, each share convertible into one share of common stock. A failure to consider the potential conversion of the preferred shares would lead to the following result: earnings per share of common in Company A are $1.00. In Company B, assuming the dividends on preferred are $300,000, earnings per share of common are $1.40. With conversion, earnings per share of common are only $1.00, the same as in Company A.

Investors managing their own money or managing money on behalf of others in a competitive market can usually be relied upon to make a serious effort to understand the relative attractiveness of different financial assets which might be owned. This effort is made easier and its results more reliable by the free availability of relevant information. The existence of convertible issues is clearly relevant, and earnings per share need to take account of potential conversions. The strictures of the Accounting Principles Board about the revelations of earnings per share, both undiluted and diluted, seem helpful in this connection. There seem to be no *a priori* grounds for believing that in stock valuation models earnings for undiluted shares would be either better or worse than earnings for shares fully diluted. For the time being, the choice between undiluted and diluted earnings probably should be resolved through a process of brute empiricism. That is, one should seek to find out which choice leads to the more successful identification of undervalued and overvalued issues. Perhaps, in some future and happier time, Miller and Modigliani will write another noted article indicating that this, too, doesn't make any difference. In the meantime, we can rue the fact that the financial literature dealing with valuation models does not deal with this subject in an analytical or theoretical way.

Forecasting Problems

The ultimate purpose of valuation models is to help in the selection of portfolios which will produce superior results. The key word in the preceding sentence is "will." Whatever their guise may be, valuation models are designed to produce or to assist in producing forecasts of the behavior of individual securities.

Since valuation models are based upon regression equations, the forecasting problem is forecasting the level of the independent variables. It is easy to forecast three of the four independent variables typically found in valuation models because of their great temporal stability. Normally, there is very little change from year to year or even from one five-year period to the next in the marketability, the riskiness, or the dividend-payout ratio of stocks in mature companies. Simple extrapolations of recent data on these variables produce good results. Most people will accept this conclusion with respect to marketability and dividend-payout ratios, but perhaps some will question the assertion regarding the stability of measures of risk. The research underlying the assertion that the riskiness of stocks does not change markedly through time is in Marshall Blume's[22] work and in Brealey's book, *An Introduction to Risk and Return from Common Stocks*.[23] In chapter 3, "Risk—Its Nature and Persistence," Brealey presents a variety of data which leads him to the conclusion: "Altogether, therefore, there is considerable evidence that the relative volatility exhibited by any stock has tended to persist over time. It is reasonable to suppose that this will continue to be true in the future."[24]

In sum, the valuation models tell us that we need to forecast four independent variables: earnings, risk, dividend-payout ratios, and marketability. Other evidence indicates that the forecasting problem is simple except for forecasting earnings. Since this is such an overwhelmingly important subject, chapter 9 is devoted to it.

CONCLUSIONS

Most valuation models have several things in common: (1) they include the same independent variables; (2) they monotonously achieve high correlations between the independent variables and the dependent variable, usually the price-earnings ratio; and (3) they almost uniformly fail in their primary purpose—providing superior rates of return by identifying under- and overvalued securities, although some studies have reported success for brief periods.

The standard independent variables are estimates of growth rates in earnings, estimates of the riskiness of the investment derived from measures of temporal instability in earnings, estimates of the dividend-payout ratio, and estimates of marketability (usually measured by trading volume). Although these variables explain the current structure of price-earnings ratios, they have not proved useful as forecasting devices. Part of the problem is that the relationship between the independent and the dependent variables changes through time, but the most important failure is the failure to forecast earnings accurately.

8

Measuring Earnings

INTRODUCTION

IN REFERRING TO changes in prices of stocks on the New York Stock Exchange in 1970, Niederhoffer and Regan state, "Unmistakably, the most important factor separating the best from the worst performing stocks was profitability."[1] Forty-five of the 50 stocks which had the largest percentage increase in price had increases in earnings; 4 of the 50 stocks with the largest percentage decreases in price had increased earnings.

Brealey reached the same general conclusion by another route. He tested his plausible view that "A company that produces a major increase in earnings is more likely to provide investors with a pleasant surprise than with a disappointment."[2] The converse would be true for a company with a reduction in profits. As evidence of this view, he cites a study of 48 stocks selected at random from those reviewed by the *Value Line Investment Survey* each year for 14 years, 1950–63. If at the beginning of each year an investor had selected the eight stocks which subsequently had the greatest percentage increase in earnings, he would have had an annual return of 30.4 percent. In contrast, the eight stocks with the smallest gain in earnings, produced an annual return of only 1 percent.

The relationship even seems to hold for aggregate profits and comprehensive stock averages. In a fine example of casual empiricism, Jack W. Cox noted that from the first quarter of 1958, a low point, through the second quarter of 1959, profits rose 156 percent and the

Standard & Poor's "500" Index rose 145 percent from its trough in the last quarter of 1957 to a peak in the second quarter of 1959. During the period 1961–66, profits rose 208 percent, while stocks rose 190 percent from 1960 to 1968. During the 1970–72 recovery, profits rose 33 percent and the Standard & Poor's "500," 37 percent.[3]

It has, perhaps, been adequately established in the preceeding paragraphs and earlier chapters that the earnings of a company ultimately determine the value of its stock. It would be fortunate, therefore, if investors could know what those earnings are. Unfortunately, it is almost never easy and sometimes not even possible to "know" the earnings of a corporation. The two fundamental sources of this ignorance are: (1) the lack of congruence between accounting principles and economic principles relevant for the determinination of earnings; and (2) the variety of accounting principles which can be applied. These comments about accounting stem from chronic discontent rather than from any knowledge about how to improve accounting practices.

The first point is discussed excellently by Treynor in his article "The Trouble with Earnings":[4]

The analyst treats earnings as if it were an economic concept. In view of his purpose—attaching economic value to the firm—he can scarcely do otherwise.

. . . The accountant defines it (earnings) as what he gets when he matches costs against revenues, making any necessary allocation of costs to price periods; or as the change in the equity account over the period. These are not economic definitions of earnings but merely descriptions of the motions the accountant goes through to arrive at the earnings number.[5]

It is simple to specify, in principle, what a corporation should report as its income or earnings. Many years ago economists defined personal income, and an analogy to that definition will serve for the corporation. Income is defined as the change in the net worth of the person during a period plus the value of his consumption. For a corporation, the analogous definition would be a change in its net worth plus the value of dividends or other distributions to stockholders. This definition is equivalent to saying that the income of a corporation is the change in the discounted value of its future earnings plus the value of its dividends and other distributions. Such changes can arise through internal investment by the firm, through changes in the rate at which future earnings are discounted, or through changes in the economic environment such as in taxes, tastes, technology, or other things.

The above definition may seem satisfactory until one thinks about it. Then, the circularity is clear. Present earnings cannot satisfactorily be explained in terms of a change in the values of future earnings until that change is defined. The best operational definition is the change in the market value of the firm's common stock. That change is the financial community's consensus regarding the change in the present value of future earnings. The market definition and the conventional accountant's definition can differ radically. Many things which affect the future earning power of the firm do not affect accounting income in the current period.

Though it is easy to define corporate earnings or income in theory, it is extremely difficult in fact. The primary task of financial analysts is to carry out this difficult task. In each year or period, the analyst must seek to ascertain the change in the net worth of the corporation, or equivalently, the change in the value of its future earnings. The analyst has at his disposal the kinds of numbers produced by accountants. Although these help, they convey an ambiguous message, as indicated in subsequent sections of this chapter. The analyst does not of course limit himself to the information provided by accountants; ingenious and competent analysts make use of many other kinds of information. The rest of this chapter is devoted to a discussion of the analyst's difficulties, but the chapter stops short of prescribing the sure road to a correct determination of corporate earnings and to the acquisition of great wealth.

The following section of this chapter deals with the major types of discretion allowed to corporations by the "generally accepted accounting principles." The next section deals with additional sources of ambiguity. The third section deals with some of the special problems created by mergers.

AMBIGUITY IN REPORTED INCOME BECAUSE OF NUMEROUS ACCOUNTING OPTIONS

Investors, and the public in general, often seem to attach great importance to reported earnings per share. This was eloquently stated in an article in *Forbes Magazine*[6] in 1967:

. . . the annual net earnings figure tends to have a magical significance—not only for the ordinary investor but for security analysts and even for acquisition-minded managements. It becomes, in effect, what grades are for the student—a measure of excellence or lack of excellence, of progress or lack of progress.[7]

Historically, accounting has been a flexible art, permitting many options for coping with different situations. While there is obvious justification for this discretion, the result is a fuzziness in data on reported earnings per share. In recent years, criticism of accounting techniques has increased. Sudden bankruptcies such as Yale Express in 1965, Westec in 1966, and the Penn Central Transportation Company in 1970 have stimulated this criticism. In the instances cited, what were reported as profits in years immediately prior to the bankruptcies were in fact losses. As *Forbes Magazine* pointed out in the 1967 article, businessmen and accountants were facing "a growing credibility gap."[8] However, as *Fortune* editorialized in 1970:

The basic problem is not dishonesty on the part of the corporation or their auditors, but the amorphous nature of accounting itself. The wide range of accounting options permits companies enormous leeway, with various paths to take in consolidating earnings of subsidiaries, depreciating assets, evaluating inventory, accounting for various drilling costs. Thus identical earnings figures for two similar companies with identical sales do not necessarily represent equal performance by management.[9]

Table 8-1 is a useful introduction to a discussion of differences in reported income that are allowed by accounting practices which are "in conformity with generally accepted accounting principles." This table is from a talk given by Leonard Spacek[10] in 1959.

It indicates that two companies doing identical things can choose to report earnings per share of $0.80 or $1.79 or almost anything in between. And, it should be added that Mr. Spacek's six kinds of discretionary treatment are not exhaustive.*

The importance of the differences in choices with regard to the six kinds of accounting procedures varies enormously among industries. For example, treatment of inventory can have an important impact on reported profits in the meat-packing industry while it has a negligible impact in the airline industry. Depreciation policy can have an enormous impact in the airline industry and a negligible impact in

---

* It has been estimated that over one million earnings figures can be generated from the same basic data. R.J. Charles, "Financial Information and the Securities Market," *Abacus,* vol. 1, no. 1 (September 1965), pp. 3–30.

TABLE 8–1
Accounting Magic (all "in conformity with generally accepted accounting principles")

	Company A Col. 1	Company B's Profits are Higher because of: Use of Fifo in Pricing Inventory Col. 2	Use of Straight-Line Depreciation Col. 3	Deferring Research Costs Over 5 Years Col. 4	Funding Only the Pensions Vested Col. 5	Use of Stock Options for Incentives Col. 6	Including Capital Gain in Income Col. 7	Company B Col. 8
Sales in units	100,000 units $100 each							100,000 units $100 each
Sales in dollars	$10,000,000							$10,000,000
Costs and expenses—								
Cost of goods sold	$ 6,000,000							$ 6,000,000
Selling, general and administrative	1,500,000							1,500,000
LIFO inventory reserve	400,000	$(400,000)						—
Depreciation	400,000		$(100,000)					300,000
Research costs	100,000			$(80,000)				20,000
Pension costs	200,000				$(150,000)			50,000
Officers' compensation—								
Base salaries	200,000							200,000
Bonuses	200,000					$(200,000)		—
Total costs and expenses	$ 9,000,000	$(400,000)	$(100,000)	$(80,000)	$(150,000)	$(200,000)	$ —	$ 8,070,000
Profit before income taxes	$ 1,000,000	$ 400,000	$ 100,000	$ 80,000	$ 150,000	$ 200,000	$ —	$ 1,930,000
Income taxes	520,000	208,000	52,000	42,000	78,000	104,000	—	1,004,000
Gain on sale of property (net of income tax)	—						$150,000	150,000
Net profit reported	$ 480,000	$ 192,000	$ 48,000	$ 38,000	$ 72,000	$ 96,000	$150,000	$ 1,076,000
Per share on 600,000 shares	$ .80	$ .32	$ .08	$ .06	$ .12	$ .16	$ .25	$ 1.79
Market value at—								
10 times earnings	$ 8.00	$3.20	$ .80	$ .63	$1.20	$1.60	$2.50	$17.93
12 times earnings	$ 9.60	$3.84	$ .96	$ .76	$1.44	$1.92	$3.00	$21.52
15 times earnings	$12.00	$4.80	$1.20	$ .95	$1.80	$2.40	$3.75	$26.90

( ) Denotes deduction

Source: Spacek, "Business Success," p. 27.

the advertising industry. This variation among industries makes it impossible in comparing reported incomes for different firms to use simple rules of thumb to achieve comparability in reported income. What is needed is an awareness of the problem and the ability to understand the impact of differences in accounting treatment in particular industries and even in particular companies.

Although differences among industries are rather obvious, it should also be emphasized that there are important differences within industries. For example, IBM depreciates its computers much more rapidly than do the many leasing firms which buy IBM equipment in order to lease to others. Similarly, in the airlines industry, Delta Airlines depreciates its 727s over 10 years, whereas United uses a 16-year period. Another example is in the steel industry. For years, Inland Steel strained to minimize reported income while several other firms in the industry choose accounting practices which in themselves resulted in higher reported income.

There are other important kinds of discretionary treatments which still are in conformity with generally accepted accounting methods. Mr. Spacek's example above indicates that corporations may choose to fund all of the accrued liabilities under a pension plan for providing retirement benefits, while other corporations may choose to fund only those portions of the liabilities which are fully vested. Even more important, perhaps, is the discretion in the choice of assumptions regarding the rates of return which will be earned on the pension fund assets. For corporations with large pension funds, assumptions regarding rates of return which will be earned can have a great impact on reported earnings. Since pension fund assets exceed $1 billion for several firms and are in the hundreds of millions of dollars for many more, this is not a negligible item. Some firms have traditionally made conservative assumptions regarding the rates of return that would be earned on their pension fund assets and have consequently had a relatively high level of annual contributions to the pension fund and a correspondingly low level of reported income. One motive, aside from conservatism, for maximizing the annual contribution to the pension fund is the fact that the pension fund assets are sheltered from corporate income taxes. Other firms, with strong demands for funds for internal investment, have made much less conservative assumptions regarding the rates of return on pension fund assets and have had correspondingly smaller annual contributions and higher reported incomes.

The following hypothetical example shows how two firms, identical except for their assumptions regarding rates of return on pension fund assets, can have substantially different reported earnings per share. Company A assumes the rate of return on its pension assets will be 5 percent compounded annually. Company B assumes a 3 percent rate. If the growth in pension fund liabilities is estimated at 5 percent, Company B will have to charge current income with a provision for pensions, thereby reducing reported earnings. Table 8–2 illustrates this,

TABLE 8–2

	Company A	Company B
Pension fund assets	$50,000,000	$50,000,000
Assumed return on assets	2,500,000	1,500,000
Earnings before contributions		
to pension fund	10,000,000	10,000,000
Contribution		1,000,000
Net earnings (before taxes)	10,000,000	9,000,000

assuming pension fund assets of $50 million. These differences among firms need to be kept in mind by financial analysts in comparing earnings per share.*

Perhaps even more dramatic is the change in reported earnings per share that can be achieved by single firms through *changing* the assumptions they make regarding rates of return on pension fund assets. In recent years, one large manufacturer of electrical equipment made large out-of-court settlements of treble damage cases arising from alleged violations of the antitrust laws. This firm substantially offset the effect of these settlements on reported income by a sharp upward revision in the assumed rate of return on its pension fund assets. The example is cited not to indicate that the firm was engaged in "questionable practices," but rather to indicate the very substantial discretion which firms have in choosing how to calculate reported income.

Another important opportunity to influence reported income is provided from time to time by the choice between charging certain outlays against current income or against earned surplus. Another of the electrical equipment manufacturers chose to offset its out-of-court settlements in the same set of lawsuits by charging its settlement costs against earned surplus rather than against current income.

---

* The assumption with regard to the rate of return on pension fund assets has other effects not included in table 8–2.

Still another opportunity for choice is provided in the specification of the time period for the recognition of sales revenue. A revelation of the possible consequences of this choice in *Barrons*[11] apparently had a dramatic impact on stock prices in 1970. Land development companies can choose to report as revenue the total sales price of a piece of land at the time that the sales contract is signed and the first payment is made, or a company can report as current revenue only monies actually received. Since many land development companies require only a small initial payment on pieces of land whose sale prices may be thousands of dollars, this choice can obviously have a large impact on reported revenues and apparent profits. When *Barrons* revealed that certain land companies were including in current revenue the total sales prices of land which was sold, the stocks of some of these companies fell sharply within the week following publication, at a time when the general market was strong.*

Still another kind of ambiguity provided by the range of options available under generally accepted accounting principles is the definition of extraordinary or nonrecurring items. Companies are permitted to use their judgement in deciding whether a given outlay, for example, is to be treated as an ordinary business expense or as a nonrecurring or extraordinary item. After the bankruptcy of the Penn Central Transportation Corporation, it was revealed that the management had chosen to make current earnings before extraordinary items look relatively favorable by treating certain items of expense as extraordinary items. There was nothing illegal in this choice; it was made in accordance with generally accepted accounting principles. Nevertheless, the Penn Central management seemed to be straining to maximize reported earnings in order to reassure the investing public, and they were helped in this effort by their decisions regarding nonrecurring or extraordinary items.

The treatment of income of subsidiaries varies among companies, and the variation affects reported income. Some parent companies include in their income a proportion of their subsidiaries' income equal to the proportion of the subsidiaries which is owned by the parent. Other parent corporations credit their income account only with dividends received from the subsidiary.

The preceding discussion is merely illustrative of the broad range

* Methods of reporting land sales were studied by both the S.E.C. and the Accounting Principles Board in 1972. Presumably, in the future there will be greater uniformity in accounting practices.

of discretionary items and is not exhaustive. Security analysts can be expected to be aware of these varieties of options available to American corporations, and undoubtedly they generally succeed in penetrating the veil of illusion which corporations inevitably create in reporting their income. Financial analysts yearn for greater standardization and precision in reporting income, but they can rejoice in the relatively great precision and standardization that exists for American corporations as compared with corporations in almost all other countries. The disclosure requirements imposed by the Securities and Exchange Commission and the New York Stock Exchange make American financial statements fine examples of candor and scientific objectivity by comparison with financial statements of many, perhaps all, other countries.

OTHER ELEMENTS OF AMBIGUITY IN REPORTED INCOME OR EARNINGS PER SHARE

Not all of the ambiguity in earnings per share is due to the range of choices that corporations are permitted by generally accepted accounting principles. Some ambiguity is created even when no choices are present.

Consider, for example, two different corporations making the same kinds of packaged food products. They report the same earnings per share and have the same capital structure. One manufacturer provides large scale distributors—primarily food chains—with products which are sold under the label of the distributor. The second firm sells its products under its own label which is heavily advertised and widely and favorably known. Generally accepted accounting principles require that the advertising of the second firm be treated as an expense. Yet, such advertising could and probably does create a very valuable asset, namely, the consumer franchise which is provided by an established brand name. If other things were equal for the two companies, the existence of this consumer franchise for the second company would justify a higher market valuation for its shares. Reported earnings per share, however, would not help the financial analysts arrive at this judgement.

The realism of the situation postulated in the preceding paragraph was documented by the antitrust suit brought against the Borden Company by the Federal Trade Commission.[12] The Borden Company sold evaporated milk under its own label for a higher price than evaporated milk which was sold to distributors for distribution under their label. The FTC claimed that this two-price system violated the Robinson-Patman Act. Part of Borden's defense was based on the claim that the Borden label conveyed valuable information to consumers for which they willingly paid and that this was a rational choice on the part of consumers. In order to prove their claim, Borden carried out a study in which consumers were allowed to choose between Borden milk and milk with an unknown label which contained the same objective information as the Borden label. Price differences between the two labels were varied systematically. For all differences in price which were tested, a large majority of consumers bought milk with the Borden label and justified their choice by reference to the knowledge which the brand name conveyed regarding the reliability and quality of the product. The survey merely documented what can be observed in almost any grocery store; brand names have significance for many consumers and can benefit the corporation which distributes the labeled merchandise.

The treatment of research and development expenditures is an example of ambiguity created in part by choices the corporation may make and in part by other things. Corporate managements are permitted to treat outlays for research and development as expenses chargeable against income in the current year, or they are permitted to capitalize them and write them off over a period of years. The choice obviously can affect current reported income. This fact is generally recognized, but another element of ambiguity in the treatment of research and development expenditures has not received equally widespread comment. Corporations are permitted to capitalize their expenditures for research and development, but they are not allowed to establish assets in excess of the amount expended for research and development. That is, if $1 million were spent in a given year for research and development, the corporation would not be allowed to capitalize more than $1 million.* This is true whether the outlay results in the invention of the wheel, fire, the transistor, or something else worth more than $1 million. Also, the outlay can be capitalized even if nothing of any commercial value is discovered or developed. In valuing a company's shares and in interpreting its reported income, financial analysts should try to form some judgment as to the value of ideas generated and under development in the corporation.

Another kind of expenditure which creates valuable assets of long

* The treatment of patents is similar. They are carried on the books at cost.

life and which accountants do not permit to be recognized are outlays for the creation of human capital. These outlays may be for executive development or for improving the quality of employees who are not executives. Human capital is an extraordinarily important factor of production. When economists attempt to account for the increase in production in the United States, there is a large fraction of the increase which cannot be accounted for by changes in measurable inputs of capital and man hours. This fraction of the increase in production is generally attributed to an increase in the quality of human capital employed. Workers and executives are highly trained. It is currently a rather popular view to attribute the frequent superiority of American corporations in competition with foreign corporations to the superiority of the management methods and skills of the American corporation. This is the view elaborated in Servan-Schrieber's book, *The American Challenge*.[13] The view that the skill of the work force makes a great deal of difference does not need belaboring; it is rather obvious. Yet, expenditures by a corporation to develop the skill of its workers and executives must be treated as a current expense, even though they create assets of great value and long life. International Business Machines provides an excellent example. As Sidney Davidson said, ". . . one of the very biggest assets of giant IBM is its sales force. The company has spent millions of dollars and millions of man hours obtaining and developing that main resource. Yet nowhere is that resource carried on IBM's books as an asset. Human capital is carried at zero."[14]

Outlays by corporations to discharge their "social" responsibilities or to enable them to act as good "corporate citizens" obviously have an adverse impact on reported income, but they may have a beneficial, though unmeasurable and unreported, impact on future profitability.

MERGERS

The United States in recent years has had the greatest merger movement in its history, whether measured by number of mergers, volume of assets, or in any other plausible way. Some of the firms which have been most active in acquiring other firms have had common stocks whose prices have provided some of the most thrilling experiences available to investors in the entire field of investments. Stocks of such companies as Ling-Temco-Vought, Litton Industries, and Gulf and Western, went up and down in recent years with exhilarating or distressing speed. The very rapid changes in value of these stocks have been attributed in part to the lack of understanding by investors of reported earnings per share for these corporations.

Some of the confusion that might arise in interpreting earnings per share for a company with an active and successful program for acquiring other companies is illustrated by the choice between accounting for such acquisitions by a pooling-of-interests or by a purchase-of-assets method. An exhaustive and illuminating discussion of this subject is provided by Opinions 16 and 17 of the Accounting Principles Board.[15] The discussion here is much briefer and is designed merely to indicate the nature of the problem.

Under pooling of interests, the stock of one company is acquired in exchange for stock of another company and the assets and liabilities of the acquired company are merged at book value with the assets and liabilities of the acquiring company. Typically, the book values of the assets are far below their market value and the value of the stock for which the assets are exchanged. A pooling of interests permits the acquiring company to create "instant earnings" by disposing of newly acquired assets at market prices which are in excess of book cost. Also depreciating the acquired assets on the basis of their unrealistically low book values results in over-stating earnings.

When pooling of interests came into vogue in the mid-40s, book values of assets were generally close to costs. Price levels were approximately the same as they had been 20 years earlier. The situation is very different today and as a result there has been substantial criticism of the use of the pooling-of-interests method.

The alternative is the purchase method of accounting. Under this approach, the cost of the acquisition is the entire payment, including the contingent considerations. The identifiable assets of the acquired company are valued currently when included in the balance sheet. If the total value is less than the total payment, the difference is labeled "goodwill." Recent rulings of the Accounting Principles Board specify that goodwill must be amortized, i.e., charged against income.* While this also creates problems in interpreting the income statement, purchase accounting clearly represents the transaction more accurately than a pooling of interests.

---

* The purchase method of accounting has been used at times because it results in negative goodwill. If charged as a credit to income, instant earnings can be created. The new rulings recognize this fact and specify that negative goodwill be prorated against the value of identifiable assets until its value is zero.

CONCLUSIONS

The intent of the preceding discussion is to emphasize the folly of attaching any great significance to reported earnings per share. To believers in efficient markets, it is not surprising that there is evidence that investors, on the average, are sophisticated in their interpretation of reported earnings. Ray Ball[16] analyzed the effects of changes in accounting techniques on stock prices. The types of changes studied included changes in depreciation policy, inventory methods, consolidation policy, accounting for investments, and the method of taking revenue into account. His sample was 197 firms making 267 accounting changes between 1947 and 1961. Using an approach similar to that described earlier in the study of stock splits,* Ball concluded that the market is not fooled by accounting magic and ". . . that accounting data are unimportant relative to the aggregate supply of information."[17] The stocks of firms which made accounting changes, on the average, performed badly relative to the market as long as 11 years prior to the changes. By the time of the earnings announcement based on the changes, almost all of the adverse information had been

FIGURE 8–1

Abnormal Performance (Relative to the Market) 267 of Firms Changing Accounting Techniques

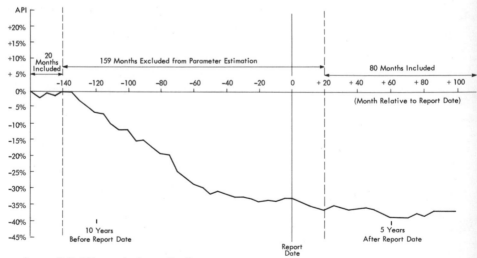

Source: Ball, "Changes in Accounting."

---

* See chapter 4, pp. 83–86.

anticipated and there was little further change in the stock price. The behavior of the "Abnormal Performance Index" (API) of the stocks making changes is shown in figure 8–1.* The average abnormal performance is approximately −32 percent over the 160 months preceding the change date. This, of course, does not represent the experience of any one firm and the performance varies with the type of change, the disclosure, and the effect on income. The evidence seems clear, however, that the market appears to impound information before the date of accounting changes.

Another aspect of investors' sophistication was studied by Lorie and Halpern.[18] It is often alleged that shareholders of acquired companies are misled by complicated securities, sometimes called "funny money." To test this, Lorie and Halpern looked at rates of return to the recipients of funny money in mergers in manufacturing and mining between 1955 and 1967. The study included 117 mergers in which the assets of the acquired firms were over $10 million and were paid for by complicated securities. Some of their results are presented in table 8–3.

The mean rate of return on the "funny money" was 77.3 percent on an annual basis for the six-month period prior to the merger. The corresponding rate of return on the Standard and Poor's Composite Index was 7.9 percent. In the first year after the merger, the mean annual rate of return on "funny money" was 9.3 percent as compared to 7.7 percent on the Index. These results hardly suggest that investors have been deceived about the values of their holdings acquired in mergers. As Lorie and Halpern state, "Despite unquestioned departures from the optimum in financial reporting, the evidence presented above indicates that investors have on the average been able to pierce the accountants' veil of illusion and have made rewarding investments."[19]

Reassuring as these findings may be, the flexibility of accounting techniques lends a note of unreality to the concept of reported earnings. Flexibility is no doubt necessary and desirable, and disclosure in financial statements has been improved in recent years. However, reported earnings need to be examined carefully and to be interpreted in the light of other, generally available information.

---

* The Abnormal Performance Index measures the cumulative departure of the price of a stock from what the price would have been if the relationship between the price of the stock and the market had been "normal."

TABLE 8–3

Rates of Return on "Funny Money" and the Standard & Poor's Composite Index, 1955–1967 (rates in percent per annum, compounded annually)

From	To	Number of Observations	"Funny Money"					Standard & Poor's Composite Index	
			Mean Rate of Return at Mean Wealth Ratio	Standard Deviation of Wealth Ratio	Minimum Rate of Return	Maximum Rate of Return	Percent Greater than Market Index	Mean Rate of Return at Mean Wealth Ratio	Standard Deviation of Wealth Ratio
6 months prior to merger	Date of merger	117	77.28	0.370	−50.25	566.36	0.821	7.87	0.087
Date of merger	1 year after merger	115	9.34	0.274	−51.90	92.71	0.443	7.73	0.099
Date of merger	2 years after merger	82	9.52	0.380	−45.57	41.29	0.537	7.38	0.125
6 months prior to merger	1 year after merger	115	28.74	0.582	−42.23	145.45	0.748	7.53	0.100
6 months prior to merger	2 years after merger	82	18.17	0.627	−40.43	70.82	0.744	6.67	0.107

Source: Lorie and Halpern, "Conglomerates," p. 160

9

Predicting Earnings

INTRODUCTION

CHAPTER 7 INDICATED that the prediction of future earnings is critical in security valuation. The other variables determining the relative values of different issues of common stock tend to be relatively stable through time; earnings do not. The extreme importance of forecasts of earnings has been documented many times. Brealey cites two studies bearing on this point in his excellent chapter on earnings and stock prices.[1] One study by Latane and Tuttle[2] indicates that on the average over 17 percent of the variation in price changes is explained by changes in earnings during the 14 years from 1950 to 1963. As indicated in the last chapter, Brealey cites this study of 48 stocks selected at random from the stocks reviewed by the Value Line Investment Survey. The average annual price appreciation of the stocks selected was 12.2 percent. In contrast, the eight stocks with the greatest percentage improvement in earnings in each year had an average annual rate of return of 30.4 percent while the eight companies with the smallest improvement in earnings had, on the average, rates of return of only 1 percent. Brealey cites another study which confirms the value of predicting earnings changes correctly. Kisor and Messner[3] studied 800 companies for the four-year period 1962–66. They compared the performance of two types of portfolios with the Standard & Poor's Industrial Index for twelve-month periods. In the first period, March 1962 to March 1963, a portfolio with equal dollar amounts invested in companies whose changes in earnings were superior to the average of all 800 stocks for the year 1962 appreciated 4.3 percent more than

157

the index. On the other hand, a similar portfolio of stocks of companies whose earnings behaved less well than the average depreciated 12 percent relative to the index. The results for the other 16 periods which Kisor and Messner studied are similar.

This chapter discusses the value of historical earnings as predictors of future earnings. It then turns to discussion of the predictions of financial analysts and the value of interim reports.

HISTORICAL EARNINGS AS A PREDICTOR OF FUTURE EARNINGS

When the random-walk or efficient market hypothesis was first discussed in the financial community, there was general incredulity. The disbelief was based upon an initial misconception that a random walk implied a senselessness or irrationality in the marketplace. Once it became clear, however, that a random walk was consistent with a theory of totally rational behavior and an efficient market, acceptance of the notion of a random walk in stock prices became much more general. Such randomness would exist even if prices were completely determined by corporate earnings which, in turn, were the result of the interplay of real economic forces with marked temporal patterns such as seasonal variations, cyclical changes, and secular trends.

Such a line of thought is consistent with the expectation that a study of changes in the earnings per share of common stocks would reveal definite patterns through time. If that proved to be true, a study of these patterns would be valuable in predicting future changes in earnings. (Such prediction would not, on the average, lead to superior rates of return, given the efficiency of the stock market.) Financial analysts have routinely studied historical changes in earnings in order to guide them in formulating views about earnings in future years.

It was with great shock, therefore, that I. M. D. Little's original work, "Higgledly Piggledy Growth,"[4] was received in both the academic and financial communities. Little reported on his study of earnings for British firms and found that changes in earnings, like prices, followed a random walk. This meant that successive changes in earnings per share were statistically independent and that the study of the sequence of historical changes in earnings per share was useless as an aid in predicting future changes. In other terms, historical rates of growth in earnings provide no clue to future rates of growth.

Little's work was criticized on methodological grounds. The search for such blemishes was almost certainly spurred by general disbelief in the validity of his conclusions. Professor Little responded in good spirit to the criticisms and revised his study in collaboration with A. C. Rayner. The result was a small book, *Higgledy Piggledy Growth Again*.[5] Little and Rayner expanded the coverage of the earlier work and remedied the shortcomings in the methods of analysis, but the conclusions were much the same: Changes in earnings for British corporations followed a random walk.

One explanation which was offered for the apparently bizarre findings was that the quality of British accounting information was so low that the results reflected events in the accounting world rather than in the real world in which the corporations operated. People believing this felt that the study of earnings of American corporations would produce quite different results, since standards of accounting in the United States are "higher" and there presumably is a greater correspondence between reported earnings and "real" earnings. It also seemed plausible that even if short-run changes in earnings were erratic, there might be discernable trends in the long run. American data were studied by Murphy,[6] Lintner and Glauber,[7] and Brealey.[8] In order to relieve the reader's suspense before reviewing these studies, the reader should know that the results for American firms are about the same as for British firms. Changes in American earnings, like changes in British earnings, follow a random walk.

Murphy studied the correlation between relative rates of growth of earnings per share in successive periods between 1950 and 1965 for 344 companies in 12 industries. He computed the correlations for successive, one-year, two-year, and five-year periods. In 340, or 69 percent of the tests, he found no significant correlation in successive growth rates of earnings per share of companies in an industry. In 25 percent of the tests, the correlations were significantly negative. Only 6 percent of the tests showed significant positive correlation.

Lintner and Glauber tested the possibility that the results of the study of British data were caused by focusing on relatively short-run rates of growth in earnings. Possibly, random exogenous events caused highly erratic fluctuations in short-term growth rates which would not be present in growth rates during longer periods of time. Another possible explanation of the British results was the fact that the British economy during the long period after World War II was alternately dampened and stimulated by the British government in an attempt to adjust to successive problems of inflation, unemployment, and adverse balance of payments. The American economy had had a more stable period of economic growth and this greater stability would perhaps be reflected in more persistent and observable trends in earnings of individual corporations. Also, the effects of any instability might be removed by including the Federal Reserve Board Index of Industrial Production as a separate variable in analyzing changes in earnings. Lintner and Glauber therefore tested the persistence of the relationship between changes in earnings of individual corporations and changes in the Federal Reserve Board Index. This seemed promising since the belief that some companies can outperform the economy with some consistency is basic to the concept of growth stocks.

Lintner and Glauber used a sample of 323 companies having positive earnings in the years 1945–65. For each company, they calculated the five-year trend in earnings per share for each of the four five-year periods. The correlation coefficients between changes in earnings in adjacent five-year periods are given in table 9–1. Two of the numbers

TABLE 9–1

Correlation Coefficients between Earnings Changes of All Companies (adjacent five-year periods)

Period	*Five-Year Growth Rates*	*Five-Year Growth Relative to FRB*	*Five-Year Growth Rates Net of FRB*
1946–50 and 1951–55 05		.08	.10
1951–55 and 1956–60 00		.03	.15
1956–60 and 1961–65 12		.08	.14

Source: Linter and Glauber, "Higgledy Piggledy Growth in America?"

in the second column are positive, but quite low; the third number is zero. Those in the third column are the correlations when growth is measured relative to industrial production rather than to time. The fourth column gives the results of correlations between growth trends when the level of industrial production is held constant. The correlation coefficients are slightly larger; adjustment for changes in the economic environment is of some help. But the correlations are still extremely low.

Finally, in a desperate effort to discover the temporal patterns which everyone had believed to exist, Lintner and Glauber studied various other financial series. In addition to using several forms of reported earnings (some before interest and taxes, some after interest and before taxes, some after interest and taxes, and so forth), Lintner and Glauber studied the degree of interdependence between growth rates in sales, dividends, and other variables during successive periods of time. As one might expect, growth rates in sales tend to be more stable than the other financial series, but the highest interperiod correlation explains less than 10 percent of the variance.

Lintner and Glauber's results were generally negative. They did find that if stocks are divided into quintiles according to the reliability of the relationship between the growth rate of operating income and industrial production, correlations between growth rates in successive periods are statistically significant for companies with the most reliable relationship. For the 64 companies with the steadiest growth rates in 1956–60, the correlation coefficient between the rates in 1956–60 and 1961–65 was 0.41. For the 67 firms with the least steady growth, it was only 0.07. This is a relatively weak finding in any absolute sense,* but among the negative findings of the entire study, this emerges as one of the few straws one may clutch in a quest for evidence of temporal patterns or persistence in performance of individual corporations in successive periods of time.

Brealey's findings are even more negative. He looked at percentage changes in earnings of approximately 700 industrial companies. Correlations for each of 14 adjacent years during the period 1945–64 were generally very low and usually negative. The average was −0.06. Correlations did not increase when percentage changes in earnings in one year were correlated with changes in earnings in the second successive year, nor were the results improved when industries were studied individually. When Brealey compared the actual number of companies experiencing a given number of years' growth of earnings in excess of the mean rate of growth with the expected number of companies, assuming complete randomness, he found an extraordinarily close correspondence between the two distributions. Similarly, when the actual number of runs of good years and bad years was compared with the expected number of runs of good or bad years, assuming randomness, the degree of correspondence was striking. Brealey cites the Lintner and Glauber findings which indicate that the correlation between growth rates in successive periods is modestly

---

* For the 64 firms with relatively well-defined growth rates, only 16 percent of the variance of the growth rates in the second period was explained.

positive for firms with the steadiest rates of growth. For Brealey, as for Lintner and Glauber, this is one of the few bits of evidence that for some companies during some periods there are significant departures from randomness in successive changes in earnings.

None of the foregoing evidence in support of the hypothesis that corporate earnings follow a random walk is meant to imply that it is impossible to forecast corporate earnings. The randomness in corporate earnings merely means that one's ability to forecast changes in earnings will not be significantly enhanced by studying changes in historical rates of growth in earnings. This is generally true, but there may be some kinds of companies—those with the steadiest rates of growth in earnings—for which analysis of historical growth rates does have some predictive power. These negative implications are clear; positive implications with respect to promising methods of forecasting are less clear.

The explanation of the random walk in security prices is plausible and satisfying, being based upon the rationality of investors and the efficiency of the market in which they operate. The explanation of the very substantial degree of randomness in corporate earnings is less satisfactory. That is, it seems both less plausible theoretically and less amply documented by empirical work. Most explanations of the randomness of successive changes in corporate earnings are simple, and they are based upon the obvious fact that corporate fortunes can be favorably or adversely affected by an extremely large number of events, many of which are beyond the control of corporate management. The variety of events is large and merely suggested by mentioning some of the more obvious such as strikes, changes in the general level of economic activity, unexpected, favorable research and development activities, mineral discoveries, natural disasters, political disasters, changing impacts of commercial rivalries, changing tastes, and so forth.

Although it is sometimes claimed that the apparent randomness of changes in corporate earnings is attributable to the great competitiveness of our society, even firms with substantial monopoly power are subject to many rude and unexpected shocks or pleasant surprises which could cause their earnings to change in erratic or random fashion. The one kind of shock to which they are less susceptible is that arising from changing fortunes among commercial rivals. Those who find it hardest to believe the evidence or conjectures about randomness in changes in corporate earnings frequently resort to the assertion that corporations with superior management are better able to dominate their companies and economic environments so that persistent upward trends in corporate earnings will be achieved with noticeable regularity. Although it is true that truly superior management can anticipate changes more successfully and adapt more quickly, the regularity of growth in earnings would depend to some extent on superior management's not being paid what it is worth. If the management receives compensation equal to the marginal value of its impact on corporate earnings, the earnings of even the best-managed companies could be expected to have irregular rates of change in earnings.

PREDICTIONS OF SECURITY ANALYSTS

Whether the proffered explanations of the apparent randomness of changes in corporate earnings are satisfactory or not, corporate earnings for most companies do not seem to depart significantly from a random walk. As has already been stated, this means that the naïve extrapolation of recent rates of change in corporate earnings is not likely to be useful. Yet, security analysts in many financial institutions produce forecasts of corporate earnings which are not significantly different from those that would have been produced by the naïve extrapolation of recent historical trends. The correspondence between forecasts by analysts and those that would have been produced by extrapolation is probably not deliberate. In trying to form their own expectations regarding the future, especially when the company is large and complicated, the analysts find their expectations being colored or constrained, perhaps subconsciously, by reference to what has been happening recently. It is almost too much to expect an analyst, perhaps operating in San Francisco and responsible for forecasting earnings for Standard Oil (New Jersey) as well as earnings for many other companies, to make forecasts wildly at variance with recent experience.

Cragg and Malkiel measured the degree of correlation between historic growth rates in earnings and forecasts of earnings.[9] Their study was based upon forecasts of earnings for 185 corporations given by five financial institutions. The forecasts were made at the end of 1962 and 1963. Each forecast was an average annual rate of growth expected over the next five years. There are many ways in which to measure historic growth rates, and they produce considerable variation in the correlations between growth rates and earnings predictions.

Nevertheless, almost any measure of historic growth rates accounts for over one half of the variation in earnings forecasts. Their relevant correlations are given in table 9–2.

TABLE 9–2
Predictions and Past Growth Rates[a] (correlations of predicted with past growth rates)

	1962				1963				
	A	B	C	D	A	B	C	D	E
g_{p1}	.78	.68	.75	.41	.85	.73	.84	.56	.67
g_{p2}	.75	.67	.72	.51	.79	.69	.80	.58	.76
g_{p3}	.77	.71	.82	.61	.75	.72	.79	.70	.74
g_{p4}	.34	.37	.59	.44	.33	.45	.70	.75	.58
g_{c1}	.55	.46	.65	.32	.63	.52	.61	.30	.58
g_{c2}	.67	.60	.68	.18	.72	.58	.73	.20	.56
g_{c3}	.75	.63	.73	.17	.79	.66	.76	.17	.57
g_{c4}	.82	.68	.79	.24	.83	.69	.79	.29	.60

[a] g_{p1} is 8–10 year historic growth rate supplied by A
g_{p2} is 4–5 year historic growth rate supplied by A
g_{p3} is 6 year historic growth rate supplied by D
g_{p4} is preceding 1 year growth rate supplied by D
g_{c1} is log-regression trend fitted to last 4 years
g_{c2} is log-regression trend fitted to last 6 years
g_{c3} is log-regression trend fitted to last 8 years
g_{c4} is log-regression trend fitted to last 10 years.
Source: Cragg and Malkiel, "The Consensus and Accuracy of Some Predictions," p. 73.

Cragg and Malkiel went on to analyze the accuracy of forecasts of earnings. Correlations between predicted and realized growth rates were low,* although most were significantly greater than zero. These statistics are summarized in table 9–3. Their main conclusion follows from all of the foregoing:

Evidence has recently accumulated that earnings growth in past periods is not a useful predictor of future earnings growth. The remarkable conclusion of the present study is that the careful estimates of the security analysts participating in our survey, the bases of which are not limited to public information, perform only a little better than these past growth rates. Moreover, the market price-earnings ratios themselves were not better than either the analysts' forecasts or the past growth rates in forecasting future earnings growth.[10]

The authors provide the usual warnings about the limited generality of their findings.

---

* The predictions of *C* are an exception, but Cragg and Malkiel attribute this to the fact that *C* concentrated on large, relatively stable companies.

TABLE 9–3
Accuracy of Predictions

I. 1962 Predictions Compared with Growth of Actual Earnings
1962–1965

Predictor	A	B	C	D	g_{p1}	g_{p2}	g_{p3}	g_{p4}
Correlation	.07	.16	.66	.45	.22	−.01	.23	.16
Number of observations	185	185	60	178	168	140	140	145

II. 1962 Predictions Compared with Growth of Normalized Earnings
1962–1965

	A	B	C	D	g_{p1}	g_{p2}	g_{p3}	g_{p4}
Correlation	.26	.32	.68	.45	.23	.16	.38	.09
Number of observations	180	180	59	175	164	136	138	142

III. 1963 Predictions Compared with Growth of Actual Earnings
1963–1965

Predictor	A	B	C	D	E	g_{p1}	g_{p2}	g_{p3}	g_{p4}
Correlation	.05	.16	.78	.47	.29	.20	.31	.22	.55
Number of observations	185	185	62	182	125	167	143	138	169

IV. 1963 Predictions Compared with Growth of Normalized Earnings
1963–1965

	A	B	C	D	E	g_{p1}	g_{p2}	g_{p3}	g_{p4}
Correlation	.27	.29	.70	.34	.49	.36	.52	.41	.32
Number of observations	180	180	61	177	123	163	139	136	165

Source: Cragg and Makliel, "The Consensus and Accuracy of Some Predictions," p. 78.

INTERIM EARNINGS AS PREDICTORS OF ANNUAL EARNINGS

Those who have observed the limited usefulness of historic growth rates and of most analysts' efforts to peer into the future have sometimes been satisfied with trying to understand the very short-term implications of very recent information. If one accepts the view that it is difficult consistently to do better than assume that the future will be like the present, it becomes especially worthwhile to have current information. Thus, the interest in earnings reports by quarters is substantial.

David Green and Joel Segall[11] were among the first to make an empirical study of the contribution of reports on earnings in the first quarter to predictions of changes in annual earnings. Green and Segall chose a random sample of 46 companies from those whose stocks were listed on the New York Stock Exchange in January 1964. Three naïve extrapolations of earnings for 1964 on the basis of reported earnings for the first quarter were compared with three naïve extrapolations based solely on previous annual earnings. The various models will not be described in detail. A typical one using interim reports assumed that earnings for 1964 would differ from earnings for 1963 by the same percentage that the first-quarter earnings for 1964 differed from the first-quarter earnings for 1963. Green and Segall are ingenious people and they looked at many of the very numerous possibilities for deriving useful information from reports of first-quarter earnings. Nevertheless, they concluded tentatively that first-quarter reports are of little help in forecasting annual earnings per share. Surprisingly, the model with the lowest average of relative forecast errors*—18 percent—assumed that earnings in 1964 would be the same as in 1963. There is some evidence, however, that first-quarter reports may be helpful in forecasting earnings for companies which will experience large and unusual changes in earnings. For the ten companies with the greatest percentage change in earnings, the use of first-quarter earnings reports reduced the average relative forecast error from 31 percent (assuming 1964 earnings the same as those in 1963) to 23 percent.

Brown and Niederhoffer[12] challenged Green and Segall's findings. They alleged that they were puzzled by the finding that knowledge of first-quarter earnings is not useful despite the fact that earnings for the first quarter are about one fourth of the annual earnings being forecast. Using a sample of 519 firms from the Compustat tapes, Brown and Niederhoffer broadened the study to see if reports of quarterly earnings improve the predictions of annual earnings at any time in the reporting year. These investigators found that the quarterly earnings were helpful. That is, forecasts of annual earnings based upon information in quarterly earnings were in some respects more accurate than forecasts of annual earnings made solely on the basis of annual earnings in preceding years. As one would hope, increasing the number of interim reports used in the predictions decreased the average relative forecast errors, although the errors were still quite large. For 1964, the smallest average error using first-quarter earnings was 17 percent; after two quarters, it was 14 percent. For 1965, the comparable average errors were 18 percent and 14 percent.

In subsequent issues of the *Journal of Business*, Brown and Niederhoffer and Green and Segall exchanged humorous though pointed criticism of each others' works.[13] Perhaps a fair summary of their successive articles would be that the use of data on quarterly earnings will not make predictions of annual earnings less accurate than reliance on annual earnings alone, and some improvement is common.

---

* The sign of the error is ignored.

This is merely a logical necessity and not a discovery of any of the authors involved. Careful and ingenious use of data on quarterly earnings seems to be able to produce small increments in the accuracy of forecasts of annual earnings, but it is not clear that these increments are of practical importance. The subject has not been exhausted; but, for the time being, security analysts cannot expect to make dramatic improvements in forecasts of annual earnings by reliance on information on quarterly earnings.

CONCLUSIONS

Conclusions with respect to the prediction of earnings are both encouraging and discouraging. The remarkably general failure of security analysts to predict earnings with greater accuracy than can be achieved by various forms of simple extrapolations of historical data means that there is a great opportunity for enormous profit for anyone who can predict earnings accurately. A variety of evidence indicates that vastly superior rates of return can be earned by anyone who has this superior capacity to predict earnings.

The conclusions about prediction are discouraging in that they indicate the great difficulty of the task. Changes in earnings seem to follow a random walk, meaning that the simple extrapolation of historical trends are not likely to be very useful in predicting future changes in earnings. Clearly, however, historical earnings will continue to be useful in predicting future levels.

section three

PORTFOLIO
MANAGEMENT

10

The Theory of Portfolio
Management

INTRODUCTION

THE BOOK THUS FAR has dealt with the behavior of the stock market as a whole and with the valuation of individual securities. The final section of the book deals with portfolio management. Perhaps it is necessary at the outset to indicate why this is a separate subject. It might appear that the selection of a portfolio would follow obviously and easily from the prior process of valuing securities.

That this is not true is evident from reflection on the behavior of investors. Almost all choose to hold groups of common stocks rather than the single stock which offers the greatest expected return. This suggests that "attractiveness" does not consist exclusively of expected return. If that were all that mattered, investors would put as much of their resources as possible into the single security offering the greatest expected return.

Since 1952, investors have come to understand much better another dimension of attractiveness and the reasons why the rational and professional management of portfolios consists of much more than the listing of securities in order of the magnitude of their expected returns. The great event in 1952 was the publication by Harry Markowitz of his now celebrated article "Portfolio Selection."[1] Markowitz's great contribution was to analyze the implications of the fact that investors, though seeking high expected returns, generally wish to avoid risk. Since there is overwhelming evidence that risk aversion characterizes most investors and especially most large investors, rationality in portfolio management demands that account be taken not only of expected returns for a portfolio but also of the risk that is incurred. Although the expected return on a portfolio is directly and obviously related to the expected returns on the component securities, it is not possible to deduce the riskiness of a portfolio simply by knowing the riskiness of individual securities. The riskiness of portfolios depends not only on the attributes of securities considered individually but also on the interrelationships among them. It is primarily for this reason that portfolio management is a separate subject.

Another reason for the treatment of portfolio management as a separate subject is that it depends upon the needs and tastes of individual investors. It is possible to estimate expected returns for individual securities without regard to any investor, but it is impossible to construct a portfolio which is optimum for an individual investor without taking his needs and tastes into account. The output of security analysts is essential for portfolio management, or at least portfolio managers make use of the output of security analysts, but this output must be analyzed with reference to the tastes and financial circumstances of individual investors in the construction of portfolios. Although security analysis can be impersonal, portfolio management cannot.

The next section of this chapter discusses Markowitz's portfolio theory, the basis of all scientific portfolio management. The following section discusses the subject of the optimality of a portfolio for the individual investor.

THE MARKOWITZ CONTRIBUTION

The portfolio theory developed by Markowitz can be summarized as follows: (1) the two relevant characteristics of a portfolio are its expected return and its riskiness; (2) rational investors will choose to hold efficient portfolios which are those which maximize expected returns for a given degree of risk or, alternatively and equivalently, minimize risk for a given expected return; (3) it is theoretically possible to identify efficient portfolios by the proper analysis of information for each security on its expected return, the variation or variance in that return, and the relationships between the return for each security and that for every other security; and (4) there is a specified, manageable computer program which utilizes inputs from security analysts in the form of the three kinds of necessary information about each security in order to specify a set of efficient portfolios. The program indicates the proportion of an investor's fund which should be allocated to each security in order to achieve efficiency, i.e., the maximization of return for a given degree of risk or the minimization of risk for a given expected return.

Efficient Portfolios

The notion of efficient portfolios is simply illustrated in figure 10–1.

FIGURE 10–1
Hypothetical Efficient Frontier

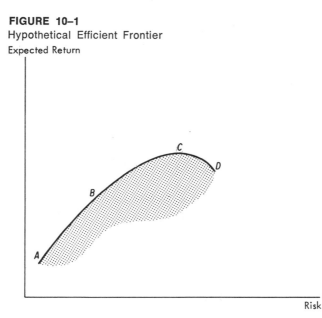

The vertical axis measures the expected return on a portfolio; its associated risk is measured along the horizontal axis. The shaded area represents all possible portfolios that can be obtained from a given set of securities. The portfolios lying on the curve *ABC* are efficient because they offer the maximum return for a given level of risk and minimum risk for a given level of return. The portfolio at point *D* is on the boundary of the feasible set, but is not efficient, because the portfolio on the curve *ABC* offering the same expected return is less risky. Similar statements can be made for all portfolios within the shaded area. The Markowitz analysis assumes that any rational investor will prefer efficient portfolios to all other portfolios. The particular portfolio that an investor prefers above all others—including others which are efficient—depends on his needs and tastes. In more technical terms, the choice depends on the investor's utility function, a subject discussed in the third section of this chapter.

Portfolios and Securities

Let us now examine the relationship of a portfolio to its component securities. First, what is the relationship between the return on a portfolio and the returns on the component securities? Fortunately, this relationship is quite simple. The return on a portfolio is simply the weighted average of the returns on its component securities, the weight of each security being the fraction of the total value of the portfolio which is invested in it. The following example illustrates this: let us assume that a total of $100 is invested in three securities. The proportions, X_i, invested in each are given in the second column of table 10–1. The third column indicates the rates of return, R_i. The sum of the products of these two columns is the rate of return on the

TABLE 10–1
The Calculation of the Rate of Return on a Portfolio

Security (i)	Proportion Invested (X_i)	Rate of Return (R_i)	X_iR_i
1	0.5	0.10	0.050
2	0.3	0.20	0.060
3	0.2	0.05	0.010
Total	1.0		0.120

portfolio, R_p. In this case, the rate of return on the portfolio is $(0.5)(0.10) + (0.3)(0.20) + (0.2)(0.05) = 0.120$, or 12 percent. Symbolically,

$$R_p = X_1R_1 + X_2R_2 + X_3R_3 = \sum_{i=1}^{3} X_iR_i$$

A complication arises because portfolio managers are concerned with future outcomes. If the rates of return on individual securities could be known with certainty, the rate of return on any portfolio could be predicted accurately and rates on all securities would be equal. Since the future is uncertain, portfolio managers must base their selections on forecasts of future outcomes. Suppose an analyst made the following forecast for a specific security:

TABLE 10–2
Forecast of Rate of Return

Rate of Return	Likelihood
8%	Very likely
5%	Possible, but not likely
12%	Possible, but not likely

The forecast of 8 percent is the analyst's "best" estimate, but he cannot be certain. He may be able to state his feelings about the security more precisely so that a picture like that in figure 10–2 can be drawn.

FIGURE 10–2
Analyst's Forecast of Possible Rates of Return for Security A*

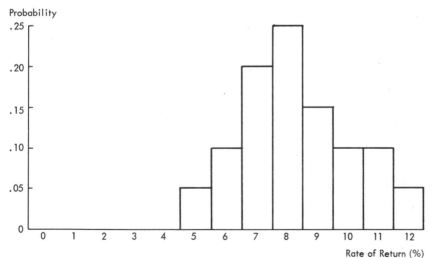

* In figure 10–2, the numbers on the horizontal axis represent the midpoints of class intervals. Thus, for example, "5" means at least "4.5" and less than "5.5."

This "probability distribution" represents the probabilities that the security will provide specified rates of return over some designated future period. The probabilities must, of course, sum to one.

In the example, there is a probability of 0.05 that the return will be 5 percent or 12 percent, and 0.25 that it will be 8 percent. The mean of the distribution, or the "expected" rate of return, is simply the weighted average of the possible returns, the weights being equal to the probabilities. Here, the expected or average return is 8.3 percent. The expected return on a portfolio can now be stated as the weighted sum of the expected returns on the individual securities. Again, the weights are the proportions invested in each security.

Unfortunately, the relationships between estimates of risk for individual securities and estimates of risk for portfolios are not so simple. For the time being, the measure of risk which we will use is variability as measured by the variance. This is defined as the weighted sum of the squared deviations of a variable around its expected value where the weights are the probabilities that the deviations will occur. It provides a measure of the spread or dispersion of the distribution.

The square root of the variance is the standard deviation. Its meaning is straightforward for normal (bell-shaped) distributions. The chances that an outcome will be in the range of the expected value (E) plus or minus one standard deviation (σ), are about two out of three. The chances that it will be between $(E + 2\sigma)$ and $(E - 2\sigma)$ are approximately 95 out of 100. (These statements do not hold for nonnormal distributions, but the standard deviation is still a useful measure of deviation from expected value.) In computations, the variance is more convenient to use than the standard deviation, but the results are usually stated in terms of the latter.* Portfolios which are efficient in the mean-variance plane are efficient in the mean-standard deviation plane, and vice versa.

Although the expected rate of return on a portfolio is simply a weighted average of the expected rates on the component assets of the portfolio, the variance of a portfolio is not simply a weighted average of the variances of the component assets. The variance of each asset matters, but it is also necessary to know the relationships among changes in the rates of return on the component assets. The following examples indicate intuitively why this is so. (All of these examples refer to portfolios of only two assets, but the principles apply equally to portfolios of more than two assets. For the purpose of simple exposition, it will be assumed that the securities in the portfolios pay no dividends or interest so that changes in prices determine completely the rates of return. Therefore, the charts refer to changes in prices through time.)

---

* The arithmetic is such that the standard deviation per dollar of investment does not change with the amount invested, while the variance per dollar invested increases with the amount invested.

In the first example, the two assets move together in perfect lock-step. Although the amplitudes of the price movements are different, the price changes are perfectly correlated. This means that one can specify with perfect accuracy the price change in either security from knowledge of the price change in the other. In this example, the correlation is positive; when security i goes up or down 1 percent, security j inevitably goes up or down by one half of 1 percent. If one assumes equal initial investments in each security, the portfolio as a whole goes up or down three fourths of 1 percent. Using the customary formula for computing the variance, one discovers that the variance of this portfolio is 3.1 percent, while the variance for security i is 5.5 percent and the variance for security j is 1.4 percent.

FIGURE 10–3

Percentage Changes in Prices of Securities i and j (with a correlation of 1.0)

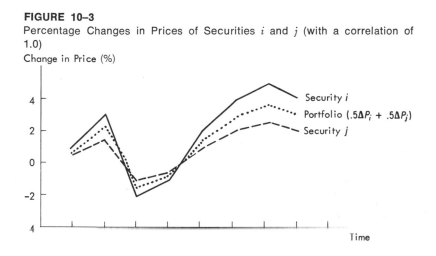

In the next example, the securities again move in perfect lockstep, but the directions of the movements are opposite. When security i goes up 1 percent, security j goes down one half of 1 percent, and vice versa. If equal amounts were initially invested in each security, the value of the portfolio would go up or down by only one fourth of 1 percent as compared to three fourths of 1 percent in the preceding example. The variances for security i, for security j, and for the portfolio as a whole are 5.5 percent, 1.4 percent, and 0.3 percent, respectively.*

---

* In this example, if the variances for the two securities were equal, changes in the price of security i would be exactly offset by changes in the price of security j, and the variance of the portfolio would be zero.

FIGURE 10–4

Percentage Changes in Prices of Securities i and j (with a correlation of -1.0)

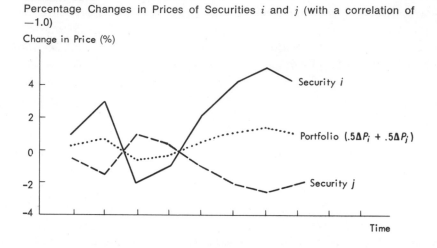

The third example is more realistic in that the securities move to-gether to some degree but not in perfect lockstep. This is true of most listed securities. When stocks go up and down together in perfect lock-step, diversification does not reduce the variance of the portfolio, since movements of individual securities are never offsetting. When the movements are contrary, the offsetting is maximized as is the effect of diversification on the reduction in variance. When the lockstep is not perfect, i.e., when the correlation is between $+1.0$ and -1.0,

FIGURE 10–5

Percentage Changes in Prices of Securities i and j (with positive correlation less than 1.0)

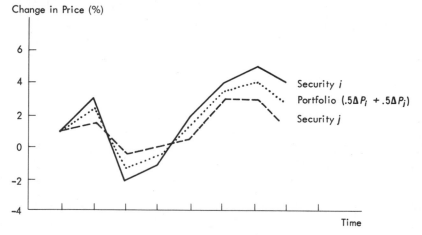

the movements in individual securities are partially offsetting. This is what makes diversification useful in reducing risk as measured by the variance in returns on the portfolio.

At this point, it seems necessary to reveal the formula for computing the variance of a portfolio from knowledge of the movements of its component assets. For simplicity, we present the formula for two securities, i and j.* The variance of the portfolio, σ_p^2, is given by the following equation:

$$\sigma_p^2 = X_i^2 \sigma_i^2 + X_j^2 \sigma_j^2 + 2 X_i X_j \operatorname{cov}_{ij}$$

where

X_i = the proportion invested in security i;
X_j = the proportion invested in security j;
σ_i^2 = the variance of the rate of return on security i;
σ_j^2 = the variance of the rate of return on security j; and
cov_{ij} = the covariance between the rates of return on i and j.

An explanation and proof that the variance of the portfolio can be calculated in this way can be found in either Sharpe[2] or Markowitz.[3]

An understanding of this formula is worthwhile. Although it refers to a portfolio of only two securities, it has great generality, since groups of securities can be considered as a single security in thinking about and analyzing the problems of portfolio management. For example, if one is interested in understanding what the addition of a security does to the variance of an existing portfolio, one can think of the existing portfolio as a single security. The simple formula then has great expository power.

Most of the terms of the equation are clear and familiar, but the final term contains the covariance between securities i and j. As the word suggests, the covariance is a measure of the extent to which two securities covary or move together. The term also has a very precise mathematical meaning which can easily be illustrated in figure 10–6. The first diagram indicates the relationship between the rates of return of i and j at four different points in time. It is possible to draw

---

* The formula is readily extended to the n security case;

$$\sigma_p^2 = \sum_{i=1}^{n} \sum_{j=1}^{n} X_i X_j \operatorname{cov}_{ij},$$

where cov_{ii}, the covariance of a security with itself ($i = i, j = i$), is equal to its variance, σ_i^2.

FIGURE 10–6
Relationship between Rates of Return of Securities *i* and *j*

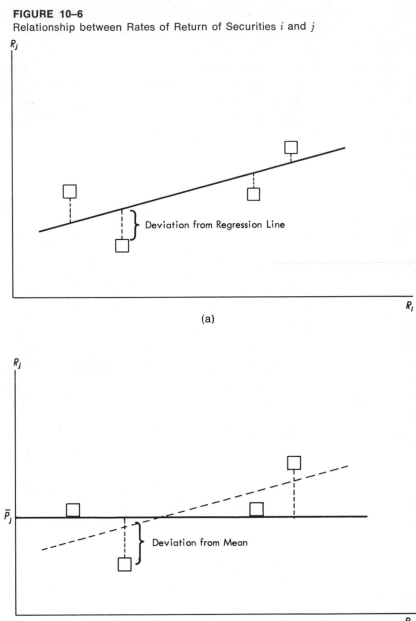

(a)

(b)

a line which indicates the *average* relationship for these four times. This line has been drawn in such a way that the squared vertical distances of the points from the line are minimized and the line is appropriately named a least-squares regression line.

It is also possible to measure the squared deviations of the points around the mean or average rate of return of security j. This is illustrated in the second chart in figure 10–6. The total variance in the rate of return of security j (the average of the squared deviations from the mean) is thus composed of two parts: (1) that attributable to deviations from the regression line; and (2) that attributable to variations in the rate of return of security i or to the forces that caused them. A measure of the extent to which the prices of the two securities move together is given by the following formula:

$$\rho = \sqrt{1 - \frac{\sigma_{j \cdot i}^{2}}{\sigma_{j}^{2}}}$$

where $\sigma_{j \cdot i}^{2}$ = the variance of the rate of return of security j, *after* allowing for the relationship to the rate of return of security i, or that part of the total variance attributable to the deviations from the regression line, and σ_{j}^{2} = the total variance of the rate of return of security j or deviations about its mean. As the formula indicates, if the deviations around the regression line, $\sigma_{j \cdot i}^{2}$, are equal to the deviations around the mean, the value of the expression or the correlation is zero. In other words, knowledge of the variation in the rate of return of security i does not help to explain or predict the variation in the rate of return of security j. If, on the other hand, all of the points lie precisely on the regression line, the correlation would be 1.0. The expression itself defines the familiar correlation coefficient which has a value between 0 and $+1.0$ when the two variables generally move in the same direction, and a value between 0 and -1.0 when they generally move in opposite directions.

The covariance between i and j is a first cousin to the correlation between i and j, being simply the correlation coefficient multiplied by the standard deviation of i and by the standard deviation of j.* In

---

* It is difficult to have an intuitive feeling about the absolute value of the covariance since its size depends not only on how closely i and j covary, but also on the ampitude of the fluctuations in i and j. The correlation coefficient is the covariance standardized by dividing it by the product of the standard deviations of i and j.

other words, the covariance between i and j equals the correlation between i and j times the standard deviation of i times the standard deviation of j. Using the conventional symbols the relationship is expressed as follows:

$$\mathrm{cov}_{ij} = \rho_{ij}\sigma_i\sigma_j$$

In order to see how different values of the covariance or correlation affect the variance of a portfolio, consider the following simple examples: Assume that two assets (single securities or portfolios) have the same rates of return and variances and that equal amounts are invested in each. If the rates of return are 5 percent and the variances are 2 percent, the expected return on the portfolio is 5 percent. The formula for the variance tells us that:

$$
\begin{aligned}
\sigma_p^2 &= X_i^2\sigma_i^2 + X_j^2\sigma_j^2 + 2X_iX_j\rho_{ij}\sigma_i\sigma_j \\
&= (.25)(.02) + (.25)(.02) + (.5)\rho_{ij}(\sqrt{.02})(\sqrt{.02}) \\
&= .01 + .01\rho_{ij}.
\end{aligned}
$$

This illustrates the critical importance of the interrelationships of securities. If there is no correlation ($\rho = 0.0$), the variance of the portfolio is 1 percent, or less than that of a portfolio fully invested in only one of the securities. If the correlation is perfect and positive ($\rho = 1.0$), the portfolio variance is 2 percent, the same as that of a single security. If the correlation is perfect and negative ($\rho = -1.0$) the variance of the portfolio is zero. If there is perfect correlation, the expression for the variance can be factored, and in this special case the standard deviation of the portfolio is linearly related to the amounts invested in each security.* If the correlation is not perfect, the standard deviation of a portfolio is not a linear function of the amounts invested in each asset.

Since investors like to avoid risk and since negative correlation or covariance between a security and a portfolio reduces the variance of the portfolio, such securities, if they exist, would be highly valued.

---

* For example, if the correlation between i and j is perfect and positive, $\rho_{ij} = +1$; the variance of the portfolio is:

$$\sigma_p^2 = X_i^2\sigma_i^2 + X_j^2\sigma_j^2 + 2X_iX_j\sigma_i\sigma_j = (X_i\sigma_i + X_j\sigma_j)^2.$$

and the standard deviation is:

$$\sigma_p = X_i\sigma_i + X_j\sigma_j.$$

On the other hand, securities which are highly correlated with a portfolio do not contribute much to the kind of risk reduction which is the purpose of diversification. In an intermediate position are securities with low positive covariances with the other securities in the portfolio.†† In subsequent chapters there will be an expanded discussion of measurement of riskiness for individual securities and the relationship of such risk to rates of return.

The Efficient Frontier

It has been seen that the attractiveness of a portfolio depends upon both its expected return and its riskiness. Risk, as measured by the variance in rates of return on a portfolio, depends upon the variances of the individual securities and the covariances of each security with each other security. Now it is possible to understand more fully what is meant by an efficient portfolio. The following diagram indicates

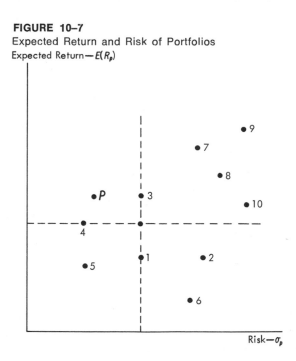

FIGURE 10–7
Expected Return and Risk of Portfolios
Expected Return—$E(R_p)$

Risk—σ_p

---

†† A portfolio made up of two securities will have a standard deviation smaller than that of either security alone if the correlation is less than the ratio of the smaller standard deviation to the larger. See Sharpe, *Portfolio Theory*, p. 48.

the risk and rates of return for ten portfolios, each consisting of a single different security. Clearly, portfolio 3 is preferred to portfolio 1. It offers a higher return for the same risk. Similarly, portfolio 1 is preferred to portfolio 2, since it offers a lower risk for the same rate of return. If the securities are not perfectly correlated—and they are not in this example—portfolios made up of combinations of these securities can have smaller variances for given returns or larger returns for given variances than the single-security portfolios. Portfolios having such characteristics would lie in the region above and to the left of the portfolios consisting of single securities. For example, portfolio *P* might represent a combination of portfolios 3 and 4.

For any given group of securities, the feasible set of portfolios consists of all single-security portfolios and all possible combinations of them. Those which are efficient will plot along the upper border of the feasible set. This border is called the efficient frontier of portfolios of risky assets and is represented by the curve *ABC* in figure 10–8.

FIGURE 10–8
The Feasible Set and Efficient Frontier

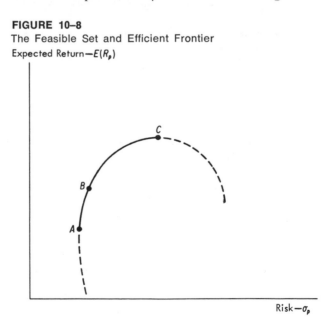

The efficient frontier will be concave from below. That is, all points on the border between, say, *A* and *B* in figure 10–8 will lie on or above a straight line connecting the two points. To see why this is so, consider figure 10–9. Portfolios which are combinations of *A* and

FIGURE 10–9
The Efficient Frontier—Possible and Impossible

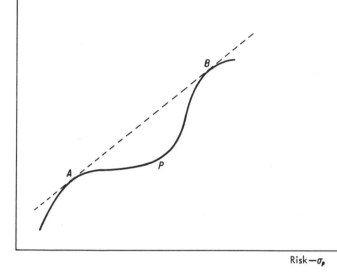

Expected Return—$E(R_p)$

Risk—σ_p

B will have values of $E(R_p)$ and σ_p which plot along or above the dotted line, AB. If the returns on A and B are perfectly correlated, combinations will lie on the line AB, since, for any combination, both the return and the standard deviation will be a linear function of the amount invested in A (or B). If the returns on A and B are not perfectly correlated, combinations will plot above the line AB, because the variances (and standard deviations) will be smaller when correlation is imperfect, and combinations will therefore be upward and to the left of the line connecting A and B. In either case, the combinations would be preferred to portfolios on the convex curve, APB, and the latter cannot be part of the efficient frontier.

Although the efficient frontier can be linear in the $E(R_p)$, σ_p plane, it will never be linear in the $E(R_p)$, σ_p^2 plane. The $E(R_p)$, σ_p^2 border will always have more curvature.* This is illustrated in figure 10–10.

The efficient frontier is linear between A and B when σ_p is the unit on the horizontal axis whereas it is concave throughout if σ_p^2 is the unit.

------

* As we mentioned earlier, the efficient set will be the same in the mean-standard deviation and mean-variance planes.

FIGURE 10–10
Expected Return Related to σ_p and σ_v^2

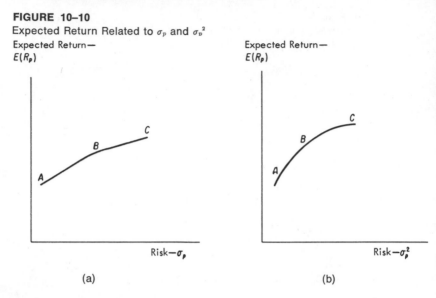

(a)   (b)

Lending and Borrowing

A natural extension of the Markowitz analysis was to consider the problem of building portfolios which included riskless assets and portfolios purchased in part with borrowed funds as well as portfolios of risky assets paid for in full with the investor's equity.

Recall that the efficient frontier for portfolios made up of many risky assets is typically concave from below in the plane whose axes are risk (as measured by the standard deviation) and expected return. For any given period of time, there are assets whose rates of return can be predicted with virtual certainty. Since nuclear holocausts, natural disasters, and revolution are conceivable, the word "virtual" is necessary in the preceding sentence. Nevertheless, most investors have an extraordinarily great confidence that they can predict accurately the rate of return on securities of the federal government for any period which is equal to their maturity. For example, Treasury bills maturing in one year have a precisely predictable rate of return for one year.*

The introduction of riskless assets into portfolios has interesting consequences. In the following diagram the return on a risk-free asset

---

* For government securities with periodic interest payments, the prediction of the rate of return to maturity is somewhat less certain since the rates that will exist when interest payments have to be reinvested cannot be known with certainty.

FIGURE 10–11
The Efficient Frontier with Lending

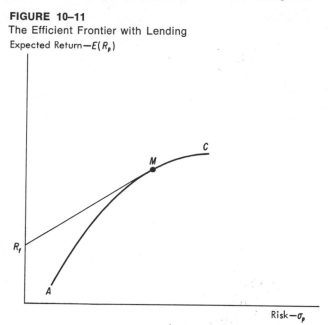

Expected Return—$E(R_p)$

Risk—σ_p

is designated by R_f on the vertical axis. Sharpe[4] and Tobin[5] pointed out that if this alternative exists, it is possible to select portfolios at any given point on the line R_fB defined by the return on the riskless asset and the point of tangency with the efficient frontier of portfolios of risky assets. This follows from the preceding discussion of the combinations of assets.

As we stated above, the rate of return on a portfolio of any two assets, A and B, is always a linear function of the amounts invested in the assets. The formula for the variance of such a portfolio is as follows:

$$\sigma_p^2 = X_i^2\sigma_i^2 + X_j^2\sigma_j^2 + 2X_iX_j\rho_{ij}\sigma_i\sigma_j$$

If the riskless asset is represented by i, and the portfolio of risky assets at the point of tangency by j, it is easy to see that only the second term of the equation has a positive value. The value of the first term is zero because the return on the riskless asset has zero variance; the third term has a value of zero because the return on the riskless asset has a standard deviation of zero. It is also true that the variance of the portfolio of risky assets is a parameter which is given. Thus, the variance of the combined portfolio depends exclusively on the proportion which is invested in the risky assets; or, equivalently, the proportion invested in the risk-free asset.

Since

$$\sigma_p{}^2 = X_j{}^2\sigma_j{}^2;$$

then

$$\sigma_p = X_j\sigma_j$$

In other words, portfolio risk measured by the standard deviation is linearly related to the proportion invested in j (or i). Investing entirely in the risk-free asset is possible; investing entirely in the risky assets at the point of tangency is possible; and achieving portfolios at any point on a straight line between these points is also possible. Clearly, portfolios on this line are preferred to portfolios on the curve AB consisting solely of risky assets, since the former provide more return for given risk.

Sharpe[6] pointed out further that it is possible to hold efficient portfolios on the line R_fB beyond the point of tangency if borrowing is allowed. If one makes the simplifying assumption that one can borrow for the purpose of buying financial assets at the same rate that the investor receives on the risk-free asset, the efficient portfolios beyond the point of tangency lie on a linear extrapolation of the line to the point of tangency. This is illustrated in figure 10–12. Any point on the line R_fBD is now attainable by combining the portfolio of

FIGURE 10–12
The Efficient Frontier with Lending and Borrowing

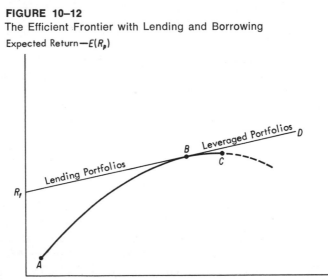

risky assets at the point B with the riskless asset, or by levering the portfolio B by borrowing and investing the funds in B. Portfolios on R_fBD are preferred to portfolios between A and B and between B and C since they offer greater return for a given level of risk or less risk for a given level of return. The efficient frontier is now linear in its entirety. The line R_fBD is Sharpe's capital market line. It relates the expected return on an efficient portfolio to its risk as measured by the standard deviation.

In the diagram above, there is only one portfolio of *risky* assets which is optimal, and it is the same for all investors. Since there is only one portfolio of risky assets which is optimal, it must be the market portfolio. That is, it includes all assets in proportion to their market value. We can now describe the capital market line mathematically in terms of the risk-free rate of interest and the return on the market portfolio. The equation is:

$$E(R_p) = R_f + \frac{[E(R_M) - R_f]}{\sigma_M} \sigma_p.$$

This says the expected return on an efficient portfolio is a linear function of its risk as measured by the standard deviation. The slope of the line has been called the price of risk. It is the additional expected return for each additional unit of risk.

In figure 10–13, the pure rate of interest is 4 percent. The expected return on portfolio M is 10 percent, and its standard deviation is

FIGURE 10–13
The Capital Market Line
Expected Return– $E(R_p)$

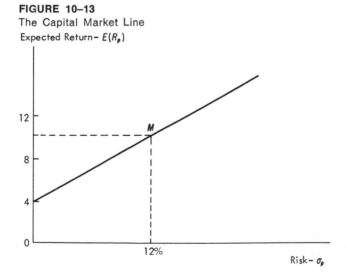

Risk– σ_p

12 percent. An investor who chooses this portfolio earns a reward of 6 percent (10 percent minus 4 percent) for bearing a risk corresponding to a standard deviation of 12 percent. The slope of the line (0.06/0.12) is 0.5. In other words, each additional unit of risk is rewarded with an additional one-half unit of expected return.

In Sharpe's model, individual needs and tastes will determine only the amount of borrowing or lending. The fact that this choice is independent of or separate from the optimal combination of risky assets is called the "separation theorem."[7]

Two qualifications should be noted. If only lending is allowed, the separation theorem will not hold. Consider, for example, figure 10–14.

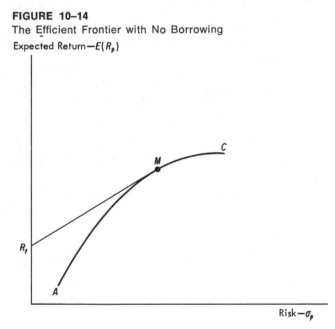

FIGURE 10–14
The Efficient Frontier with No Borrowing
Expected Return—$E(R_p)$

The efficient set of portfolios is not limited to those on the line R_fM. It also includes portfolios of risky assets between M and C. A particular investor might prefer one of the latter to portfolios on R_fM. In other words, there is no single optimum combination of risky assets.

The second qualification is that the efficient frontier of portfolios of risky assets can have linear segments. If the frontier is linear at the point of tangency, there is again, more than one optimum portfolio of risky assets. This is illustrated in figure 10–15. Portfolios B and

FIGURE 10–15
The Efficient Frontier with a Linear Segment

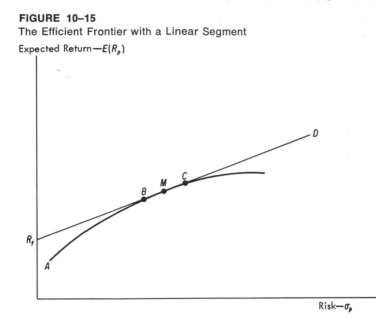

Expected Return—$E(R_p)$

R_f

Risk—σ_p

C, and all those on the line between them, are efficient portfolios of risky assets. Their returns are, of course, perfectly correlated.

UTILITY, RISK AVERSION, AND OPTIMALITY

Markowitz provided the world with a way of analyzing data on each security so as to specify all of the portfolios which were optimum or "efficient" in the sense that no other portfolio could be superior in both dimensions. Specification of an efficient portfolio means indicating the proportion of the investor's assets that should be allocated to each security included in his portfolio. Rational investors who are risk averse would choose to hold one of the efficient portfolios. This section of the chapter discusses the problem that each investor faces in deciding which of the efficient portfolios is optimum for him.

The previous sections of this chapter have been based on the assumption that most investors like high rates of return but dislike risk. The definition of efficient portfolios follows from this. Given predictions about individual securities and their interrelationships, the efficient set is the same for all investors. Since investors' preferences for return vis-à-vis risk are likely to differ, we now need to discuss the ways in which an investor chooses an optimum portfolio from those which are efficient. Optimization implies that something is maximized. We have said that the fact that almost all investors diversify indicates that they do not seek to maximize expected gain, rate of return, or wealth. The underlying principle that guides their behavior is the maximization of expected utility. Utility will be maximized when a given combination of expected return (or wealth) and risk is preferred to all other combinations.

It is now time to relate ideas about efficient portfolios to ideas about utility functions. A utility function is the relationship between wealth and utility. Since money, like other things, has diminishing marginal utility, the relationship looks like figure 10–16. That is, utility increases

FIGURE 10–16
The Utility of Wealth

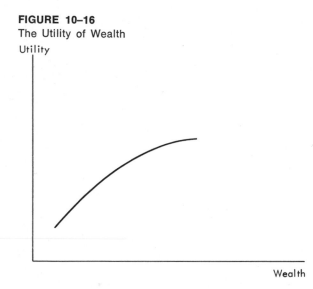

at a decreasing rate as wealth increases. Each additional (marginal) unit of wealth provides less of an increment in utility than the preceding unit. Thus, the curve is concave from below. It would be convenient if it could be shown that portfolios which are efficient in terms of their means and variances were portfolios which maximized the expected utility of the investor. If that were true, all of the individual things about portfolio management which seem plausible would be shown to be consistent with each other.

In beginning the task of attempted reconciliation between utility theory and efficient portfolios, it is unfortunately necessary to characterize the relationship between wealth and utility more explicitly. All that has been said so far is that the curve representing this relationship is concave from below. A concave curve can be described by several mathematical functions. It is not unusual to use some extremely simple quadratic equation such as the following:

$$U(R_p) = a + bR_p - CR_p{}^2$$

where U is the utility of a portfolio, R_p is the rate of return on a portfolio, and a, b and c are constants, b and c being positive, whose values will depend upon the preferences of the investor.

If the utility function is represented by the foregoing equation, it can be shown that expected utility depends only on the mean and variance of the probability distribution of future returns.[8] In other words, for investors whose utility functions are quadratic, the mean-variance approach to portfolio selection is valid. A portfolio which is efficient in terms of the mean and variance will be one which maximizes expected utility.

Since investors like to increase their expected wealth and like to avoid risk or uncertainty, it is possible to imagine different combinations of expected gain and risk which are valued equally by an investor. That is, an investor will be willing to assume greater risk, if he achieves greater expected wealth. The combinations of expected gain and risk which are valued equally lie on a so-called indifference curve which has the shape indicated in figure 10–17.

Each investor has, of course, not a single indifference curve but an infinitely large family of them. Each curve represents the set of expected gains and risks which are equally valued and each investor will seek to invest so that he acquires the greatest expected utility. In figure 10–17, the investor obviously would prefer indifference curve U_3 to U_2, U_2 to U_1, and so forth.

The individual investor is now conceptually prepared to select the optimum portfolio from those constituting the efficient set. The optimum portfolio (i.e., the one which maximizes expected utility) is the one at the point of tangency between the efficient frontier and an indifference curve. In figure 10–18 it can be seen that the investor can do no better than choose the portfolio at point A on the efficient frontier, since no other portfolio is on as high an indifference curve.

This happy reconciliation between utility theory and portfolio theory has a few theoretical blemishes. Some have pointed out that a utility function or relationship which is quadratic is one which eventually will have utility declining as wealth increases. This is of course unsatis-

FIGURE 10–17
Hypothetical Example of the Relationship between Preferences for Expected Return and Risk

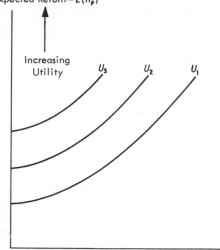

FIGURE 10–18
The Optimal Portfolio with Lending or Borrowing

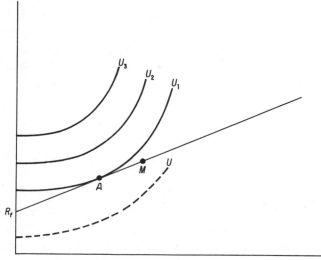

factory, since one of the few things which economists know for sure is that people always prefer more money to less money. There are two escapes from this difficulty. One is to forget about what happens eventually and assume that the relevant range of wealth is one in which utility continues to rise.[9] This is illustrated in figure 10–19.

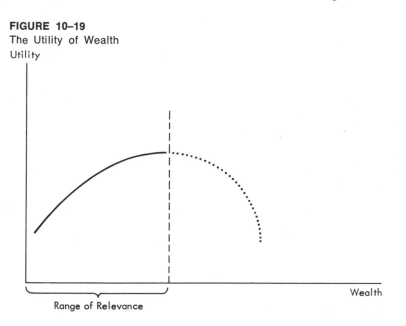

FIGURE 10–19
The Utility of Wealth

Another escape is to say that concavity does not necessarily imply that the relationship is quadratic and that other equations can preserve the concavity without ever implying a maximum value from which utility will decline as wealth increases. The difficulty with these other curves is that efficiency in terms of the mean and variance of a portfolio does not necessarily imply maximization of expected utility. Markowitz has shown, however, that many utility functions can be reasonably approximated by the quadratic.[10]

Another theoretical blemish is the assertion by some that the mean-variance criteria for portfolio selection are inadequate. For example, Baumol[11] has argued that some efficient portfolios may be unacceptable if the best outcomes associated with them are worse than the worst outcomes associated with other efficient portfolios. He considers two portfolios, A and B, which have the characteristics given below. If the returns are normally distributed, $E(R_p) \pm \sigma_p$ can be

TABLE 10–3
Possible Outcomes for Portfolios *A* and *B*

	A	*B*
$E(R_p)$	8%	15%
σ_p^2	4%	16%
σ_p	2%	4%
$E(R_p)$ + σ_p	10%	19%
$E(R_p)$ – σ_p	6%	11%

Source: Baumol, "Expected Gain-Confidence Limit Criterion."

viewed as confidence limits. Baumol's point is that no one should choose portfolio *A* since the best plausible outcome provides a lower rate of return (10 percent) than the worst plausible outcome (11 percent) for portfolio *B*.

A different line of criticism has been advanced by Arditti and others.[12] They argue that investors may be interested in characteristics of distributions of rates of return additional to the mean and variance. In particular, they argue that skewness may be of importance. That is, if the rates of return on the portfolios have the same mean and variance, but different skewness, investors may prefer the distribution which is more skewed to the right.

CONCLUSIONS

One is not excused from reaching tentative conclusions simply because the theoretical development of a field is still rudimentary. A conclusion which is consistent with much that has been observed in the real world and which is satisfying theoretically is the one with which we started: namely, that portfolios which are efficient in terms of their means and variances necessarily maximize expected utility which can be represented by a quadratic equation. Markowitz, perhaps, does the best job of showing that his efficient portfolios are very close to optimum or come very close to maximizing expected utility, even if things other than the mean and variance of the distributions of returns make a difference to or affect the expected utility of investors.[13] Even if the investor is concerned about the magnitude of the expected loss, the maximum expected loss, the probability of a loss, or other attributes of the distribution, the portfolios selected according to those criteria will be very similar to portfolios selected according to their means and variances.

This chapter has been abstract and general. It has indicated the great contribution of Harry Markowitz in defining the efficient set of portfolios for risk-averse investors. These are the portfolios which maximize expected return for given risk or which minimize risk for given expected return. There has been discussion of the ways in which expected returns and risks for individual securities contribute to the expected returns and risks of portfolios. There has also been discussion of utility theory in an effort to show that maximizing expected utility is consistent with risk aversion and provides a way for the individual investor to choose an optimum portfolio from the efficient set in light of his own resources, needs, and tastes.

Almost certainly, the discussion has been at such a high level of generality that it provides little concrete guidance for real investors. After some more similar, general, and abstract discussion of related topics, such as capital asset pricing and risk, we hope to provide some help in translating these general concepts into usable investment procedures.

11

Further Developments in Markowitz's Work: The Capital Asset Pricing Model and Other Things

INTRODUCTION

MARKOWITZ'S WORK dealt with the problem of building efficient portfolios of risky assets. One practical problem required immediate attention; the volume of computations necessary to compute an efficient portfolio was excessive. This problem has been solved. The solution is discussed in the next section of this chapter. The solution has implications for the measurement of risk and is a natural bridge to a major subject: the determination of the price of risk.

A SIMPLIFICATION OF THE MARKOWITZ MODEL

In order to define Markowitz's efficient set of portfolios, it is necessary to know for each security its expected return, its variance, and its covariance with each other security. If the efficient set were to be selected from a list of only 1,000 securities, the volume of necessary inputs and the computational costs would be intolerably large. It would be necessary to have 1,000 statistics for expected return, 1,000 variances, and 499,500 covariances.* It is not realistic to expect security analysts to provide this volume of inputs. If 20 analysts were responsible for the 1,000 stocks, each analyst would be responsible for providing almost 25,000 covariances. The volume of work would

---

* The formula for determining the number of covariances is: $\dfrac{N(N-1)}{2}$.

be intolerable and, furthermore, it seems to be quite difficult to have an intuitive feeling about the significance of a covariance.

Because of this practical difficulty, the Markowitz portfolio model was exclusively of academic interest until William Sharpe suggested a simplification which made it usable.[1] Since almost all securities are significantly correlated with the market as a whole, Sharpe suggested that a satisfactory simplification would be to abandon the covariances of each security with each other security and to substitute information on the relationship of each security to the market. In his terms, it is possible to consider the return for each security to be represented by the following equation:

$$R_i = a_i + b_i I + c_i$$

where R_i is the return on security i, a_i and b_i are parameters, c_i is a random variable with an expected value of zero, and I is the level of some index, typically a common stock price index. In words, the return on any stock depends on some constant (a) plus some coefficient (b) times the value of a comprehensive stock index (say, the S & P "500") plus a random component. Sharpe's simplication reduces the number of estimates that the analyst must produce from 501,500 to 3,002 for a list of 1,000 securities.*

There have been other efforts at simplification derived from Sharpe's ideas. Cohen and Poague[2] suggested that several indexes rather than a single index be used, with the return for each security being related to the index most appropriate for it—perhaps some index of production which is a component of the aggregate Index of Industrial Production of the Federal Reserve Board. Their empirical results suggest that the cost of using simplifications—either Sharpe's or theirs—is small. That is, the portfolios which are efficient as a result of their simplified processes are very similar to the efficient portfolios that result from Markowitz's more complex process. Furthermore, if results are evaluated in terms of the two criteria, expected return and risk, the efficient portfolios from the simple process are insignificantly worse than the efficient portfolios from the complex process.

Sharpe's idea that the return on a security varies with its sensitivity to changes in the market (as measured by b) implies something about the pricing of assets and the relationship of price to this sensitivity.

---

* The number of estimates necessary for the Markowitz model is $\dfrac{N(N + 3)}{2}$; the Sharpe simplification requires $3N + 2$.

These ideas were subsequently elaborated by Sharpe in a now-famous article on the price of risk, which is discussed in the next section.

THE DETERMINATION OF PRICES OF FINANCIAL ASSETS

In his article entitled "Capital Asset Prices: A Theory of Market Equilibrium under Conditions of Risk,"[3] Sharpe considered the relationship between portfolio theory and the determination of the prices of financial assets. Portfolio theory is normative in that it tells how investors should behave. It tells us nothing about the way prices of individual assets adjust to reflect differences in risk. Capital market theory is positive. It describes the market relationships which will result in equilibrium if investors behave in the manner prescribed by portfolio theory. These relationships provide the clue to the relevant measures of risk for portfolios and for individual assets.

The Assumptions

Sharpe's simplifying assumptions are the following: risk aversion; identical time horizons and expectations of all investors with respect to each financial asset; identical borrowing and lending rates; neither taxes nor transaction costs; and, rational investors who seek to hold portfolios efficient in the Markowitz sense. At first, the assumptions underlying Sharpe's model for determining asset prices seem so restrictive or even absurd that the model itself appears unworthy of serious consideration. At the very least, however, the model is useful for understanding some forces which affect asset prices; at the most, the lack of reality in the assumptions will be found to have far less practical importance than most persons would at first believe. After discussing the model, we will look at the assumptions in more detail.

In the preceding chapter we discussed Sharpe's capital market line which relates the expected return on an efficient portfolio to the risk-free rate and the return on the market. The equation was as follows:

$$E(R_p) = R_f + \frac{[E(R_M) - R_f]}{\sigma_M} \sigma_p$$

where $E(R_p)$ is the expected return on a portfolio, R_f is the risk-free return, $E(R_M)$ is the expected return on the market (Index), σ_p is the standard deviation in returns on the portfolio, and σ_M is the standard deviation in returns on the market. Since this holds only for *efficient* portfolios, it does not describe the relationship between the rates of return on individual assets (or inefficient portfolios) and their standard deviations.

Sharpe's capital asset pricing model states that the expected return on *any* asset (or portfolio) is related to the riskless rate and the return on the market as follows:

$$E(R_i) = R_f + [E(R_M) - R_f]\beta_i$$

where R_i is the return on the asset (or portfolio), R_f is the return on a riskless asset, R_M is the return on the market, and β_i (the beta coefficient) is a measure of the sensitivity of the return on the asset to movements in the market. This relationship is similar to, but not the same as, the capital market line which holds only for efficient portfolios. Here, risk is measured by beta rather than by the standard deviation. For efficient portfolios, the two relationships are equivalent. By definition, the riskiness of efficient portfolios is determined exclusively by market movements and their returns are linearly related to both the standard deviation and beta.

The capital asset pricing model or equation is represented graphically in figure 11–1.

If the risk-free rate were 4.0 percent, the expected return on the market were 10 percent, and B_i were 0.5, the expected return on i would be as follows:

$$
\begin{aligned}
E(R_i) &= .04 + 0.5(.10 - .04) \\
&= .04 + 0.5(.06) \\
&= .07
\end{aligned}
$$

The risk premium for asset i is equal to β_i (its beta coefficient) times the risk premium on the market. In this example, since $\beta_i = 0.5$, the risk premium on asset i is .03 and the total return is this premium plus the rate on the riskless asset, or .07.

The above equation and figure deal with the *expected* return on an asset. The relationship between the actual risk premium on an asset (the actual return minus the riskless rate of return) and returns on the market is represented by a regression equation directly derived from the equation dealing with expectations. It is as follows.

$$R_i - R_f = a_i + b_i(R_M - R_f) + c_i$$

where R_i is the actual return on asset i, R_f is the riskless rate of return, a_i is a constant, b_i is the sensitivity of i to the market, R_M is

FIGURE 11–1

The Capital Asset Pricing Model (relationship between expected return and risk for *any* asset or portfolio)

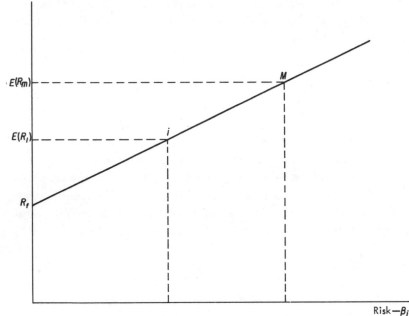

the return on market, and c_i is a term representing variability in R_i not associated with variations in R_M. If actual returns were exactly what was "expected," the value of a_i and c_i would be zero and R_i would be completely explained by R_M, R_f and b_i. Even if random disturbances caused departures from expectations in any single period, on the average a_i and c_i would be equal to zero.

The Sharpe model presents a simple and intuitively appealing picture of financial markets. All investors hold efficient portfolios and all such portfolios move in perfect lockstep with the market. Portfolios differ only in their sensitivity to the market. Prices of all risky assets adjust so that their returns are appropriate, in terms of the model, to their riskiness. This riskiness is measured by a simple statistic, beta, which indicates the sensitivity of the asset to market movements.

If there should be a momentary disequilibrium such that the price of an asset were "too high," causing expected returns to be "too low," investors would sell the asset and its price would return to the equilibrium level. And, the converse would be true for assets whose prices were "too low" and whose expected returns were consequently "too high."

THE REALISM OF THE MODEL

The attractions of a religion based upon faith in Sharpe's model are obvious. There is an understandable predisposition to be a "believer." Yet one is naturally deterred initially by the lack of realism of the assumptions underlying the model. There are two ways to assess the practical implications of this lack of realism. One is to examine the assumptions themselves to see whether their apparent absurdity or lack of realism is as great as seems true at first glance. Another approach is to ignore the realism of the assumptions and to see whether predictions based upon the model are confirmed by experience. Fortunately, it is now generally understood that the value of a model lies in its predictive or explanatory power and that the model cannot be judged by reference to the realism of its underlying assumptions. This point has been expressed with great clarity and persuasiveness by Milton Friedman in a famous essay:[4]

. . . the relevant question to ask about the "assumptions" of a theory is not whether they are descriptively "realistic," for they never are, but whether they are sufficiently good approximations for the purpose in hand. And this question can be answered only by seeing whether the theory works, which means whether it yields sufficiently accurate predictions.[5]

Therefore, we shall pause only briefly to comment on the realism of the underlying assumptions before passing to the more important task of determining the explanatory or predictive power of the model.

Efficient Portfolios

Sharpe's capital market line describes the relationship between risk and rate of return for efficient portfolios. All are perfectly correlated with the market, and, as a consequence, the market is the only source of variation (or risk) for all of them. Either the beta coefficient or the standard deviation is a practical, theoretically satisfying measure of risk.

Most portfolios are not perfectly efficient, and, consequently, they are not perfectly correlated with the market. Thus, part of the variation in returns on such portfolios is not attributable to variation in the market. Whereas the beta coefficient is sufficient to indicate the relative volatility (riskiness) of efficient portfolios, it may not be sufficient to indicate the relative variability (riskiness) of inefficient portfolios.

The total variability of inefficient portfolios or of a single asset is greater than that indicated by the beta coefficient. Thus the question arises as to the appropriate measure of their risk. The standard answer of modern financial theory is that the proper measure of *total* risk for a single asset is a measure of its total variability. But, the measure of risk which determines its risk *premium* is its contribution to the variability of a diversified portfolio. The answer is based on the premise that most investors dislike risk and therefore hold diversified portfolios. The contribution of an asset to the riskiness of a portfolio—its systematic risk—is measured by the familiar beta coefficient, since the beta coefficient of a portfolio is simply a weighted average of the coefficients of its component securities, each individual coefficient being weighted by the value of its security as a percent of the portfolio's total value.

In other words, the risk premium which an asset commands depends upon only that part of its variability which is associated with general market movements and not upon its independent variability. We are led to the startling conclusion that there is no risk premium for an asset if its rate of return has no correlation with rates of return on the market as a whole. The relationship between the beta coefficient of an asset and its correlation with the market is as follows:

$$\beta_{iM} = \frac{\rho_{iM}\sigma_i\sigma_M}{\sigma_M{}^2}$$

where β_{iM} is the beta coefficient between asset i and the market; ρ_{iM} is the correlation coefficient between asset i and the market; σ_i is the standard deviation of i; and, $\sigma_M{}^2$ is the variance of the market.

The equation makes it clear why the beta coefficient would be zero if there were no correlation between asset i and the market. Thus, even if returns on asset i were extremely variable, its beta coefficient would be zero and asset i would not increase the variability or riskiness of a diversified portfolio. And, modern portfolio theory would say that such an asset would not provide a risk premium. The conformity of the world with this theory is discussed in the next chapter.

Single assets are inefficient portfolios. What is true for single assets is true for other inefficient portfolios. The total risk (variability) is greater than that caused by movements in the market. Thus, beta is not a good measure of total risk. But, beta is the proper measure of that part of total risk which can be expected to produce a risk premium. Beta measures so-called systematic risk or volatility—the risk that cannot be eliminated by diversification. Nonsystematic risk can be eliminated by diversification.

Other Assumptions

The assumption of risk aversion seems quite reasonable. The extraordinarily general tendency of investors to hold portfolios of assets rather than the single asset with the greatest expected return is *prima facie* evidence of risk aversion. Although there may be a few investors who enjoy and value risk *per se,* it is difficult to believe that they are numerous or important. Certainly, financial institutions, which accounted in 1970 for more than 60 percent of the value of public trading on the New York Stock Exchange, are not managing investments on behalf of their beneficiaries or clients for the fun of taking chances. The assumption of risk aversion seems well founded.

The next assumption—identical expectations and time horizons for all investors with respect to all assets—is extremely troubling. Much trading on the New York Stock Exchange arises because of differences in expectations. There is accumulating evidence that the ability to have superior forecasting ability and accompanying superior rates of return on one's investments is rare. Some believers in the efficient market hypothesis even advocate that investors not spend the time or money necessary to form independent expectations. Yet they will do it, and one certainly cannot assert that the assumption of identical expectations is realistic. If the assumption is abandoned, we can no longer say, in the context of Sharpe's model, that all investors face the same capital market line. There is no single optimum portfolio of risky assets, and portfolios which are efficient for one investor need not be efficient for another.

Equally unrealistic is the assumption of identical borrowing and lending rates for the investor. The risks involved in lending money to the federal government are less than the risks of lending money to ordinary investors, and investors therefore pay higher rates of interest on borrowed funds than they receive through investment in riskless assets. The effect of the lack of realism of this assumption, unlike that of some of the others, is easily portrayed geometrically. The market line of Sharpe's model has the same slope throughout. If one grants that the investor pays a higher rate of interest to borrow than he earns by lending, the extrapolation beyond the point of tangency should be a line with a smaller slope as in the figure below. Efficient portfolios lie on the line segments $R_l A$ and BD or on the curve AB. (See figure 11–2.) R_l is the lending rate and R_b is the borrowing rate.

FIGURE 11–2

The Relationship between Expected Return and Risk with Different Lending and Borrowing Rates

Expected Return— $E(R_p)$

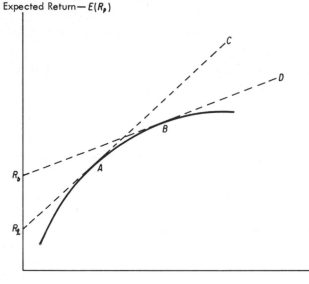

Risk— σ_p

The amount of reduction in the slope of the line beyond the point of tangency obviously depends upon the magnitude of the difference between the borrowing rate for the investor and the lending rate, and this difference depends in part upon the credit rating of the investor. It is also realistic to acknowledge that the rate paid by the investor depends in part on the amount borrowed. This results in an extrapolation beyond the point of tangency which is curvilinear rather than linear.

The final assumption of Sharpe's model is the absence of taxes. The presence of taxes clearly has normative implications for individual investors, since it is after-tax returns which are relevant. Optimum portfolios for taxpayers will not be the same as optimum portfolios for tax-exempt institutions, and optimum portfolios for taxpayers with high marginal rates will not be the same as for those with low marginal rates. The effect of taxes is the same as that of differing expectations. Investors face different capital market lines. The market line for the taxpayer obviously has a different point of tangency on the frontier of efficient portfolios of risky assets and a different intercept on the vertical axis. Despite the obvious point that investors must take account of their own taxes, the implication for the operation of the market for financial assets is not important.

Empirical Evidence on the Explanatory Power of the Model

After this commentary on the lack of realism of the assumptions underlying Sharpe's model, we can now consider the usefulness of the model itself. The two primary implications of Sharpe's model are: (1) that the rate of return on efficient portfolios will be a linear function of their riskiness, as measured by their standard deviation; and (2) that the rate of return on individual assets will be determined by their contribution to the riskiness of portfolios, as measured by the beta coefficient of the returns on the individual assets and the returns on the market.* These implications are borne out in part by observation.

The most visible professionally managed portfolios are mutual funds, and it is not surprising, therefore, that most research in the field of investments relating to portfolios is based upon mutual funds. Earlier, in chapter 4, studies of mutual funds were discussed to see whether their performance was consistent with the efficient market hypothesis. Here, the performance of mutual funds is discussed to test the explanatory power of Sharpe's capital asset pricing model.

There are two excellent studies of mutual fund performance which explicitly discuss the nature of the relationship between the rate of return on portfolios and their riskiness through time. Both are in substantial conformity with the implications of Sharpe's model. The first study was by Sharpe himself.[6] He computed average annual rates of return and standard deviations of those returns for 34 mutual funds for the years 1954–63. The model implies that higher risk portfolios, on the average, will have higher returns. Sharpe's inquiry indicates

---

* More specifically, the risk premium on any asset (or portfolio) will be a linear function of its riskiness as measured by its beta.

that this was true for the 34 funds during the period studied. The correlation between the average returns and their standard deviations was +0.836 indicating that about two thirds of the differences in returns were "explained" by differences in risk.

Further, the relationship between returns and risk was approximately linear, as implied by the model, except for the region of high risk. A possible explanation is that the high-risk portfolios were less efficiently diversified than the others.

This study provides fragmentary support for the view that the capital asset pricing model is a useful explanation of the relationship between portfolio theory and the determination of prices in the market despite the lack of realism of the underlying assumptions.

The second study was by Michael Jensen.[7] His analysis was based on market sensitivity (beta coefficients) rather than standard deviations. As we saw earlier, this allows for the possibility of inefficient portfolios. On the basis of returns on 115 open-end mutual funds for the period 1955–64, he concluded that high returns are associated with high volatility or systematic risk. He also found evidence that beta coefficients are valid measures of risk.

In sum, these two studies of the performance of mutual funds indicate that most of the variation in their rates of return is explainable by differences in their riskiness and, further, that rates of return are approximately a linear function of their riskiness.

Evidence on the second implication of Sharpe's model is less satisfactory. Since all rational investors will hold efficient portfolios, the risk premium on individual assets should depend on the contribution each makes to the riskiness of such a portfolio. The algebra is fairly simple, especially when the relationship is written in the extended form which most authors pass over in their quest for brevity. The relationship is usually written as follows:

$$E(R_i) - R_f = [E(R_M) - R_f]\beta_i$$

Since $\beta_{iM} = \dfrac{\rho_{iM}\sigma_i}{\sigma_M}$, it is easy to see that the riskiness of each asset depends upon the correlation of its return with the market and the standard deviation of its return relative to the standard deviation of the market. If the correlation with the market is 1.0, the riskiness of the individual asset is equal to the ratio of its standard deviation to the standard deviation of the market. If the correlation is 1.0

and the standard deviation of the asset returns is equal to that of the market, the risk premium on the individual asset will be equal to that on the market as a whole. If the correlation with the market is zero, the risk premium will be zero, since such an asset will not add anything to the riskiness of an efficient portfolio.

There have been various efforts to see whether the risk premium on individual assets is explained by the preceding equation. The studies are far from satisfactory in two senses: (1) the evidence is not what true believers would have wished; and (2) the studies suffer from methodological blemishes.

The studies which bear most directly on this point are those of Douglas[8] and Lintner.[9] Both found that the risk premium depended not only on the contribution of each asset to the risk of an efficient portfolio but also to some extent upon independent variability. Recall that this independent variability should not produce a risk premium according to the Sharpe model and the equation cited above.

Scholes and Miller in their review article dealing with this subject conclude that the definitive tests of the second implication of the Sharpe model remain to be carried out.[10] They point out in exhaustive detail the methodological requirements of a definitive test and the shortcomings of the Lintner and Douglas studies. Their conclusion is that much of the apparent conflict between the Douglas-Lintner results and capital market theory is due to bias in the testing procedures. Also, they argue that *ex post* returns could be related to residual variance or nonsystematic risk, although there was no such relationship *ex ante*. The capital market line and the relationship between expected return and perceived risk are of course *ex ante* concepts which cannot be observed.

CONCLUSIONS

Markowitz's original work on portfolio theory has been extended in two important ways. Sharpe indicated the consequences of including riskless assets in the population of assets among which an investor's funds were to be allocated. The inclusion of the riskless asset changes the set of opportunities available to the investor, permitting the creation of portfolios superior to those consisting solely of risky assets with respect to both risk and rate of return. In other words, efficient portfolios including the riskless asset dominate efficient portfolios of risky assets only, with the one exception noted above.

The second major extension of Markowitz's work is also primarily attributable to Sharpe. How are prices of financial assets determined in a world of rational, risk-averse investors with identical expectations operating in a world of perfect markets and without taxes? The resulting model of capital markets is based upon unrealistic assumptions but nevertheless has considerable predictive and explanatory power. The two major testable implications of the model have been tested to a limited extent. The first implication—that rates of return on efficient portfolios will be linearly related to their standard deviations— has been tested by studies of mutual funds and the results are in general conformity with the implications of the model.

The second implication—that risk premiums on individual assets will be determined by the contribution of each to the risk of an efficient portfolio—has been tested with indecisive results. Studies have indicated that risk premiums are in part determined by the independent variability of individual assets, and this finding is contrary to the implications of the Sharpe model. The studies themselves have been subject to valid criticism, and more satisfactory studies remain to be carried out.

The choice of a measure of risk for actual portfolios, not merely perfectly efficient ones, is more complicated. For the purpose of seeing how much risk an investor endured or is likely to endure, measures of total variability in the past or prospective total variability in the future are appropriate. Since inefficient portfolios by definition vary in part for reasons other than movements in the market, the beta coefficient is an inadequate measure of the risk incurred and the standard deviation is acceptable.

If the purpose of the measurement is the evaluation of portfolio performance, both a measure of the risk (volatility) attributable to the market and a measure of total variability can be useful. The beta coefficient provides the basis for one kind of bench mark, namely, the average return on efficient portfolios with equal systematic risk. A measure of total variability on the other hand, provides a better measure of total risk and provides the basis for comparing actual returns with those that would have been achieved on the average from an efficient portfolio of equal total risk.

The capital asset pricing model is interesting and controversial. The controversy centers around the proper measurement of risk, the stability of such measures, and their relationship to rates of return. These subjects are discussed in the next chapter.

12

Risk: Measurement,
Stability, and Relationship
to Return

IN THE EARLY AFTERMATH of the publication of Sharpe's work on the price of risk, a new industry was created to manufacture and distribute beta coefficients. This coefficient was intuitively simple; it measured the sensitivity of the return on an asset or portfolio to changes in returns on the market. Further, it was *the* measure of risk and was therefore in itself sufficient to explain differences in returns among securities and portfolios. A by-product of the manufacture of betas was the manufacture of alphas which are discussed below. This new industry is the primary subject of this chapter, although the subject is first placed in the context of the more general subject—risk and its relationship to return.

SOME EARLY EMPIRICAL STUDIES OF RISK AND RETURN

Bonds

There are two major works on rates of return on bonds which attempt to relate these returns to differences in the riskiness of the asset. The first is a large study by Hickman[1] on realized rates of return for all new corporate issues during the period 1900 to 1943.* Hickman measured the average realized rates of return for bonds of different quality classes as measured by a composite of ratings, assigned by four investment agencies: Moodys, Fitch, Standard Statistics, and

---

* A more precise description of the sample can be found in chapter 2, pp. 41–42.

Poor's.* These quality ratings are intended to indicate differences in the riskiness of bonds—the degree of confidence that one can have in predicting actual realized rates of return.

Hickman's main conclusion is that, on the average, low-grade bonds outperformed high-grade bonds, i.e., rates of return were higher on low-grade bonds. (This was not true of low grades during the Great Depression.) His work indicates the expected relationship between risk and return—the greater the risk, the higher the average realized rates of return (table 12–1). For bonds of the highest quality (least risk),

TABLE 12–1

Realized Life-Span Yields for Bonds Classified by Agency Rating at Offering (1900–1943)

Total Offerings	Agency Rating								
	I	*II*	*III*	*IV*	*V*	*VI*	*VII*	*I-IV*	*V-IX*
	Realized Yield (Percent, per Year)								
Large issues[a]	5.1	5.0	5.0	5.7	5.6	9.2	23.4	5.2	8.6
Small issues	4.7	5.1	6.0	5.6	5.7	10.3	16.2	5.7	7.8

[a] Issues of five million or more.

Note: Figures for grades VIII and IX are not given separately since they are based on a very small number of offerings. Bonds with no rating are also excluded.

Source: Hickman, *Corporate Bond Quality and Investor Experience*, table 39.

the average realized rate of return for the period 1900 to 1943 was 5.1 percent for large issues and 4.7 for small issues; for bonds of the lowest quality (greatest risk), the returns were 23.4 percent and 16.2 percent respectively. Bonds of intermediate quality or riskiness on the average provided intermediate rates of return.

Fisher studied bond yields in an effort to explain risk premiums.[2] He started with the observation that different bonds provide different realized yields and therefore different risk premiums. The latter are defined as the difference between the market yield and the pure rate of interest. Under the conventional assumptions regarding risk aversion by investors, he tried to explain the premiums (higher yields) on some bonds by measuring their greater riskiness. Fisher's hypothesis was that the average risk premium depends on the risk of default and

---

* The composite is a median of individual coded ratings. The rating 1 was assigned to the top grade under each system, the rating 2 to the next grade, etc. See Hickman, *Corporate Bond Quality*, p. 4.

the marketability of the bonds. Risk of default depends, in turn, upon three things: (1) the variability* of corporate earnings after all charges and taxes over the preceding nine years; (2) the length of time since creditors were forced to take a loss; and (3) the ratio of the market value of the common stock of the corporation to the par value of its debt. Marketability is simply measured by the market value of the corporation's publicly traded bonds.

The hypothesis was tested for domestic industrial corporations by cross-section regressions† for five dates: December 31 of 1927, 1932, 1937, 1949, and 1953. For each of these cross sections, the regressions explained approximately three fourths of the variance in the risk premiums. Also, the estimated coefficients were relatively stable over time. For each period, risk premiums are positively related to variability in earnings and negatively related to the length of the period of solvency, the equity-debt ratio, and marketability. (Table 12–2.)

TABLE 12–2
Regression Equations for Estimating Logarithm of Average Risk Premium on a Firm's Bonds as a Linear Function of Logarithms of Earnings Variability, Period of Solvency, Equity/Debt Ratio, and Bonds Outstanding

| | | | | | Coefficient of Logarithm of | | |
| | Number of Obser- | | Con- | Earnings Vari- | Period of | Equity/ Debt | Bonds Out- |
Date	vations	R^2	stant	ability	Solvency	Ratio	standing
1927	71	.756	0.874	+.233	−.269	−.404	−.169
1932	45	.726	1.014	+.248	−.067	−.531	−.286
1937	89	.731	0.949	+.286	−.254	−.491	−.271
1949	73	.786	0.711	+.228	−.124	−.426	−.329
1953	88	.773	1.012	+.228	−.300	−.474	−.363
Total.	366	.750	0.987	+.307	−.253	−.537	−.275

Source: Fisher, "Determinants of Risk Premiums," table 1.

Fisher's findings are not surprising. They are consistent with Hickman's findings and the general theory of investment. The greater the risk or uncertainty of return, the greater the average return or risk premium.

---

* Variability is measured by the coefficient of variation (the standard deviation divided by the mean).

† The regressions are least-square equations, linear in the logarithms of the variables. The coefficients can therefore be interpreted as elasticities. That is, a coefficient indicates the estimated percentage change in the dependent variable associated with a 1 percent change in an independent variable.

Bonds Compared with Stocks

It is perfectly clear that bonds are less risky than stocks when both classes of securities are issued by the same corporation. Since bond-holders have a prior claim to the earnings and assets of the corporation, the rates of return on bonds are less variable and more confidently predicted than rates of return on the common stock. This fact is so obvious that it has not been studied and does not require study.

A more interesting question is whether bonds as a whole are less risky than stocks, and what the relationship is between rates of return on bonds and rates on stocks. It is possible, though not true, that bonds are issued only by corporations whose earnings are extremely uncertain, while corporations with only common stock in their capital structure have extremely stable and predictable earnings. It is thus theoretically possible that bonds as a group are as risky as common stocks. In the real world, things are not this way, since debt-equity ratios tend to be highest for corporations with relatively stable earnings—the utilities, for example. Thus, we would expect to find that, on the average, rates of return for bonds are less than for stocks because returns on bonds are more predictable or less risky. If one compares the results of buy-and-hold policies for bonds and stocks for the period January 1926 to December 1965, investments in bonds would have outperformed investments in stocks in only 23 of the 820 possible holding periods of one or more years.* For the most part, the periods when investment in bonds would have been profitable are of short duration. The exceptions are six periods when the initial investment was made prior to 1931. The lesson is obvious. If one can predict a major depression, investment in bonds can be relatively rewarding by providing superior rates of return. Otherwise, stocks provide higher returns.

Common Stocks

Things have proceeded satisfactorily so far. Average rates of return on low-class bonds have been greater than rates on high-class bonds, and rates on common stocks have on the average generally exceeded rates on bonds. All of this is in accordance with what we would expect in a market dominated by risk-averse investors who expect to receive, and on the average actually receive, superior returns for holding assets

---

* These comparisons are based on tables 2–2 and 2–9.

of greater riskiness. When we turn to common stocks themselves, the results are less clear cut and satisfactory.

Unfortunately, there is no long-established commercial service which provides generally accepted ratings of the riskiness of common stocks. Investigators have usually provided their own rankings. Let us start with the work of Shannon Pratt.[3] Pratt ranked all common stocks on the New York Stock Exchange according to the variability (standard deviation) of their monthly rates of return during two preceding periods of three and five years. For the three-year periods, Pratt ranked stocks for 372 different dates, beginning in January 31, 1929 and ending December 31, 1959. For the five-year periods, there were 348 periods, beginning in January 31, 1931. He then divided common stocks into quintiles on the basis of their historical variability in order to determine the average rate of return for each quintile during subsequent holding periods of one, three, five, and seven years.

His major finding can be easily summarized. If the first quintile includes the stocks with the least variable returns, the second quintile on the average generally has a higher rate of return than the first, the third generally has a higher return than the second, and the fourth generally has a slightly greater return than the third. The performance of the fifth quintile varies. In some instances, it has a lower rate of return than the fourth and a return not very different from the third. In other words, the relationship between risk as measured by historic variability and future returns is somewhat as we would expect, but not completely. Returns generally rise with risk as measured by historic variability, but at a decelerating rate. And, there is some suggestion that rates for the most variable quintile are less than for less variable quintiles.

These results require interpretation or explanation. The results are vaguely disturbing in that they represent a break in the smooth progression from very high-quality bonds with relatively low returns to low-quality bonds, to common stocks, and to common stocks of various degrees of riskiness. The fact that average rates of return on stocks of the lowest quality or with the greatest historic variability are lower than for stocks of higher quality or with smaller historic variability must be discussed.

There are two explanations which preserve the integrity of earlier and more theoretical discussions of risk and return. First, as was explained in the last chapter, according to modern portfolio theory, the risk premium of an individual asset is not measured by its own variability considered in isolation but rather by the contribution which it makes to the variability or riskiness of a diversified portfolio to which it is added. An individual stock with very great variability would be expected to have a rate of return not much greater than that of bonds of high quality if the returns on the stock were not highly correlated with returns on the market as a whole and it therefore did not *add* much to the riskiness of a diversified portfolio. In fact, a common stock whose returns were not correlated at all with returns on the market would be expected to have returns equal to those on a riskless asset.

It is plausible to assert that stocks of the lowest quality or with the greatest historic variability have returns which are less highly correlated with the market than stocks of higher quality and less historic variability. The stocks of the highest quality are often stocks of very large and widely diversified corporations—stocks such as American Telephone, General Electric, General Foods, Standard Oil Company (New Jersey) and so on. These great corporations are often deemed to be "blue chips" or of "investment grade," the implication being that they are of high quality and have rates of return which can be predicted with greater confidence than can those of stocks of lesser quality. Since each of these corporations is very large, and since the profitability of each depends upon levels of demand in almost all parts of the country and in many different industries, it is not surprising that rates of return on these stocks are highly correlated with movements in the general economy and in the market as a whole.

By contrast, stocks of the lowest quality or with the greatest variability are often stocks of relatively small and immature companies whose profitability depends to a greater degree upon things other than the great tides in the movement of the general economy and the general market. It is easy to think of exceptions, but the generalization seems valid. If that is so, the stocks of lowest quality and with greatest historic variability may well have returns that are not highly correlated with the market and which consequently do not contribute as much to the riskiness of diversified portfolios as might be surmised on the basis of their total variability. This explanation amounts to saying that historic variability does not determine the risk premium of an individual asset, and that the deficiency in the measure has important consequences for the stocks with the greatest variability.

There is another explanation of the low average returns on stocks of low quality and great variability. These stocks may represent a kind of lottery ticket to many investors who are willing to accept lower expected returns than they would accept for stocks of higher quality in order to have some chance of very large gain. A person who buys a lottery ticket accepts negative expected returns in order to have some possibility of extremely great rates of return—say, 1 million percent. Low-quality stocks do not present possibilities of such extreme enrichment, but the possibility of very large gains may be sufficient to explain the low average returns on these stocks. Such behavior is not inconsistent with maximization of expected utility as has been shown in a famous article by Friedman and Savage.[4]

There is another form of this explanation. We have already mentioned the fact that the distribution of returns for individual stocks is usually skewed to the right. This positive skewness is to be expected since it is possible to make investments which increase in value by more than 100 percent—especially if the holding period is several years—while it is difficult to make investments which decrease in value by more than 100 percent. (It is theoretically possible to make such investments if one sells short or buys on margin, but instances of such extreme losses are rare.) Positive skewness forces us to consider whether there are attributes of the distributions of returns other than the mean and variance which are of importance to investors. There has not been any divine revelation that investors care only about means and variances; it is quite possible that they like or dislike positive skewness. If they like it, we would expect to find that positive skewness is inversely related to rates of return; if they dislike it, we would expect to find a positive relationship between skewness and the rate of return. It is not absurd to think that there may be a skewness premium (or discount) just as there is a risk premium.

This subject has been studied in a variety of ways. Mosteller and Nogee in some experimental studies found that some investors are willing to pay a high premium for positive skewness.[5] Some of their experimental subjects were willing to accept expectations of loss in order to have some chance of very large gains. The widespread popularity of lotteries attests to the pervasiveness of this attitude. Of more direct relevance is the work of Arditti who studied the relationship between measures of positive skewness and rates of return on common stocks.[6] Arditti concluded that rates of return are positively correlated with variance but inversely correlated with skewness.

Arditti's work makes it necessary to recognize explicitly that the willingness of investors to purchase particular assets depends upon all of their feelings about those assets. For many investors and for almost all academic writers about investment, these feelings are adequately described by the mean of the subjective probability distribution of rates of return—the expected return—and by some measure of dispersion of that probability distribution—the risk. This leads to the familiar references in the academic literature to efficient frontiers which are defined in terms of the mean (expected return) and the dispersion (typically measured by the variance or standard deviation and called risk). However, other things about the probability distribution, say, positive skewness, can be considered relevant by investors, and Arditti tells us explicitly that positive skewness is valued and therefore is negatively associated with the required rate of return. Such a finding could explain why Pratt's study indicated that the most volatile stocks had on the average lower returns than somewhat less volatile stocks.

Despite various plausible explanations of Pratt's findings, most serious work has centered on efforts to test and perhaps confirm the theoretically satisfying capital asset pricing model of Sharpe. Since this model indicates that the beta coefficient is *the* measure of risk and fully accounts for risk premiums, the work has dealt with problems of estimating beta, its stability, and its relationship to rates of return.

Portfolios

Now let us consider the relationship between the riskiness of portfolios and their returns. First, we will consider those most visible of professionally managed portfolios, mutual funds.

Although rates of return on mutual funds have been measured and studied many times, the relationship between their riskiness and their rates of return have been studied less often. Perhaps the best study is that by Michael Jensen.[7] Jensen studied 115 mutual funds for the period 1955–64. In addition, annual data for 56 of the 115 funds were available for the preceding ten years, 1945–54. Jensen was interested in studying evidence concerning the efficiency of the market for securities as well as the ability of mutual fund managers to pick individual securities. We are interested here only in the results bearing on the relationship between the riskiness of the funds and their rates of return.

Jensen's main relevant findings were as follows:

1. Estimates of systematic risk (the beta coefficients) seem to be insensitive to the length of the period for which the estimates are made and to be stationary through time.

2. The relationship between systematic risk and return for mutual funds is consistent with the implications of Sharpe's model— that is, returns seem to be a linear function of risk as measured by the beta coefficient.

If one could assume that mutual funds were efficient portfolios, the returns would also be a linear function of the standard deviation of the returns. This is equivalent to the systematic risk of the portfolio, which in turn, is determined exclusively by the proportion of the portfolios invested in the risk-free asset. (See chapters 10 and 11.) Of course for efficient portfolios, systematic risk is the only risk there is. All of the variations in the returns of the portfolio are accounted for by movements in the market. Thus, one can say that risk is a linear function of either the standard deviation or of the beta coefficient, since the statements would be equivalent.*

For inefficient portfolios (and mutual funds may be inefficient), it is necessary to distinguish between the variability which is attributable to the market and measured by the beta coefficient and the total variability which can be measured by the standard deviation or the variance. Sharpe's main message with respect to the risk premiums of individual assets or portfolios was that only systematic risk counted. (See chapter 11.) Therefore, although we can be indifferent as to whether we use the beta coefficient or the standard deviation for efficient portfolios, we must use only systematic risk as measured by the beta coefficient for portfolios in the real world, since they may not be efficient.

Jensen's study indicates that on the average mutual funds with greater risk as measured by their beta coefficients with the market, had higher returns than funds with less risk. Estimates of systematic risk and net returns for funds classed by type are given in table 12–3. On the average, rates of return increase with the degree of risk (β).

Jensen's finding was confirmed subsequently in a study of mutual funds by Friend, Blume, and Crockett.[8] In their study of 299 leading funds for the years 1960–68, they found that high-risk funds emphasizing growth had higher average rates of return than low-risk or medium-risk funds. These results are summarized in table 12–4. In a postscript the authors indicate that in the declining market during 1969–70, the high-risk funds *always* suffered the greatest losses. All of this is in accordance with our expectations regarding the relation-

---

* It will be recalled that Sharpe, in his study of mutual funds, assumed the portfolios were efficient and therefore used the standard deviation as his measure of risk. (See chapter 4.)

TABLE 12–3
Average and Median Values of Systematic Risk and Net Return for Various Classes of Funds (data are for 1964)

Type of Fund [a]	No. of Funds in Class	Average Values		Median Values	
		$\hat{\beta}$	$_{10}R^*_{1964}$	$\hat{\beta}$	$_{10}R^*_{1964}$
Growth.	31	.970	1.018	.919	1.043
Growth-income	30	.941	1.004	.940	.998
Income-growth	15	.856	1.037	.834	1.059
Income.	9	.674	.754	.845	.790
Balanced	30	.645	.860	.603	.848

[a] As classified by Wiesenberger *Investment Companies.*
Source: Jensen, "Risk, Pricing of Capital Assets," p. 223.
* Annual return compounded continuously for 10 years ending 1964.

TABLE 12–4
Investment Performance of Mutual Funds (January, 1960–June, 1968)

Risk Class (Beta Coefficient)	Number in Sample	Mean Beta Coefficient	Mean Variance	Mean Return
Low risk (β = .5 to .7).	28	.614	0.000877	0.091
Medium risk (β = .7 to .9).	53	.786	0.001543	0.106
High risk (β = .9 to 1.1).	22	.992	0.002304	0.135

Source: Friend, Blume, Crockett, *Mutual Funds and Other Institutional Investors,* Appendix table 3–2, p. 150.

ship between risk and rate of return in a market dominated by risk-averse investors.

These results find further support in the *Institutional Investor Study Report of the Securities and Exchange Commission.*[9] The study is of particular interest because it deals with portfolios administered by bank trust departments and life insurance companies as well as those of registered investment companies. The findings which are relevant in the context of this chapter are summarized in tables 12–5 through 12–8.

Table 12–5 presents average monthly rates of return for 236 open-end registered investment companies for the period January, 1960 to December, 1969.* The funds are classified by volatility which is measured by the beta coefficient between fund returns and the Stan-

* There are at least nine observations for each of the funds.

TABLE 12–5

Rates of Return and Volatility of 236 Open-End Registered Investment Company Funds

Period	Volatility Range (Beta Range)	No. Funds	Average Values (Unweighted)	
			Monthly Return (Percent/Month)	Volatility Measure (Beta)
January 1960–	0–0.4	4	0.40	0.20
December 1969	0.4–0.8	43	0.57	0.69
	0.8–1.0	63	0.69	0.91
	1.0–1.2	56	0.69	1.08
	1.2+	70	0.81	1.51
	Total	236	0.70	1.08
January 1960–	0–0.4	7	0.50	0.18
December 1964	0.4–0.8	53	0.82	0.65
	0.8–1.0	44	0.83	0.91
	1.0–1.2	34	0.64	1.10
	1.2+	20	0.90	1.28
	Total	158	0.78	0.88
January 1965–	0–0.4	4	0.17	0.22
December 1969	0.4–0.8	28	0.37	0.69
	0.8–1.0	69	0.63	0.92
	1.0–1.2	50	0.60	1.09
	1.2+	85	0.93	1.53
	Total	236	0.69	1.13

Source: *Institutional Investor Study Report of the Securities and Exchange Commission*, table IV–104.

dard and Poor's "500" Index. Table 12–6 contains the same figures for 125 of the funds with complete data for the period. On average, there is a positive relationship between volatility (risk) and rates of return.

Table 12–7 presents rates of return by volatility class for 48 pooled employee benefit and common trust funds managed by 40 of 50 bank trust departments administering the largest amounts of total assets at the end of 1967.* The period covered is 1967–69.

The findings with respect to separate accounts of life insurance companies are summarized in table 12–8. The numbers refer to 80 accounts created in the period 1965–69. The length of the period covered varies among accounts.

At first glance, the table suggests that in contrast to rates of return

---

* At the end of 1969, approximately $130 billion of common stock were in these funds. This was 70 percent of the assets administered by all bank trust departments.

TABLE 12–6

Rates of Return and Volatility for 125 Open-End Registered Investment Company Funds

Period	Volatility Range (Beta Range)	No. Funds	Average Values (Unweighted) Monthly Return (Percent/Month)	Volatility Measure (Beta)
January 1960–	0–0.4	3	0.43	0.23
December 1969	0.4–0.8	35	0.63	0.68
	0.8–1.0	44	0.79	0.91
	1.0–1.2	30	0.86	1.07
	1.2+	13	1.05	1.33
	Total	125	0.78	0.91
January 1960–	0–0.4	4	0.60	0.16
December 1964	0.4–0.8	47	0.83	0.65
	0.8–1.0	43	0.82	0.91
	1.0–1.2	22	0.73	1.11
	1.2+	9	1.14	1.30
	Total	125	0.82	0.85
January 1965–	0–0.4	3	0.17	0.26
December 1969	0.4–0.8	22	0.46	0.69
	0.8–1.0	46	0.68	0.91
	1.0–1.2	30	0.73	1.08
	1.2+	24	1.20	1.41
	Total	125	0.74	0.99

Source: *Institutional Investor Study Report of the Securities and Exchange Commission*, table IV–103.

TABLE 12–7

Rates of Return and Volatility of 27 Employee Benefit Funds and 21 Common Trust Funds Managed by 40 Bank Trust Departments, 1967–69

Volatility Range (Beta Range)	No. Funds	Average Values (Unweighted) Monthly Return (Percent/Month)	Volatility Measure (Beta)
0.4–0.8	7	0.33	0.65
0.8–1.0	19	0.49	0.92
1.0–1.2	20	0.48	1.09
Over 1.2	2	1.42	1.39
Total	48	0.50	0.97

Source: *Institutional Investor Study Report of the Securities and Exchange Commission*, table V–22.

TABLE 12–8

Rates of Return and Volatility of 80 Separate Accounts of Life Insurance Companies, 1965–1969

Volatility Range (Beta Range)	No. Accounts	Average Values (Unweighted)	
		Monthly Return Percent/Month	Volatility Measure (Beta)
0–0.4.	3	0.53%	0.20
0.4–0.8.	13	0.32	0.64
0.8–1.0.	30	0.42	0.93
1.0–1.2.	24	0.54	1.08
Over 1.2	10	0.36	1.36
Total.	80	0.44	0.95

Source: *Institutional Investor Study Report of the Securities and Exchange Commission.* table VI–116.

on portfolios of registered investment companies and bank trust departments, the rates for separate accounts of life insurance companies do not exhibit any clear cut relation to volatility. On closer inspection, this supposition seems unfounded. The monthly returns are unweighted averages of the individual fund returns. Since there are only three funds in the lowest risk class, little importance can be attached to its average. In the highest risk class there are 10 funds, but the average number of observations per fund is only 27.1 as compared to 41–52 for the other classes. If these two classes are disregarded, the expected relationship between risk and return is present.

THE BETA (AND ALPHA) COEFFICIENTS

In the late 1960s and early 1970s, there was a general and enthusiastic endorsement of the value of beta coefficients as a measure of risk and an indicator of reasonable expectations of the returns on portfolios, given specified behavior of the market. Beta coefficients were embedded in an intricate, comprehensive, and plausible theory and had the further advantage of an esoteric name. Some leading brokerage firms and others began to manufacture and distribute betas on a large scale.

Controversies quickly arose. One of the least important was over the method of estimating betas for individual assets. The practical importance of the differences between the best and worst estimates was never large.[10]

Of greater apparent importance, initially, was the instability of betas for individual stocks. Even betas produced by the most sophisticated methods were quite unstable. Betas based on actual data for a previous period, say, two years, typically accounted for less than one third of the variation among betas of the same stocks in the future.

The seriousness of this fact is not great when one realizes that one is interested in betas for portfolios rather than for their component assets. The law of large numbers helps somewhat. Estimates of beta are sometimes too high and sometimes too low. These discrepancies are partially offsetting with the result that estimates for portfolios are often quite good predictors of future betas for portfolios.

The virtue of the historical beta as a predictor of the future beta is quite sensitive to the correlation between the actual portfolio and the market index for which the beta is relevant. If the correlation were 1.0, the historical beta would be a perfect predictor. That is, if a portfolio always moved in perfect lockstep with the market index, the beta of the portfolio would always predict the portfolio's response to the market. A portfolio with a beta of 0.5 would move up and down half as fast as the market, a portfolio with a beta of 0.75, three fourths as fast, and so forth.

Skepticism about the value of betas became acute in some financial institutions when they calculated betas for their own portfolios and discovered that future reactions to the market were quite different from expectations created by the historical betas. A portfolio supposed to decline only half as much as the market sometimes declined much more and sometimes much less. This was true whether the historical beta for the portfolio was estimated by calculating its own average sensitivity to the market in the past or whether it was considered to be a weighted average of the betas of the component assets.

The beta manufacturers as well as the academic creators of the underlying theory were quick to seek an explanation, and two explanations were found. One was obvious and accepted, and the other was complex and controversial.

The first explanation is already somewhat familiar. Just as betas for individual stocks are poor predictors of future sensitivity to market movements, so are betas of other inefficient portfolios, even though they be composed of many stocks. Historical betas are accurate predictors of highly diversified, efficient portfolios; they are poor predictors of inefficient portfolios.

Investors who believe that markets are efficient and who themselves are risk averse will seek to hold efficient portfolios. Since it is a trivially simple task to create efficient portfolios, betas can be for them effective tools. For other investors, betas and most of the other apparatus of the modern science of investment are of less use.

The second explanation is based on other disturbing departures in the real world from Sharpe's model of the determination of risk premiums. As has been stated, according to Sharpe, the expected risk premium on any asset is the product of the risk premium on the market and the asset's beta coefficient. Returns in the real world are not determined in quite that way.

A model, more complicated than Sharpe's, but not fundamentally in conflict with it, states that the expected return on an asset is expressed by the following relationship:

$$E(R_i) = E(R_z)(1 - \beta_i) + E(R_M)\beta_i$$

where the symbols have their familiar meaning except for the new symbol R_z. This symbol refers to the return on a portfolio designed so as to have no correlation with the market.* R_z is often called the "beta factor" or the "second factor," since it is incorporated in a two-factor model of returns and has a coefficient which is a function of beta.[11]

The main finding of Black, Jensen, and Scholes is that the risk premium on an asset is not strictly proportional to its beta. For the periods of their study, the returns on stocks with high betas were lower than would be expected on the basis of Sharpe's one-factor model; the returns on low beta stocks were higher.

A practical implication of the two-factor model is that during the period of the study, 1926–66, superior returns for any level of risk could have been obtained, by levering low-risk (beta) stocks to the desired level of risk.

Those who questioned the usefulness of betas, either because of their instability or because they were not related to returns in exactly the way implied by Sharpe's model, should think again. Efficient portfolios have stable betas and the relationship between betas and returns, though more complex than implied by Sharpe, is still rational and observable and useful in managing money.

---

* This portfolio also has the lowest variance of all portfolios which have no correlation with the market.

Alpha

The regression form of Sharpe's capital asset pricing model is as follows:

$$R_i - R_f = a_i + b_i(R_M - R_f) + c_i$$

where the symbols have their familiar meaning. The *expected* return on an asset depends exclusively on its beta; but the real world is untidy, and allowance must be made for departures from theoretical expectations. Nevertheless, Sharpe's model implies that the average value of a_i and c_i will be zero.

The work of Black, Jensen, and Scholes indicates that that was not true for New York Stock Exchange Stocks for the period 1926–66.[12] Alphas (a's) were positive for stocks with low betas and were negative for stocks with high betas. Thus, the former stocks were more rewarding for the risk—as measured by beta—to which they subjected their owners.

The firms which manufacture and distribute betas also manufacture and distribute alphas, once considered only an incidental by-product. Now, while betas are valued because they enable the investor to control his risk, alphas are valued because they may indicate opportunities for superior or inferior return for a given degree of risk.

CONCLUSIONS

Adam Smith and undoubtedly his forebears understood that risk was related to rates of return. People do not like risk and if they expect to incur it, they expect to be paid. This payment is now called the risk premium or price of risk.

Prior to William Sharpe's article, "Capital Asset Prices: A Theory of Market Equilibrium under Conditions of Risk,"[13] discussions of risk and its relation to return were theoretically casual or exercises in brute empiricism. Hickman and Fisher showed that realized rates of return on lower-class bonds were higher than on higher-class bonds. Various authors pointed out that rates on common stock were generally higher than on bonds. Pratt and others pointed out that generally stocks whose returns were more variable had average returns higher than those on less variable stocks.

Sharpe's article finally provided a theoretically satisfying definition of risk and gave focus to most subsequent, serious work and controversy. He pointed out that rational, risk-averse investors in an efficient market would hold efficient portfolios (in Markowitz's sense of the term), and that therefore the proper measure of risk was the contribution of an asset to the riskiness of an efficient portfolio. That measure is the beta coefficient. The cult of beta and the beta industry quickly flowered.

Skeptics pointed out two weaknesses in beta orthodoxy: (1) betas are unstable; and (2) returns are not proportional to betas. It is true that betas of individual stocks and other inefficient portfolios are unstable. Betas of efficient portfolios, however, are stable. Indeed, they are perfectly stable by definition. Large, diversified portfolios, such as unspecialized mutual funds and many pension funds, are sufficiently efficient to have quite stable betas.

The fact that returns are not strictly proportional to betas—a proportionality implied by Sharpe's capital asset pricing model—was explained by Black, Jensen, and Scholes.[14] By expanding Sharpe's model to include a second factor—returns on a portfolio uncorrelated with the market—they explained the fact that high-beta stocks had returns lower than Sharpe would have led one to expect and low-beta stocks had higher returns.

Beta remains a valuable tool and the beta industry, consequently, is in good health.

13

The Evaluation of the
Performance of Portfolios

IN 1970, financial institutions and investment advisers managed more than $350 billion in assets on behalf of others. Bank trust departments managed almost $300 billion; and mutual funds, closed-end investment companies, investment advisers, and brokers with discretionary accounts accounted for more than $100 billion, in addition. It is not surprising that a strong interest has developed in objective and rational measures of the relative skill with which these financial agents discharge their responsibilities on behalf of their clients.

The first major effort to specify a system of objective measurements was carried out by a group of academic authors on behalf of the Bank Administration Institute (BAI).[1] Although the study leaves some questions unanswered and provides some answers which are controversial, it does cover much of the necessary ground. The next section of this chapter discusses the major findings of that study. The final section of the chapter deals with some of the controversial answers and some of the unanswered questions.

THE STUDY OF THE BANK ADMINISTRATION INSTITUTE

The study of the Bank Administration Institute was written by academic specialists with the advice and help of a group of bankers experienced in investments. That fact is important to interpreting subsequent statements in this chapter which refer to the unanimous opinions of the academic committee and of the so-called steering committee of practical men.

Rate of Return

There was unanimous agreement—which must be expected by the readers of this book—that it is desirable to evaluate performance in two dimensions: rate of return and risk. After an introductory chapter, the second chapter of the report discusses measuring the rate of return.

The authors unanimously agreed that the rate of return should be based upon changes in the market value of assets held and the value of dividends, interest, and other payments received. (It is pleasant to reflect that it is no longer necessary, for most purposes, to discuss the book value of assets.) In some contexts it may be necessary to distinguish between dollars in the form of interest and dividends and dollars in the form of capital gains. Clearly, it is returns after taxes which matter to the investor. When taxes exist and are different for different kinds of dollars, returns from the various sources must be segregated to allow accurate computation of relevant taxes. Also trustees of personal trusts must deal even-handedly with lifetime beneficiaries and "remaindermen." Lifetime beneficiaries receive *income* (dividends, interest, and so forth), and remaindermen receive *principal*. Trustees must choose investments which divide the total return in a reasonable way between the conflicting claims of the two classes of beneficiaries.

Similarly, many trustees of endowed institutions feel that they are legally proscribed from spending principal or capital gains. Trustees feeling such legal constraints understandably prize income dollars more highly than other dollars since the former can be either spent or reinvested while the latter cannot be spent. Considerable doubt was cast upon the necessity for such concern or restraint by trustees of endowed institutions in a recent serious study on the subject undertaken at the behest of The Ford Foundation.[2] This study suggests that the law of trusts does not apply to endowed institutions, and that trustees have considerable latitude in defining income to include capital gains.

Despite the fact that some investors need to take account of taxes and others need to distinguish between some kinds of dollars and others, the following discussion refers to investors who pay no taxes and who need make no such distinctions. This group certainly includes the managers of private, noninsured pension funds whose assets exceed $150 billion and also probably includes many endowed institutions. The problem of generalizing the comments in the following pages to include investors subject to taxes is not difficult. The obvious adjustments are to measure returns after taxes and to be sure that comparisons among portfolios be limited to those whose owners or beneficiaries are in similar tax brackets.

Keeping in mind that the discussion relates to tax-exempt investors, the gentle reader can now proceed to a consideration of the problem of measuring returns. One prominent candidate for the role of such measurement is the internal rate of return. This is the rate of return which is calculated in finding the yield to maturity of a bond. It is the rate of discounting of the cash flows associated with an investment which makes their algebraic sum equal to zero. The following hypothetical example makes this clear.

If a $100 bond paying 5 percent at the end of each year is purchased for $87.53, and sold at the end of three years for $100, the cash flows are as follows:

TABLE 13–1
Example of Calculation of the Internal Rate of Return

Year	Cash Flows (Year End)	Present Value (Discounted at 10 Percent)
0	–$ 87.53	–$87.53
1	+ 5.00	+ 4.545
2	+ 5.00	+ 4.130
3	+ 105.00	+ 78.855
		$\Sigma = 0$

The 10 percent rate of discount makes the algebraic sum of the cash flows equal to zero and is the internal rate of return. It measures the performance of the initial investment and assumes any additions to the original investment earn the same rate of return.

The internal rate of return is an interesting and useful number. It tells the rate at which the assets of a fund are growing because of returns on investments. All prudent fund managers and investors will want to know the internal rate of return on their investments.

Nevertheless, the internal rate of return is not ideal for evaluating the relative skill with which different portfolios are managed. Its blemish is that it is affected by some things which the fund manager does not control. To use a number for the purpose of evaluating the fund manager when the number is affected by things not controlled by that manager is obviously a mistake. The thing which affects the internal rate of return and which the fund manager typically does not control is the time at which new funds are received for investment and the time at which funds must be disbursed to the owner or beneficiary.

For illustration, consider two fund managers of two portfolios on January 1, 1973. The two fund managers on that date have identical judgements about investments with the result that the portfolio managed by each has the same percentage distribution of funds among particular assets. On January 2, the first fund manager receives for investment a large amount of money from the trustor or the individual investor; the second fund manager does not. The first fund manager distributes the new capital among existing assets so as to preserve the same percentage distribution. For six months the market goes up very rapidly providing large positive returns for both portfolios. On July 2, the first fund manager must make a large payment from the fund and the second fund manager receives a large check for investment. After the disbursal and the new investment, both fund managers continue to have identical judgements and portfolios with identical distributions of funds among particular assets. The market then goes down rapidly for six months. For the year 1973, the first fund manager's portfolio will have had a higher internal rate of return than that of the second fund manager's portfolio despite the fact that at every moment in time each had identical judgements and exhibited identical skills. It is that shortcoming of the internal rate of return which must be eliminated.

There has been some misunderstanding in the financial community about the use of the word "time" or "timing" in discussing this subject. Obviously, the fund manager can control shifts between common stocks and cash or fixed-dollar assets in an effort to judge the timing of general market movements, and any measure of the fund manager's skill should reflect his skill in making such judgements. The fund manager, however, does not control the time at which funds are received or at which they must be disbursed, and the measure should not reflect this timing.

There is an easy way to make the measurement of the rate of return insensitive to the timing of receipts and disbursals. In the BAI report, this measure has the possibly confusing name, "time-weighted rate of return." Although the name may be confusing, the principle is not. The time-weighted rate of return is logically equivalent to the rate of return on mutual fund shares which are bought and redeemed at net asset value per share. The investor who purchases shares in a mutual fund can measure the rate of return on his investment by knowing the price he paid, the value of payments received, and the price of the shares at the end of the period in question. He does not need to know the time or amount of new investments in the fund by other investors who bought shares or the time or amount of disbursals from the fund to shareowners who redeemed their shares. The individual investor's rate of return is totally insensitive to those injections of capital into or withdrawals of capital from the fund.

And so it is with the time-weighted rate of return for portfolios other than mutual funds. The way in which the time-weighted rate of return is calculated is illustrated in the BAI report, and their illustration is reproduced in figure 13–1 and table 13–2.

FIGURE 13–1

Changes in Value of a Fund with Net Investment and Disinvestment

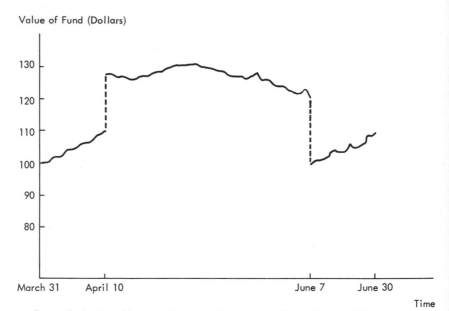

Value of Fund (Dollars)

Source: Lorie et al., *Measuring Investment Performance of Pension Funds*, p. 75.

Fluctuations in the value of a hypothetical fund are shown in figure 13–1 and the fund values and cash flows are summarized in table 13–2.[3] The market value of the fund increased from $100 on March 31 to $110 on April 10. There were no contributions or withdrawals

TABLE 13–2
Summary of Fund Values and Cash Flows

	March 31	April 10	June 7	June 30
Value of fund before				
contribution.	$100	$110	$120	$105
Net contribution	0	15	–25	0
Value of fund after				
contribution.	100	125	95	105

Source: Lorie et al., *Measuring Investment Performance of Pension Funds*, p. 76.

during the period. On April 10, there was a $15 contribution, raising the fund value to $125. On June 7, the $125 fund was worth $120, and there was a withdrawal of $25. No further contributions or withdrawals were made through June 30, when the value of the fund was $105. The time-weighted rate of return for the period March 31 to June 30 is a weighted average of the internal rates of return for each of the three subperiods.*

The academic specialists and the steering committee unanimously recommended that the time-weighted rate of return be used in evaluating the skill with which pension fund assets are managed. Obviously, the time-weighted rate of return is also useful for other kinds of portfolios.

It can be costly to calculate the time-weighted rate of return precisely. The internal rate of return requires only that one know the value of the portfolio at the beginning of a period and at the end, and the time and amount of all flows into and from the fund. To calculate the time-weighted rate of return, one needs to know not only those things but also the market value of the fund at the time of each cash flow. Determining that market value for hundreds or thousands of different funds many times a week or month could be quite burdensome. As a result, the BAI report suggests two methods of approximation, each providing estimates of the time-weighted rate of return which would very seldom be in error by more than ten basis points per year. The methods are the linked internal rate of return method and the regression method. The former requires the

---

* In terms of an annual rate of interest compounded continuously it can be calculated as follows:

$$i = \left(\frac{365}{91}\right) \ln \left[\left(\frac{110}{100}\right) \left(\frac{120}{110 + 15}\right) \left(\frac{105}{120 - 25}\right) \right]$$

The term 365/91 converts the quarterly rate to an annual rate.

determination of the market value of assets once a month; the latter, once a quarter.*

Risk

It will not be surprising to any reader who has persisted to this point that the BAI report recommends that performance must take account not only of the rate of return on assets but also of the risk to which the investor has been subject. It is undesirable or unwise for all investors to subject themselves to the same degree of risk, and therefore not all investors should expect the same rate of return. The elderly widow whose primary objective is the protection of her assets from loss cannot expect as high a return as the more venturesome young physician whose primary objective is to maximize the value of his holdings 25 years in the future. If one knew only the rates of return on the widow's and the physician's respective portfolios, one would not be in a position to judge the skill with which their investment advisers had done their work.

It is desirable to measure risk for another reason. In judging the significance of any observed difference in the rates of return on two portfolios, it is desirable to be able to distinguish between differences which can reasonably be attributed to random fluctuations in returns on each portfolio and differences which could only be attributed reasonably to differences in the skill with which the portfolios have been managed. This is an ancient and ordinary problem in statistical inference and all of the usual principles apply in this context. The distinction between random differences and other differences can be made only if there is knowledge of the variability in each series. Any observed difference for any particular period between rates on two different portfolios can more confidently be attributed to differences in skill if rates on each portfolio have been rather constant than if rates have been extremely variable. Since estimates of risk are typically based on variability in rates of return, measurements of risk seem to be useful in distinguishing between random and other differences in rates as well as for the more primary purpose of evaluating rates in terms of risks which were assumed.

Some of the difficulties of measuring risk have been discussed in chapter 12, and we will not repeat that discussion. The Bank Adminis-

---

* For details of these methods, see BAI report, pp. 21–26. Computer programs for producing these estimates are available from the BAI in a library of programs tied to the BAI report and entitled COMVEST.

tration Institute recommends the use of the mean absolute deviation of the time-weighted rates of return as its measure of risk. The mean absolute deviation is preferred to the standard deviation because the former is more stable through time and therefore is a more reliable estimate of risk.

It can and has been argued that a more appropriate measure of risk is the beta coefficient—the measure of the sensitivity of the portfolio to market movements rather than a measure of total variability such as is provided by the mean absolute deviation. As has already been discussed, in his theoretical articles William Sharpe argued that risk premiums depend only on systematic risk (sensitivity to market movements) and that risk should therefore be measured by the beta coefficient of rate of return on market returns.* If all investors held perfectly diversified portfolios, Sharpe's argument is persuasive. If all portfolios are perfectly diversified, risk as measured by the beta coefficient is equivalent to risk as measured by the standard deviation or the mean absolute deviation.

We must recognize, however, that some investors do not hold efficiently diversified portfolios. If a portfolio is imperfectly diversified, not all variations in rates of return will be accounted for by movements in the market. Some measure of total variability is therefore justified.

The evaluation of portfolio performance in terms of total dispersion measures not only the manager's ability to pick winners but also his ability to diversify efficiently. In contrast, if risk is measured by market sensitivity alone, performance evaluation depends only on the manager's ability to choose investments with higher rates of return than others with similar levels of systematic risk. Since total risk cannot be smaller than systematic risk, evaluation in terms of total dispersion will be less favorable than evaluation in terms of systematic (undiversifiable) risk, in a period when the rate of return on the market exceeds that on the riskless asset. Conversely, if the return on the riskless asset is greater than the return on the market, evaluation in terms of total dispersion will be more favorable to portfolio managers.[4]

Combining Measurements of Rate of Return and Risk

It is easy to rank things if only one criterion is relevant; it is more difficult if there is more than one. Since two criteria are necessary for evaluating portfolio performance, the problem of combining these

---
* See chapter 11, pp. 203–5.

criteria is sufficiently difficult to warrant discussion, and an excellent discussion has been provided by Bower and Wippern.[5]

Consider the four portfolios whose risks and returns for a given period are represented in the following diagram:

FIGURE 13–2
The Relationship between Risk and Return for Four Hypothetical Portfolios

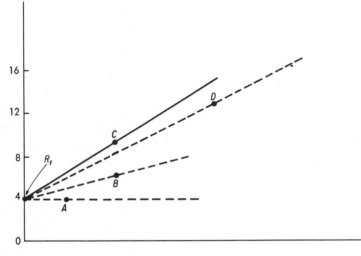

It is clear that portfolio C is superior to portfolio B in that C provides more return for the same risk. It is not immediately clear whether D is superior or inferior to any of the other portfolios; the same can be said for portfolio A. Although D provides more return, it also provides more risk; A provides less risk and less return. Whether the additional return for D is adequate compensation for the additional risk and whether the reduced risk for A is worth the foregone return are the interesting questions for which the answers may not be intuitively obvious.

The standard answer is to talk about the amount of return per unit of risk and to judge that portfolio superior which provides the most return per unit of risk. The reasoning behind that answer is simple. In figure 13–2 assume that the risk-free rate of return is 4 percent. If that is true, portfolio C is superior to all other portfolios, using the criterion of return per unit of risk. This can be seen by drawing rays from the risk-free rate of return through the points representing each of the portfolios. The ray passing through portfolio C has the greatest slope and this, of course, is just a geometric reflection of the fact that the additional return per unit of risk is greatest for that portfolio. Portfolio C is considered best because it would be possible by appropriate combinations of it with the risk-free asset or by buying on margin to achieve a rate of return superior to that for any other portfolio while having only the same degree of risk. For example, by combining portfolio C with the risk-free asset, it would be possible to move the portfolio down the ray passing through portfolio C to a point directly above portfolio A, thus achieving a greater return than that on portfolio A for the same degree of risk. Similarly, by buying portfolio C on margin, it would be possible to move up the ray which passes through portfolio C to a point directly above portfolio D, thus achieving a rate of return superior to that on portfolio D for equivalent risk. In this sense portfolio C is the "best" portfolio of the four.

Though this is in some ways a satisfying conclusion, there are some difficulties. For example, a particular investor may not be allowed to buy on margin and therefore he may not be able to move along the ray passing through portfolio C in order to achieve a higher return from that portfolio. Given that limitation, the investor might prefer portfolio D to portfolio C, even though the skill with which C is managed is in some sense superior to that with which D is managed.

Another difficulty has to do with the proper measurement of the additional return per unit of risk. There seems to be general agreement that the rate of return on a portfolio should be expressed as a risk premium by subtracting from the rate of return the risk-free rate of interest. In order to determine the rate of return per unit of risk, this risk premium should be divided either by a measure of total variability such as the standard deviation or mean-absolute deviation or by a measure of volatility or sensitivity to the market such as the beta coefficient. The choices between these two measures of risk can be better made if the relationship between them is understood. (For an extended discussion, see Bower and Wippern, "Risk Return Measurement," pp. 421–23.) The beta coefficient is related to the standard deviation algebraically as indicated by the following equation:

$$\beta_{im} = \frac{\rho_{im}\sigma_i}{\sigma_m}.$$

This equation makes clear the importance of something we have discussed earlier.* If all portfolios were "efficient," all would be perfectly correlated with the market, and the beta coefficient of each would be simply the ratio of the standard deviation of the individual portfolio to the standard deviation of the market. Since the standard deviation for the market would be constant across portfolios, rankings of portfolios according to the standard deviation would be identical to rankings according to the beta coefficient. Unfortunately, not all portfolios are perfectly correlated with the market so that rankings according to one risk measure can be different from rankings according to another.

In studies of mutual funds, Treynor has used an index based on volatility to rank funds.[6] His method is easily illustrated. In figure 13–3 the returns on two funds are plotted against a market index.

FIGURE 13–3
The Relationship between Historical Rates of Return on Funds and Rates of Return on the Market
Return on Fund (%)

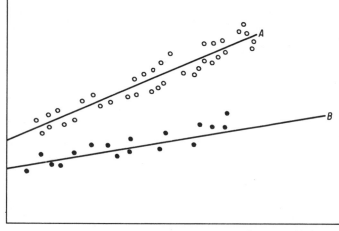

Return on Market Index (%)

The circles represent the returns on fund A, and the dots, the returns on fund B. Each point represents the return for a year. The two regression lines fitted to these points are Treynor's "characteristic" lines. The volatility of the fund is given by the slope of the characteristic

---

* See chapter 11, pp. 208–9.

line. If the line for fund B were parallel to and below that for fund A, fund B would obviously be inferior, since it would provide a lower return for the same volatility. In the diagram above, all we can deduce so far is that fund A is more volatile. To rank funds, Treynor draws a horizontal line through the risk-free rate of interest. This is illustrated in figure 13–4. Since the intersection (X) of this line with the charac-

FIGURE 13–4
A Diagrammatic Illustration of the Treynor Index for Ranking Funds
Return of Fund (%)

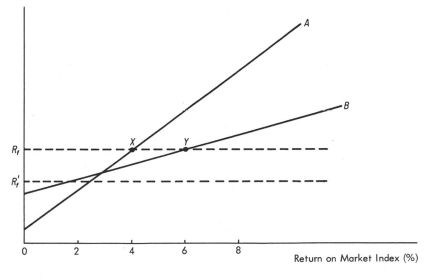

teristic line for fund A is to the left óf that (Y) for fund B, fund A is superior. Treynor shows this mathematically, but it is also obvious geometrically since a ray rotated through X until it is parallel to the characteristic line for fund B could be achieved by combining fund A with the riskless asset.

The horizontal distance to the point of intersection—$R_f X$ for fund A and $R_f Y$ for fund B—is the Treynor index of fund performance. It is read off the horizontal axis as a percentage; the smaller the percentage the better the relative performance. The index indicates the rate of return on the market index required to make the fund's expected return equal to the risk-free rate of return. In the example above, it is 4 percent for fund A and 6 percent for fund B. It is in this sense that fund A is superior. It is important to recognize, however, that a fund's ranking will depend upon the level of the risk-free rate of interest. In the diagram above, if the riskless asset earned a return of R_f' instead of R_f, fund B would be superior by the Treynor measure.

Sharpe's[7] method is similar, but he uses the standard deviation to compute the reward-to-variability ratio as a means of ranking funds. For example, in figure 13–5 each point represents the average return

FIGURE 13–5
The Relationship between the Average Return on Funds and Risk (σ)

Return on Fund (%)–R_p

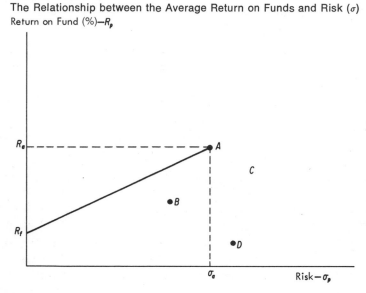

on a fund for some period, and the standard deviation of returns for subperiods. Since the slope of the line from R_f, the risk-free rate of interest, to point A is the steepest, fund A has the highest ranking. This is Sharpe's reward-to-variability ratio and is given by

$$\frac{R_a - R_f}{\sigma_a}.$$

The Treynor index is equivalent to

$$\frac{R_a - R_f}{\beta_a}$$

and is therefore a reward-to-volatility ratio.

It is probably true that almost all investors are concerned, and sensibly so, about all variability in rates of return and not merely about the variability caused by market movements. If an investor has very low rates of return on his portfolio and has had enormous variability from period to period, he is probably right not to be comforted by the investment adviser's assertion that the low rate of return is understandable and acceptable because only very little risk was assumed, as any fool could tell by noting the low beta coefficient. This defense of the low rate of return seems quite inadequate in view of the very great variability in rates of return which existed. The investment adviser should be held responsible for that variability and should not be excused on the grounds of low sensitivity of the portfolio to movements in the general market.

There are other logical problems in the measurement of performance, and Bower and Wippern deal with them well. Some of these problems have to do with the adequacy of the standard deviation as a measure of total variability. The Bank Administration Institute recognized the problem but denied its importance on the grounds that correlations among different measures of variability are very high. The Institute's study indicated correlations for 595 common stocks listed on the New York Stock Exchange throughout the period March 29, 1926 to March 31, 1966 were in excess of 0.7 between such measures as the standard deviation, the mean-absolute deviation, the semistandard deviation, the absolute deviation, and the beta coefficient. The only measure that had correlations with the others below 0.7 was the probability of loss.[8] Bower and Wippern did not find equally high correlations and found significant differences in rankings of funds according to the measure of variability used.[9] For example, for a sample of 34 mutual funds for the 1954–63 period, they found a rank correlation of −0.149 between indexes of unfavorable variation and standard deviations.

More important, Bower and Wippern felt that the measures of performance when applied to mutual funds were not helpful in predicting future performance. That is, superiority in one period did not seem to be associated with superiority in a subsequent period. This may not be a criticism of the method of evaluating performance; it may merely reflect the efficiency of markets in which mutual funds operate and the consequent extreme difficulty of achieving a consistent superiority (or inferiority).

BENCH MARKS

Most investors are interested in evaluating portfolio managers in order to know to whom to entrust their funds. For that purpose, it is necessary to rank portfolio managers in terms of some appropriate bench mark.

There are three main possibilities. The first is the naïvely selected portfolio with a risk approximately equal to that of the actual portfolio. The use of "naïve" models or bench marks is a familiar technique in economics, meteorology, and perhaps elsewhere. In economics, it is now ordinary practice to evaluate economic forecasts by reference to naïve forecasts such as would be produced by assuming that next year will be like this year or that next year will be different from this year by the same percentage that this year differed from last. In meteorology, it is commonplace to evaluate weather forecasts by reference to such naïve models as one which postulates that the next day will be like the current day or one that selects a forecast for the next day at random with probabilities proportionate to the historic relative frequency of different kinds of weather.

Such a naïve bench mark is easily provided for the purpose of evaluating portfolio performance. Sharpe's capital asset pricing model provides a theoretical basis for such a bench mark. The model indicates the rate of return for every degree of riskiness that would be produced on the average by combining riskless assets with randomly selected groups of risky assets. The capital market line is illustrated in figure 13–6 for the period 1955–64 and is taken from Jensen's study of mutual funds.[10] Jensen uses the logarithms of the terminal wealth ratios rather than rates of return. The logarithms represent the annual continuously compounded rate of return. The line $R_f M Q$ is the capital market line, where R_f is the risk-free rate of interest and M represents the return on the market. Jensen uses β as his measure of risk, but this does not change the capital market line since total risk and undiversifable or systematic risk are equivalent for naïvely selected, efficient portfolios.

The difference between each portfolio's performance and the market line can be measured and the managers of these portfolios can be ranked in terms of that measurement. For example, in figure 13–7, portfolio A is above the capital market line, having a rate of return of 10 percent compared with only 8 percent for a portfolio of similar risk on the market line. Portfolio A could be ranked relative to any other with the same degree of risk by comparing the deviations from the capital market line. To rank portfolio A relative to, say, portfolio B, the differentials should be measured relative to the excess return, or risk premium on the

FIGURE 13–6
Scatter Diagram of Risk and (Net) Return for 115 Open-End Mutual Funds in the Ten-Year Period

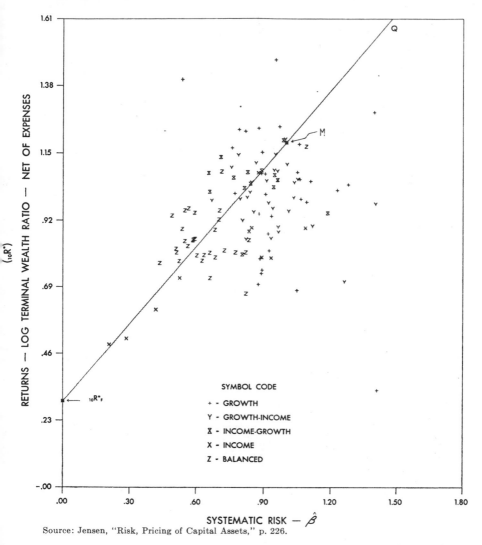

SYSTEMATIC RISK — $\hat{\beta}$

Source: Jensen, "Risk, Pricing of Capital Assets," p. 226.

naïvely selected portfolio of equal riskiness. In this instance, it is $\dfrac{10 \text{ percent} - 8 \text{ percent}}{8 \text{ percent} - 4 \text{ percent}}$, or 0.5 percent for portfolio A. The relative differential for portfolio B is $\dfrac{14 \text{ percent} - 12 \text{ percent}}{12 \text{ percent} - 4 \text{ percent}}$, or 0.25 percent. Portfolio A is therefore superior to portfolio B.

FIGURE 13–7

The Comparison of Fund Performance to That of Randomly Selected Portfolios

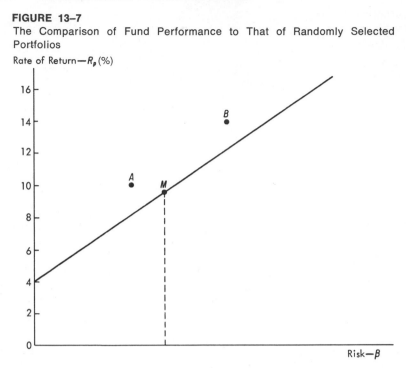

A second bench mark is obviously provided by the average performance of the group of actual portfolios which are considered comparable. For example, it would be appropriate to judge the performance of each mutual fund having capital appreciation as its objective with the average performance of all other such funds. In the Jensen study, it would have been possible to draw a regression line to represent the relationship between risk and rate of return for the mutual funds actually studied. A simplified illustration of this line and the relationship is given in figure 13–8.

The line PT is the regression line fitted to the fund observations. Its slope, in this instance, is flatter than that of the capital market line R_fQ. The ranking can be based on deviations of each fund from PT in much the same way that funds could be ranked according to their deviations from Sharpe's capital market line. Rankings by one method may differ from those by the other because of differences in the slopes of the two regression lines. For example, fund A in the diagram is superior to fund B when compared to the capital market

FIGURE 13–8

The Comparison of Performance among Funds

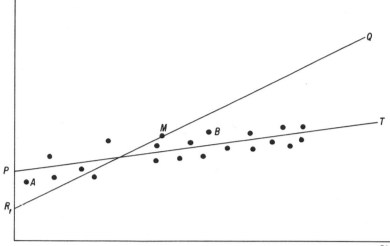

line, but inferior to fund B when compared to the regression line for fund returns alone.

Making comparisons among funds is appealing to many investors for another reason. For example, if a trustor—say, almost any of the largest corporations—entrusts part of its corporate pension fund to each of several trustees and gives them identical policy prescriptions, it is quite easy to judge the trustees relative to each other simply on the basis of the rates of return. This is possible if one assumes that the trustees have tried to or do indeed follow very similar policies with respect to risk.

The third possible bench mark is the reward-to-variability ratio (or its counterpart, the reward-to-volatility ratio) which has already been discussed.

MEASUREMENTS OF DIFFERENT PARTS OF THE PORTFOLIO

The chapter has so far discussed measurements of risk and return for the whole portfolio in evaluating the skill with which it has been managed. One might ask at this point whether it is also necessary to measure the risk and return separately for the different classes of assets in the portfolio. Is it necessary, for example, to measure the risk and return on the equity portion, on the bonds, on convertible securities, and so forth?

One of the maxims of Markowitz which should be given great weight is that investors should think of themselves as choosing portfolios rather than securities so that the performance of investors should be judged by the total portfolio rather than by individual securities or groups of securities. Although it is fairly standard practice to measure the risk and return for different kinds of assets, the purpose should be diagnosis rather than the overall evaluation of portfolio management. Such separate measurements can cast light on the reasons for superior or inferior performance, and such potential illumination is discussed in the next chapter. At this point, perhaps all that is necessary is to show why such measurement should not be relied upon to indicate the skill with which a total portfolio is managed.

The basic objection to reliance on measurements for separate classes of securities is that they fail to take account of the relationships and interactions among classes of securities. Just as it is foolish to attempt to measure the risk and return on an individual asset apart from its relationships to the rest of the portfolio, so it is foolish to measure the risk and return for individual groups of assets apart from their relationships to the other parts of the portfolio. In fact, one of the clear lessons of portfolio theory is the impossibility of getting a meaningful measurement of the riskiness of an individual asset—or group of assets—apart from the other assets with which they are combined to form an investor's portfolio. The most dramatic example would be a security or group of securities which are negatively correlated with the portfolio. Viewed in isolation, such securities might seem very risky with the consequent expectation of a large risk premium. Viewed together with the rest of a portfolio, such securities would correctly be judged to be risk reducing and consequently would be expected to have a very small or even negative risk premium.

REACHING A CONCLUSION

The ultimate purpose of evaluating a portfolio manager is almost always a conclusion about his superiority or inferiority. Clearly, the measurements of performance, period by period, which have been discussed are the raw materials for this ultimate judgement; but, equally clearly, they do not automatically lead to it. The problem exists because performance in any period is affected not only by the skill of the portfolio manager but also by random influences. Just as in acceptance sampling, one typically does not reject a supplier because of one deficient batch or unit, so an investor should not reject or discard an adviser because of poor performance in any single period. Contrariwise, the investor should be slow to distribute gold stars or enlarged responsibilities on the basis of superior performance in any one period.

There is an interesting question as to when the investor is justified in reaching the conclusion that his trustee or adviser is *truly* superior or inferior. There is no completely satisfactory answer to that question, but the judgement can be reached sooner and with greater confidence if the margins of superiority or inferiority are large and stable than if they are small and erratic. The principles of sequential sampling which have proved so useful in acceptance sampling for mass-produced items in industry might also be applied here.

14

Diagnosing the Causes
of Performance

INTRODUCTION

SOME INVESTORS undoubtedly will be satisfied with a simple evaluation of the skill with which their trustee or investment adviser has managed a portfolio. If the evaluation is favorable, the investor can relax and congratulate himself on his wise choice. If the evaluation is unfavorable, the investor can seek a new trustee or new adviser. He may not want to understand the causes for his adviser's success or failure.

Most large investors and especially most large trustors of employee pension plans are not content with a mere summary evaluation and wish to understand the causes. Such an understanding may be just as helpful in achieving better performance as a switch to another adviser or trustee believed to have greater investment ability. In fact, if evidence concerning the likelihood that superior performance in any one period will be followed by superior performance in a subsequent period is taken seriously, understanding the causes of investment performance will do more to improve it than switching from one trustee or adviser to another.

Perhaps the best way to diagnose the causes of performance is to list the factors which can affect it. For most investors, the following factors are relevant:

1. Skill in selecting particular assets.
2. Skill in switching between classes of assets, primarily between equities and fixed-dollar assets.

248

3. Efficiency of diversification.
4. Degree of adherence to prescribed policies with respect to risk.
5. Transaction costs.
6. Taxes.
7. Management fees.

This chapter deals with these factors.

SKILL IN SELECTING PARTICULAR ASSETS

An investor's skill in selecting assets of a particular class, say, common stocks, is properly judged by comparing the rate of return on these assets with other assets of the same degree of riskiness. For portfolios of common stocks having a small degree of risk or the same degree of risk as the market as a whole, the bench mark is easily defined. There are some details that need to be taken care of, but they are not difficult.

The market portfolio which is used in defining Sharpe's capital market line includes all common stocks with the value of each being proportional to its market value. If the bench mark is to be the capital market line, and it is a good one, either the New York Stock Exchange Composite Index or the Standard & Poor's "500" is a reasonable first approximation.[1] Each is a value-weighted index of prices of stocks on the New York Stock Exchange. Although the Standard & Poor's Composite Index does not include all stocks, the market value of the included stocks is about 80 percent of the total value of all common stocks. As a consequence, the movements in the Standard & Poor's Index are highly correlated with movements in the New York Stock Exchange Composite Index, and the correlation coefficient between the two indexes is close to 1.0. For example, for the period January 1939 to December 1966, the correlation between closing values of the two indexes on the last Friday of the month is 0.913. The estimated regression coefficient is 0.865.

The reason for calling these indexes only first approximations is that the universe of stocks available for investments is far more extensive than those listed on the New York Stock Exchange. About 1,200 stocks are listed on the American Stock Exchange and there are more than 10,000 reasonably actively traded stocks in the over-the-counter market. Although the number of stocks not listed on the New York Stock Exchange vastly exceeds the number so listed, the market value of stocks on the New York Stock Exchange at the end of 1970 was about 70 percent of the total value of publicly traded stocks in the United States.

A better bench mark for evaluating the skill of individual investors in picking stocks would be a combination index of stocks listed on the New York Stock Exchange and American Stock Exchange. A still better index would include the over-the-counter stocks. A still better one would include bonds and other things. Unfortunately, the official index of the American Stock Exchange is not a value-weighted index, and the index of the over-the-counter stocks is not inclusive or necessarily representative.* Someone would do the financial community a great service by constructing a value-weighted index that included stocks not on the New York Stock Exchange. In the meantime, investors seeking a bench mark can probably struggle along without major error by using one of the value-weighted indexes for the New York Stock Exchange.

An argument can be made for using an index in which each stock receives equal weight. In computing the tables of rates of return on common stocks listed on the New York Stock Exchange (see chapter 2), Fisher and Lorie gave equal weight to each stock. Such an index provides perhaps the simplest naïve model with which to compare the performance of actual portfolios of common stocks. It is the model which corresponds to the dramatic and implausible picture of a man picking stocks by throwing darts or by some more rigorous random process. An index based upon equal weighting shows the results of an investment policy based on random selection with equal probabilities of selecting each stock; the value-weighted indexes correspond to an investment policy based on random selection with probabilities of selection proportional to market value.†

It is impossible to state categorically which kind of index provides the best bench mark, but it is worth noting that the choice can have practical consequences. The study of mutual fund performance by

---

* The OTC average published by the National Quotation Bureau includes 35 stocks selected from those with largest market value, largest number of stockholders, and most extensive quotation records. The average is computed in the same way as the Dow Jones averages, with an adjustment in the divisor for splits. In 1971, the National Association of Security Dealers began to release comprehensive averages of over-the-counter stocks through the use of its automated quotation service (NASDAQ). It is not yet possible to say much about these new averages except that they are a great improvement in terms of comprehensiveness over what has heretofore been available.

† For a fuller discussion, see chapter 3.

Friend *et al* shows that their sample of 136 mutual funds on the average had an annual rate of return compounded monthly of 10.7 percent for the period January 1960 through June 1968. This was inferior to the annual rate of 12.4 percent based on portfolios of stocks with equal weights and was superior to the annual rate of 9.9 percent based on indexes of stocks with weights proportional to market value.[2] The margins of inferiority and superiority were probably not so great as to justify a confident conclusion that managers of mutual funds picked stocks better or worse than a random process with either equal probabilities of selection or probabilities proportional to market value. Most observers would probably conclude that mutual funds demonstrated neither superiority nor inferiority during the period under study. Nevertheless, it is worth keeping in mind that the choice of index can make a difference and that occasionally it might even be important.

Another point worth remembering is that transaction costs, dividends, and management fees must be properly treated. The return on the actual portfolio should, of course, include dividends and rights, and the bench marks therefore should include dividends and rights.

There are transaction costs in managing actual portfolios, but there are no transaction costs attributed to the hypothetical portfolios represented by market indexes. This problem is a bit more difficult. Returns on actual portfolios should be calculated after deducting all transaction costs, but comparisons with the indexes should be made only after crediting back to the actual portfolios unavoidable transaction costs. The portfolio manager cannot avoid the cost of investing new capital or of disinvesting for the purpose of making payments to beneficiaries. On the other hand, transaction costs incurred in order to shift funds among particular assets in response to changing expectations could be avoided by a more passive policy. Returns on common stock portfolios should be judged with avoidable costs included and unavoidable costs excluded.

Management fees should not be considered in measuring rates of return for diagnostic purposes. The purpose of the diagnosis is to evaluate the skill of the investor in judging the prospects for particular stocks, and the management fee is not relevant for that evaluation. Obviously, the size of the management fee will be taken into account in judging the wisdom of continuing to retain an adviser or trustee, but the fee itself should not be allowed to cloud the evaluation of performance.

If the actual portfolio of common stocks is riskier than the market as a whole, the bench mark is harder to define. Sharpe's capital market line provides the theoretical bench mark based on the linear extrapolation of the line between the risk-free asset and the portfolio of risky assets. The linear extrapolation is based upon the assumption that investors can borrow at the same rate as the federal government and that the rate is independent of the amount borrowed. Neither of those assumptions is valid. The invalidity is not a serious deficiency of Sharpe's capital asset pricing model in its more general role of explaining the relationship between the risk of particular assets and their rates of return, but it can be a significant blemish in defining a bench mark for the purpose of evaluating an investor's skill in selecting common stocks.

There are various ways to deal with this problem. First, the extrapolation of the capital market line could be based upon a more realistic assumption about the cost of borrowed funds for the purpose of buying on margin. This greater realism would result in lower rates of return for given degrees of risk. Another solution would be to use as bench marks comprehensive portfolios of common stocks whose average riskiness was greater than that of the market as a whole. For example, the New York Stock Exchange Index of Industrial Stocks or the Standard & Poor's Index of 425 industrial stocks might be used. Each is a comprehensive index and each has a beta coefficient with the market as a whole which is usually greater than 1.0.

By combining the two adjustments, it should be possible to generate bench marks appropriate for evaluating actual portfolios of common stocks with regression coefficients of as much as 2.0. This should suffice for virtually all institutional investors such as pension funds and mutual funds, and should suffice for all but the most venturesome individual investors.*

SKILL IN SWITCHING BETWEEN CLASSES OF ASSETS

Conventional discussions of investments usually identify two major problems. The first is selecting particular assets in each asset class and the second is deciding the allocation of funds between asset classes,

---

* Only four of the 136 funds studied by Friend, Blume, and Crockett had beta coefficients over 1.1. Ibid., p. 56. In Jensen's study, six of the 115 funds had beta coefficients above 1.1; the highest was 1.4. Michael Jensen, "Risk, the Pricing of Capital Assets, and the Evaluation of Investment Portfolios," *Journal of Business,* vol. 42, no. 2 (April 1969), pp. 207–9.

primarily between stocks and bonds. The second problem is often referred to as the *timing* problem. Successful coping with the timing
problem results in extensive switches from equities to short-term debt
instruments just prior to large, general declines in the prices of common stocks, and to a reverse movement of funds just prior to large,
general advances. Very high marks for timing would have gone to
those investment managers who switched from common stocks to
Treasury bills in the fall of 1968 and who made the reverse switch
in the late spring of 1970. The New York Stock Exchange index declined 18 percent from a high of 61.3 in November 1968 to a low
of 50.2 in May 1970. During this period, the yield on six-month
Treasury bills averaged 6.8 percent.

Although there is very little evidence to support the belief that actual investors consistently play the timing game successfully, many
investors continue to try and perhaps some consistently succeed. Skill
in making the judgement with respect to timing can be extremely
rewarding. Switches in and out of the market at major peaks and
troughs, even if the alternative holding were only cash, would have
produced high annual rates of return during the 1960s.

The report of the Bank Administration Institute suggests a statistic
for judging the skill with which the timing problem is handled.[3] The
statistic is the difference between two rates of return. The first is the
actual rate of return on a portfolio during the period in question.
The second is the hypothetical rate of return that would have been
earned on the portfolio if the allocation of funds between equities
and fixed-dollar assets which existed at the beginning of the period
had been maintained throughout the period. A simple example should
make this clear. Assume that the assets in portfolio A were distributed
as in table 14–1. If the rate of return on equities were 10 percent,

TABLE 14–1
Distribution of Assets in Portfolio A

	Equities	*Debt*
End of preceeding period	30%	70%
Period being evaluated	50%	50%

and that on bonds 5 percent, the actual return on the portfolio (assuming the switch to equities was made at the outset of the period) would
be $0.5(0.10) + 0.5(0.05)$, or 7.5 percent. The hypothetical rate of

return—that which would have been earned with no reallocation of funds—was $0.3(0.10) + 0.7(0.05)$, or 6.5 percent. Thus the reallocation was profitable.

EFFICIENCY OF DIVERSIFICATION

According to modern portfolio theory, investors on the average cannot expect to be compensated for incurring avoidable risk. If all investors believe that markets are efficient and understand the portfolio theory of Markowitz and Sharpe, all will seek to hold highly diversified portfolios which, by definition, have eliminated avoidable risk. This is equivalent to saying that all investors will hold portfolios which are perfectly correlated with very general market indexes so that fluctuations in the value of portfolios will be determined solely by general market movements.

Opportunities for superior or inferior performance are made possible only by departures from that theoretical goal. Naturally, any portfolio which is perfectly correlated with the market will lie on the capital market line and its manager will be judged to be neither inferior nor superior by reference to that bench mark. Imperfect correlation (i.e., the existence of avoidable risk) provides opportunities for success or failure. We are not interested here in judging success or failure, but rather in understanding its causes. If a portfolio consistently lies above the capital market line, there are a number of possible causes such as adeptness in switching from equities to fixed-dollar assets and back, or superiority in picking assets within each class. The latter will inevitably be accompanied by correlations with the market significantly below 1.0. More often such departures from perfect correlations will be accompanied by inferior performance and will be one plausible explanation of it. True believers in efficient markets will insist upon efficient diversification (high correlations with the market) and will find that goal easy to achieve.

DEGREE OF ADHERENCE TO PRESCRIBED POLICIES

Some investors may not be satisfied with overall measures of success or failure or even with plausible explanations of them. Some investors may take seriously the division of responsibility between those who prescribe policy and those who execute it. Trustees of endowed funds, for example, have the responsibility for prescribing investment policy and have an understandable interest in seeing whether their prescription has been followed. There is an unverified story that Casey Stengel once fined a player for hitting a home run when he had been ordered to bunt. The fine is understandable, since those responsible for policy need to have confidence that it is being carried out, and they should not be pleased by departures from policy even when the departures prove it to be successful.

The prescription of policy is frequently so vague or ambiguous that determining the degree of conformity to it is impossible. When ambiguity is avoided, the prescription is often so general that conformity is meaningless. For example, a prescription of policy in terms of proportions of portfolios to be in equities and in fixed-dollar assets is easily adhered to, but the range of discretion remaining to the investment manager is often so great as to render the policy of little value.

As a result of the development of modern portfolio theory, there is an incipient but perceptible trend to prescribe investment policy in terms of beta coefficients (i.e., measures of systematic risk) and measures of the percent of total risk which is systematic (i.e., coefficients of determination). For example, an investment manager can be directed to have a portfolio which moves up and down as fast as the market, half as fast, or once and a half as fast. Policy makers may feel that their collective wisdom is adequate to judge the general economic outlook and to prescribe the associated appropriate investment policy. (They may also recognize that committees are not efficient agents for selecting particular assets and executing particular orders.) When such policy makers expect rising corporate profits and declining interest rates, they may choose an aggressive policy which is expressed through a beta coefficient greater than 1.0. Expectations of declining profits and rising interest rates would naturally lead to specifying a defensive policy, operationally defined as a beta coefficient of, say, 0.2. Such policy prescriptions are operationally meaningful and are capable of being carried out. It is relatively easy for investment managers to achieve almost any specified beta coefficient, and policy makers can hold their agents responsible for doing that. It is also possible to prescribe the amount of unsystematic risk which is to be incurred.

TRANSACTION COSTS

At the present time, the purchase and sale of 100 shares of stock on the New York Stock Exchange costs approximately 4 percent.*

---

* Transaction costs include not only brokerage fees but the spread between bids and offers and transfer taxes.

There are quantity discounts, and transaction costs can be substantially less. Turnover rates on large professionally managed portfolios vary enormously. During the 1960s, rates for mutual funds ranged from 17.3 percent per year to 55.6 percent per year. Rates for private non-insured pension funds and for life insurance companies ranged from 9.7 percent to 23.1 percent and from 9.8 percent to 28.1 percent respectively.* Trading volume on the New York Stock Exchange in 1969 was 3,174 million shares, 21 percent of the total shares listed. Since institutional investors account for only about one third of the ownership of shares on the New York Stock Exchange and account for more than 50 percent of the trading volume, it is reasonable to conclude that on the average institutional investors had turnover ratios of approximately 35 percent.

Given the existing commission structure for buying and selling stock and the range of turnover ratios which exist, transaction costs could be an insignificant percentage of the asset value of the portfolio in any year or a rather important percentage. Since rates of return are based upon interest, dividends, and capital gains after all relevant costs, it is interesting to analyze the impact of transaction costs on realized rates of return.

Obviously, since rates of return are measured after transaction costs, it is not necessary to adjust rates of return any further. It may be worthwhile, however, in diagnosing the cause of ultimate results to see whether all of the trading activity was useful. An obvious way to make that determination is to see what rates of return and risk would have been if the investment manager had gone fishing and been utterly passive in his professional role. It is quite easy to determine what rates of return would have been if the assets in the portfolio at the beginning of the period in question had been retained throughout the period. This rate can be compared with the actual rate. If the actual rate after all relevant costs exceeded the hypothetical rate, there was net benefit from the trading. If the hypothetical rate were greater, the trading was disadvantageous.

A more refined question has to do with comparisons between actual trading and degrees of activity other than total inaction. Analysis directed at the more refined question might indicate that trading was

---

* Friend, Blume, and Crockett, *Mutual Funds and Other Institutional Investors,* p. 118. The turnover rate is defined as the average of purchases and sales divided by the average market value of stockholdings at the beginning and at the end of the period.

advantageous in rising markets and disadvantageous in falling markets, or the reverse; that trading was advantageous in stocks in certain industries and not in others; or even that trading was advantageous or disadvantageous in particular stocks which the manager followed particularly closely. In all of these analyses, it is necessary to distinguish between results which should be attributed to sampling fluctuations and results which should be attributed to more basic and manageable causes. Even in the absence of a scientific distinction of this sort, it should be revealing and possibly instructive to both the beneficiary or client and to the investment manager to know whether shifts among securities produced results superior to total inaction.

From time to time, students of investments or actual investors (sometimes the categories overlap) believe that they have schemes for selecting stocks or timing investments which will produce superior results. If transaction costs are ignored, it is easy to be misled. A dramatic example is the filter technique of Alexander.[4] When transaction costs were excluded, the filter technique seemed to provide rates of return substantially in excess of those obtainable by buying and holding securities. When transaction costs were taken into account, the superiority of the filter technique disappeared and an inferiority of impressive magnitude appeared.[5]

Reference has already been made to the necessity of seeing to it that rates of return for actual portfolios be compared with bench marks—say, market indexes—only after proper adjustment for transaction costs. It is unrealistic to assume zero transaction costs for the bench-mark portfolio. Nevertheless, once the stocks in such a portfolio are acquired, the transaction costs needed to maintain it would typically be quite small. Costs would be incurred when stocks are originally acquired with new funds, when stocks are sold to pay beneficiaries, or when interest or dividends are reinvested. It is doubtful that the practical importance of this problem is sufficient to warrant refined calculations of what these costs would be, but rough approximations would almost certainly be better than the assumption that no transaction costs were necessary.

When the bench mark is other professionally managed portfolios, transaction costs for a particular portfolio may appear to be "low" or "normal" or "acceptable." Yet it is possible that all of the portfolios have had excessive trading and transaction costs. Those who believe that passivity is prudent because of the efficiency of markets will always want to compare the transaction costs of any group of portfolios with those of a hypothetical portfolio in which transaction costs were minimized.

TAXES

Often, academic discussions of the theory of portfolio management achieve lucidity through the simplication of assuming no taxes. For some important classes of portfolios, the assumption is realistic. Pension funds, charitable endowments, and some investment companies pay no taxes or virtually no taxes. For many other investors, however, taxes are of great importance and must be carefully considered by professional portfolio managers. Measurements of the rates of return on common stocks listed on the New York Stock Exchange revealed the very great impact of taxes. The terminal wealth of a tax-exempt investor who made initial equal investments in each stock listed in January 1926 and reinvested dividends would have been 2.26 times that of the investor in a moderately high tax bracket and 1.36 times that of the investor in a low tax bracket.[6]

Obviously rates of return should be measured after deduction of all associated costs, and these certainly include taxes. Thus, measurements of rates of return will indicate the success or failure of the manager. For diagnostic purposes, it is interesting to know whether taxes were dealt with sensibly. The magnitude of the tax liability depends upon the following:

1. Whether the gain is realized or unrealized.
2. Whether the gain is long term or short term.
3. Whether the return is in the form of capital gains or dividends or interest.
4. Whether the gain is realized sooner, rather than in some subsequent year.
5. Whether the realized gain is offset by realized losses.

MANAGEMENT FEES

Management fees are easily judged. Given the riskiness of the assets being managed, did the realized rate of return exceed the rate on randomly selected portfolios of equal riskiness by an amount less than, equal to, or greater than the management fee? This simple measurement is enough unless there are nonpecuniary advantages or disadvantages attached to the management of one's own investments.

Some investors are undoubtedly willing to pay someone in order to be relieved of the possible agony of managing one's own investments, and others will require an extra margin of superiority for the investment advisor because the investor has been deprived of the fun of playing the investment game. Perhaps of greater importance are the political implications for some investors of the divestiture of direct responsibility for investments. Many corporations, for example, find that their dealings with labor unions are simplified if responsibility for managing the employee pension fund is in other hands, particularly large institutions of impeccable reputation.

15

A Note on Investment Counselling

INTRODUCTION

THERE ARE MANY fine investment counselling firms, and their staffs
are honorable, conscientious, and sophisticated. Yet, most of their resources are devoted to security analysis and to portfolio management
rather than to investment counselling. Investment counselling is advis-
ing an investor regarding investment policy. Portfolio management
is the execution of policy. Security analysis provides some of the information traditionally considered necessary for portfolio management.

Those who have found the evidence regarding the efficiency of markets convincing, as have the authors of this book, will believe that
the most important investment decision—the one with the greatest
impact on results—is the choice of policy with respect to risk. Rates
of return of mutual funds, for example, vary consistently and substantially almost entirely because of differences in risk. There is no substan-
tal evidence (some would say no evidence) that the managers of
any mutual fund consistently display superior judgment in picking
assets of a given degree of risk.

If all of these statements are valid, investment counselling becomes
important and almost certainly more important than security analysis
or even portfolio management.

THE NEEDS AND RESOURCES OF INVESTORS

Many trustees and investment counsellors make only rudimentary efforts to analyze the needs, resources, and tastes of their clients, whether they be individuals, corporate trustors of pension funds, endowed institutions, or others. In view of the importance of investment policy, the lack of any systematic, sophisticated analysis of the relevant circumstances of the investor is unfortunate.

For example, actuaries for large corporations typically provide estimates of the characteristics of the firm's employees for only a year or two into the future, although longer-term estimates are sometimes provided. Such data can be the raw material for estimating the liabilities of the corporate pension fund. Of course, there is uncertainty regarding the size of the work force, its composition by age and job classification, its retirement benefits, and so forth, but actuaries can and should provide probability distributions of these variables and a summary probability distribution of the fund's liabilities.

When such information is combined with distributions of rates of return resulting from different investment strategies, it becomes possible to simulate the operation of the fund, indicating the likely range of requirements for corporate contributions year by year and other things of interest to the trustor. On the basis of such simulations, the trustor and trustee have the raw material for a rational choice of investment policy.

The declining firm with a relatively old work force almost certainly should choose a different policy from the rapidly growing firm with a relatively young work force. The former has great need for liquidity and a relatively short horizon, indicating the desirability of a portfolio of relatively low risk. The latter company has virtually no possibility of needing liquidity in the near term, is therefore relatively immune to the impact of near-term fluctuations in the value of its pension fund, and can (should?) bear relatively high risk with the associated relatively high expected return. Management science is beginning to enable actuaries to play a more useful role in helping trustees and trustors choose an investment policy more rationally.

Similar techniques can be applied to other classes of investors. Universities, for example, have to choose expenditure policies as well as investment policies. Simulation permits trustees to see the probable effects of different combinations of such policies on annual expenditures from endowments and annual changes in their market value.

Simulations do not prevent pleasant or unpleasant surprises, nor do they automatically produce wise decisions regarding the relative importance of near-term and more remote needs, but simulations provide the raw material for a decision-making process that is likely to be superior to the short-term, ad hoc, formless intuition that is commonplace.

The first example of such simulations known to the authors, was undertaken at the University of Rochester. A hypothetical example derived from their work shows the probable range of annual expenditures from endowment and the probable range of year-end values of endowments from a policy of spending 5 percent of the year-end value of the endowment and assuming that the distribution of rates of return on the portfolio during the next 40 years would be the same as during the preceding 40 years. The assumed mean of the returns is 8.8 percent and the standard deviation is 10.8 percent. (Figure 15–1.)

FIGURE 15–1
Expenditure Profile of a Hypothetical Endowment Assuming Annual Expenditures Equal to 5 Percent of the Market Value of the Endowment at the Beginning of Each Year

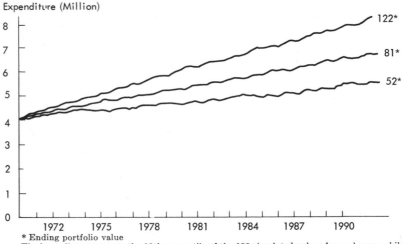

* Ending portfolio value
     The lower line represents the 20th percentile of the 100 simulated values for each year while the middle and top lines represent the 50th (median) and 80th percentiles.

The firm of O'Brien Associates, Inc. has done serious work on a system for understanding the interrelationships between actuarial assumptions and returns based on market simulations. The following hypothetical example is taken from their work:

FIGURE 15–2
Assumptions Used in Example Simulation

1. *Work Force Projection Model*
   Work force growth = 1 percent per annum
   Salary scale growth = 3½ percent per annum
   Male/female hiring ratio = 1:3
2. *Actuarial Liability Computation*
   Discount rate = 3½ percent per annum
3. *Investment Portfolio Projection Model*
   Capital market assumptions
   Mean equity market return = 9½ percent per annum
   Standard deviation of equity market return = 16 percent per annum
   Riskless rate of return 4½ percent per annum
   Investment policy parameters
   Portfolio diversification = 95 percent
   Turnover = 20 percent per annum
   Dividend yield = 3.0 percent per annum
   Relative equity exposure (β) range = 0.0–1.2
   Mean independent return (α) = 0.0 percent per annum

FIGURE 15–3
Impact of Investment Policy on Annual Pension Plan Cost

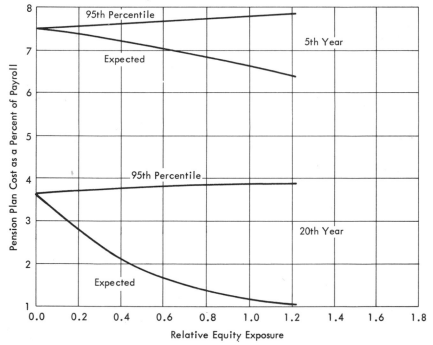

Other actuarial assumptions and assumptions about returns on the market would, of course, produce different results. Those analyses and simulations provide the basis for a more rational basis for the choice of an investment policy than the casual intuitive process which is now typical.

Individuals, too, need better investment counselling than they often receive. The problem is especially difficult for small investors, but even large investors typically manage their portfolios or have them managed with only unsystematic regard for their current and prospective needs, resources, and tastes. Portfolios should change in response to changes in earned income, life style, number of dependents, and attitudes towards risk. Marriages, divorces, children, grandchildren, and many other factors should determine investment policy. Yet, they seldom are systematically taken into account.

Perhaps, the point has been sufficiently made. In efficient markets, investment counselling is the most important investment function, and the available tools of scientific investment have been insufficiently used to perform it well.

THE SPECIFICATION OF INVESTMENT POLICY

Investment counsellors and trustees do not ignore the choice of investment policy. In fact, they typically produce a written statement of policy and occasionally refer to it. Current practice deserves criticism not only because of the casual, intuitive process by which policy is chosen, but also because of the ambiguity and vagueness of its expression. These deficiencies are often so pronounced that the policy neither provides meaningful guidance to the portfolio manager nor the effective means for controlling him and evaluating his performance.

Many trust departments and investment counselling firms rely on three criteria to give operational meaning to statements of policy:

1. A list of securities eligible for purchase—the so-called "buy" list.
2. A diversification requirement, usually specifying the maximum percentage of a portfolio that can be invested in the securities of a single company and the maximum percentage that can be invested in a single industry.
3. A maximum percentage that can be invested in equities.

These three criteria are designed to restrict investments to under-valued securities, to control risk through diversification and a maximum commitment to equities, and to deal with the timing problem by changing the maximum permissible commitment to equities. Although there is remarkably little evidence that "buy lists" outperform other securities of similar risk, the three criteria combined do provide some control over portfolio managers.

Yet, the control is crude and inexact. Portfolios can be and are constructed from the same "buy list," with the same percentage in equities and full compliance with the criteria for diversification, and yet have quite different characteristics. More than one trust department and investment counselling firm foresaw the 1969–70 bear market and sought unsuccessfully to effect appropriate modifications in portfolios through changes in "buy lists" and reductions in maximum, permissible levels of investment in equities. The control mechanism frequently failed, if portfolio managers, not sharing the pessimism of their policy makers, shifted to equities more sensitive to market movements than those previously held. Reducing the proportion of a portfolio in equities from 80 percent to 60 percent will not make the portfolio less vulnerable to a market decline, if the equities held have substantially higher beta coefficients than those formerly held.

A more precise prescription of policy could be achieved through the use of beta coefficients and correlation coefficients. The prescription of a beta coefficient would perform two functions. It would control the relative riskiness of all portfolios and would permit a controlled adjustment in absolute levels of systematic risk in response to convictions of policy makers regarding future, major market movements. The prescription of a correlation coefficient would control diversification and thus the proportions of total risk that would be unsystematic—that is, caused by something other than movements in the market. A "buy list" can also be used, but its value should be frequently tested.

Since the use of beta and correlation coefficients provides a precise prescription of investment policy, it is easy both to audit the degree of compliance of portfolio managers and to evaluate their performance in light of the precisely stated, theoretically relevant constraints on their choice of investments. Thus, the institution employing the portfolio managers is enabled to discharge its inescapable responsibility of having a policy for each portfolio, knowing whether the policy is being followed, and evaluating the performance of those who execute policy.

The use of beta and correlation coefficients in the spring of 1969 would have permitted prescient policy makers to make sure that portfolio managers reduced to a prescribed degree the vulnerability of their portfolios to the coming sharp decline in the market. The institution employing these managers could avoid embarrassing or even absurd ignorance of the degree to which their portfolio managers were adapting to the anticipated decline.

The value of the beta coefficient in measuring the sensitivity of a diversified portfolio to market movements has been discussed at length. The use of the correlation coefficient in prescribing and controlling policy has only been mentioned. The correlation between the return on a portfolio and the return on a comprehensive market index measures the extent to which the return on the portfolio is determined by the market. A correlation coefficient of 0.9, for example, would mean that 81 percent (0.9^2) of the change in value of a portfolio was caused by a change in the index. Eighty-one percent of the total risk in the portfolio would be systematic; 19 percent would be unsystematic and attributable to the lack of complete or efficient diversification.

Very high correlations would be appropriate for portfolios for which low risk was appropriate or for portfolios whose managers had not *demonstrated* the ability to discriminate between undervalued and overvalued stocks. In efficient markets, there is no expected reward for bearing unsystematic risk. Portfolio managers should not, therefore, be permitted to incur such risk in the absence of evidence that they possess that very rare thing, consistently superior judgment about investments.

CONCLUSION

The relatively high degree of efficiency of American security markets makes investment counselling the most important of the investment functions. That is, the choice of an investment policy is likely to have a greater influence on results than either security analysis or portfolio management. Yet, investment counselling is typically treated casually despite the availability of theories and techniques that could make it more precise and rational.

Glossary

Abnormal Performance Index (API). An abnormal performance index measures the behavior of stock prices not explained by their normal relationships to general market movements. The normal relationship of the return on a security to the return on the market is described by the market model:

$$R_i = a_i + \beta_i R_M + e_i$$

where R_i is the return on the security, R_M is the return on the market, a_i and β_i are parameters, and e_i is a random variable with an expected value of zero. Abnormal behavior will result in values of e_i different from zero and nonrandom.

Alpha (α_i). Alpha is the constant term in the equation relating the risk premium on an asset to the risk premium on the market. Its *expected* value is zero, but its actual value may differ from zero. It is this possibility that explains investors' efforts to identify under- or over-valued securities, i.e., those with nonzero alphas.

Beta Coefficient (β). The beta coefficient measures sensitivity of rates of return on a portfolio or on a particular security to general market movements. If the beta is 1.0, a 1 percent increase in the return on the market will result, on average, in a 1 percent increase in the return on the particular portfolio or asset. If beta is less than 1.0, the portfolio or asset is considered to be less risky than the market. Beta is the regression coefficient of the rate of return on the market in the market model equation,

$$R_i = \alpha_i + \beta_i R_M + e_i.$$

An estimate of the beta coefficient of a portfolio is a weighted average of the betas of the portfolio's component assets.

The Beta Factor (R_z). In Sharpe's capital asset pricing model, the expected risk premium on an asset depends on the expected risk premium on the market multiplied by the asset's beta coefficient.

267

In a more elaborate model (attributable to Black, Jensen, and Scholes), the expected return on an asset depends also on the expected return on a portfolio not correlated with the market (R_z) multiplied by $(1 - \beta)$. This second factor is called the beta factor.

The Capital Asset Pricing Model. The capital asset pricing model describes the way prices of individual assets are determined in markets where information is freely available and reflected instantaneously in asset prices—that is, efficient markets.

Prices are determined in such a way so that risk premiums are proportional to systematic risk, which is measured by the beta coefficient.

Capital Market Line. The capital market line in the Sharpe model is the ray from the risk-free rate of return (R_f) that is tangent to the efficient frontier of risky assets. It describes the relationship between expected rates of return on efficient portfolios and risk as measured by σ_p. All efficient portfolios lie on this line if lending and borrowing are permissible at the (same) risk-free rate.

The mathematical relationship is

$$E(R_p) = R_f + \left[\frac{E(R_M) - R_f}{\sigma_M} \right] \sigma_p.$$

The slope of the line,

$$\left[\frac{E(R_M) - R_f}{\sigma_M} \right],$$

is the reward per unit of risk.

Characteristic Line. A characteristic line relates the return on an asset or portfolio to the return on a market index. The slope, β, measures volatility, or sensitivity to market movements.

Coefficient of Variation $\left[\dfrac{\sigma_x}{\bar{x}} \right]$. The coefficient of variation is the standard deviation divided by the mean, or

$$\sqrt{\frac{\Sigma(x_i - \bar{x})^2}{N}} \Big/ \bar{x}$$

It is a measure of the *relative* spread of a distribution about its mean. Coefficients of variation can be compared, since they are relative measures.

For example, if the standard deviation of a distribution of rates of return were 2 percent, and the mean were 5 percent, the coefficient of variation would be 0.02/0.05 or 0.4 percent.

Compounding. Compounding is the arithmetic process of finding the final value of an investment or series of investments when compound interest is applied. That is, interest is earned on the interest as well as on the initial principal.

Continuous Compounding. The annual rate of return compounded continuously is the natural logarithm $(\log_e)$ of the ratio of the value of the investment at the end of the year to the value at the beginning.

For example, if the wealth ratio were 1.1, its natural logarithm would be 0.09531. The annual rate of return compounded continuously would be 9.531 percent. This is easily converted to an annual rate of return compounded annually using the formula $e^x - 1$, where x is the annual rate compounded continuously.

If the period is other than one year, the annual rate compounded continuously can be found by dividing the logarithm of the wealth ratio by the number of years in the period.

Correlation Coefficient (ρ). A simple correlation coefficient is a measure of the degree to which two variables move together. If the relationship is causal, it can be interpreted as a measure of the degree to which knowing the value of one variable helps to predict the value of the other.

The coefficient is the square root of 1 minus the unexplained variance of one variable, given its relationship to the other, divided by its total variance. Symbolically, for the variables, x_i and x_j

$$\rho_{ij} = \sqrt{1 - \frac{s_{i \cdot j}^2}{s_i^2}}$$

The square of the correlation coefficient is the coefficient of determination. It measures the percentage of the total variance of i explained by its relationship to j.

Covariance (Cov_{ij}). Covariance is a measure of the degree to which two variables move together. A positive value means that on average, they move in the same direction. The covariance is related to, but not the same as, the correlation coefficient. It is difficult to attach any significance to the absolute magnitude of the covariance.

Symbolically, the covariance between two variables, x_i and x_j, is

$$\frac{\Sigma(x_i - \bar{x})(x_j - \bar{x}_j)}{N}$$

The covariance is also equal to $\rho_{ij}\sigma_i\sigma_j$, so its magnitude depends not only on the correlation, but also the standard deviations of the two variables. Stated alternatively, the correlation coefficient is the covariance standardized by dividing it by the product of σ_i and σ_j.

Deviation, Residual $(x_i - \bar{x})$ **or** (e_i). A deviation is the amount by which a particular value differs from some other value such as the average, or mean. Deviations can also be related to values, such as normal trend values, or to theoretical values one would expect on the basis of an historical relationship among the variables. This type of deviation is usually called a residual. Deviations from the mean are used to compute the variance and standard deviation of a distribution. A deviation from an expected value, given the existence of a relationship with one or more other variables, is the error term in a regression equation. In the two variable case, $y = a + bx + e_i$, e_i is a residual (which is a random variable with a mean of zero).

Diminishing Marginal Utility of Wealth. Marginal utility is the amount of additional satisfaction associated with an additional amount of something such as money or wealth. If successive increments in satisfaction decline as the level of wealth increases, there is diminishing marginal utility. This implies risk aversion, because, at a given level of wealth, the gain in utility associated with some increment in wealth is less than the loss in utility associated with a decrement of the same amount of wealth.

Dispersion.   Dispersion is the spread of a distribution about its average, or mean value. The greater the spread, the greater the variability. It can be measured either absolutely or relatively. Common absolute measures are the standard deviation, the variance, and the semi-interquartile range. The most common measure of relative dispersion is the coefficient of variation (the standard deviation divided by the mean).

Diversification.   Diversification is the spreading of investments over more than one company or industry to reduce the uncertainty of future returns caused by unsystematic risk.

Efficient Frontier.   The efficient frontier is the locus of all efficient portfolios. If neither lending nor borrowing is allowed, it is that part of the boundary of the feasible set that includes only efficient portfolios of risky assets. If lending and borrowing are permissible, the efficient frontier is the ray drawn from the risk-free rate to the point of tangency on the efficient frontier of risky assets. This line is called the capital market line.

Efficient Market.   An efficient market is one in which prices always fully reflect all available, relevant information. Adjustment to new information is virtually instantaneous.

Efficient Portfolio.   An efficient portfolio is one that is fully diversified. For any given rate of return, no other portfolio has less risk, and for a given level of risk, no other portfolio provides superior returns. All efficient portfolios are perfectly correlated with a general market index, except portfolios with beta coefficients above 1.0 and which do not achieve that relatively high risk by levering an efficient portfolio. Such portfolios lie on the curved frontier of portfolios consisting exclusively of risky assets.

Expected Rate of Return.   The expected rate of return on an asset or portfolio is the weighted arithmetic average of all possible outcomes, where the weights are the probabilities that each outcome will occur. It is the expected value or mean of a probability distribution. For example, the expected return on a portfolio, $E(R_p)$, is the weighted average of all possible returns, R_i, each weighted by its probability. Mathematically, $E(R_p) = \Sigma p_i R_i$.

Feasible Set.   The feasible or attainable set includes all individual securities and all combinations (portfolios) of two or more of these securities available to the investor within the limits of the capital available to him.

Filter Rules.   A filter rule is a simple mechanical rule for deciding to buy or sell assets. An x percent filter rule for investing states that if the price of a security rises at least x percent, buy and hold the security until its price falls by x percent from a subsequent high. The security should then be sold or sold short until the price rises by x percent from a subsequent low.

For example, if the filter is 5 percent and the price of Security A rises from a low of 100 to 105, the security should be purchased. If the price rises to 110 and then declines to 104½, the stock should be sold or sold short. This position should be maintained until the price rises by 5 percent above a subsequent low. The filter need not be the same percentage for buy and sell signals.

Gini's Coefficient of Variation. Gini's coefficient of variation is the mean difference between all possible pairs of observations divided by the mean. Symbolically, it is:

$$\sum_{i=1}^{N} \sum_{j=1}^{N} \frac{(x_i - x_j)}{N} \bigg/ \bar{x},$$

where $i \neq j$.

Geometric Mean (M_g). The geometric mean is the nth root of the product of n observations. It is the correct measure to use when averaging annual rates of return, compounded annually, over time.

   In calculating the average of rates of return, it is necessary to take the geometric mean of wealth ratios in order to allow for negative rates. The average rate of return is then the geometric mean minus one. For example, if the annual rates of return for two years were 10 percent and 8 percent, the average annual rate of return would be

$$\sqrt[2]{1.1 \times 1.08} - 1$$

or .0899. If the annual rates for two years were 100 percent and -50 percent, the average annual rate of return would be

$$\sqrt[2]{2.0 \times 0.5} - 1 = 0.0.$$

Indifference Curve. An indifference curve represents combinations of, say, risk and return, that are equally valued.

   For risk averters, indifference curves are convex from below when return is measured on the vertical axis and risk on the horizontal axis. The shape varies with the risk-return preferences of the individual.

Internal Rate of Return. The internal rate of return is analogous to the familiar yield to maturity on a bond.

   The internal rate of return is the rate of discount which makes the net present value of an investment equal to zero. In the case of a bond, if

$$P_o - \sum_{t=1}^{N} \frac{I_t}{(1 + i)^t} + \frac{P_N}{(1 + i)^N} = 0,$$

where P_o is the initial price, P_N is the terminal price, I_t is the interest in year t, i is the internal rate of return.

Intrinsic Value. The intrinsic value of an asset is the value that asset "ought" to have as judged by an investor. Discrepancies between current value and intrinsic value are often the basis of decisions to buy or sell the asset.

Investment Performance Index (IPI). An investment performance index differs from a price index in that it takes into account cash dividends and other distributions to shareholders.

Least-Squares Regression Line. A least-squares regression line minimizes the sum of the squares of the vertical deviations of observations from a line drawn through them.

For example, if a regression line is fitted to points representing pairs of values of x_i and x_j, the equation is

$$x_i = a + bx_j$$

The squared vertical distances of the actual values of x_i from the theoretical values, given its relationship to x_j are minimized. The mean values of x_i and x_j will always be a point on the regression line.

The Market Model. The market model describes the relationship between the rates of return on individual securities or portfolios and the rates of return on the market.

For example, for a particular security i, the relationship can be written as follows:

$$R_i = a_i + \beta_i R_M + e_i$$

where R_i is the rate of return on i, R_M is the rate of return on the market, a_i and β_i (beta) are parameters, and e_i is a random variable with an expected value of zero.

The model is useful for isolating "abnormal" stock-price behavior from that due to the influence of several market conditions.

The Market Portfolio. The market portfolio includes all risky assets in proportion to their market value. In the capital asset pricing model, it is the optimum portfolio of risky assets for all investors. Graphically, it is located at the point of tangency of a ray drawn from the risk-free rate of return to the efficient frontier of risky assets.

Mean Absolute Deviation. The mean absolute deviation is the average of the absolute values (the signs are disregarded) of the deviations of a group of observations from their expected value. Symbolically it is

$$\frac{\Sigma|x_i - \bar{x}|}{N}.$$

Median. The median of a distribution is the value that divides the number of observations in half. If the distribution is normal, the mean and the median will coincide. If the distribution is not normal and has positive skewness, the mean will exceed the median. If the skewness is negative, the mean will be below the median.

Multiple Correlation. Multiple correlation is a measure of the relationship between one variable (the dependent variable) and two or more other variables (the independent variables) simultaneously. It is an extension of simple correlation to include more than one independent variable.

Nominal Return. The nominal return on an asset is the rate of return in monetary terms, i.e. unadjusted for any change in the price level. The nominal return is contrasted with the real return which is adjusted for changes in the price level.

"Normalized" Earnings. "Normalized" earnings are the earnings one would expect in a "normal" or mid-cyclical year. There is no general agreement about the best way to normalize earnings, but it is not uncommon to use a moving average for three, four, or five or more years. Normalized earnings are sometimes called "steady-state" earnings.

Present Value or Worth. The present value of a payment or payments is the actual value discounted at an appropriate rate of interest. The discounting reflects the productivity of capital and the risk premium. For example, the present value of a share of stock, V_o, is the stream of future earnings discounted to perpetuity, or,

$$\sum_{t=1}^{\infty} \frac{E_t}{(1 + i)^t}$$

where E_t are the earnings in period t and i is the rate of discount.

Probability Distribution. A probability distribution is a distribution of possible outcomes with an indication of the subjective or objective probability of each occurring.

Random Selection. Random selection is similar to picking stocks by throwing darts at a stock listing.

Technically, random selection means that each element in the relevant population has a known and positive probability of selection. For example, if an index were based on 10 randomly selected stocks from a population (list) of 1000, the stocks could be selected with equal probabilities or, say, with probabilities proportional to the market value of the outstanding shares of each of the 1000 firms.

Random Walk. A random walk implies that there is no discernible pattern of travel. The size and direction of the next step cannot be predicted from the size and direction of the last or even from all the previous steps. If one wanted to find a random walker, the best place to look would be the starting point.

Random walk is a term used in mathematics and statistics to describe a process in which successive changes are statistically independent. The serial correlation is zero.

The changes are a random variable with an expected value of zero.

Regression Analysis. Regression or correlation analysis is a statistical technique for estimating the relationship between one variable (dependent variable) and one or more other variables (independent variables).

The relationship estimated, usually a least-squares regression equation, is often used to predict the value of the dependent variable, given the values of the independent variable, or variables.

Regression Coefficient. A regression coefficient indicates the responsiveness of one variable to changes in another. If the relationship between two variables is described by a straight line, the regression coefficient is the slope of the line.

The regression coefficient between rates of return on an asset and rates of return on the market is called the beta coefficient.

Reward-to-Variability Ratio. The reward-to-variability ratio is the risk premium on an asset per unit of risk as measured by the variability or standard deviation. Sharpe used this measure to rank mutual funds.

Risk Aversion. Risk aversion means riskiness matters and is disliked. A risk averter will hold a portfolio of more than one stock in order to reduce risk for a given expected return.

Technically, the utility function of a risk averter will depend on rate of return *and* risk and will not be linear. This implies diminishing marginal utility of wealth.

A risk-averse investor will incur additional risk only if he *expects* a higher rate of return.

Risk-free Rate of Return (R_f). The risk-free rate of return is the return on an asset that is virtually riskless. For example, Treasury bills maturing in one year have a precisely predictable nominal rate of return for one year. The risk premium on an asset is the rate of return in excess of the risk-free rate. The risk-free rate is normally used in portfolio theory to represent the rate for lending or borrowing.

Risk Neutrality. Risk neutrality means risk doesn't matter. A risk-neutral investor cares only about rate of return and would hold a portfolio of one asset—the one with the highest expected rate of return. Risk neutrality implies constant marginal utility of wealth. The utility function for such an investor is linear. It is represented by the equation $U = a + bE(R)$, where U is the utility of the return on an asset and where $E(R)$ is the expected return on the asset.

Risk Premium $(R_i - R_f)$. The risk premium on an asset is the actual return minus the riskless rate of return. In Sharpe's capital asset pricing model, the risk premium for any asset is proportional to its beta—the measure of sensitivity to general market movements.

If R_i is the rate of return on an asset, and R_f is the riskless rate, $R_i - R_f$ is the risk premium.

Runs. A run is a sequence of changes in the value of a variable, all having the same sign. The number of runs in a sequence of changes is the number of reversals in sign plus one.

For example, if price changes are classified as zero, positive, or negative, a sequence of $++-++0--$ would include 5 runs.

Sampling. Sampling is the process of selecting a subset of a population. It may or may not be random. The usefulness of a sample depends upon its representativeness, or the degree to which one can make inferences about the excluded population on the basis of the sample.

The Semistandard Deviation. The semistandard deviation is analogous to the standard deviation, but only the observations below the mean are taken into account. The deviations, $(x_i - \bar{x})$, are all negative. The measure is relevant if one is interested only in downside or adverse risk.

The Separation Theorem. The separation theorem states that the choice of an optimum portfolio is independent of, or separate from, the optimal combination of *risky* assets. The latter is the same for all investors if lending and borrowing are allowed. Individual needs determine only the amount of borrowing or lending.

Serial Correlation (ρ). Serial correlation measures the degree to which what happens next is related to what happened previously.

Serial correlation is measured by the simple correlation coefficient between two variables, one being the successive value of the other. Serial correlation can also be measured with lags. For example, a change in the price of a stock can be serially correlated with the change before the last one as well as with the last one.

Skewness. Skewness is a measure of the asymmetry of a distribution. A normal distribution is symmetrical and has no skewness. If there are more observations to the left of the mean, the skewness is positive; if more to the right, negative.

Standard Deviation. The standard deviation is a commonly used measure of dispersion. It is the square root of the variance. It is based on deviations of observations from the mean and is therefore in the same units as the observations. A measure of relative dispersion is the standard deviation divided by the mean (the coefficient of variation). This is often useful in comparing distributions that differ substantially in the magnitude of the numbers.

The formula for the standard deviation, σ, is

$$\sqrt{\frac{\Sigma(x_i - \bar{x})^2}{N}}$$

For a probability distribution,

$$\sigma = \sqrt{\Sigma P_i [x_i - E(x)]^2}$$

Statistical Independence. If two variables are statistically independent, the correlation between them is not significantly different from zero. That is, the changes in the two variables are unrelated. Knowledge of the changes in one is of no value in predicting the other.

For example, the weak form of the efficient market hypothesis asserts the statistical independence of successive price changes. Current prices reflect and impound all of the implications of the historical sequence of prices so that a knowledge of that sequence is of no value in forming expectations about future price changes.

Systematic Risk. Systematic risk is the volatility of rates of return on stocks or portfolios associated with changes in rates of return on the market as a whole. It can be estimated statistically from the market model. The percentage of total variability that is systematic is given by the coefficient of determination and the degree of responsiveness to market movements is measured by beta.

Time-weighted Rate of Return. The time-weighted rate of return is a weighted average of the internal rates of return for subperiods dated by the contribution or withdrawal of funds from a portfolio. To calculate it, one needs to know the value of the portfolio at the time of each cash inflow or outflow and the dates on which these occur. Rates of return on mutual fund shares are time-weighted rates of return.

Treynor Index. The Treynor index of fund performance is the reward per unit of risk as measured by volatility or beta. It indicates the rate of return on the market index required to make the expected rate of return on a fund equal to the risk-free rate.

Unsystematic Risk. Unsystematic risk is the variability not explained by general market movements. It is avoidable through diversification. Only inefficient portfolios have unsystematic risk.

Utility Function. A utility function describes the relationship for an individual between various amounts of something such as wealth and the satisfaction it provides.

If one's preferences are known, his utility functions can often be approximated by precise mathematical equations. The signs and values of its derivatives indicate the direction and magnitude of changes in utility associated with changes in the amount of the good possessed.

Variance (σ^2). The variance of a distribution is a measure of variability based on squared deviations of individual observations from the mean value of the distribution. Its square root, the standard deviation, is a commonly used measure of dispersion.

The formula for the variance is,

$$\sigma^2 = \frac{\Sigma(x_i - \bar{x})^2}{N}$$

If the distribution is of future outcomes that are not known with certainty, the variance is a weighted average of the squared deviations and the weights are the probabilities of occurrence. That is,

$$\sigma^2 = \Sigma P_i[x_i - E(x)]^2$$

Volatility. Volatility is that part of total variability due to sensitivity to changes in the market. It is systematic and unavoidable risk. It is measured by the beta coefficient.

Efficient portfolios have no additional risk, and volatility is the only source of variability in rates of return.

Wealth Ratio $\left(\dfrac{W_t}{W_o}\right)$. A wealth ratio is the terminal value of an investment divided by its initial value. It is used in calculating rates of return.

The wealth ratio is expressed as W_t/W_o where W_t refers to the terminal value and W_o to the initial value. The annual rate of return compounded continuously is

$$\log_e \frac{\left(\dfrac{W_t}{W_o}\right)}{n},$$

where n is the number of years in the period. The annual rate of return compounded annually is $e^x - 1$, where x is the annual rate compounded continuously.

Weighting. Weighting is the specification of the relative importance of each of a group of items that are combined. For example, stocks included in indexes may be equally weighted or weighted according to value.

Notes

Chapter 1

1. New York Stock Exchange, "The Demand for Corporate Equity: Projections for 1975 and 1980," *Perspectives on Planning,* no. 5 (January 1970), p. 2.
2. New York Stock Exchange, *1972 Fact Book,* p. 27.
3. American Stock Exchange, *Amex Databook,* 1971, p. 18.
4. New York Stock Exchange, *1972 Fact Book,* p. 52.
5. See Sidney Horner and Martin L. Liebowitz, *Inside the Yield Book. New Tools for Bond Market Strategy* (New York: Prentice-Hall and New York Institute of Finance, 1972).
6. Donald T. Regan, *A View from the Street* (New York, N.Y.: New American Library, 1972), especially chaps. 1 and 2.
7. Ezra Solomon, "Economic Growth and Common Stock Value," *Journal of Business,* vol. 28, no. 3 (July 1955), pp. 213–21.
8. Ibid., p. 217.
9. J. Fred Weston, "The Stock Market in Perspective," *Harvard Business Review,* vol. 34, no. 2. (March–April 1956), pp. 71–80.
10. Arthur F. Burns, "Progress Towards Economic Stability," *American Economic Review,* vol. 50, no. 1 (March 1960), pp. 1–19.
11. Theodore A. Andersen, "Trends in Profit Sensitivity," *Journal of Finance,* vol. 18, no. 4 (December 1963), pp. 637–46.
12. Reuben A. Kessel, "Inflation-Caused Wealth Redistribution: Test of Hypothesis," *American Economic Review,* vol. 46, no. 1 (March 1956), pp. 128–41: Reuben A. Kessel and A. A. Alchian, "The Meaning and Validity of the Inflation-Induced Lag of Wages behind Prices," *American Economic Review,* vol. 50, no. 1 (March 1960), pp. 43–66; and "Inflation and Stock Prices" (paper prepared for the Seminar on the Analysis of Se-

curity Prices, University of Chicago, May 1965).

13. John M. Keynes, *A Treatise on Money,* vol. 2 (New York, N.Y.: Harcourt and Brace, 1930).

14. Irving Fisher, *The Purchasing Power of Money* (rev. ed., New York, N.Y.: The McMillan Co., 1925).

15. Earl J. Hamilton, "Profit Inflation and the Industrial Revolution, 1751–1800," *Quarterly Journal of Economics,* vol. 56 (February 1942), pp. 256–73; and "Prices as a Factor in Business Growth," *Journal of Economic History,* vol. 12 (Fall 1952), pp. 325–49.

16. Wesley Clair Mitchell, *A History* of the Greenbacks with Special Reference to the Economic Consequences of Their Issues (Chicago, Ill.: University of Chicago Press, 1903).

17. Kessel and Alchian, "Inflation-Induced Lag of Wages," p. 64.

18. Milton Friedman and Anna Jacobson Schwartz, *A Monetary History of the United States 1867–1960,* a study by the National Bureau of Economic Research (Princeton, N.J.: Princeton University Press, 1963).

19. Beryl W. Sprinkel, *Money and Markets* (Homewood, Ill.: Richard D. Irwin, Inc., 1971).

Chapter 2

1. W. Braddock Hickman, *Corporate Bond Quality and Investor Experience,* a study by the National Bureau of Economic Research (Princeton, N.J.: Princeton University Press, 1958); David Durand, *Basic Yields on Corporate Bonds, 1900–1942* (New York, N.Y.: National Bureau of Economic Research, 1942); David Durand and Willis J. Winn, *Basic Yields of Bonds, 1926–47: Their Measurement and Pattern* (New York, N.Y.: National Bureau of Economic Research, 1947); Frederick R. Macaulay, *The Movement of Interest Rates, Bond Yields and Stock Prices in the United States Since 1856* (New York, N.Y.: National Bureau of Economic Research, 1938).

2. John P. Herzog, "Investor Experience in Corporate Securities: A New Technique for Measurement," *Journal of Finance,* vol. 19 (March 1964), p. 46.

3. Lawrence Fisher and James H. Lorie, "Rates of Return on Investments in Common Stocks," *Journal of Business,* vol. 37, no. 1 (January 1964), pp. 1–24.

4. Lawrence Fisher and James H. Lorie, "Rates of Return on Investments in Common Stocks: The Year-By-Year Record, 1926–65," *Journal of Business,* vol. 41, no. 3 (July 1968), pp. 291–316.

5. Lawrence Fisher and James H. Lorie, "Some Studies of Variability of Returns on Investments in Common Stocks," *Journal of Business,* vol. 43, no. 2 (April 1970), pp. 99–134.

6. For an excellent discussion of the relevant formulas see Grant and Ireson, *Principles of Engineering Economy,* (4th ed. New York, N.Y.: Ronald Press, 1960), chap. 6.

7. Alfred Cowles III, and Asso-

ciates, *Common Stock Indexes, 1871–1937,* Cowles Commission Monograph (Bloomington, Ind.: Principia Press, 1938).

8. Fisher and Lorie, "Rates of Return."

9. Fisher and Lorie, "Rates of Return: Year-By-Year Record."

10. A. J. Merrett and Allen Sykes, "Return on Equities and Fixed Interest Securities, 1919–1966," *District Bank Review* (June 1966), pp. 29–44.

11. Ibid.

12. Fisher and Lorie, "Studies of Variability of Returns."

13. Hickman, *Corporate Bond Quality.*

14. Roman L. Weil, "Realized Interest Rates and Bondholders' Returns," *American Economic Review,* vol. 60, no. 3 (June 1970), pp. 502–11.

15. Lawrence Fisher and Roman L. Weil, "Coping with the Risk of Interest-Rate Fluctuations: Returns to Bondholders from Naïve and Optimal Strategies," *Journal of Business,* vol. 44, no. 4 (October 1971), pp. 408–31.

16. Edgar Lawrence Smith, *Common Stocks as Long-Term Investments* (New York, N.Y.: The Macmillan Co., 1924). Smith's work was updated in 1954 by Winthrop B. Walker. His results,

which appeared in *A Re-examination of Common Stocks as Long Term Investments* (Portland, Maine: The Anthoensen Press, 1954), cover the period 1923–1951 and support the earlier findings.

17. Donald L. Kemerer, "For Long-Term Investment: Stocks or Bonds," *Commercial and Financial Chronicle,* February 1, 1951. Reprinted in H. K. Wu and A. J. Zakon, eds., *Elements of Investments, Selected Readings* (New York, N.Y.: Holt, Rinehart & Winston, 1965), pp. 91–101.

18. Lawrence Fisher and Roman Weil, "Coping with the Risk of Interest-Rate Fluctuations: Returns to Bondholders from Naïve and Optimal Strategies," *Journal of Business,* vol. 44, no. 4 (October 1971).

19. This performance index was presented in Lawrence Fisher, "Some New Stock-Market Indexes," *Journal of Business, Security Prices: A Supplement,* vol. 39, no. 1, part 2 (January 1966), pp. 191–225.

20. Fisher and Weil, "Coping with the Risk of Interest-Rate Fluctuations," p. 408.

21. Merrett and Sykes, "Return on Equities."

Chapter 3

1. "Index Numbers," *Encyclopedia of Social Sciences,* vol. 7, pp. 154–69; Alfred Cowles III and Associates, *Common Stock Indexes, 1871–1937,* Cowles Commission Monograph (Bloomington, Ind.: Principia Press, 1938);

Irving Fisher, *The Making of Index Numbers: A Study of Their Varieties, Tests, and Reliability* (Boston and New York: Houghton Mifflin Co., 1922).

2. Benjamin F. King, "Market and Industry Factors in Stock Price

Behavior," *Journal of Business, Security Prices: A Supplement,* vol. 39, no. 1, part 2 (January 1966), pp. 139–90.

3. Lawrence Fisher and James H. Lorie, "Some Studies of Variability of Returns on Investments in Common Stocks," *Journal of Business,* vol. 43, no. 2 (April 1970), pp. 99–134.

4. Eugene F. Fama et al., "The Adjustment of Stock Prices to New Information," *International Economic Review,* vol. 10, no. 1 (February 1969), pp. 1–21.

5. Paul Cootner, "Stock Market Indexes—Fallacies and Illusions," *Commercial and Financial Chronicle* (September 29, 1966), p. 18.

6. Lawrence Fisher, "Some New Stock Market Indexes," *Journal of Business, Security Prices: A Supplement,* vol. 39, no. 1, part 2 (January 1966), pp. 191–225.

7. Robert D. Milne, "The Dow Jones Industrial Average Reexamined," *Financial Analysts Journal,* vol. 22, no. 6 (November–December 1966), p. 86.

8. Ibid., p. 86.

9. Ibid., p. 86.

10. Cowles, *Common Stock Indexes.*

11. Irwin Friend, Marshall Blume, and Jean Crockett, *Mutual Funds and Other Institutional Investors* (New York, N.Y.: McGraw-Hill Book Co., 1970), p. 19.

Chapter 4

1. Paul A. Samuelson, "Proof That Properly Anticipated Prices Fluctuate Randomly," *Industrial Management Review,* vol. 6 (Spring 1965), pp. 41–49.

2. Benoit Mandelbrot, "Forecasts of Future Prices, Unbiased Markets, and Martingale Models," *Journal of Business, Security Prices: A Supplement,* vol. 39, part 2 (January 1966), pp. 242–55.

3. Karl Pearson and the Right Honorable Lord Rayleigh," The Problem of the Random Walk," *Nature,* vol. 72, no. 1865, pp. 294, 318, and 342.

4. Louis Bachelier, "Théorie de la Spéculation," (Paris: Gauthier–Villars, 1900).

5. Holbrook Working, "A Random Difference Series for Use in the Analysis of Time Series," *Journal of the American Statistical Association,* vol. 29 (March 1934), pp. 11–24.

6. Alfred Cowles and Herbert E. Jones, "Some A Posteriori Probabilities in Stock Market Action," *Econometrica,* vol. 5 (July 1937), pp. 280–94.

7. Maurice G. Kendall, "The Analysis of Economic Time Series, Part I: Prices," *Journal of the Royal Statistical Society,* vol. 96, part 1 (1953), pp. 11–25.

8. Harry V. Roberts, "Stock Market 'Patterns' and Financial Analysis: Methodological Suggestions," *Journal of Finance,* vol. 14, no. 1 (March 1959), pp. 1–10.

9. M. F. M. Osborne, "Brownian Motion in the Stock Market," *Operations Research,* vol. 7 (March–April 1959), pp. 145–73.

10. Arnold B. Moore, "Some Characteristics of Changes in Com-

mon Stock Prices," in Paul H. Cootner, *The Random Character of Stock Market Prices* (Cambridge, Mass.: The M.I.T. Press, 1964), pp. 139–61.

11. Eugene F. Fama, "The Behavior of Stock Market Prices," *Journal of Business,* vol. 38, no. 1 (January 1965), pp. 34–105.

12. Clive W. J. Granger and Oskar Morgenstern, "Spectral Analysis of New York Stock Market Prices," *Kyklos,* vol. 16 (1963), pp. 1–27.

13. Sidney S. Alexander, "Price Movements in Speculative Markets: Trends or Random Walks," *Industrial Management Review,* vol. 2 (May 1961), pp. 7–26; also by Alexander, "Price Movements in Speculative Markets: Trends or Random Walks, No. 2," *Industrial Management Review,* vol. 5 (Spring 1964), pp. 25–46,

14. Fama, "The Behavior of Stock Market Prices."

15. Eugene F. Fama and Marshall E. Blume, "Filter Rules and Stock Market Trading," *Journal of Business, Security Prices: A Supplement,* vol. 39, no. 1, part 2 (January 1966), pp. 226–41.

16. See, for example, Paul H. Cootner, "Stock Prices: Random versus Systematic Changes," *Industrial Management Review,* vol. 3, no. 2 (Spring 1962), pp. 24–45; Robert A. Levy, "Random Walks: Reality or Myth," *Financial Analysts Journal,* vol. 25 (November–December 1967), pp. 69–76; Michael C. Jensen, "Random Walks: Reality or Myth—Comment," *Financial Analysts Journal,* vol. 25 (November–December 1967), pp. 77–85; James C. VanHorne and

George G. C. Parker, "Technical Trading Rules: A Comment," *Financial Analysts Journal,* vol. 24 (July–August 1968), pp. 128–31.

17. Miles M. Dryden, "Filter Tests of U.K. Share Prices," *Applied Economics,* vol. 1 (1970), pp. 261–75.

18. Ibid., p. 269.

19. A. James Boness, "A Theory and Measurement of Stock Option Value" (Ph.D. diss., University of Chicago, 1962).

20. Carl Sprenkle, "Warrant Prices as Indicators of Expectations and Preferences," *Yale Economics Essays,* vol. 1 (1961), pp. 178–231.

21. Arnold B. Moore, "A Statistical Analysis of Common Stock Prices" (Ph.D. diss., University of Chicago, 1962).

22. Samuelson, "Proof That Properly Anticipated Prices Fluctuate Randomly."

23. Mandelbrot, "Forecasts of Future Prices."

24. Eugene F. Fama, "Efficient Capital Markets: A Review of Theory and Empirical Work," *Journal of Finance,* vol. 25, no. 2 (May 1970), pp. 383–417.

25. Eugene F. Fama et al., "The Adjustment of Stock Prices to New Information," *International Economic Review,* vol. 10, no. 1 (February 1969), pp. 1–21.

26. Ibid., p. 17.

27. Myron S. Scholes, "The Market for Securities: Substitution versus Price Pressure and the Effects of Information on Share Prices," *Journal of Business,* vol. 45, no. 2 (April 1972), pp. 179–211.

28. Ray Ball and Philip Brown, "An Empirical Evaluation of Ac-

counting Income Numbers," *Journal of Accounting Research,* vol. 6, (Autumn 1968), pp. 159–78.

29. Roger N. Waud, "Public Interpretation of Discount Rates Changes: Evidence on the 'Announcement Effect'," *Econometrica,* vol. 38, no. 2, pp. 231–50.

30. Irwin Friend et al., *A Study of Mutual Funds,* prepared for the Securities and Exchange Commission by the Securities Research Unit, Wharton School of Finance and Commerce, University of Pennsylvania (Washington, D.C.: U.S. Government Printing Office, 1962).

31. William F. Sharpe, "Mutual Fund Performance," *Journal of Business, Security Prices: A Supplement,* vol. 39, no. 1, part 2 (January 1966), pp. 119–38.

32. William F. Sharpe, "Capital Asset Prices: A Theory of Market Equilibrium Under Conditions of Risk," *Journal of Finance,* vol. 19, no. 3 (September 1964), pp. 425–42; also by Sharpe, "Risk Aversion in the Stock Market: Some Empirical Evidence," *Journal of Finance,* vol. 20, no. 3 (September 1965), pp. 416–22.

33. John Lintner, "Security Prices, Risk, and Maximal Gains from Diversification," *Journal of Finance,* vol. 20, no. 4 (December 1965), pp. 587–616.

34. Sharpe, "Mutual Fund Performance," p. 137.

35. Ibid., p. 138.

36. Michael C. Jensen, "The Performance of Mutual Funds in the Period 1945–64," *Journal of Finance,* vol. 23, no. 2 (May 1968), pp. 389–416.

37. Michael C. Jensen, "Risk, The Pricing of Capital Assets, and the Evaluation of Investment Portfolios," *Journal of Business,* vol. 42, no. 2 (April 1969), pp. 167–247.

38. Irwin Friend, Marshall Blume, and Jean Crockett, *Mutual Funds and Other Institutional Investors, A New Perspective,* A 20th Century Fund Study (New York, N.Y.: McGraw-Hill Book Co., 1970).

39. Peter J. Williamson, "Measuring Mutual Fund Performance," *Financial Analysts Journal* (November–December 1972), pp. 78–84.

40. Victor Niederhoffer and M. F. M. Osborne, "Market Making and Reversal on the Stock Exchange," *Journal of the American Statistical Association,* vol. 61 (December 1966), pp. 897–916.

41. Scholes, "The Market for Securities."

42. James H. Lorie and Victor Niederhoffer, "Predictive and Statistical Properties of Insider Trading," *Journal of Law and Economics,* vol. 11 (1968), pp. 35–53.

43. Ibid., p. 52.

Chapter 5

1. Charles G. Callard, "The Third Yield," *Financial Analysts Journal,* vol. 24 (January–February 1968), pp. 114–20; idem, "Stock Price Outlook During Coming Decade," *The Commercial and*

Financial Chronicle, vol. 212, no. 7016 (July 30, 1970), pp. 1, 14–17.

2. See, for example, M. J. Gordon and Eli Shapiro, "Capital Equipment Analysis: The Required Rate of Profit," *Management Science* (October 1956), pp. 102–10; Walter Morton (Testimony during A.T.&T. Rate Hearings before the Federal Communications Commission, May 2, 1966).

3. Guilford C. Babcock, "The Concept of Sustainable Growth," *Financial Analysts Journal,* vol. 26 (May–June 1970), pp. 108–14; idem, "The Trend and Stability of Earnings" (paper prepared for the Seminar on the Analysis of Security Prices, University of Chicago, November 1970).

4. Richard Martin, "Looking for Losers," *Wall Street Journal,* vol. 50, no. 71, pp. 1, 16.

5. James H. Lorie and Victor Niederhoffer, "Predictive and Statistical Properties of Insider Trading," *Journal of Law and Economics,* vol. 11 (1968), pp. 35–53.

6. Marshall E. Blume, "The Assessment of Portfolio Performance— An Application of Portfolio Theory" (Ph.D. diss., University of Chicago, 1968); Shannon Pratt, "Relationships Between Risk and Rate of Return for Common Stocks" (D.B.S. diss., Indiana University, 1966); Richard A. Brealey, "Some Implications of the Comovement of Corporate Earnings" (paper prepared for the Seminar on the Analysis of Security Prices, University of Chicago, November 1968).

7. Geoffrey P. Clarkson and Allan H. Meltzer, "Portfolio Selection: A Heuristic Approach," *Journal of Finance,* vol. 15, no. 4 (December 1960), pp. 465–80.

8. Richard A. Brealey, *An Introduction to Risk and Return from Common Stocks* (Cambridge, Mass.: M.I.T. Press, 1968), p. 115.

9. Fischer Black, "Implication of the Random Walk Hypothesis for Portfolio Management," Financial Note 13A, Associates in Finance, December 11, 1969.

Chapter 6

1. Merton H. Miller and Franco Modigliani, "Dividend Policy, Growth, and the Valuation of Shares," *Journal of Business,* vol. 34, no. 4 (October 1961), pp. 411–33.

2. The classic statement appears in John Burr Williams, *The Theory of Investment Value* (Cambridge, Mass.: Harvard University Press, 1938). The book was reprinted in 1964 by North-Holland Publishing Co., Amsterdam. All references are to this edition.

3. Ibid., p. 15.

4. Ibid., pp. 57–58.

5. M. J. Gordon, "Dividends, Earnings, and Stock Prices," *Review of Economics and Statistics,* vol. 41, no. 1 (May 1959), pp. 96–105.

6. Ibid., pp. 102–3.

7. Frederick Lutz and Vera Lutz, *The Theory of Investment of the Firm* (Princeton University Press, 1951), pp. 155 ff.

8. James E. Walter, "Dividend Policies and Common-Stock Prices," *Journal of Finance,* vol. 11, no. 1 (March 1956), pp. 29–41.

9. Miller and Modigliani, "Dividend Policy."

10. Ibid., p. 414.

11. Gordon, "Dividends, Earnings, and Stock Prices," and "The Savings, Investment, and Valuation of a Corporation," *Review of Economics and Statistics,* vol. 44 (1962), pp. 37–51. See also Miller and Modigliani, "Dividend Policy," p. 424, n. 18; and John Lintner, "Dividends, Earnings, Leverage, Stock Prices, and the Supply of Capital to Corporations," *Review of Economics and Statistics,* vol. 44, no. 3 (August 1962), pp. 255–56.

12. Ross Watts, "The Information Content of Dividends" (Ph.D. diss., University of Chicago, 1971).

13. William F. Sharpe, *Portfolio Theory and Capital Markets* (New York., N.Y.: McGraw-Hill Book Co., 1970), especially chap. 3.

Chapter 7

1. Merton H. Miller and Franco Modigliani, "Dividend Policy, Growth, and the Valuation of Shares," *Journal of Business,* vol. 34, no. 4 (October 1961), pp. 421–22.

2. Fischer Black, "Yes, Virginia, There Is Hope: Tests of the Value Line Ranking System" (paper prepared for the Seminar on the Analysis of Security Prices, University of Chicago, May 1971).

3. Volkert S. Whitbeck and Manown Kisor, Jr., "A New Tool in Investment Decision-Making," *Financial Analysts Journal,* vol. 19 (May–June 1963), pp. 55–62.

4. Ibid., p. 60.

5. Ibid., p. 58.

6. Some support for this view comes from Manown Kisor, Jr. and Stanley Levine, "Simulated Results from a Valuation Model Using Objectively Determined Proxies for Analysts' Expectations" (manuscript).

7. David M. Ahlers, "SEM: A Security Evaluation Model," in Kalman J. Cohen and Frederick S. Hammer, eds., *Analytical Methods in Banking* (Homewood, Ill.: Richard D. Irwin, Inc., 1966), pp. 305–36.

8. Ibid., p. 317. This form of the equation has also been used by Whitbeck. See Volkert S. Whitbeck, "An Iterative Version of a Stock Valuation Model" (paper presented to the Seminar on the Analysis for Security Prices, Center for Research in Security Prices, University of Chicago, May 1968).

9. Cohen and Hammer, *Analytical Methods in Banking*, p. 314.

10. Ibid., p. 316.

11. Ibid., p. 316.

12. Ibid., p. 324.

13. Ibid., p. 333.

14. B. G. Malkiel, "Equity Yields, Growth, and the Structure of Share Prices," *American Economic Review,* vol. 53, no. 5 (December 1963), pp. 1004–31.

—

15. Leslie G. Peck, "The Goldman, Sachs & Co. Valuation Model" (manuscript).
16. Ibid., p. 3.
17. Ibid., p. 4.
18. David Durand, "Growth Stocks and the Petersburg Paradox," *Journal of Finance,* vol. 12, no. 3 (September 1957), pp. 348–63.
19. See, for example, M. J. Gordon, *The Investment Financing and Valuation of the Corporation* (Homewood, Ill.: Richard D. Irwin, Inc., 1962).
20. Charles C. Holt, "The Influence of Growth Duration on Share Prices," *Journal of Finance,* vol. 17, no. 3 (September 1962), pp. 465–75.
21. Whitbeck and Kisor, "A New Tool," p. 56.
22. Marshall E. Blume, "The Assessment of Portfolio Performance: An Application of Portfolio Theory" (Ph.D. diss., University of Chicago, 1968).
23. Richard A. Brealey, *An Introduction to Risk and Return from Common Stocks* (Cambridge, Mass.: The M.I.T. Press, 1969), chap. 3.
24. Ibid., p. 46.

Chapter 8

1. Victor Niederhoffer and Patrick Regan, "Earnings Changes, Analysts' Forecasts, and Stock Prices," *Financial Analysts Journal* (May–June 1972), pp. 65–71.
2. Latané and Tuttle cited in Richard A. Brealey, *Introduction to Risk and Return from Common Stocks* (Cambridge, Mass.: M.I.T. Press, 1969), p. 84.
3. *Wall Street Journal,* July 31, 1972, p. 17.
4. Jack L. Treynor, "The Trouble with Earnings," *Financial Analysts Journal,* vol. 28, no. 5 (September–October 1972), pp. 41–46.
5. Ibid., p. 41.
6. "What *Are* Earnings? The Growing Credibility Gap," *Forbes Magazine,* May 15, 1967, pp. 28–31, 34, 39, 42, 44.
7. Ibid., p. 28.
8. Ibid., p. 28.
9. "It's Time to Call the Auditors to Account," *Fortune* (August 1970), p. 98.
10. Leonard Spacek, "Business Success Requires an Understanding of the Unsolved Problems of Accounting and Financial Reporting" (Address to the Financial Accounting Class, Graduate School of Business, Harvard University, September 25, 1969). Leonard Spacek was then managing partner of Arthur Andersen & Co.
11. Abraham J. Briloff, "Castles of Sand?" *Barron's,* February 2, 1970.
12. *FTC* v. *The Borden Company* (Docket No. 7129).
13. J. J. Servan-Schreiber, *The American Challenge* (New York, N.Y.: Atheneum, 1968).
14. Sidney Davidson, in Dennis V. Waite, "'Radical' Accountants Add Ideas," *The Chicago Sun Times,* January 18, 1970.
15. Accounting Principles Board, *Business Combinations* (Opinion no. 16), August 1970; and *Intangible Assets* (Opinion no. 17), August 1970.
16. Raymond J. Ball, "Changes in

Accounting Techniques and Stock Prices" (Manuscript, University of Chicago, 1971).

17. Ibid., p. 2.

18. James H. Lorie and Paul Halpern, "Conglomerates: The Rhetoric and the Evidence," *Journal of Law and Economics,* vol. 13, no. 1 (April 1970), pp. 149–66.

19. Ibid., p. 163.

Chapter 9

1. Richard A. Brealey, *An Introduction to Risk and Return from Common Stocks* (Cambridge, Mass.: M.I.T. Press, 1969).

2. Henry A. Latané and Donald L. Tuttle, "An Analysis of Common Stock Price Ratios," *Southern Economic Journal,* vol. 33 (January 1967), pp. 343–54.

3. Manown Kisor, Jr. and Van A. Messner, "The Filter Approach and Earnings Forecasts—Part One" (Manuscript, June 1968).

4. Ian M. D. Little, "Higgledy Piggledy Growth," Institute of Statistics, Oxford, vol. 24, no. 4 (November 1962).

5. Ian M. D. Little and A. C. Rayner, *Higgledy Piggledy Growth Again* (Oxford: Basil Blackwell, 1966).

6. Joseph E. Murphy, Jr., "Relative Growth in Earnings per Share—Past and Future," *Financial Analysts Journal,* vol. 22 (November–December 1966), pp. 73–76.

7. John Lintner and Robert Glauber, "Higgledy Piggledy Growth in America?" (paper presented to the Seminar on the Analysis of Security Prices, University of Chicago, May 1967); and "Further Observations on Higgledy Piggledy Growth," (paper presented to the Seminar on the Analysis of Security Prices, University of Chicago, May 1969).

8. Richard A. Brealey, "The Character of Earnings Changes" (paper presented to the Seminar on the Analysis of Security Prices, University of Chicago, May 1967).

9. J. G. Cragg and Burton G. Malkiel, "The Consensus and Accuracy of Some Predictions of the Growth of Corporate Earnings," *Journal of Finance,* vol. 23, no. 1 (March 1968), pp. 67–84.

10. Ibid., p. 83.

11. David Green, Jr. and Joel Segall, "The Predictive Power of First-Quarter Earnings Reports," *Journal of Business,* vol. 40, no. 1 (January 1967), pp. 44–55.

12. Philip Brown and Victor Niederhoffer, "The Predictive Content of Quarterly Earnings," *Journal of Business,* vol. 41, no. 4 (October 1968), pp. 488–97.

13. David Green, Jr. and Joel Segall, "Brickbats and Strawmen: A Reply to Brown and Niederhoffer," *Journal of Business,* vol. 41, no. 4 October 1968), pp. 498–502; idem, "Return of Strawman," *Journal of Business,* vol. 43, no. 1 (January 1970), pp. 63–65; Victor Niederhoffer, "The Predictive Content of First-Quarter Earnings Reports," *Journal of Business,* vol. 43, no. 1 (January 1970), pp. 60–62.

Chapter 10

1. Harry M. Markowitz, "Portfolio Selection," *Journal of Finance,* vol. 7, no. 1 (March 1952), pp. 77–91.
2. William F. Sharpe, *Portfolio Theory and Capital Markets* (New York: McGraw-Hill Book Co., 1970), pp. 37–44.
3. Harry M. Markowitz, *Portfolio Selection, Efficient Diversification of Investments,* Cowles Foundation, Monograph No. 16 (New York: John Wiley & Sons, 1959), pp. 72–101.
4. William F. Sharpe, "A Simplified Model for Portfolio Analysis," *Management Science,* vol. 9, no. 2 (January 1963), pp. 277–93.
5. James Tobin, "Liquidity Preference as Behavior Towards Risk," *Review of Economic Studies,* vol. 6, no. 1 (February 1958), pp. 65–86.
6. Sharpe, "A Simplified Model."
7. Tobin, "Liquidity Preference."
8. The proof of this assertion is in Sharpe, *Portfolio Theory,* pp. 196–201.
9. Markowitz, *Portfolio Selection, Efficient Diversification of Investments,* pp. 288–89.
10. Ibid., pp. 282–86.
11. William J. Baumol, "An Expected Gain-Confidence Limit Criterion for Portfolio Selection," *Management Science,* vol. 10, no. 1 (October 1963), pp. 174–82.
12. Fred D. Arditti, "Risk and the Required Return on Equity," *Journal of Finance,* vol. 22, no. 1 (March 1967), pp. 19–36; and Clayton P. Alderfor and Harold Bierman, Jr., "Choice with Risk: Beyond the Mean and Variance," *Journal of Business,* vol. 43, no. 3 (July 1970), pp. 341–53.
13. Markowitz, *Portfolio Selection, Efficient Diversification of Investments,* pp. 287–97.

Chapter 11

1. William F. Sharpe, "A Simplified Model for Portfolio Analysis," *Management Science,* vol. 9, no. 1 (1963), pp. 277–93. This approach was suggested, but not explained in detail, by Markowitz, *Portfolio Selection: Efficient Diversification of Investments* (New York: John Wiley & Sons, 1959), pp. 96–101.
2. Kalman J. Cohen and Jerry A. Poague, "An Empirical Evaluation of Alternative Portfolio Selection Models," *Journal of Business,* vol. 40, no. 2 (April 1967), pp. 169–93.
3. William F. Sharpe, "Capital Asset Prices: A Theory of Market Equilibrium under Conditions of Risk," *Journal of Finance,* vol. 19, no. 3 (September 1964), pp. 425–42.
4. Milton Friedman, "The Methodology of Positive Economics," *Essays in Positive Economics* (Chicago: The University of Chicago Press, 1953).
5. Ibid., p. 15.
6. William F. Sharpe, "Risk Aversion in the Stock Market: Some Empirical Evidence," *Journal of Finance,* vol. 20, no. 3 (Septem-

ber 1965), pp. 416–22; and "Mutual Fund Performance," *Journal of Business, Security Prices: A Supplement,* vol. 39, no. 1, part 2, (January 1966), pp. 119–38.

7. Michael C. Jensen, "Risk, the Pricing of Capital Assets, and the Evaluation of Investment Portfolios," *Journal of Business,* vol. 42, no. 2 (April 1969), pp. 167–247.

8. George W. Douglas, *Risk in the Equity Markets: An Empirical Appraisal of Market Efficiency* (Ann Arbor: University Microfilms, 1968).

9. John Lintner, "Security Prices and Risk: The Theory and a Comparative Analysis of A.T.&T. and Leading Industries" (paper presented at the Conference of Regulated Public Utilities, University of Chicago, 1965).

10. Merton H. Miller and Myron S. Scholes, "Rates of Return in Relation to Risk: A Re-examination of Some Recent Findings," in Michael C. Jensen, ed., *Studies in the Theory of Capital Markets* (New York, N.Y.: Praeger Publishers, 1972).

Chapter 12

1. W. Braddock Hickman, *Corporate Bond Quality and Investor Experience,* A study by the National Bureau of Economic Research (Princeton, N.J.: Princeton University Press, 1958).

2. Lawrence Fisher, "The Determinants of Risk Premiums of Corporate Bonds," *Journal of Political Economy,* vol. 67, no. 3 (June 1959), pp. 217–37.

3. Shannon Pratt, "Relationships Between Risk and Rate of Return for Common Stock" (D.B.S. diss., Indiana University, 1966).

4. Milton Friedman and Leonard J. Savage, "The Utility Analysis of Choices Involving Risk," *Journal of Political Economy,* vol. 41, no. 4 (August 1948), pp. 279–304.

5. F. Mosteller and P. Nogee, "An Experimental Measure of Utility," *Journal of Political Economy,* vol. 59, no. 5 (October 1951), pp. 371–404.

6. Fred. D. Arditti, "Risk and the Required Return on Equity," *Journal of Finance,* vol. 22, no. 1 (March 1967), pp. 19–36.

7. Michael C. Jensen, "Risk, the Pricing of Capital Assets, and the Evaluation of Investment Portfolios," *Journal of Business,* vol. 42, no. 2 (April 1969), pp. 167–247.

8. Irwin Friend, Marshall Blume, and Jean Crockett, *Mutual Funds and Other Institutional Investors* (New York, N.Y.: McGraw–Hill Book Co., 1970).

9. U.S. Congress, *Institutional Investor Study Report of the Securities and Exchange Commission,* vol. 2, 92d Cong., 1st sess., 1971, H. Doc. No. 92–64, part 2.

10. Lawrence Fisher, "Good Betas and Bad Betas: How to Tell the Difference" (paper prepared for the Seminar on the Analysis of Security Prices, University of Chicago, November 1971).

11. Fischer Black, Michael C. Jen-

sen, and Myron S. Scholes, "The Capital Asset Pricing Model: Some Empirical Tests," in Michael C. Jensen, ed., *Studies in the Theory of Capital Markets* (New York: Praeger Publishers, 1972).

12. Ibid.

13. William F. Sharpe, "Capital Asset Prices: A Theory of Market Equilibrium under Conditions of Risk," *Journal of Finance,* vol. 19, no. 3 (September 1964), pp. 425–42.

14. Black, Jensen, and Scholes, "Capital Asset Pricing Model."

Chapter 13

1. James H. Lorie et al., *Measuring the Investment Performance of Pension Funds for the Purpose of Inter-Fund Comparison* (Park Ridge, Ill.: Bank Administration Institute, 1968).

2. William L. Cary and Craig B. Bright, *The Law and the Lore of Endowment Funds* (New York: Ford Foundation, 1969).

3. Lorie et al., *Measuring Investment Performance of Pension Funds,* pp. 75–75.

4. For a fuller discussion, see Eugene F. Fama, *Risk and the Evaluation of Pension Fund Portfolio Performance,* Supplement to Lorie et al., *Measuring Investment Performance of Pension Funds,* pp. 16–21.

5. Richard S. Bower and Donald F. Wippern, "Risk-Return Measurement in Portfolio Selection and Performance Appraisal Models: Progress Report," *Jour-*

nal of Financial and Quantitative Analysis, vol. 4, no. 4 (December 1969), pp. 417–47.

6. Jack L. Treynor, "How to Rate Management of Investment Funds," *Harvard Business Review,* vol. 43, no. 1 (January–February 1965), pp. 63–75.

7. William F. Sharpe, "Mutual Fund Performance," *Journal of Business, Security Prices: A Supplement,* vol. 39, no. 1, part 2 (January 1966), pp. 119–38.

8. Lorie et al., *Measuring Investment Performance of Pension Funds,* p. 32.

9. Bower and Wippern, "Risk-Return Measurement," pp. 424–25.

10. Michael C. Jensen, "Risk, The Pricing of Capital Assets, and The Evaluation of Investment Portfolios," *Journal of Business,* vol. 42, no. 2 (April 1969), pp. 167–247.

Chapter 14

1. For the results of some empirical tests using different indexes, see Keith V. Smith, "Stock Prices and Economic Indexes for Generating Efficient Portfolios," *Journal of Business,* vol. 42, no. 3. (July 1969), pp. 326–36.

2. Irwin Friend, Marshall Blume,

and Jean Crockett, *Mutual Funds and Other Institutional Investors* (New York: McGraw–Hill Book Co., 1970), p. 19.

3. James H. Lorie et al., *Measuring the Investment Performance of Pension Funds for the Purpose of Inter-Fund Comparison* (Park

Ridge, Ill.: Bank Administration Institute, 1968).

4. Sidney S. Alexander, "Price Movements in Speculative Markets: Trends or Random Walks," *Industrial Management Review*, vol. 2 (May 1961), pp. 7–26; idem, "Price Movements in Speculative Markets: Trends or Random Walks, No. 2," *Industrial Management Review*, vol. 5 (Spring 1964), pp. 25–46.

5. Eugene F. Fama and Marshall E. Blume, "Filter Rules and Stock Market Trading," *Journal of Business, Security Prices: A Supplement*, vol. 39, no. 1, part 2 (January 1966), pp. 226–41.

6. Lawrence Fisher and James H. Lorie, "Rates of Return on Investments in Common Stocks: The Year-By-Year Record, 1926–65," *Journal of Business*, vol. 41, no. 3 (July 1968), pp. 291–316.

Complementary Readings

We list below some books and articles which should prove helpful to readers interested in further exploration of the subjects discussed in our book.

I. The Behavior of the Market

Baumol, W. J. *The Stock Market and Economic Efficiency.* New York: Fordham University Press, 1965.

Brealey, Richard A. *An Introduction to Risk and Return from Common Stocks.* Cambridge, Mass.: M.I.T. Press, 1969.

Brealey, Richard A. *Security Prices in a Competitive Market: More about Risk and Return from Common Stocks.* Cambridge, Mass.: M.I.T. Press, 1971.

Brigham, E. F., and Pappas, J. L. "Rates of Return on Common Stock." *Journal of Business,* July 1969.

Cootner, P. H. *The Random Character of Stock Prices.* Cambridge, Mass.: M.I.T. Press, 1964.

Eiteman, S. J.; Dice, C. A.; and Eiteman, D. K. *The Stock Market.* 4th ed. New York: McGraw-Hill, 1966.

Fama, Eugene F. "The Behavior of Stock-Market Prices." *Journal of Business,* vol. 37, January 1965, pp. 34–105.

Fama, Eugene F. "Efficient Capital Markets: A Review of Theory and Empirical Work." *Journal of Finance,* May 1970.

Fisher, Lawrence, and Lorie, James H. "Rates of Return on Investments in Common Stock: The Year-by-Year Record, 1926–65." *Journal of Business,* vol. 41, no. 3, July 1968, pp. 291–316.

Fisher, Lawrence, and Lorie, James H. "Some Studies of Variability of Returns on Investments in Common Stocks." *Journal of Business,* vol. 43, no. 2, April 1970, pp. 99–134.

Friedman, Milton. "Factors Affecting the Level of Interest Rates." Savings and Residential Financing 1968 Conference Proceedings, September 1968, pp. 10–27.

Jensen, Michael C. "Random Walks: Reality or Myth—Reply." *Financial Analysts Journal,* vol. 23, November 1967, pp. 69–85.

Jensen, M. C., and Bennington, G. A., "Random Walks and Technical Theories: Some Additional Evidence." *Journal of Finance,* May 1970.

Kemmerer, Donald L. "For Long-Term Investment: Stocks or Bonds." *Commercial and Financial Chronicle,* February 1, 1951.

Kessel, Reuben A. "The Cyclical Behavior of the Term Structure of Interest Rates." Occasional Paper 91. National Bureau of Economic Research, New York: Columbia University Press, 1965.

Kessel, Reuben A. "Inflation-Caused Wealth Redistribution: A Test of a Hypothesis." *American Economic Review,* March 1956.

Latané, Henry A., and Tuttle, Donald L. "Market Averages and Portfolio Performance." *Security Analysis and Portfolio Management,* chap. 7. New York: The Ronald Press Co., 1970.

Levy, Robert A. "Conceptual Foundations of Technical Analysis." *Financial Analysts Journal,* July–August 1966.

Levy, Robert A. "Random Walks: Reality or Myth." *Financial Analysts Journal,* vol. 24, January–February 1968, pp. 69–77.

Malkiel, Burton G. *The Term Structure of Interest Rates: Theory, Empirical Evidence and Applications.* Morristown, N.J.: General Learning Press, 1970.

Samuelson, P. A. "Rational Theory of Warrant Pricing." *Industrial Management Review,* Spring 1965.

Scholes, Myron S. "The Market for Securities: Substitution versus Price Pressure and the Effects of Information on Share Prices." *Journal of Business,* vol. 45, no. 2, April 1972.

Seligman, Daniel. "Playing the Market with Charts." *Fortune,* vol. 65, February 1962, pp. 118, 168ff.

Sprinkel, B. *Money and Markets.* Homewood, Ill.: Richard D. Irwin, Inc., 1971.

West, S., and Miller, N. "Why the New NYSE Common Stock Indexes?" *Financial Analysts Journal,* May–June 1967.

II. The Valuation of Securities

Bauman, W. Scott, "Investmnt Return and Present Values." *Financial Analysts Journal,* vol. 25, November–December 1969, pp. 107–20.

Benishay, H. "Variability in Earnings—Price Ratios of Corporate Equities." *American Economic Review,* March 1961.

Brigham, E. F., and Pappas, J. L. "Duration of Growth, Changes in Growth Rates, and Corporate Share Prices." *Financial Analysts Journal,* May–June 1966.

Friend, Irwin, and Puckett, Marshall. "Dividends and Stock Prices." *American Economic Review,* September 1954, pp. 656–82.

Graham, B.; Dodd, D. C.; and Cottle, S. *Security Analysis.* New York: Mc-Graw-Hill, 1961.

Holt, C. C. "The Influence of Growth Duration on Share Prices." *Journal of Finance,* September 1962.

Kaplan, Robert S., and Roll, Richard. "Investor Evaluation of Accounting Information: Some Empirical Evidence." *Journal of Business,* vol. 45, no. 2, April 1972, pp. 225–57.

Malkiel, Burton G. "Equity Yields, Growth, and the Structure of Share Prices." *American Economic Review,* December 1963.

Miller, M. H., and Modigliani, F. "Dividend Policy, Growth, and the Valuation of Shares." *Journal of Business,* October 1961.

Molodovsky, N. "Building a Stock Market Measure— A Case Story." *Financial Analysts Journal,* January–February 1969.

Soldofsky, Robert M. "Growth Yields." *Financial Analysts Journal,* vol. 17, no. 5, September–October 1961, pp. 43–47.

Weston, F. T., and Davidson, S. "What Will Accounting Changes Do to Earnings?" *Financial Analysts Journal,* September–October 1968.

Williams, John B. *The Theory of Investment Value.* Cambridge: Harvard University Press, 1938.

Williams, W. D. "A Look Behind Reported Earnings." *Financial Analysts Journal,* January–February 1966.

III. Portfolio Management

Arditti, F. D. "Another Look at Mutual Fund Performance." *Journal of Financial and Quantitative Analysis,* June 1971.

Baumol, William J. *Portfolio Theory: The Selection of Asset Combinations.* Morristown, N.J.: General Learning Press, 1970.

Blume, Marshall E. "Portfolio Theory: A Step Toward its Practical Application." *Journal of Business,* April 1970.

Bower, R. S., and Bower, D. H. "Risk and Valuation of Common Stock." *Journal of Political Economy,* May–June 1969.

Bower, R. S., and Wippern, R. F. "Risk-Return Measurement in Portfolio Selection and Performance Appraisal Models: Progress Report." *Journal of Financial and Quantitative Analysis,* December 1969.

Dietz, P. O. *Pension Funds—Measuring Investment Performance.* New York: Columbia University and the Free Press, 1966.

Fama, E. F. "The Behavior of Stock Market Prices." *Journal of Business,* January 1965.

Fama, E. F., and Miller, Merton H. *The Theory of Finance.* New York: Holt, Rinehart and Winston, 1972.

Friedman, M., and Savage, L. J. "The Utility Analysis of Choices Involving Risk." *Journal of Political Economy,* August 1948.

Friend, Irwin, and Blume, Marshall. "Measurement of Portfolio Performance under Certainty." *American Economic Review,* vol. 60, no. 4, September 1970, pp. 561–75.

Friend, Irwin, and Vickers, D. "Portfolio Selection and Investment Performance." *Journal of Finance,* September 1965.

Jensen, Michael C. *Studies in the Theory of Capital Markets.* New York: Praeger Publishers, 1972.

Lintner, J. "Security Prices, Risk and Maximal Gains from Diversification." *Journal of Finance,* December 1965.

Markowitz, H. *Portfolio Selection: Efficient Diversification of Investments.* New York: John Wiley, 1959.

Robichek, A. A. "Risk and the Value of Securities." *Journal of Financial and Quantitative Analysis,* December 1969.

Robichek, A. A.; Cohn, R. A.; and Pringle, J. J. "Returns on Alternative Investment Media and Implications for Portfolio Construction." *Journal of Business,* vol. 45, no. 2, July 1972.

Samuelson, P. A. "General Proof that Diversification Pays." *Journal of Financial and Quantitative Analysis,* March 1967.

Sharpe, William F. "Capital Asset Prices: A Theory of Market Equilibrium under Conditions of Risk." *Journal of Finance,* vol. 19, September 1964, pp. 425–42.

Sharpe, William F. *Portfolio Theory and Capital Markets.* New York: McGraw-Hill, 1970.

Sharpe, William F. "A Simplified Model for Portfolio Analysis." *Management Science,* January 1963, pp. 277–93.

Tobin, A. "Liquidity Preference as Behavior Towards Risk." *Review of Economic Studies,* February 1958.

Treynor, J. L. "How to Rate Management Investment Funds." *Harvard Business Review,* January–February 1965.

There are several good anthologies of essays from the periodical literature:

Archer, Stephen H., and D'Ambrosio, Charles A. *The Theory of Business Finance: A Book of Readings.* New York: Macmillan, 1967.

Fredrickson, E. Bruce. *Frontiers of Investment Analysis.* Scranton, Pa.: International Textbook Co., 1971.

Fredrickson, E. Bruce, ed. *Frontiers of Investment Analysis.* 2d ed. Scranton, Pa.: International Textbook Co., 1971.

Lorie, James H., and Brealey, Richard A. *Modern Developments in Investment Management: A Book of Readings.* New York: Praeger, 1972.

Wu, H., and Zakon, A. J. *Elements of Investments.* 2d ed. New York: Holt, Rinehart and Winston, 1972.

Index

A

Abnormal performance index (API), 154, 156, 267
Absolute deviation, 241
Accounting principles, 144–50
Accounting Principles Board, 139, 153
Actual earnings, 137
Advertising costs, 150
After-tax rate of return on common equity, 102
Ahlers, David, 131
Ahlers model, 131–33
Alchian, A. A., 17–19
Alexander, Sidney S., 77, 257
Allocation of securities in portfolio, 248, 252–54
Alphas, 211, 226, 267
American Stock Exchange, 249–50
  market value of shares listed on, 4
  movement in, 52
  number of shares listed on, 4
American Stock Exchange Price Level Index, 37, 63–64
Andersen, Theodore A., 16–17
Arditti, Fred D., 196, 217–18
Arithmetic mean, 29, 57–59
  bias, 59
Asset valuation; see Security valuation
Averaging, 52, 57–59
  arithmetic mean, 57–59
  geometric mean, 57–59
  indexes distinguished, 57

Avoidable risk, 254

B

Babcock, Guilford C., 102–3
Bachelier, Louis, 72
Ball, Ray, 87, 154
Bank Administration Institute (BAI) study, 253
  evaluation of portfolio performance, 228–41
Bank trust departments, portfolios administered by, 220–23
Base-weighted aggregative index, 62
Baumol, William J., 195–96
Behavior of market, 1 ff.
Bench marks
  average performance of group, 244–45
  evaluating skill of individual investors, 250–52
  evaluation of portfolio performance, 241–45
  naïve, 242–44
  rates of return compared with, 257
  reward-to-variability ratio, 245
  reward-to-volatility ratio, 245
Bernhard, Arnold, 128
Beta coefficients, 91 n, 201–5, 207–8, 210–11, 218–20, 223–25, 227, 235, 237–38, 241, 252, 255, 265–67
Beta factor, 225, 267–68
Black, Fischer, 108, 225–27

Blume, Marshall, 77, 94, 140, 219, 256 n
Bonds
  common stock investments compared, 47–50
  quality ratings, 211–12
  rates of return on, 19, 26–27, 41–50
  risk in relation to rate of return, 211–13
    common stock compared, 214
  20-year bond portfolio, rate of return on, 47–48
  weighted average realized yields, 42, 46
Boness, A. James, 80
Borden Company, 150–51
Borrowing, 186–91, 194, 205–6
Bower, Richard S., 236–37, 241
Brealey, Richard A., 106–7, 140, 142, 157, 159, 161–62
Brown, Philip, 87, 166
Brownian motion, 72
Burns, Arthur F., 16
Business cycles, 21–22
Buy-and-hold policy, 79, 134

C

Callard, Charles, 101–3
Capital asset pricing model, 89, 91, 198–210, 218, 225–27, 252, 268
  assumptions, 205–7
  borrowing, 205–6
  efficient portfolios, 203–5
  empirical evidence on explanatory power of, 207–9
  graphic representation, 202
  lending, 205–6
  mutual funds, performance of, 207–8
  naïve bench mark basis, 242
  realism of, 203–9
  risk aversion, 205
  taxes, 206–7
Capital-market line, 189, 203, 242, 252, 268
  equation for, 189, 200
  market portfolio used in, 249
Capital structure, 116–17
Cash flows
  components of, 114
  discounting rate, 114, 122–24
  dividends, 115–22
  earnings, 118–22
Center for Research in Security Prices (CRSP), tapes of, 82
Characteristic lines, 238–39, 268
Charles, R. J., 145 n
Clarkson, Geoffrey, 106

Coefficient of determination, 255
Coefficient of variation, 40, 132, 213 n, 268
Cohen, Kalman J., 199
Combination Index, 66, 250
Common stocks
  bond investments compared, 47–50
  high quality, 215–16
  low quality, 215–17
  New York Stock Exchange listing, rates of return on, 30–36
  not listed on New York Stock Exchange, rates of return on, 36–37
  prices of; *see* Stock prices
  rates of return on investment in, 26–41; *see also* Rates of return
  ratings of riskiness of, 215
  risk in relation to rate of return, 214–18
    bonds compared, 214
  value of listed issues, 27–28
  variability of, 37–46, 215–18
Compounding, 28–29, 268
Compustat tapes, 82, 166
Corporate bonds; *see* Bonds
Corporate earnings; *see* Earnings *and* Earnings per share
Corporate profits, 19
  declines in, 9–10
  gross national income in relation to, 16
  sensitivity of, increase in, 20
  sensitivity of, measuring of, 16–17
Correlation coefficients, 67, 75, 77–78, 160, 204, 265–66, 269
Correlations
  growth rates of earnings per share, 159–61
  historic growth rates and forecasts of earnings, 163
  indexes, 67
  return with market, 208–9
  securities, 182
  stock price changes, 75
Covariance of security, 179–183, 198, 269
Cowles, Alfred, 30–31, 65, 72
Cox, Jack W., 142
Cragg, J. G., 163–64
Crockett, Jean, 94, 219, 256 n
Current-earnings-plus-future-investment-opportunities approach, 115
Cyclical relationships, 14–17

D

Davidson, Sidney, 152
Debt-equity ratio, 101

Depreciation, 145, 147
Descriptive statistics, 4–5
Determinants of level of stock prices, 5–10
Diagnosing causes of portfolio performance, 248–59
Diluted earnings, 139
Diminishing marginal utility of wealth, 136, 192, 269–70
Disclosure requirements, 150
Discounted cash-flow approach, 115
Discounting rate, 6–8, 116
  cash flows, 114, 122–24
  certain world, 122
  changes, 87
  uncertain world, 123, 127
Dispersion, 40–41, 176, 218, 270
Diversification, 41–42, 178–79, 183, 205, 264–65, 270
  degree of, 107
  efficiency of, 249, 254
Dividend-payout ratio, 117, 119, 126, 130, 140
  in equilibrium, 129
  Whitbeck-Kisor model, 129–30
Dividend yield, 101, 132
Dividends, 117–18, 251
  changes in, 122
  importance of, 118
Douglas, George W., 209
Dow Jones Averages, 37, 52, 56, 57, 59, 63, 75, 250 n
  bias in, 57
  geometric average, 59
Dow Jones Industrial Average, 8, 52–55, 60–62, 65–69, 89
  computation of, 60–61
  criticisms of, 61
  stock split adjustment, 60–61
  weighting, 55
Dryden, Miles M., 79
Durand, David, 126 n, 135

E

Earnings, 11
  correlation between historic growth rates and forecasts, 163
  defined, 136–37, 144
  discretionary methods of treatment of, 144–50
  expected change in, 6–7
  measuring, 142–56
  predicting, 157–67
  random walk, 158–59, 162–63
  value of stock determined by, 142–43
Earnings per share, 102, 135, 139

Earnings per share—*Cont.*
  ambiguity in
    accounting options, 144–50
    other elements, 150–52
  correlation in growth rates, 159–61
  importance attached to, 144–45
  patterns in, 158
  variability of, 104
Economic principles, accounting principles in relation to, 143
Efficient frontier, 172–73, 183–88, 270
Efficient market, 97, 270
Efficient market hypothesis, 70–97; *see also* Random walk *and* Stock prices
  conditions necessary for efficiency, 80–81
  defined, 98
  development of theory of, 70
  implications of, 98–110
  portfolio management, 105–10
  quest for a theory, 79–96
  security analysis, 99–105, 108–9
  semistrong form, 71, 88, 97
    tests of, 82–87
  strong form, 71, 97
    tests of, 87–96
  weak form, 71, 72–74, 80, 87, 97
    early tests of, 75–79
Efficient portfolios, 172–74, 183, 191, 198, 227, 270
  capital asset pricing model, 203–5
  expected return on, 200–201
Endowed institutions, 122, 229
Endowment funds, 254
Equal-weighted index, 55, 68
Evaluation of portfolio performance
  average performance of group, 244–45
  Bank Administration Institute study, 228–41
  bench marks, 241–45
  beta coefficient, 235
  internal rate of return, 230–31, 233
  market sensitivity, 235
  mean absolute deviation, 235
  measurements of different parts of portfolio, 245–46
  mutual funds, 238–41
  purpose of, 246
  rate of return, 229–34
    risk combined with, 235–41
  risk, 234–35
    rate of return combined with, 235–41
  time-weighted rate of return, 231–34
  total dispersion measures, 235

F

Fama, Eugene F., 75–78, 80, 83,
  85–87 n
Feasible set, 184, 270
Federal Reserve Banks, 87
Federal Reserve Board, 23, 88
Federal Trade Commission, 150–51
Filter technique, 77, 79, 257, 270–71
Financial analysts; *see* Security analysts
Financial Analysts Journal, 95
Financial assets, determination of prices
  of, 200–203
Financial institutions
  assets managed or controlled by, 26
  holdings of, 5–6
  security analysis, 99
Fisher, Lawrence, 17–18, 21 n, 30–32,
  34, 36–38, 40, 44, 46–49, 59,
  65–66, 83, 86–87 n, 212–13, 226,
  250
Footnotes, 277–90
Forbes Magazine, 144–45
Ford Foundation, The, 229
Forecasts
  annual earnings, 131
  earnings, 157–67
  error in, 14–15, 132
  rate of return, 175
  security valuation models; *see* Se-
    curity valuation
Fortune, 145
Frequency distribution of wealth ratios,
  38–42, 53–54
  skewness of, 37, 40, 59, 196, 217–18
Friedman, Milton, 22, 203, 217
Friend, Irwin, 69, 88, 94–95, 219,
  251–52 n, 256 n
Funny money, 155–56

G

General Electric, 216
General Foods, 216
Generally accepted accounting princi-
  ples, 144–50
Geometric mean, 29, 57–59, 64, 271
  bias, 59
Glauber, Robert, 159–62
Glossary, 267–76; *see also specific terms
  in index*
Goldman, Sachs & Company, 133
Gordon, M. J., 117, 121, 126 n
Government bonds, rate of return of,
  8–9
Granger, Clive W. J., 75
Great Britain; *see also* United Kingdom
  accounting standards, 159

Great Britain—*Cont.*
  earnings of corporations, 158–60
  postwar economy, 159–60
  random walk hypothesis, 158
Green, David, 165–66
Gross National Product (GNP), 13–16,
  138–39
  decline in, 15
Growth rate, 126, 133
  security valuation, 134–36
  short-term, 159
Growth stocks, 118

H

Halpern, Paul, 156
Hamilton, Earl J., 17–18
Herzog, John P., 17
Hickman, W. Braddock, 41, 43, 46–47,
  211–13, 226
Holt, Charles, 136

I

Income defined, 143
Indexes; *see* Stock market indexes *or
  specific name or type*
Indifference curve, 193, 271
Inefficient portfolios, variability of,
  204–5
Inflation, 8, 17–20
Insider trading, 103
Internal rate of return, 230–31, 233,
  271
Intrinsic value, 80, 99, 114, 271
  variables, impact of, 99
Investment committees
  lists of approved securities, 106
  recommendations of security analysts,
    consideration of, 106
Investment companies, 258
Investment counselling, 30, 108, 110,
  260–66
  beta coefficients, 265–66
  correlation coefficients, 265–66
  criteria of investment policy, 264–65
  defined, 260
  diversification, 264–65
  importance of, 260
  individual investors, 264
  needs and resources of investors,
    261–64
  pension plan costs, 263
  simulation techniques, 261–64
  specification of investment policy,
    264–66
  universities, 261–62

Investment performance index (IPI), 64–65, 271
  price index distinguished, 64–65
Investment policy; *see* Investment counselling

J–K

Jensen, Michael, 83, 86–87 n, 90–95, 208, 218–19, 225–27, 242–43
Journal of Business, 166
Kemerer, Donald, 49
Kendall, Maurice G., 72
Kessel, Reuben A., 17–19
Keynes, John M., 17–18
Kisor, Manown, Jr., 138, 157–58

L

Latané, Henry A., 157
Leading indicators, 21–22
Lending, 186–91, 194, 205–6
Life insurance companies, portfolios administered by, 220–23
Limited-horizon models, 133–34
Linked internal rate of return method, 233–34
Lintner, John, 89, 159–62, 209
Little, I. M. D., 158–59
Lorie, James H., 21 n, 30–32, 34, 36–38, 40, 44, 46, 96, 103, 156, 232 n
Lutz, Frederick, 117
Lutz, Vera, 117

M

Malkiel, B. G., 133, 163–64
Management fees, 249, 251, 258–59
Mandelbrot, Benoit, 70, 80
Market model, 84 n, 272
Markowitz, Harry, 171, 179, 195–97, 246, 254
Markowitz portfolio theory, 172–91; *see also* Portfolio
  borrowing, 186–91, 194
  capital market theory distinguished, 200–210
  computer program, 172–73
  efficient frontier, 172–73, 183–88
  efficient portfolios, 172–74
  estimates necessary for, 199 n
    simplification of, 199
  lending, 186–91, 194
  relationship of portfolio to component securities, 174–83

Markowitz portfolio theory—*Cont.*
  simplification of, 198–200
  summary of, 172–73
Mean-absolute deviation, 235, 241, 272
Mean deviation, 40
Mean wealth ratios, 37, 53
Measuring earnings, 142–56
Median, 272
Meltzer, Alan, 106
Mergers, 152–53, 156
Merrett, A. J., 31, 36, 50
Merrill Lynch, Pierce, Fenner & Smith Inc., 82 n
Messner, Van A., 157–58
Miller, Merton H., 115, 119–21, 129–30, 139, 209
Mitchell, Wesley Clair, 17–18
Modigliani, Franco, 115, 119–21, 129–30, 139
Money supply
  changes in, 22
  stock prices in relation to, 22–25
Monopolistic access to information, 88, 96
Moody's Investors Service, 27, 211
Moore, Arnold B., 75, 80
Morgenstern, Oskar, 75
Mosteller, F., 217
Murphy, Joseph E., Jr., 159
Mutual funds, 88, 250–51
  assets of, 26
  bench mark for performance valuation, 90–91
  capital asset pricing model, 207–8
  high-risk, 219
  performance analyses, 88–97, 238–41
  random portfolios, comparison with, 90–96
  rates of return, 88–89
  risk, 89, 91–96
  risk in relation to rate of return, 218–23
  Treynor index, 238–41
  turnover rates, 256
  variability in rates of return, 89

N

National Association of Security Dealers Automated Quotation service (NASDAQ), 250 n
National Bureau of Economic Research, 9–10, 21
National economy
  empirical relationships with stock market, 10–20
  stock market and, 3–25

National Quotation Bureau, 36–37,
250 n
New York Stock Exchange, 31, 54, 62,
65, 79, 91, 94, 118, 136, 142, 165,
205, 215, 226, 241, 249–50, 258
costs of trading on, 255–56
disclosure requirements, 150
movements in, 52
number of shares listed on, 4–6
rates of return on common stocks
listed on, 27, 30–36
trading volume, 256
value of shares listed on, 4–6
variability in prices of stocks listed
on, 53
New York Stock Exchange Composite
Index, 9, 37, 63, 66, 67 n, 249
New York Stock Exchange Index of
Industrial Stocks, 252
Niederhoffer, Victor, 96, 103, 142, 166
Nogee, P., 217
Normalized earnings, 132, 137, 273
defined, 129

O

Optimality, 191–94, 206–7
Osborne, M. F. M., 72, 75, 77, 96
Over-the-counter securities, 4–5, 52,
249–50
automated quotation systems, 108
rates of return on, 37

P

Payout ratio, 117, 126, 132
Pension funds, 122, 147–48, 256,
258–59, 263
Petersburg Paradox, 135–36
Poague, Jerry A., 199
Portfolios
covariance between securities, 179–83
diversification; *see* Diversification
efficient frontier, 183–86
estimates of risk, 176
management fees, 249, 258–59
optimality, 206–7
performance analyses, 88–97
performance of
diagnosing causes of, 248–59
evaluation of, 228–47
factors affecting, 248–59
rates of return on, 174
relationship to component securities,
174–83
risk-free assets, 186–91
riskiness, 107, 171–72, 186–91
selection of particular assets for,
249–52

Portfolios—*Cont.*
skill in, 249–52
taxes, 249, 258
transaction costs, 249, 255–58
turnover rates, 256
variance of, 176–81
formula, 179
Portfolio management, 105–10, 169 ff.
adherence to prescribed policies, 249,
254–55
defined, 260
diversification degree, 107
economies of scale, 100
Markowitz theory, 172–91; *see also*
Markowitz portfolio theory
simplification of, 198–200
needs and tastes of individual investors, 172
optimality, 191–94
prices of financial assets in relation
to, 200–203
risk aversion, 191–92
risk level of portfolio, 107
switching between classes of assets,
248, 252–54
tasks performed in, 109–10
tax status of investor, 108
theory of, 171–97
transaction costs, 108
utility theory, 192–95
Portfolio manager; *see* Portfolio
management
Pratt, Shannon, 215, 218, 226
Predicting earnings, 157–67
accuracy of, 165
historical earnings, 158–63
interim earnings, 165–67
security analysts, 163–65
value of, 157
Present value, 114, 273
Price-earnings ratio (P-E), 10, 13–14,
117–18, 126, 128, 133
cyclical behavior of, 137–38
decline in, 10
specification in security valuation,
136–40
Whitbeck-Kisor model, 129
Prices; *see* Stock prices
Probability distribution, 175, 193, 218,
273
Profits; *see* Corporate profits *and*
Earnings

Q–R

Quadratic utility functions, 193, 195
Quarterly earnings as predictors of annual earnings, 166–67

Random portfolios, mutual funds compared with, 90–96
Random sampling, 53–54
Random selection, 273
Random walk, 83 n, 273; *see also* Efficient market hypothesis
   controversy over, 70–71
   corporate earnings, 158–59, 162–63
   early beginnings, 71–75
   stock prices, 162
   transformation to efficient market hypothesis, 97
Rates of return, 8, 51, 69, 126
   accurate measurement of, 26–27
   actual versus hypothetical, 253–54, 256
   annual compounding, 28–29, 268
   arithmetic mean, 29
   bench marks, comparison with, 257
   bonds, 20–21, 26–27, 41–50
     common stocks compared, 214
     risk in relation to, 211–13
   common stock investments, 26–41
     bonds compared with, 214
     listed on New York Stock Exchange, 30–36
     not listed on New York Stock Exchange, 36–37
     risk in relation to, 214–18
   compounding, 28–29, 268
   errors in use of, 28–29
   evaluation of portfolio performance, 229–34
     risk combined with, 235–41
   forecast of, 175
   mutual fund
     performance analysis, 88–89
     risk in relation to, 218–23
   over-the-counter securities, 37
   portfolio, 174
     risk in relation to, 218–23
   reinvestment of dividends, effect of, 31–35
   stocks, 20–21
   time-weighted, 231–34, 275
   variability in, 37–46
Rayner, A. C., 159
Readings, complementary, 291–94
Regan, Donald, 9, 142
Regression analysis, 133, 135, 138, 140, 181, 201, 213, 233–34, 273
Regression coefficients, 252, 273
Retained earnings, 117, 120–21
Reward-to-variability ratio, 245, 274
Reward-to-volatility ratio, 245

Risk, 123, 183
   alphas, 226
   beta coefficient, 223–25
   bonds, return on, 211–13
     common stocks compared, 214
   common stocks, return on, 214–18
     bonds compared, 214
   estimate of, 123, 176
   evaluation of portfolio performance, 234–35
     rate of return combined with, 235–41
   measure of, 123–24, 202–4, 210
     disagreement about, 114
   mutual fund performance, 91–96
     analysis of, 89
   mutual fund rate of return in relation to, 218–23
   portfolio management, 107
   portfolio rate of return in relation to, 218–23
   portfolio selection, 171–72
   price of, 189
   stability measures, 140
Risk aversion, 121, 171, 191–92, 197, 200, 212, 274
   capital asset pricing model, 205
Risk-free assets, 186–91, 209
Risk-free rate of return, 8, 274
Risk premiums, 116, 204, 208–10, 212–13, 215, 235, 274
Roberts, Harry V., 72–75, 77
Roll, Richard, 83, 86–87 n
Runs, 274

S

Sampling, 52–54, 274
   adequacy of indexes based on, 52
   concentration of value in few companies, 52–53
   indexes based on, 52
   small samples, 52–54
   stock exchange listings, 52
Samuelson, Paul A., 70, 80
Savage, Leonard J., 217
Scholes, Myron S., 86–87, 209, 225–27
Schwartz, Anna Jacobson, 22
Secondary offerings, effect on stock prices of, 86–87, 96
Secular relationships, 10–14, 158
Securities and Exchange Commission (SEC), 88, 103–4
   disclosure requirements, 150
   secondary offerings, 87
Security analysis, 99–105, 108–9
   approaches to, 101–3

Security analysis—*Cont.*
  evaluation of, 105
  financial institutions, 99
  implications, 100–105
  originality, 101, 103, 109
  purpose of, 114
Security analysts
  function of, 144
  predictions in earnings, 163–65
    accuracy of, 165
Security valuation, 111 ff.; *see also*
    Cash flows
  Ahlers model, 131–33
  approaches to, 115
  critical issues in, 134–40
  current-earnings-plus-future-invest-
    ment-opportunities approach, 115
  determinants of, 6–7
  discounted cash-flow approach, 115
  earnings as determination of, 142–43
  forecasting problems, 140
  growth in earnings, 134–36
  limited-horizon models, 133–34
  models, 99–100, 125–41
  Petersburg paradox, 35–36
  specification of price-earnings ratio,
    136–40
  stream-of-dividends approach, 115–22
  stream-of-earnings approach, 115,
    117–22
  theory of, 113–24
  Value Line ratings, 127–29
  Whitbeck-Kisor model, 129–31
Segall, Joel, 165–66
Semistandard deviation, 241, 274
Separation theorem, 190, 274
Sharpe, William F., 89–91 n, 95, 123,
    179, 183 n, 187–90, 199–203,
    206–7, 209–11, 219 n, 225–26, 235,
    240, 242, 252, 254
Simulation techniques in investment
    policies, 261–64
Skewness of distribution, 37, 40, 59 n,
    196, 217–18, 275
Smith, Adam, 80, 226
Smith, Edgar Lawrence, 47, 49 n
Solomon, Ezra, 13–14
Spacek, Leonard, 145–47
Specification of investment policy,
    264–66
Speculation, 10, 13–14
Sprenkle, Carl, 80, 224
Standard & Poor's, 212
Standard & Poor's indexes
  Composite Index, 89, 91, 155–56, 249
  Corporate AAA Bond Yields, 47
  Index, 13, 47, 52, 88

Standard & Poor's indexes—*Cont.*
  arithmetic mean as basis, 57
  Index of 425 industrial stocks, 132,
    252
  Industrial Index, 14, 157
    geometric average, 59
  "500" stock index, 54, 62, 65–69,
    87, 131, 143, 220–21, 249
    advantages, 62
    Dow Jones Average compared, 62
Standard deviation, 28, 40, 91 n, 130,
    132, 176, 181–83, 201, 203, 207–8,
    210, 219, 235, 237–38, 241, 275
Stock Exchange of London, value of
    stocks listed on, 27–28
Stock market
  behavior of, 1 ff.
  empirical relationships with national
    economy, 10–20
  movements in, 51, 53
  national economy and, 3–25
  summary measure of behavior of, 51
Stock market indexes, 51–69; *see also*
    specific names of indexes
  averages distinguished, 57
  averaging, 52, 57–59
  importance of, 65–69
  problems involved in, 51–52
  purpose, 51
  relationships among, 65–69
  sampling, 52–54
  types of, 60–65
  volatility of, 68–69
  weighting, 52, 55–57
Stock prices; *see also* Efficient market
    hypothesis
  changes in, 142, 157
  correlation between changes, 75
  determinants of level of, 5–10
  economic growth in relation to, 13
  filter technique, 77, 79
  gross national product in relation to,
    14–15
  intrinsic value, 80, 99
  leading indicator, 21–22
  money supply in relation to, 22, 25
  random walk controversy, 70–71,
    162; *see also* Efficient market
    hypothesis secondary offerings,
    effect of, 86–87, 96
  time series, 72–74
  United Kingdom, trends in, 79
  variability in, 104
Stock splits, 63
  adjustments for, 56, 60, 64
  stock prices, effect on, 83–86
Stock valuation; *see* Security valuation

Stream-of-dividends approach, 115–22, 133
  certain world, 125–26
  uncertain world, 126
Stream-of-earnings approach, 115, 117–22, 133
  certain world, 125–26
  discounting rate, 122–24
  uncertain world, 126
Subjective probability distribution, 218
Sykes, Allen, 31, 36, 50
Systematic risk, 204–5, 218–19, 235, 255, 275

T

Tax-exempt investors, 230, 258
  terminal wealth of, 31
Taxes, 121–22, 206–7, 229, 249, 258
  rates of return, effect on, 31
Terminal wealth, 31
  bond investment and common stock investment compared, 49
Terminal wealth ratios, 242
Time-weighted rate of return, 231–34, 275
Timing problem, 4, 20–25, 65, 72–74, 128, 253
Tobin, James, 187
Total dispersion measures, 235
Total risk, 235, 255
Trading volume, 256
Transaction costs, 108, 121–22, 249, 251, 255–58
Treasury bills, 253
  market study, 83 n
  90-day, 8–9
  180-day, 8
  rate of return, 8–9, 186
Treynor, Jack L., 143, 238
Treynor Index, 238–41, 275
Turnover ratios, 256
  sales to total capital, 102
Tuttle, Donald L., 157

U

Uncertainty, conditions of, 6–8
  discounting rate, 123, 127
  security valuation, 113–14, 121
United Kingdom; *see also* Great Britain
  rates of return on common stock, 31, 36
  rates of return on investments in, 50
  stock price trends, 79

University of Chicago, Center at the Graduate School of Business of, 82 n
Unsystematic risk, 276
Utility of wealth, 192, 195
Utility function, 192–93, 276
Utility theory, 192–95

V

Valuation of securities; *see* Security valuation
Value Line "1400" Composite Average, 57, 59, 64
Value Line Investment Survey, 142, 157
Value Line ratings, 127–29
Value-weighted indexes, 55–56, 249–50
Variability, 37–46, 53, 89, 104, 176, 213, 215–19
Variables in security valuation models, 127–34; *see also specific models*
Variance, 176–81, 198, 276
  formula, 179
Volatility, 68–69, 140, 276
  ranking of funds based on, 238–40

W–Y

Walker, Winthrop B., 49 n
Wall Street Journal, 103, 107 n
Walter, James, 118
Watts, Ross, 122
Waud, Roger N., 87
Wealth ratios, 53–54, 276
  frequency distributions of, 38–42, 53–54
  mean, 37
Weighting, 52, 55–57, 276
  adjustment for stock splits, 56
  equal, 55
  methods of, 55
  reason for, 55
  value as basis, 55–56
Weil, Roman L., 21 n, 47–49
Weston, J. Fred, 14
Whitbeck, Volkert S., 138
Whitbeck-Kisor model, 129–31
  Ahlers model distinguished, 132
Williams, John Burr, 115–17
Williamson, Peter J., 95
Wippern, Donald F., 236–37, 241
Working, Holbrook, 72
Yields on bonds; *see* Rates of return

This book has been set in 11 and 10 point Baskerville, leaded 2 points. Section numbers and titles are 16 point Helvetica. Chapter numbers are 30 point Helvetica and chapter titles are 18 point Helvetica. The size of the type page is 26 by 45 picas.